the drama of

Luigi Pirandello

the drama of

Luigi Pirandello

Domenico Vittorini
author of (the modern italian novel)

with a foreword by
Luigi Pirandello

NEW YORK / RUSSELL & RUSSELL

To
MARY CURTIS ZIMBALIST

Founder of the
Curtis Institute of Music
in Philadelphia.

Foreword

New York 30 VII 1935 XIII

Mio caro Vittorini,

tra I tanti Pirandello che vanno in giro da un pezzo nel mondo della critica letteraria internazionale, zoppi, deformi, tutti testa e niente cuore, strampalati sgarbati lunatici e tenebroni, nei quali io, per quanto mi sforzi, non riesco a riconoscermi neppure per un minimo tratto (il piu imbecille di tutti credo che sia quello di Benedetto Croce), ha voluto anche lei metterne su uno, tutto suo, non per il gusto di storpiarmi e poi mostrarmi zoppicante; non per il gusto di presentarmi mascherato da una testa d'elefante e col cuore atrofizzato mediante quella pompa a filtro che è la macchinetta infernale della logica; io annaspante tra le nuvole o intenebrato nelle grotte; ma anzi tutt'al contrario; e di questo, come è naturale e come può bene immaginarsi, io le sono molto grato, caro Vittorini. Molto grato perchè, tra tanti che credono di saper molto bene ciò che sono, io che non lo so affatto e ho sempre rifuggito dal saperlo come da una soperchieria a tutta la vita che mi si muove dentro di continuo, trovo in lei uno che mi fa andar dritto sulle gambe e mi dà tanto cuore quanto me n'abbisogna per amare e compatire questa povera umanità, sia quando ragiona e sia quando sragiona; uno che cerca di spiegare che se tanti mi credono strampalato è perchè mi muovo a mio modo e non come gli altri vorrebbero; sgarbato, perchè ho sdegno delle loro garbatezze; incomprensibile, perchè non sanno ancora vedere e pensare e sentire come me.

Comunque, caro Vittorini, zoppo, deforme, tutto testa e niente cuore, strampalato sgarbato lunatico e tenebrone, io esisto e seguiterò ad esistere, e loro no. È vero che questa non è una cosa che abbia per me molta importanza. Uomo, ho voluto dire agli uomini qualche cosa, senz'alcuna ambizione, tranne forse quella di vendicarmi d'esser nato. Ma pure la vita, anche per tutto quello che m'ha fatto soffrire, è così bella! (Ed ecco un'altra affermazione senza nemmeno un'ombra di logica, ma tuttavia così vera e sentita.) Basta, io la ringrazio cordialmente, caro Vittorini, dello specchio che con questo suo libro lei mi presenta, in cui con tanto gradimento io posso rimirarmi.

LUIGI PIRANDELLO

Foreword

(*Translation*)

New York 30 VII 1935 XIII

Dear Vittorini,
   The world of international literary criticism has been crowded for a long time with numerous Pirandellos—lame, deformed, all head and no heart, erratic, gruff, insane, and obscure—in whom, no matter how hard I try, I cannot recognize myself, not even in the slightest degree. (The most senseless of these phantoms I believe to be the one fashioned by Benedetto Croce.) You too have now decided to present your own Pirandello, not for the pleasure of maiming me and then exposing me as I limp along; not for the pleasure of showing me masked with the head of an elephant and my heart atrophied by that infernal pump which is the machine of logic, lost in the clouds or wandering in the murky bowels of the earth. Indeed, you have done just the opposite of this, and as is natural and as you can well imagine, I am very grateful to you, dear Vittorini. I am very grateful because, among so many who think they know so well what I am, I, who have no conception of what I am and have always refrained from trying to find out for fear of offending all the life which continually seethes within me, find in you one who makes me walk upright on my own legs and grants me as much heart as I need to love and pity this poor humanity of ours, both when it is rational and when it is irrational; one who tries to explain that if so many believe me erratic, it is because I move in my own way and not as others would like me to; gruff because I grow indignant with their affectations; incomprehensible because they do not yet know how to see, to think, to feel as I do.

   At any rate, dear Vittorini, lame, deformed, all head and no heart, erratic, gruff, insane and obscure, I exist and I shall continue to exist, while they will not. It is true this is not a matter of great importance for me. A man, I have tried to tell something to other men, without any ambition, except perhaps that of avenging myself for having been born. And yet life, in spite of all that it has made me suffer, is so beautiful! (And here is another positive statement without even a shadow of logic, and yet so true and deeply felt.) Well, I thank you cordially, dear Vittorini, for the mirror of this book which you place before me, in which I can behold myself with so much gratification.

LUIGI PIRANDELLO

Preface

THE present book was grown out of a course on the works of Luigi Pirandello, and was made possible by a grant from the University of Pennsylvania which enabled me to go to Italy to collect material and to obtain a fresh perspective on the contemporary theatre.

Italian criticism is on the road to Damascus as far as Pirandello is concerned. After years of silence and incomprehension, critics are beginning to feel that Pirandello is the only truly gigantic figure in the world of Italian letters of today.

I have looked at Pirandello first in the light of contrasts and similarities that can be gathered around him from the background of the Italian literary tradition. There are writers to whom his tormented humanity bears marked resemblance. There are others to whom he is hostile to the point of being antithetical.

I have studied only those events of his life which have a direct relation to his work. Other happenings belong only to him. It may be of interest to the historically minded scholar to collect every detail of a writer's life. I have been more interested in Pirandello as a man and an artist, and I have looked upon his art as a result of his sensitiveness and of the experiences to which life subjected him. Such appears to us to be the genesis of the art of Luigi Pirandello, a modern tragedian.

I am deeply grateful to Dr. William J. Phillips of the English Department of the University of Pennsylvania for his patient and competent assistance in putting my manuscript in its present form.

The fact that Luigi Pirandello has written the Foreword to this book indicates how much I owe to him. He arrived in New York on July 20 as I was correcting the page proofs. He was most kind in granting me long interviews and in discussing with me the basic elements of his art as well as my interpretations of his plays. I can truthfully say that I have lived a few hours in the light of true greatness.

August 1935, Philadelphia   D. V.

New Preface

MANY important events have taken place since the original publication of this book in 1935. Pirandello's literary and dramatic contributions have become more widely read, dramatized and critically analyzed with keen interest.

Luigi Pirandello has been honored by having the translations of five of his major works included in Everyman's Library under the title of *Naked Masks;* a most *signficant* recognition. These works have been competently edited by Eric Bentley, who provided a new and improved English translation of *Così è (se vi pare)*, entitled *Right You Are*. Mr. Bentley has also listed five other volumes in which Pirandello's works are available in English as well as all the works that have been dedicated to him in contemporary Italian criticism.

Pirandello felt that in his art he was addressing himself to the world rather than to the inhabitants of his native and beloved Italy. We know that he did not cherish his universal thinking in vain. *Henry IV* and *Six Characters in Search of an Author* belong to the repertoire of the well-known Hedgerow Theatre Group in Rose Valley, Pennsylvania. *Six Characters in Search of an Author* also had a flattering production in the 1955-56 season in New York City.

In Italy, meanwhile, his work has received wide and enthusiastic recognition. His plays have been published in four volumes by Mondadori of Milan under the title *Maschere Nude*, the meaningful symbol that Pirandello saw as an expression of what he was attempting to say to other men.

Many books and essays have been dedicated to Pirandello as an artist after his death in 1936. Clear realization of the wide scope and depth of his ideas as well as his originality has replaced the lack of comprehension which he experienced during his three months' visit to New York.

Since Pirandello's death, the world of letters has developed greater insight into the philosophical implications of his art. We know that Pirandello considered himself a

New Preface

philosophical author as evidenced by his own comments. In the preface of *Six Characters in Search of an Author*, he wrote: "I have never been satisfied with representing the figure of a man or woman for the sheer pleasure of representing it; nor with narrating a specific event, gay or sad, for the sheer pleasure of narrating it; nor with describing a landscape for the sheer pleasure of describing it." He attributed to such objective authors the quality of being "historical" or "descriptive." He pointed out that there were other writers for whom "a human figure, an event, a landscape become enriched with a peculiar life-sense that lends to them a universal value. These are writers of a nature strongly philosophical." He added, "I have the misfortune of belonging to the latter type." It was only natural that a writer who took his art so seriously and who had studied himself so perceptively should seek a more congenial medium of expression than the naturalistic fiction of his youth. For Pirandello this medium was drama, a form of expression in which he enclosed the thought content of his life experience and in which he was to acquire full stature as an artist. He was about fifty years old when he turned to the stage.

Pirandello was a man who keenly experienced the poignant loneliness of life. In his imaginary characters, one can detect the sad vicissitudes of his life and the tormented thoughts of his searching mind. He delighted in relating the fact that he had been born near Girgenti in a place called Chaos during a raging cholera epidemic. He attributed to these circumstances the motifs of chaos and pain that are ever present in his art.

I hope that I will not be considered vain if I communicate to readers of this new edition that the copy of the first edition which I gave to the Maestro with deep gratitude and filial devotion remains on his desk; left when death claimed him on December 19, 1936.

Domenico Vittorini

January 21, 1957.

Contents

CONTENTS

CONTENTS

INTRODUCTION

I

Pirandello in the Tradition of Italian Letters

Pirandello appeared in the literary world of Italy when the movement that critics usually designate under the name of "naturalism" was in full blossom.

Naturalism was an event of paramount importance in Italian life. It focused the human mind clearly and deliberately towards the consideration and acceptance of the material and controllable aspects of reality, and it enjoined artists to seek inspiration from the objective study of life close at hand. While other currents were found side by side with naturalism, it is indisputable that this movement occupied the center of the artistic and intellectual life in the eighties.

The concern for the concrete and objective goes beyond the field of art, and it encompasses the political and social aspects of Italian life as well. In 1870 the country achieved its national unity, and this important political event was accompanied by a noticeable stir in the economic field. Italy was reëntering the currents of European thought and life from which it had been excluded after three centuries of political slavery to France and Spain.

In the drama, veering away from historical themes that had been predominant in the days of romanticism, naturalism proclaimed the value of instinctive life as the raw material of art. It would be erroneous to believe that naturalistic elements had never appeared in the theatre, but it would be equally anti-historical to ignore the significance of the naturalistic school in its attitude towards the outside world in its relation to art. The term "school" shows the nature of the process that led to the crystallization of tendencies that beforehand had represented scattered efforts, unrecognized by the official hierarchy of the arts. Naturalism gave an official sanction to realism that before had been looked at askance as an inferior art mode. In fact, realism was found primarily in dialectal and popular literatures. Comedy that assigned to itself the observation of the everyday reality was looked upon as inferior to tragedy that had inherited stateliness and grandeur from the classical drama.

To understand the interplay of the various forces that are at work in Italian literature, it is necessary to view Italian life as the expression of two antithetical points of view that act not only in the literary field, but in the political, religious, and social fields as well. For the sake of simplicity, we may call these two attitudes the rhetorical and the realistic. Behind them there is the clash between conservativism and modernity which goes on unceasingly: conservativism that clings to old forms and upholds them with the tenacity with which life defends itself to the very end; modernity that seeks and presents new values which necessarily mean the death of the old ones. This clash is a tragic struggle between the old and the new, and leaves one perplexed before the alternative of ruthlessly discarding what represented the life of yesterday or accepting the new life which victoriously advances, crushing and conquering the old one.

Italy was born at the root of the gigantic plant of Rome. Classical traditions never died out, and they were a positive asset at a time when Europe, after the turmoil of the barbaric invasions, was trying to fashion a new civilization. At the same time, however, it was inevitable that the presence of the old plant should rob the young and tender shoot of air, sunlight, and of the nourishment that the new historical soil afforded to it. The magnificent growth that one notices in the twelfth and thirteenth centuries centered around the life of the merchants who conquered European and Eastern markets and accumulated the wealth that made possible the raising of stately cathedrals and universities. It was also accompanied by the appearance of a new means of expression: the vernacular. Those centuries bear all the earmarks of greatness, and they realize a truly new political outlook through the guilds that attracted the active participation of a large part of the social body.

The central fact of which we must not lose sight, however, is that Italy was no longer classical and imperial Rome; that the typical individual of that time was no longer the togated Roman; that the vernacular was a distinct language that bore only a resemblance to classical Latin; that the economic life was no longer the same as in the days of Rome, now that the masses had been made a part of the process of production and of consumption. Yet schools and churches tried to recast Italian history in the old mold of that of Rome; they tried to stifle the vernacular by forcing on it the stately composure of Latin prose; they proclaimed the glory of the past and the misery of the present; and they pointed at the literary men of the classical period as models who had to be imitated if literature was to rise again to the heights of old. Tradition molded a new universe different from the one in which people lived, with stars and planets, trees and flowers, not as people observed them, but as the literary tradition had handed down. It was a universe filled with men who likewise bore literary stigmas. They moved, acted, felt, and spoke—— at least they tried to—as Homer or Virgil or the Provençal poets dreamed that men did or should speak. Pirandello instructs us at this point as follows: "Rhetoric and imitation are ultimately one and the same thing. They have wrought immeasurable harm in every epoch, not only of Italian literature, but of Latin, and therefore in a varying degree, of all Romance literatures." [1]

It would be absurd to imagine that in ordinary life people, the rhetoricians themselves, felt and spoke differently from people of today. The togated form was superimposed; it bred artificiality and restrained the personal and individualistic elements in art. It is strange to pass from the rhetorical prose of Dante's *Convito,* that only here and there breaks forth into a sincere outburst of passionate feelings, to the limpid and eternally modern poetry of the *Commedia.* Poetry, since it was still outside the boundary of rhetoric in Dante's day, kept the natural, spontaneous form that it possessed in the great heart and mind of the poet. The *Convito,* modeled after

[1] "L'opera di Alberto Cantoni," *Nuova Antologia,* 1906, pp. viii, ix.

Latin prose, is opaque and often dull in its medium of expression.

More striking contradictions are found in writers of a later period when rhetoric held an indisputable sway in literature. If Politian and Tasso succeeded in letting their poetic genius reveal itself, they did so by breaking the rules of rhetoric that had forced them to sing of epic battles for which their temperament was totally unfit. As epic poems, Politian's *Stanzas* and Tasso's *Jerusalem Delivered* are failures. The greatness of the two works is revealed through the exquisite treatment of the love theme and through their poetry of nature where dewy mornings and delicately green vistas pass before us with a resonance that speaks of great poetry. It must not be forgotten, however, that these elements had nothing to do with wars and battles, and that they were condemned by the custodians of the Temple of Rhetoric as in the case of Tasso. The failure of Politian and Tasso as epic poets was quite natural, because in the fifteenth and sixteenth centuries the greatest exploit of man was not that of waging a war as in the days of primitive Greece and Rome.

In the theatre, the struggle between rhetoric and realism was intense and bitter. Rhetoric carefully codified by Giraldi and Speroni in the sixteenth century made it easy to write many tragedies, but it interfered with the creation of real drama. The classical drama of that century was stillborn since the erudite efforts of Trissino, Giraldi, and Speroni were utterly barren of results. If we wish to find a significant dramatic work, we must turn to Machiavelli's *Mandragola* and to Bruno's *Candelaio,* two comedies that with a steady hand dissect the moral lowness of their times and indulge in a laughter that is tragically painful.

The fundamental blunder in the attitude of learned humanists like Trissino, Giraldi, and Speroni consisted in their confusing culture and art. If we depart from the usual criterion of literary evaluation by relegating the rhetoricians to the background and placing the realists in the foreground, we see that the harvest of realism in the drama of the sixteenth century is very abundant. We can admire it in the

Commedia dell'arte with its genial and grotesque elements, and in the comedies of the quixotic Aretino, and those of Lasca and Cecchi. We should find even more and important material if we were to go to the rustic farce and the popular comedy that flourished in Tuscany, a dramatic production to which criticism has given scant attention.

The two currents, that of rhetoric and that of realism, continued distinct and hostile until we find them in the eighteenth century represented by the tuneful and courtly Metastasio and the charmingly realistic Goldoni. These two dramatists stand near each other in an almost antithetical light: Metastasio providing his sentimental, historical dramas for the court of Vienna; Goldoni moving in his dear old Venice among his contemporaries and studying them with his good-natured humor and with a smile that is deeper than it seems.

Pirandello, at least in the beginning of his career, links himself to the naturalism of the eighties. The crystallization of the naturalistic movement into a definite set of æsthetic principles meant the defeat of the rhetorical attitude within the walls of the citadel of official criticism and art. Naturalism became a conscious effort to recognize the æsthetic value of life in its entirety by bringing it into the precincts of art without the veils of rhetoric. It meant the rising to the height of dignified art of subjects pertaining to life in the province. Romanticism in Italy had fought the first battle in behalf of popular literature, although it had failed to realize its goal since on the whole it took to an evanescent art lost in the distances of history. This was particularly true in the theatre where the historical theme assigned to drama did not blossom into significant works. Naturalism resumed the battle for a modern art, and succeeded in defining its nature and having its importance recognized by all men who called themselves modern.

The naturalism whence Pirandello derives is that of the south, that of Sicily, to be more exact. The naturalism of the north was different in that it was more intellectual. The poet Carducci, for instance, disguised his realism under the renewed garb of a genial and personal classicism, although he

7

expressed a sanguine love for the earth. On the other hand, for Giovanni Verga and Luigi Capuana, Sicilians like Pirandello, naturalism meant Sicily—Sicilian life with all its color and richness of human pathos. Verga showed the way to Pirandello in his *Cavalleria Rusticana* (*Rustic Knighthood*) and in the *La Lupa* (*The She-Wolf*), where the most absolute objectivity is applied to the theme of instinct, only relieved by the element of the picturesque.

The drama of Luigi Pirandello has developed from that realistic nucleus, as have other aspects of the contemporary theatre, in that modern playwrights have never forgotten that their works have to reach a public that lives in contact with the daily life. This realistic nucleus is found even in the lyrical drama of Dario Niccodemi and Massimo Bontempelli, and in the fantastic drama of Alberto Casella as well as in the historical drama of Sem Benelli. The practical concern which naturalism stressed has been very beneficial to the contemporary drama, since it has prevented it from being unduly evanescent.

This is particularly true of the theatre that goes by the name of "grotesque," with which Pirandello is usually identified, and in which fantasy predominates to a spasmodic degree. The theatre of the grotesque expresses a frenzied state of mind that forces man to burst into laughter before the harrowing contradictions of life. It flourished especially during the War, and it assumed the form of contrast between essence and appearance, between the face and the mask, the pathetic and the ludicrous. The formula and the æsthetic background of this dramatic form were afforded both by Pirandello's fiction and by his ideas of the grotesque elucidated in his volume *Umorismo* (*Humor*). The content was given by the sentiment of each individual writer.

The best of the immediately modern Italian drama was produced by working around the æsthetic nucleus of the grotesque. Around it can be gathered *La maschera e il volto* (*The Mask and the Face*) by Chiarelli, *Marionette, che passione!* (*Marionettes of Passion*) by Rosso di San Secondo, *L'uomo che incontrò sè stesso* (*The Man Who Met Himself*) by Antonelli, *Ridi, pagliaccio (Laugh, Clown, Laugh)* by Martini and the section of the drama of Luigi Pirandello that corresponds to the genial intuition of the grotesque, which we have chosen to call the drama of "being and seeming."

The art of Luigi Pirandello is a challenge to many categorical assertions as to the meaning and character of Italian literature. Some critics have stated that Italian literature has always sought the grandiose and that it is both turgid and hollow, with no interest in introspection and ideas. Others, following a diametrically opposed point of view, have stressed the so-called realistic traits of the Italian people and have pointed out the sensuous character and the absence of idealism in the annals of Italian letters. Before the vast mass of the literary production of a people that reflects its life thought over a period of seven centuries, both statements could be amply documented, a fact that would destroy the validity of both claims, proving the 'uselessness and unscientific character of many a demonstration.

Pirandello is a realist. In his long and great career as a writer he has sought to portray individuals as such rather than to present them through the concept of man, stately but abstract. He has always molded his art after the individuals that he has met, known, and studied, who have touched both his sense of humor and his heart. His powerful imagination and his genius have done the rest in transporting them from the tumult of life into the serenity of his art.

We are not using the term "realist" in the usual sense of the word. Pirandello is a realist in the sense that he tries to encompass within the scope of his art the basic, instinctive needs of man together with the secret torment of his soul and the mobile life of his intellect. Man is one in his various attributes, and Pirandello has pictured to us the drama of humanity as he sees it and feels it. In so doing he has joined the ranks of the great who have from time to time appeared under all skies.

II

Pirandello, Man and Artist

In Luigi Pirandello, the artist and the man are so closely interwoven as to make it imperative to know him intimately in order to understand his art.

Judging from his outward appearance, he is a continental gentleman accustomed to the life of European capitals, notably Rome, Berlin, and Paris. He is distinguished, well-dressed, affable, but not cordial. I should not say that Pirandello is a kindly person. He has been too embittered by experience to be such. His intellect is too sharp, and it goes too directly into the darkest sides of all questions for him to possess the happy gift of kindness. Kindness, like the kingdom of heaven, is of the poor in spirit. If in the end he proves to be friendly to his characters, the latter have been perplexed for a long time, gazing hesitatingly at the quizzical face of their author.

Following is a presentation of one of his characters that might be viewed as a self-portrait: "A good-looking, well-preserved man, although in his fifties. Penetrating eyes, full of life, and on his still fresh lips an almost youthful smile. Cold, reflective, entirely deprived of those natural qualities that easily win over our sympathy and trust. Not succeeding in simulating any warmth of affection, he tries to appear at least affable, but his graciousness, in trying to be spontaneous rather than reassuring, embarrasses and sometimes disconcerts one." (*Naked*, p. 4.)

Pirandello is a thinker and a man of unusual honesty. For this reason he knows the difficulties that life offers to those who possess these two rare attributes. Men who are not given to thought and are not honest solve the difficulties of life in a very swift manner: either they do not see them or they suppress them. Pirandello has always compelled himself to stand face to face with the many contradictions that human existence offers. He has seen them, analyzed them, and grieved

10

over them even if he has outwardly appeared to laugh. He is not a kindly person, but he is extremely compassionate and sympathetic towards human weaknesses.

We are interested in the vicissitudes of his life which have a direct bearing on his art. We shall not tarry too long on his birth and childhood. That he was born at Girgenti in 1867 during an epidemic of cholera has the vividness of the picturesque, yet it is an event wholly independent of him, and one which he shared with so many other children who were born at that time.

It is necessary to have known the monotonous, sluggish, unchanging conditions of life in southern Italy during the eighties in order to understand many events pertaining to Pirandello's childhood. We should study this period of Italian and European civilization without indulging in meaningless recriminations. History, like nature, has its instincts and milestones, and is often cruel in all its awesome grandeur. The present is the child of the past, and we should feel reverence before the conditions that existed then, and the noble efforts that were made to hasten the turning and the advancing of the wheels of progress.

I think of a town where I lived when a child, and I see men and things caught alike in the tentacles of immobility: division of classes, poverty, shabby houses sleeping under the blazing sun with pots of red flowers at the small and dark windows, which made one think of hearts that bled in silence without ever losing their taste for beauty. At times the silence of the town merged with that of the fields till it was suddenly broken by the passing of a group of tattered children filling the air with shouts; then silence again, only interrupted by the beating of the hoofs of a donkey led by a peasant woman. In the mass of poor hovels stood two or three big houses, immutable in their bulky strength, always dark, dingy. I remember old servants as devoted as slaves and as sweet as mothers. At dusk they would tell us stories of ghosts and of brigands who had kidnapped our grandfathers long before we were born and had held them for ransom of flour, pork, oil, and wine. Our little hearts beat fast, and our fancy with eagerness and fright followed the brigands who lived in the woods and had long, dark beards and rifles, and rode lean, swift horses.

Pirandello knew one of these humble, tender, and unforgettable servants in Maria Stella, who was a part of the household. She used to tell little Luigi ghost stories, and she kindled his already ardent fancy. He has related to his Italian biographer, Federico Vittore Nardelli, that he often heard shouts from a dark street behind his house where rivals met and decided by the flourish of a knife who was right. He remembered that his mother had gone to the window, had hastily glanced into the street and had closed the shutters.

Imagination works most feverishly when we are in a situation and environment that know no change. The primitive and sluggish atmosphere of Sicily was bound to inspire a sensitive boy like Pirandello with the sense of the inevitable in life—there is no greater philosopher than the Italian peasant or the Sicilian donkey—and later the artist portrayed the stoic passiveness that the child had noticed in the men and women whom he saw caught in that changeless existence. Everything lasted in those distant days. People wore plain heavy clothing that was meant to do for their lifetime. The lastingness of everything meant no change, no production, but a massive solidity of life that would be a torment to us men of today and that meant a quiet, although monotonous, existence for our ancestors.

There hung over Sicily, still in a somewhat medieval economic condition, a pall of inertia broken by sudden outbursts of jealousy and of crime. A few old people still recollect this life which has for them, as it should have for us, the delicate and melancholy charm of what is no longer, but was once alive with hopes and fears, sorrows and joys, tears and smiles.

Such an environment could not but be conducive to an introspective attitude—that is typical of many Sicilians. They are smoldering fires under dark, solemn faces that often look hieratic, behind eyes composed in a fixity that bespeaks conscious restraint. It also developed a great power of observation in the future artist, an observation not of the external, decorative kind, but one that pierced through the shell of men and things, blossoming into a subtle and penetrating psychological art.

All people look, and most of them see, but only a few observe. Pirandello is among the few. Of a character very dear to his heart he has written: "All his pleasure is in observing. He seems to be absent minded and never to see anything. Mother gets provoked: What! Didn't you see this? Didn't you see that? No. He hasn't seen anything, but he has noticed, on the other hand, only he among all other persons, certain things that when he says them amaze us." (*When One Is Somebody*, p. 101.)

Fedeiico Vittore Nardelli in Pirandello's biography, called *L'uomo segreto* (*The Unknown Man*), has recorded many facts that must have left a deep impression on Pirandello as a child, since he can recollect them even today. The chief actors in the drama of Pirandello's life were his parents, his wife, Donna Antonietta, and his father-in-law. His father, Stefano, was a wealthy owner of sulphur mines in Sicily. He was bearded, extremely tall and powerful. He was very violent, and was fired upon four times. Once he had a dangerous experience with Cola Camizzi, a member of the Mafia who wanted to collect money from him. Stefano paid him not with money, but with a slap that knocked him down. The thug ambushed him and shot him in the shoulder.

Cola Camizzi appears in retrospect in one of Pirandello's dramatic sketches, *The Other Son*, as the head of a group of brigands who harass and terrorize the island. Such an experience as the one encountered by Stefano was not out of the ordinary at that time. People, especially if well-to-do, often took the law in their own hands and never went out without a rifle, even if brigands were beginning to be a romantic and hazy memory. During the political turmoil of preceding years, security was rather scarce and individuals learned how to rely on themselves for protection. Hence, the habit of carrying weapons and the feeling of physical prowess that was characteristic of the generation of Pirandello's father.

Pirandello lived his childhood in the twilight hour of heroism and grandeur that set in after the epic battles for Italian independence. Italy had been slumbering for centuries in a medieval economy that Cavour had but slightly changed. The country had attempted to solve two great problems at the same time—the political and the economic. It wanted to follow in the footsteps of industrialized countries like England and Germany, while it aspired to reach national unity. Through great sacrifices and heroism, the country had achieved its political independence, and it was asking its still rural soul to hurl itself into the turmoil of industrial life.

Pirandello's mother, Donna Caterina, was such a modest and long-suffering woman as only women of that time knew how to be. Living with a man as despotic and violent as Stefano required frequent appeal to those virtues. Her life was entirely absorbed by family duties, since women of the *bourgeoisie,* even if they belonged to well-to-do families, had to work very hard at a time when home comforts were extremely limited. Husbands in those days were not particularly given to faithfulness, and economic limitations led to the slavery of women. Today women rebel and go to court. In the past they shed tears silently, and one day Pirandello learned that the eyes of a mother are made not only to look at us with tenderness and fondness, but also to cry. That day was a great test for his character. He was only in his teens. He discovered that his father had fallen in love again with a cousin to whom he had once before been engaged. In their renewed interest, he and she met in the parlor of a convent on the excuse of visiting their common aunt, the abbess. Pirandello dashed into the parlor one day and told the woman of the grief of his mother. His father had hidden behind a green curtain, but the son could see the tips of his black shoes.

Among the events worthy of notice in his childhood is the one pertaining to the commandment that he had just learned in church: Clothe the naked. He had received from his father a new sailor suit and had proudly put it on. On his way to church he met a poor boy who was all in rags. Luigi took off his suit and gave it to him because the Bible said that that was the thing to do. The mother of the poor boy, very much disturbed, blushing and gesticulating, returned the sailor suit to Luigi's mother, and Luigi, the future humorist, learned that day that it is not easy to practise the commandments.

Pirandello has immortalized in a short story, *The Little Wax Madonna,* an event that filled his childhood with wonder and indignation. During the month of May which is dedicated to the Virgin, there was a lottery every Sunday evening after the rosary. The winner received a little wax statue of the Madonna under a glass cover. Tickets cost two *sous.* The day of the last lottery Luigi met a pale little boy, Luzzu, who had never been able to take part in the lottery because he had been sick. Luigi gave him his own ticket, crossed out his name, and inserted Luzzu's. When the ticket bearing the name of the winner was drawn, the priest, ignoring the poor boy's name, called out that of Luigi Pirandello in order to ingratiate himself with the lad's wealthy father. Luigi was surprised and indignant. He protested, he shouted, he burst into tears. It was of no use. The people took him, forced him into a procession, and they marched to the Pirandello home singing hymns. Donna Caterina, so Nardelli informs us, returned the statuette to the curate, and Luigi never went back to the church again. That fact must have impressed his mind with the irony of the situation in which the winner was refusing the prize while the people stifled his sobs and cries with the rolling of drums and with songs.

Pirandello began to write poetry at the age of sixteen, and even at that early age he had conceived a hatred for rhetoric, the refuge of young people who usually began to try their wings in poetry by following the pattern of Petrarch. Pirandello in his first poems attacked the "old words worn out with usage" that surround and hide our thought "like flies a spittle."

Fiery, impetuous, like all repressed people when they suddenly flare into bursts of passion, Pirandello at eighteen became engaged to a girl four years older than he. He was ready to give up studying and help his father in his business in order to get married. After three months' trial, Don Stefano sent him to the University of Rome. He saw that Luigi was not meant to be a business man.

As Pirandello grew up, other facts struck him and left deep imprints on his literary works as well as on his character. Among these were of paramount importance the scandal of the Roman Bank in 1894 and the repression of the uprising of the peasants at Palermo in 1898. Pirandello later wrote a novel that deals with the Roman scandal: *I vecchi e i giovani* (*The Old and the Young*). He has described as follows his impressions of those days that formed the warp and the woof of his novel: "Every evening, every morning, newsboys shouted in the streets of Rome the name of this or of that deputy in the national parliament, connecting it with a swindle or fraud against this or that bank. Yes, just so. From the Italian sky there rained mud in those days and people indulged in mud-slinging as a pastime. Mud clung everywhere on the pale and convulsed faces of assailed and assailants, on the medals once received on the battlefield, on war crosses and citations, on frock coats and on the insignia of public buildings as well as of newspaper offices." Pirandello felt powerless before such a national shame, and used his art as an outlet for his indignation.

He was equally powerless before the events that led to the declaration of martial law in Sicily in 1898 that cost so many victims among the poor peasants. He gives his own version of the situation: "Those Sicilian peasants, finding in their rage against injustice the courage to affirm with violence a right of their own, had gone to till the crown lands. Frightened by the intervention of the troops, they had hastened to ask the city government to divide the land among them. In the absence of the mayor, an official had appeared at the window, and, to ward off any possible hostile demonstration, had told them to go back and till the land; but the crowd had found the militia in their way." (Nardelli, *L'uomo se-*

16

greto, p. 97.) In the encounter, many met death at the hands of the soldiers.

The mood that colors the novel *The Old and the Young*, is the reflection of Pirandello's state of mind when he went to the University of Rome. His recollection of his student days here, as confided to Nardelli, is far from being happy or even pleasant. The historical school prevailed in the lugubrious halls of the Sapienza. Pirandello felt pity and disgust for the manner in which old Professor Nannarelli taught Italian literature and Professor Occioni, Latin literature. Fearless, and at times violent like his father, Pirandello clashed with the latter professor while in his second year at the University. The matter was referred to the faculty council with the possibility of serious consequences. The great Ernesto Monaci, one of the founders of Romance philology, whom Pirandello revered and appreciated as we all did who had the privilege of being his pupils, suggested that Pirandello go to study for his doctor's degree at Bonn in Germany.

Pirandello worked very hard at Bonn because he wanted to be able to graduate, find a position, and get married. He has always had the good or bad fortune, one hardly knows which, of taking life seriously. Three years of absence had weakened his love for his *fiancée*, but he was ready to keep his promise. Having returned from Bonn he hastened to Sicily to his *fiancée*, but the two soon realized that an abyss had opened between them. The engagement was broken by mutual consent. Pirandello then went to Rome and lived in an old abandoned convent at the top of Monte Cave, near Rocca di Papa, where a small inn had been opened. Six other literary men and artists had found refuge there: Fleres, Ojetti, Mantica, Cesareo, Vianini, and Giusti, personalities of the republic of Italian letters during Pirandello's youth. Writing absorbed his life entirely, and he wrote there *L'esclusa* (*Excluded*), one of his best novels.

Pirandello's literary career developed in a parallel line with the æsthetic school which predominated in Italy around the nineties and condemned his great art to obscurity. Those were the days in which the *Convito, Capitan Fracassa,* and *Cronaca Bizantina* made their appearance; journals that were the expression of perfect technicians of art, of men who reacted against the new democratic strain that was appearing in the Italian social body and that the reactionaries, both literary and political, were forcing into the arms of the extreme left. Pirandello, a liberal in politics, was an antirhetorician in art, a combination that by way of contrast corresponded to the position of the followers of the æsthetic school who backed political reactionary methods.

He fought stubbornly and passionately against the cult of the superman that D'Annunzio had popularized. An individual like Pirandello could not accept that superhumanity that on the wings of rhetoric and under the bewitching veils of imagery said little or nothing about man, his inner anguish and torment. The public, always ready to brush aside an individualistic and honest writer, paid him with indifference. No editor accepted Pirandello's writings for many years. His works, a great many short stories and novels, were not known until 1915, when the literary world of Europe heard through James Joyce and Benjamin Crémieux, an Irishman and a Frenchman, that there was something new and vital in the literary production of this unknown writer. Even then the Italian public was indifferent. Pirandello was not daunted, however. Like an old paladin, but without the splendor of shining armor, living in the cold flame of his own thoughts, he continued his struggle until the public was forced to take notice of him. The War compelled people to draw within themselves, and the art of Pirandello was duly appreciated after the War in the stormy years of 1918 to 1925, when Italy was on the very brink of national disintegration.

Pirandello's literary production began with poetry, developed into the novel through a form of ironical realism all his own, and finally flowed into the theatre where he produced the best that his genius had to offer to art and to mankind. There is the literature of man and of mankind—literature useful for a quarter of an hour, for an hour, for a month, for a year; and there is the literature that defies time, rising towards immortality. There are works, characters, vicissitudes, and pages that assign to Pirandello's drama a place in the latter class.

At Bonn he wrote poetry which was collected into a volume bearing the title of *Pasqua di Gea* (*Springtime of Gæa*), dedicated to Jenny, a girl he met in that city. In spite of the classical name, Pirandello strictly adhered to the inspiration that he always derived from life as humans live it.

Luigi Capuana, one of the leaders of the naturalistic school, to whom Pirandello was introduced by the gay and genial humorist Ugo Fleres, advised him to write prose. The great Verga recognized in the novels and short stories that Pirandello submitted to him not only another Sicilian islander, but also a kindred soul in his tormented way of feeling life. He must also have seen other traits that were dear to him: unadulterated art, honesty, clear thinking. He felt that with Pirandello "a new light was appearing."

Pirandello's literary dream was broken by his father, who reminded him that it was time for him to get married, and he finally agreed to marry Antonietta Portulano, a girl he had never seen. Their marriage was arranged by their parents. Portulano was a business partner of Stefano Pirandello. They had made money speculating on sulphur, and they agreed to seal another bargain with the lives of their children just as they had played on the falling and rising prices of the market.

Antonietta had received the rudimentary education that girls of the *bourgeoisie* used to receive in a convent. Her mother had died in childbirth because she had refused to have a doctor attend her, on account of her husband's jealousy. Signor Portulano was as jealous as only a Sicilian can be, if we accept Pirandello's verdict on the score.

The two were married in January 1894, after a very brief and superficial acquaintance, and they settled in Rome, where they lived on the generous allowance given to Pirandello by his father, and on Antonietta's dowry. The first years of their marriage were the most pleasant. I do not use the banal word happy because it is hard to conceive of Pirandello being in a happy

19

mood. There were three children from the union: Stefano in 1895, Lietta in 1897, Fausto in 1899. Stefano now writes poetry under the pen name of Stefano Landi, since he does not wish to exploit his father's celebrity. Fausto is an artist.

The first ten years of Pirandello's married life were absorbed by his family and by his literary activity. He was asked to contribute to the *Marzocco,* a famous publication with decidedly æsthetic tendencies, edited by Angiolo Orvieto. At first he refused, saying that his ideals were too different from those of the *Marzocco.* He finally accepted with the understanding that he would have complete freedom to do as he chose. His first article was one on Giovanni Verga, exalting the art of the great Sicilian writer. His closed, concentrated, and passionate nature made him continue his violent attacks against the predominating literary fashion represented by D'Annunzio.

Pirandello's anti-D'Annunzian attitude goes beyond the field of pure literature. It also encompasses the temperament and the moral temper of the two men. D'Annunzio was always ready to pass from one love affair to another, and even to imagine *affaires d'amour.* Like an eternal adolescent, he boasted of them, and did not hesitate to reveal even the most intimate actions and sentiments of those women whom he tied to the chariot of his lust. Pirandello, bound by pity and self-respect to his tragic family, always remained true to his wife.

A terrible blow awaited him, however, in the ruin by flood of his father's sulphur mines in which all the family fortune was invested, and in the loss, in a certain sense, of his wife. His family life became the oppressing weight, the stifling and torturing prison, that he has portrayed in the lives of so many of his characters. Donna Antonietta had suffered a great deal when Fausto was born. The serious financial reverses in which her dowry was lost found her in that weak condition, and the shock was so great that it affected her mind.

Without any other source of income except that of his pen, Pirandello was compelled to seek a position as a teacher. Thanks to an influential friend who held his literary merits

in high esteem, he was appointed Professor of Italian Literature at the Istituto Superiore Femminile di Magistero, a
sort of Teacher's College in Rome.

From 1904 on, Pirandello lived a life of torment that gave
him the sensation of being closed in an unbreakable cage,
caught there forever. Never has the feeling of the weight of
daily existence, of its unbearable character, and of the need
of liberation been expressed with more humanity and pathos
than in the work of Luigi Pirandello, as he presents the
sense of oppression experienced by his characters who are
caught in a plight from which they have no hope of extricat-
ing themselves.

His characters are the reflection of his very self, and they
are, therefore, shy, introspective and self-effacing, much in
the manner of their creator. Pirandello has never looked com-
placently at himself. If he had done so, he would never have
put on his characters' lips words like these: "I could spit at
my image when I see myself in the mirror." For this reason
he does not glorify his characters. He tells one of them con-
solingly: "I am sorry to tell you that you do not cut a very
nice figure in this comedy."

As his wife accused him of duplicity and of unfaithfulness,
he saw near himself the shadow of another man, of the one
that his wife had created, hateful and low, the one who made
her shout and go into hysterics. Pirandello must have often
wondered which of the two was the real one. The imaginary
man had as much reality and consistency for her, as well as
for him in his bruising effect, as the consciousness of his own
actual self had for him. Indeed, he was gradually forced to
acknowledge that the fictitious self was so strong as to crowd
out the real one. This sad realization gave life to the experience of one of his heroines, who goes home under an assumed
name and sees the fictitious being cloud and almost kill in her
the feelings of the real mother for her own child who looked
upon her as an intruder.

Pirandello did all that a human being could to allay his
wife's suspicions. He stayed at home constantly, and gave up
his friends, drawn into the whirl of his wife's insanity, patient

and resigned, but letting his fantasy work in the immobility to which he condemned himself. He went so far as to give his wife every penny he made, keeping for himself sixty centimes a day for carfare to school. But it was of no avail.

Donna Antonietta's derangement of the mind grew worse, and it took more and more the form of jealousy. She even left her husband and went back to Sicily for three months with her children. Gradually she became violent and passed from moods of tenderness to outbursts of fury. An old, honest, and compassionate physician advised Pirandello to keep her with him rather than send her to a sanitarium, believing that it would be better for her. Pirandello agreed and took that cross as he had taken so many others, stoically and compassionately. It was in this closed torment that was born, at least in germ, the drama of Luigi Pirandello.

He suffered everything in silence, and through his mind flashed irrational thoughts while in his heart surged a feeling of powerless revolt. When he wrote he gave vent to that tormented inner life by envying madmen who could shout whatever they wanted, who could reveal their strangest thoughts and queerest emotions with impunity. He must have written his agonizing pages while his wife frantically pounded at the door of his studio, accusing him and threatening him.

In the tortures of his daily life, near his children whose childhood and adolescence were overshadowed and saddened by the madness of their mother and by the stoical resignation of their father, he learned what it is to aspire to a life different from the one to which we are condemned. He also learned the comforting power of illusion; an illusion, however, which tantalizes us with a prospect of what life might have been and was not. His characters are the embodiment of himself pounding at the portals of the mystery of destiny as desperately as his wife pounded outside his door. Why? Why? What can a man do after asking in vain without receiving any answer? Laughter, if he can laugh, is his salvation. His heart is too bitter and his nerves too tense to respond to the soothing effect of tears.

The World War contributed, together with the circumstances of his private existence, to make life appear more irrational, absurd, and cruel. Stefano, his oldest son, mindful of his ancestors who had fought with Garibaldi, joined the army as a volunteer. Every minute marked the agony of the father who pictured what might happen. Concern over Stefano made Donna Antonietta more upset and violent. She began to persecute Lietta too, accusing her of wishing to take the reins of the household away from her. The girl tried to commit suicide with an old revolver, but the bullet lodged in the barrel and she was saved.

We can easily imagine Pirandello's life. Stefano was a prisoner in Bohemia amid suffering and privation. Fausto was in the army, dangerously ill as the result of being drafted while still recovering from an operation. Pirandello felt himself to be but a poor, crushed man who could not even have the consolation of feeling his sorrow and anguish like an ordinary mortal. His fame had spread and he could not go out in the streets of Rome without attracting an attention that offended the feeling of his own humility. One day, while dining alone at a little inn in Rome, two young men looked at him so insistently that he in a fit of rage threatened to throw a bottle at them. He has lent this experience to the hero of one of his plays, *When One Is Somebody*. It was at this time that Pirandello thought of the most agonizing cases of mental torture and enclosed them in his comedies: *As Well as Before, Better than Before; All for the Best; Man, Beast, and Virtue; Each in His Own Way; Right You Are if You Think You Are; Cap and Bells; Think It Over, Giacomino; Liolà; Mrs. Morli, One and Two;* and *The Pleasure of Honesty.* Tragedy and laughter, and the greater the tragedy the more spasmodic the laughter! Donna Antonietta's death in 1918 ended a pitiful and tragic situation.

Pirandello had turned to the theatre during the War. He was urged to do so by Angelo Musco, a great actor who was determined to make a success of his comic ability at any cost. Musco wanted a comedy and begged Pirandello to write one for him, the amusing Musco who during the War made people laugh and forget their sorrows at least for a brief time. Once

Pirandello began to write plays, he wrote passionately and relentlessly. He has confessed to Nardelli that in one year he wrote nine plays. *Think It Over, Giacomino* was written in three days; *Right You Are if You Think You Are* in six. Two great actresses, Emma Gramatica and Marta Abba, played the leading feminine rôles, while Pirandello watched most carefully how they as well as the other actors interpreted their respective parts.

Pirandello has never begged for honors nor for recognition, either from the government or from the public. He has stubbornly kept on writing, unmindful of the fact that some praised and exalted him while others jeered at him. Only late in his career as a dramatist has he received any honors. It was not until the French Government proposed to bestow the Legion of Honor on the now famous writer, that the Italian Government realized it had not taken any notice of him. In order not to be second to a foreign government, Italy hastened to give Pirandello the *commenda* of the Crown of Italy. Mussolini has given him the high *commenda* of the Order of Saint Maurice, and has made him a member of the Italian Academy. He received world recognition with the award of the Nobel prize in 1934 which has been not only the acknowledgment of his literary merit but also a vindication of his unadulterated art.

Fame and wealth have not changed him. He has remained the same modest man, determined and strong willed. In the year 1925 he set out to found a national theatre. With a small group of interested persons he took over the Odescalchi Theatre in Rome, where Guido Podrecca showed his marionettes before he paraded them all over the.world. The building was remodeled and designated to become the cradle of a new Italian renaissance in the drama. Mussolini attended the opening night when, in a gorgeous setting, Pirandello's short play, *In a Sanctuary,* was given. The Premier declared this movement sponsored by his régime. Marta Abba was engaged, and from Milan she came to Rome, where she appeared in the rôle of Ersilia Drei in *Naked* and later distinguished herself in other famous rôles. Another great actor, Ruggero Ruggeri, joined the troupe. Pirandello with his company went to England, France, and Germany. Artistically the enterprise was successful. Financially it was a fiasco; it cost Pirandello six hundred thousand *lire*.

Among all the irksome experiences of his dramatic venture, he found joy in the love of his children, who always stood by him, understanding his good and long-suffering heart, and in his tender friendship for beautiful Marta Abba. Pirandello's drama seems to be made for her with its desperate and agonizing truth. She interprets his tragic figures with a passion and an adherence to their anguish that reveals in them new beauty and depth. The author is grateful to his interpreter for giving life to his characters by living them in her flesh and soul. She is like a daughter to him.

In these last years Pirandello has lived a wandering life in France, South America, and the United States, even in Hollywood, where he will soon supervise the filming of *Six Characters*. He has no attachments, no home, no possessions. He has divided his royalties among his three children with the sense of equity and justice that has always characterized his actions. From his pen will undoubtedly flow other works before he faces the last tragedy of man—death.

III

Pirandello's Philosophy of Life

Pirandello has subjected to a pitiless but passionate *critique* man and life, exploring every fold and nook, and presenting to us convincingly the sad and pitiful spectacle of the tragedy of being human. In this he has the justification of sincerity and, above all, that of having lived the sadness with which he has enveloped life.

Standing before the panorama that the universe offers to every thinking man, Pirandello is struck by the fact that one is born plant, beast, or man by mere chance, and that one is fatefully and irrevocably closed in that form for the span of one's earthly existence. Man, however, is different from plants and animals in that he cannot entrust himself to instinct with the same subconscious and happy abandonment as can lower beings. For, as soon as man yields to instinct, he sets in motion the so-called intellect which is nothing more, in the majority of cases, than a mechanism of deception through which he attempts to give idealistic motives and terms to his instinctive actions. One can follow Pirandello step by step as he analyzes life and envelops it in the web of his pessimism, pointing out its harrowing contradictions. On the whole, Pirandello's philosophy is not very comforting. Standing pensively and grievingly before the spectacle of daily existence, he has concluded "that there is nothing to conclude, because it is so," which is a conclusion in itself.

This philosophy was fashioned after the experience and observation of many years, upon realizing that life constantly loses its bloom; that the faces of those he had once known as children had begun to look old; that the strength of these people had ebbed away; that their skin, once soft and velvety, was rough and full of wrinkles; that their eyes, once sparkling with youth, were dimmed by age. Deeply touched and perturbed, with the conviction of one who is stating an opinion that sums up his life, he concludes that "everything is

26

indefinite, fleeting, and evanescent." (*Each in His Own Way,*
p. 3.)

The author starts from the premise that our knowledge
about our very self is painfully limited. Mattia Pascal, one
of the best-drawn characters in Pirandello's fiction, states, in
looking back at his former life: "One of the few things, indeed, perhaps the only one that I knew as a positive fact
was this: that my name was Mattia Pascal." (*Mattia Pascal,*
p. 1.) Man does not know much about himself beyond an
intimate knowledge of his physical being and worldly possessions: his clothes, his money, his home, his estate.

This belief, instead of making Pirandello cling to the
tangible sides of his life and self, leads him to a complete
detachment from them. He does not understand why we give
so much importance to the gross and solid aspects of tangible
reality. He is unwilling to grant that the human body is our
most personal possession, since it decays so steadily, though
imperceptibly. Life is a short-lived dream, and shadows are
the most important element in it, since we live on memories
of what has been or in longings of what is yet to be. In the
changes that unceasingly go on in us, we cannot cling to
our tangible and actual reality, since this reality is in a constant state of flux, and therefore it offers nothing solid and
permanent.

This attitude of detachment from the tangible aspects of
life is brought about by the author's unsatisfied desire to
find something solid on which to rest, since there is in
Pirandello, as in all human beings, a great longing for life,
warm and fluid, happy and joyous. If he proclaims the glory
of abstraction, it is only after he has been violently and bitterly offended and disappointed by actual experience. There
is therefore in him and, by way of reflection, in his characters, a constant clash between his longing for the gifts of
sensuous life and the sad disappointment experienced when
his lips touch a cup that is empty, or a fruit that is withered
and bitter. This is one of the deepest *motifs* in Pirandello's
drama, and it has been beautifully realized in *Henry IV,* although it circulates in many of his plays.

27

As Pirandello looks at his fellow-men and at himself, he discovers that we are all "immobilized" in the concept that each of our friends and acquaintances forms of us. Moreover, we are also crystallized in the concept that each of us forms of himself. As we grow old and youth recedes from us, we poignantly cling to that fading image. The author has no other explanation to offer upon noticing that we cover most religiously the bald spots on our heads, we dye our hair, we straighten up when we walk in the streets, and slouch into sad figures when we are unobserved. To him a portrait is a touching attempt to stem the advancing destruction of death by holding close to us the image of what we used to be.

Man not only encloses himself in a concept, but he also immobilizes in it every one of his emotions and feelings. This is a natural though tragic necessity, and it dwarfs human sentiments. The Philosopher, a character in one of Pirandello's early plays, points out that churches are nothing but the tangible form of man's religious instinct, that "not satisfied to abide in the heart of man, it has built a house for itself—and what a house: domes, naves, columns, gold, marble, precious canvases! As a house of God, the universe is unquestionably larger and richer than a church; the spirit of man in adoration before divine mystery is incomparably more noble and precious than any altar. But this is the fate of all sentiments that wish to build a house for themselves: they are, of necessity, dwarfed and become a little childish because of their vanity." According to Pirandello, this is how the infinite which abides in man fares when it takes a tangible form, without which, however, it could not reveal itself. In the clash between the beauty of what is not and the misery of what is, we are saddened by their irreconcilable contrast.

Pirandello has gone deeply into the secret chamber of man's heart and has discovered tragic wants. He has seen that there are things that we dare not confess even to ourselves, moral deeds that lie like heavy stones in the depth of our conscience. Who can go before his fellow-men with an unveiled soul? In this realization there is an echo of the great but terrifying words: "He that is without sin among you, let him first cast a stone."

The author has also been tempted to look at his existence in retrospect, and has discovered that the ideas of his youth are no longer his, and that the beliefs of yesterday have become the illusions of today. It was inevitable that at this realization a sense of emptiness should envelop him. Every basis for his thought crumbled under him, and he felt himself wandering in a universe where extinguished stars moved in a meaningless whirl as if ready to plunge into the abyss of nothingness. One of Pirandello's characters has expressed this belief in unforgettable words: "If we think over the illusions which we no longer entertain, the things which now do not *seem* as they *used to seem,* we feel suspended in a void, since we must also argue that what we feel today, that is, the reality of today, is destined to appear as the illusion of tomorrow." (*Six Characters in Search of an Author,* p. 130.) This is all the more true since history proves that in the forward advance of progress new ideas dislodge and kill old ones, just as in life children are fated to take the place of their parents, and one generation passes over the tombstones of another.

Pirandello is not abstract in his approach to the theme of his pessimism of life. He calls our attention to such aspects of the existence of his characters as may be easily compared with those of the existence of each one of us. He recalls to our mind the day when we, like the Son in *Six Characters in Search of an Author,* discovered that our parents lived as man and woman, for themselves, outside the image of father and mother which we had conceived of them and in which they lived for us. We are also compelled to mourn with another of Pirandello's characters the fact that not even the deepest affections, not even love for our mother, can resist the fatal onslaught of life. Life is a ruinous torrent and carries along in its fury men and things, irrevocably.

No happy outlook is brought to us by observing the relations between man and his fellow-creatures. Our acts appear to others as if they were enveloped in a haze and smoke which veil the flame that glows in them when we act spontaneously. With eager earnestness and passionate conviction he points out that we grow up in the belief that we are one, a definite individual, with a clear-cut contour, with definite qualities, and with a personality. Life proves that we are not, that in reality this subjectiveness of man's perceptions create in us as many-faceted persons as are individuals who look at and know us. Closed in his subjectivism, man interprets the acts of others according to his own ideas of human behavior. The result is an incommunicability that offers one of the most recurrent and fertile *motifs* in Pirandello's theatre.

Brought face to face with the grimacing countenance of the daily tragedy, Pirandello seeks the cause of man's isolation, and he finds that words are a most inadequate means of expression. "The core of the evil is exactly here!" says the Father in *Six Characters in Search of an Author,* "In the words we use! We all have a world of things within us, each his own world. And how can we understand each other if, to the words that I say, I give the sense of things that are within me, while he who listens to them, inevitably, receives them with the sense that they have for him, from the world that he has within him?" (*Six Characters in Search of an Author,* p. 30.)

To understand the impenetrability of human beings, we must keep in mind the accusations that poor deranged Donna Antonietta hurled at her husband in her frantic state of mind. In his own flesh and soul, Pirandello lived the isolation of his characters, an isolation that leads to hostility and hatred.

All that poets have said to exalt life has appeared cold and empty to him as it echoed in his tragic soul. Man fosters the illusion of the glory of his will power, yet he has to acknowledge that his will is limited in two paramount facts: birth and death. They are both independent of his will and "between the two events many things happen that we all wish would not happen, and to which we unwillingly must submit." (*Each in His Own Way,* p. 64.) Men will say very proudly: This day which is just dawning will be ours; we shall mold it as we wish. In reality we repeat what others have done before us. Traditions and customs are there, tyrannically imposing on us what others have decreed and obeyed. We speak and must repeat the words that have always been said. "Do you believe that you live?" queries one of Pirandello's characters. "You are re-chewing the life of the dead." (*Each in His Own Way*, p. 107.)

We might argue with the author, in an imaginary conversation, that man can boast of a definite asset in human conscience. Pirandello would look at us with his wistful and whimsical eyes and say that he is aware that conscience exists in the poor of spirit who do not need it, but he is unable to find it in the over-intellectualized beings that he meets in his imaginary wanderings.

A man like Pirandello cannot think of nature in positive terms, any more than can the mariner and the aviator who know the fury of the tempest on the high sea and the slashing of the storms in midair. Both the mariner and the aviator see in nature an enemy to conquer, just as Pirandello sees in it the cause of the plight in which his characters are struggling in a vain attempt to free themselves. He calls our attention to the fact that life is monotonously, if not serenely, unfolding when, suddenly, an earthquake sows destruction and sorrow and leaves us uncertain whether human lives have more purpose than the Japanese beetles that the dark, callous, rough hand of a farmer snatches from the sweet-tasting ear of corn in order to throw them into a jar full of gasoline. Pirandello has allowed Leone Gala in *Each in His Own Rôle* to voice his deep-seated feeling that life is something that allures and hurts. Leone Gala proclaims his defense against the evil that life does to all, inevitably. Life is cruel: "You eat meat at the table. Who provides it for you? A pullet or a calf. You never think of it. We all hurt one another reciprocally; and each hurts himself. It is inevitable. It is life." (*Each in His Own Rôle*, p. 36.)

We are brought into the presence of evil and death while a ghastly spectacle unfolds before us. There are parents whose children are born imbeciles, unable to use their limbs, unable to speak. There are hospitals filled with pain, wars that kill millions, maim more millions, torture body and soul. At the fringe of this life lurks death, and it chills every joy and destroys every affection.

If the thought of nature is not comforting to Pirandello, that of modern civilization is not less barren of solace to him. He sees in it only the frantic efforts to escape the sadness of life. Man moves, builds cities, crosses the ocean, conquers the air, only because he tries to escape his inner torment, the torment of his intellect. He is engaged in a mad race for speed which is followed by disappointment because our thought moves faster than mechanical contrivances. The sad plight of Pirandello is that he cannot suggest contemplation in the oriental fashion. The peaceful life of a distant mythical past is beyond our reach, gone forever, the penalty that we pay for progress. Intimately and ultimately civilization is to Pirandello a synonym for tragic artificiality. Yet we must submit to it because there is no escape.

The element that contributes most in building the gloomy structure of Pirandello's pessimism is instinct. Man is compelled to yield to it even when he is perfectly aware of the dire consequences that it will entail. Pirandello considers instinct an acid which corrodes the best that life possesses. His drama begins where instinct ends. His characters are people who give themselves to passion and cannot live in it. They readily pass from passion to hatred, and they cling to it with a cruel and spasmodic tenacity. Their brain and their heart stand vigil on the flesh that yields; they rebel and the result is the lucid madness of the individuals that we see suffering in Pirandello's drama.

If we exclude the early plays conceived in the light of naturalistic principles, Pirandello's art presents a sensuality that is neither self-satisfied, beastly, nor wholesome. His drama opens at the moment when instinct has lost all its impetuousness, and the warmth of passion has been chilled by the cold dissecting power of the intellect. As a consequence, only reason predominates in the psychological life of the characters, and it leads them in their aimless wanderings over the bleak desert of their existence.

The background of most of Pirandello's plays is a wrong relation, the experience of which leaves his characters desperately disappointed. Instinct and lust appear paltry and despised, especially as the characters rebel at having their whole lives and beings identified with a moment of weakness. The rebellion of the characters is accompanied by a perplexed state of mind in the author, who seems unable to understand the power of something which is so devastating and yet seems so negligible and hateful when looked at with a certain objectivity. Pirandello is disconsolately silent before this perplexity, and often takes refuge in laughter. This thoughtful and grieving silence, mingled with a burst of laughter at human weakness, is reflected on Pirandello's countenance, and it forms the most appealing trait of his tragic personality.

There arises at this point the problem of morality as a substratum of Pirandello's art. Many people, especially if vowed to ethical orthodoxy at any cost, would call Pirandello immoral. Yet there is no other modern writer for whom morality is as intimately imbedded in the very texture of life and art as for Luigi Pirandello. This is evidenced by the fact that his drama is almost always brought about by the breaking of a moral law; by the fact that Pirandello never treats instinct as an aphrodisiac; by the unraveling of the plot that reaffirms the validity of the moral law. Pirandello does not need the glamour of immorality to make his art attractive, just as he never allows it to become laden down by the weight of didacticism. He is often provincial in the familiar tone of most of his plays, although he reaches the universal in the implications that he lends to the everyday occurrences on which he builds his drama.

Many may resent the drastic pessimism that is found at the basis of Pirandello's thought. Pirandello does not wish to give a universal value and meaning to his pessimistic sense of life. His exasperated subjectivism rejects any categorical and universal interpretation of it. If truth has as many aspects as there are thinking individuals, a life concept is the projection of each single experience. Pirandello refuses to be dogmatic.

Pessimism forms the background of Pirandello's drama, but the author has skilfully veiled his pessimism behind humor and laughter, relieving the extreme tension that oppresses his pitiful characters. In the foreground one sees ludicrous figures, victims of instinct and of Pirandello's sense of humor that expresses itself in laughter at human weakness, a laughter that hurts him although it relieves his tension.

In spite of the fact that the central part of Pirandello's picture of life is painted in dark hues, there shines in the distant horizon a feeble, iridescent light which is derived from the author's idealism. Like the idealists of all times, Pirandello contrasts the drab and sorrowful condition of man on earth with the vision of a perfect life lost in the distance of imagination whence all life originates. His idealism takes the form either of a cosmic and religious sense of universal life or of a lofty ideal existence to which man aspires when actual life offends him. This evanescent Platonism, which in its vagueness will not stand very close analysis, often echoes in Pirandello's drama, and it assumes greater importance in his latest plays. Idealism and pessimism are closer than we may at first surmise, since pessimism is often nothing but disappointed idealism.

Pirandello is fully aware of the existence and validity of man's ideal aspirations. He confesses: "We all have seen, in certain moments, appear and kindle within us a light that seems to emanate from other skies—which permits us to gaze into the most profound depths of our souls and gives us the infinite joy of feeling ourselves lost in a moment of eternity—eternal with it." (*Each in His Own Way*, p. 53.) That light shines for but a moment; it affords to Pirandello a fleeting instant of inner illumination and then disappears, leaving him in a night of terrifying darkness. This moment of inner illumination is the only eternity granted to man, but man makes the mistake of considering it a natural state and of attempting to enclose it into a system. It is natural that he should soon realize the futility of his efforts, since that moment cannot repeat itself. The result is a feeling of ennui, boredom, and nausea that stifles him, while he longs in vain for the region whence his dreams emanated.

Pirandello joins the Book of Ecclesiastes and the ascetics of long ago in proclaiming his indifference towards the gifts of the earth. Since this indifference rises through a life experience, it is beyond racial lines and outside the narrow boundaries of time limitations. It is universal, and as such it is to be found in the art of all those whose sensitiveness has been hurt by the rough hand of the daily life.

The sharp contrast that Pirandello feels between his aspiration and the result of his fearless and cold analysis of reality is determined by the objective character of his temperament that strips evil of any alluring quality, thus preventing him from abandoning himself to his belief in a good and primitive life. His drama often springs out of the conflict between the aspiration of his soul and the cold objectivity of his temperament.

It is not correct to stress unduly the term "idealism" in relation with Pirandello's thought. Idealism, outside the realm of true philosophy, has a literary patina of dubious alloy, and it points at the academic attitude of a dilettante who deals with imaginary problems and with fantastic solutions. Pirandello's idealism does not go beyond seeing grains of gold, our dreams, scattered among the ruins of the human heart—remains and echoes, but distant echoes, of the goodness that God has given to man. The ruins and the desolation of human life have attracted Pirandello's attention more than the glittering bits of the precious metal. If we chance to use the term "idealism," we should qualify it with the adjunct of "tragic."

Pirandello is inherently a primitive, with a complicated and over-active mind. His heart longs for peace and tranquillity, while his eyes long to see and his intellect to analyze what the lack of positive moral elements has produced in

35

life. These elements have no connection whatsoever with idealism, while they testify to Pirandello's moral approach to a life concept. His ascribing to lack of simplicity and sincerity the ludicrous and painful situations in which his characters are caught points at a deep ethical attitude, and it draws a sharp line of differentiation between Pirandello and his characters, between the point of departure of the play and the final conclusion to which he is led by his deep soul. Between the beginning that portrays Pirandello outside the precincts of the Temple of Thought, where life is mockery, and the end that shows him within the temple, in the presence of sacred life and human sorrow, there is an abyss. On one side there is Pirandello who, having reached the breaking point, bursts into broad though painful laughter; on the other there is Pirandello, the thinker and man, on whose heart experience has left deep marks and scars. Pirandello, having begun with laughter, ends by revealing to us his belief that only humility can save man from the crushing weight of his human destiny. In this fashion the element of the grotesque that permeated the plays conceived and written in the chaotic years that followed the War gives place to his attitude of passive silence with a strong religious undercurrent. Silence had been the only weapon at his disposal for many long years, and it becomes now a great force in the life of his characters.

More than an idealist, Pirandello is a modern stoic, who has found the traditional cold and stiff posture too uncomfortable and commonplace, and who has renewed stoicism, either through laughter, or through his tragic idealism. In both cases, Pirandello's art acquires a cosmic resonance which is the distinctive quality of all true and great art in which men can mirror themselves.

His art is not made out of peaceful, rhythmic life, nor is it conducive to quiet, idyllic thoughts. It bruises, it wounds, it smarts; but it presents a wide horizon of life, and it never fails to awaken in our hearts pathos and sympathy for the vicissitudes of his poor characters. His art is not made out of the plain and of the obvious, just as his characters are not pleasant people. They are not individuals that life has caught in the peaceful mold or prison of the everyday life: a nice home, a plump wife, two charming children, getting up in the morning, shaving, bathing, going to the office, lunching, going back to the office, dinner, quietly reading the newspaper while smoking a pipe, and finally going to bed. His characters have actually experienced what even our fancies dread. They have lived beyond the laws of society and humanity. They have existed in a vacuum with only their tragedy, the horror of vice in their flesh; they are, none the less, free of all fetters, primeval beings in the whirlwind of the irrational.

In spite of the statement of many critics to the contrary, the outstanding characteristic of Pirandello's thought is that of being constantly close to life. Life has always been envisaged by him in terms of man's existence on this planet. In fact, his drama centers around the consideration of what happens to a human being endowed with instinct and reason, sentiment and intellect.

In the course of literary history we find ourselves before writers who aim at transcending the actual and historical reality by losing themselves in dreams and idyls. We also meet others who do not flinch at accepting their human lot with its share of pleasure and sorrow, of ugliness and beauty. These writers followed two antithetical processes, since they either concealed what was to them the hideous countenance of daily life behind the bewitching network of their dreams, or they shunned dreams and compelled their art to portray only the massive and seamy aspects of everyday life.

In Pirandello these two processes, welded together, integrate each other, and the two planes of reality, that of the actual and that of imaginary life, are tragically fused into one. The result of this new process is, from an æsthetic point of view, that Pirandello's art can adhere more closely to life where the dispassionate observer finds a dream side by side with the most instinctive and elementary needs of man. From the point of view of sentiment, the obliteration of the boundary between the actual and the imaginary realities leads

Pirandello's characters to the high plane of pure tragedy, since they are denied an escape from the talons of the grief that tortures them.

Pirandello takes into account that it is instinctive with human beings to protect themselves by allowing their fancy to picture beautiful vistas and idyllic lands, but his tragic sense of life is so impelling and overpowering that he cannot allow his characters to abide in the fantastic realm of their imagination. If the exaltation of the characters is so great that they identify themselves with their assumed reality, the illusion is only momentary, because the author shows them the fictitious quality of their attitude and how ludicrous they look. This prevents the obliteration of the original ego, and differentiates very sharply Pirandello's art from that of the traditional idealists. In the traditional process the original personality disappeared completely to give place to a new ego, primitive in the Arcadian fashion or garbed in the long robes of Platonism. In Pirandello the two personalities remain, tragically merged into one, writhing in a grief in which the truth of art defies the truth of life.

We do not speak of obliteration of reality and personality in the same sense as does Adriano Tilgher, a brilliant critic of Pirandello and of modern art.[1] Tilgher reduces Pirandello's attitude to the old transcendentalism. He also speaks of the negation of human personality in Pirandello's characters. No true dramatic art is possible without personality, and the conscious madman is in art a well-defined dramatic character. Illusion in Pirandello is forced on his characters by external circumstances, and, therefore, is no longer illusion. It is lucid madness, grief that writhes in the heart of man tied to his daily existence like a modern Prometheus.

Pirandello had ample opportunity to study this clear and conscious madness in himself as he contrasted it with that of poor Donna Antonietta. He looked at the painful circumstances of his life, at his acts and feelings, as if they were the life and acts of another being. He saw himself just as if he were a character in a strange drama, the creation of a

[1] *Voci del tempo,* 1921; *Studi sul teatro contemporaneo,* 1923.

cruel and fantastic artist. This harrowing contemplation induced the madness that he gives to his characters. His was a terrifying madness, and he felt it beating in his own veins, tormenting his brain, searing his soul, withering his body. Yet he continued to live and to work, finding in his art a solace for the tragedy that life had assigned to him.

Part One

IN THE WAKE OF NATURALISM

IV

Introduction

In considering Pirandello's plays it has seemed convenient to us to classify them under five headings: In the Wake of Naturalism; the Drama of Being and Seeming; Social Plays; the Drama of Womanhood; and Art and Life. This classification has a twofold justification: a pragmatic, though arbitrary and subjective one, which, for the sake of clearness, groups the various plays around a central and predominating theme; and another, deeper and more significant, that corresponds to the general direction of Pirandello's development.

The line of development followed by Luigi Pirandello in his art goes from a somewhat external and even picturesque naturalism to an introspective and tormented individualism. The two stages, however, are not separated by a clear-cut line of division. On the contrary, if one looks below the surface, he discovers that the early naturalism shows traces of the later individualism, just as the introspective stage has never lost at least the memory of the time when Pirandello's art was devoted to a direct analysis of life studied at close range. Whether in the elementary humanity of the earlier plays or in the complex individuals of the later ones, we find the reflection of his tormented spirit and sad existence. This is the essential part of Pirandello's drama, and it should be constantly seen behind the division to which we have subjected his large and imposing dramatic production.

Cap and Bells should be included among the plays of "being and seeming" because of the implications that it contains, although the hero, Ciampa, bears all the outer marks of Sicilian naturalism. The same can be said of characters that are found in plays studied in other groups. The utmost has been done not to allow the formal element of divisions to interfere with seeing Pirandello's plays as an indivisible though varied whole.

Naturalism has left clearly distinguishable traces on Pirandello's art. It can be seen in his concept of life which has never failed to recognize the power of instinct, in the Sicilian setting of most of his early plays, in the presentation of elementary characters, as well as in the objective attitude that he assumes in portraying both events and characters. These traits, consciously or subconsciously, stated in theory and often denied in practice, are found in the works of the masters of Sicilian naturalism—Giovanni Verga and Luigi Capuana. They are also noticed in Pirandello's dramatic works, although the younger man has gone beyond naturalism, compelled by the bitterness of his experience to rely on his imagination and to feel detached from the instinctive side of life.

Pirandello has taken from naturalism—and not only from that of his time but from that of all time—the concept of a suffering and pitiful humanity. In his conscientious and objective method of observation he has deprived life of any lyrical and lofty attributes. He has obeyed the dictates of the naturalistic school in rendering the background of his plays with great precision, as we can readily see in *Liolà*, in *Limes of Sicily*, and in the sketches that we have grouped together considering them in the light of the school that Pirandello admired and followed in his youth. *Liolà* might have been written by Verga, if Pirandello had not broken the pledge of objectivity and if he had not allowed his humor to take hold of the situation, which ends with a cold and diabolic burst of laughter, of which the good Verga was not capable.

Many of the dramatic sketches that have been included in this section are dramatizations of short stories that had been written at an earlier date. *The Imbecile, At a Sanctuary, The Jar, The Patent, Limes of Sicily, The Duty of a Physician* had appeared under the garb of the short story until Pirandello's repressed dramatic genius urged him to recast them into plays. Other dramatic works that will be considered later have also been taken from short stories. Such are, for example, *Either of One or of No One, Think It Over, Giacomino; It Is Only in Jest, All for the Best.* In a sense the naturalistic trend in Pirandello's drama is only a reflection of an earlier stage of his art.

Pirandello in the beginning of his literary career sought strong and vivid passions. It was but natural that he should place the setting of his early works of fiction in his beloved island. In one of his plays he speaks of Sicily in these terms: "The action takes place in a city in the interior of Sicily, where, as you know, passions are strong and smolder under cover till they break forth with a fearful violence. Among all most fierce is jealousy." (*Tonight We Improvise*, p. 26.)

Pirandello owes a great deal to naturalism. The clear, detailed descriptions of his scenes afford a solid basis for his drama, while the penetrating observation and rendering of the outward appearance and gestures of his characters give a complete characterization of the latter that leaves little to the actors in interpreting them. It is also due to Pirandello's contact with naturalism that the soul is made to reflect on the physical being of the characters, with the result that the psychological study of them never degenerates into abstraction. It can be truly said that Pirandello's characters are complete personalities, and that they stand out unforgettably in one's memory, projected against the everyday life that the author has given them as a background.

Pirandello shares with Verga his tendency to describe primitive people and passions. The characters that we shall soon meet: Micuccio Bonavino, Cecè, Liolà, Chiarchiaro, are characters caught through the observation of reality close at hand and rendered with directness and objectivity. In his early plays Pirandello placed himself before odd figures that he noticed in old Sicily, described their outward characteristics, and wove a slight dramatic action on them. Only indirectly is the drama of his characters that of Pirandello, the playwright. One does not feel the presence of the author in the elementary and healthy sensuality of Liolà nor in the sketches in which he reveals a charming but external naturalism.

The author, however, felt ill at ease in these humble and limited characters, and he soon passed to an art which presents characters that show traces of an intense and passionate subjectivism. There are suggestions of this new mood in Tommaso Corsi in *The Duty of a Physician*, in Andrea Fabbri in *The Vise*, as well as in the hero of *The Man with a Flower in His Mouth*. These characters are clear examples of the author's departure from his external naturalism, and they point at a more psychological and introspective art.

Someone may be led to doubt or even to reject the relation between naturalism and the drama of Pirandello by noticing the emotional people that he takes from provincial life in Sicily. Though humble people of the lower classes, they gesticulate like persons possessed of the evil spirit, they roll their eyes excitedly, and they have a great deal of temperament and sentiment. These characters may appear as pure fantastic creations to anyone who has not known the Italian people whom Pirandello had the opportunity to observe and study in his childhood and youth. We still remember these odd figures whose gestures were exalted, whose lives were miserable, and whose thoughts were extraordinary. They were heroes of an imaginary greatness, grotesque mixtures of gentleness and violence, with strange eyes now widened in a frenzy, now soft with delicate feelings. The leveling factor of modern life has destroyed these picturesque figures, and with them a great deal of suffering and a vast amount of unwritten poetry has gone, perhaps forever.

The consideration of naturalistic elements in the drama of Luigi Pirandello is of paramount importance. The most daring situations where instinct irresistibly has led human beings into the snares that nature has set for them are found in Pirandello, as in all great artists. Instinct, however, is presented as a life force, and it affords the pattern on which the artist can weave his own introspective and speculative thoughts. The fact that the love theme predominates in Pirandello's drama must not lead us to confuse him with writers affected by eroticism. Love has constantly and justly occupied a central place in art because it has a large part in life. The greatness of the artist, however, is proportionate to the degree in which he has succeeded in making us feel the presence of the whole life of the character through his love experience. Reduced purely to love, a work is gross eroticism or ethereal Platonism.

Pirandello's early contacts with naturalism has prevented his drama from degenerating into empty lyricism. Since he often deals with characters who are forced to walk in the clouds, he has used a naturalistic setting to enhance the solidity and charm of the actual life from which his typical characters have been excluded. A lyric dramatist would give a diffused and hazy rendering of the scenery, and he would allow the concreteness of the landscape to degenerate into the diaphanous mist of idyl and symbolism. Pirandello is so concerned in rendering accurately the observable reality as even to give geographical names of the places where the action develops.

Italo Siciliano, one of Pirandello's most bitter and super-ficial critics,[1] has stated that the latter has failed as a dramatist because he did not continue to derive his inspiration from the modest, though solid world of naturalism, and has lost himself in the midst of cerebral and abstract themes. The fact is that Pirandello's naturalistic plays cannot compare with those in which he has gone beyond the limited bound-aries of this movement. If any criticism should be made, it is that Pirandello often encloses big problems in little people, with the result that they are too small for the task that he assigns to them.

In the plays that we are about to study there is nothing that bespeaks the complexity of later plays, of the cerebral process which he attributes to some of his characters in later works. We are using these plays, therefore, by way of in-troduction to the significant works of Pirandello. As time has gone on he has identified himself more and more with his characters until, in his latest plays, as, for instance, *When One Is Somebody*, he is so close to his main character as to merge completely with him. The drama of Pirandello the artist has gradually coincided with that of Pirandello the man. This explains why the analysis of life that appears in his

[1] *Il teatro di Luigi Pirandello ovvero dei fasti dell'artificio*, 1929.

latest works is infinitely deeper and more penetrating than that of the earlier plays.

Most of these are simple sketches in which the author tried his hand in passing from the short story to the drama. They are useful, however, to show the distance that separates these simple attempts at drama from the full blossom of Pirandello's art. They also serve the purpose of showing how Pirandello links himself with Sicilian naturalism while rising towards an art of his own that has made him a gigantic figure in the history of contemporary drama.

V

Humble Themes of Sicilian Life

LIMES OF SICILY

and Other Dramatic Sketches

Sicily and southern Italy naturally attracted the attention of a man who had remained so intimately a Sicilian in the intensity of his emotions which smoldered in his heart like a fire ready to burst into vivid flames. One of the jewels of this production of a minor tone is *Limes of Sicily.* It would seem opportune, however, to discuss briefly a few other dramatic sketches with a Sicilian background in order to create the proper setting for the touching story of Micuccio Bonavino, the modest and humble hero of *Limes of Sicily.*

We shall consider first four very short plays in which Pirandello appears to have assumed the objective attitude that the masters of Sicilian naturalism had advocated. He sketches from life, much in the manner of an artist who goes from place to place in search of characteristic bits that he may notice in the primitive atmosphere of Sicilian villages.

*
* *

IN A SANCTUARY

(*La sagra del Signore della nave*)

In his *In a Sanctuary* Pirandello relies especially on a pictorial technique for effect. The play brings to one's memory the celebrated painting, The Vow, by Francesco Paolo Michetti, where in a riot of colors are represented those who go to a sanctuary to make vows to the statue of a saint in the midst of clouds of incense, imploring to be healed by divine power. Pirandello has caught the vivid lights, the picturesqueness, the tumult of a festival day in a maritime city of southern Italy where people who have been miraculously saved from the wrath of the sea go to render their thanks to a renowned effigy of Christ.

There echo in the play the voices of numerous vendors, the noises of a sanguine life full of strength and violence. The sound of distant drums covers this confusion. Pirandello has transported into his play in all its truth the vividness of the old Italian fairs. We see "old men with faces baked by the sun, and short, curly beards, wearing huge, conical hats with hanging ribbons, velvet clothes worn out and discolored, a green one here, a brown one there, short trousers, heavy blue cotton stockings, rough and heavily hobnailed shoes." Here is one of the sailors: "The old sailor, tall but bent, with a wooden and almost black face, stiff and smooth gray hair, hard, angry eyes, his beard cut in an oval shape all around his face."

The author stresses the naturalistic aspects of life as he watches the flood of humanity that surges around the sanctuary: prostitutes in garish colors, profligate youths whose blood courses more rapidly under the scorching sun, pigs killed and prepared and cooked, there in the public square. There are long tables covered with white tablecloths where roast pork is served, together with abundant red wine. Wine and blood, good and bad odors are rendered with great directness and objectivity.

A slight episode is grafted on this primitive and colorful background where the religious and the beastly are not contrasted but actually merged. Among some people seated at the table to eat a fresh-killed pig, there arises a discussion about the intelligence of the pig that allows itself to be fattened in order to be killed. The intelligence of the pig is attacked by a young pedagogue, an exponent of thought and culture who is "thin, pale, and blond; he dresses in black and is sickly. A born poet, he defends his incorruptible faith in the ideal values of life and, above all, in human dignity against the irony of prolonged fasting and against the ob-

scene brutality of daily experience." Pirandello with benevolent irony contrasts him with the violent and sanguine life
that surrounds him. The idealist does not understand what
relation there is between the religious festival and the heavy
eating and drinking. What is more entertaining is that he
tries to find out from those who kill and prepare the pigs.
He grows pale and trembles when the men take hold of a
huge pig and slaughter it with a long knife that cuts the
throat of the animal while the poor beast squeals in pain
and the blood gushes out of the large wound.

The wan pedagogue teaches the humanities to the son of
Signor Lavaccara who, on that very day, has sold his fat
pig that he loved very dearly, and is still grieving over the
fate of the poor animal. He had cried when they had taken
it away from his stable. One could chat with that animal.
He had even given him a name—Nicholas. His son called
him "and he came to eat the bread from his hand; he came
like a little dog." Signor Lavaccara, "well provided with an
enormous wealth of pink flesh that shakes around him," arrives just as they are killing his hog. He frantically shouts:
"No, no! Tell him not to slaughter it. I shall give him back
his money! I shall give him back his money!" His wife closes
her ears so as not to hear the pitiful cries of the animal and
moans: "Poor Nicholas! Poor Nicholas!" So also does the
son entrusted to the care of the pedagogue, who is horrified
at the idea that the boy should have been allowed to come
there in that confusion and before that display of bestiality.
He teaches the humanities according to the old method that
consists in elevating oneself above the grossness of life. What
is a pig and its intelligence compared to the divine intelligence of man? How can Signor Lavaccara say that his
Nicholas was more intelligent than a man?

Upon hearing the romantic and platonic pedagogue offend
the memory of his dear and, to him, noble pig, Signor Lavaccara becomes furious. His idea of a pig, patterned on his
wonderful animal, is so high, its humanity so pronounced,
that he proves to the pedagogue that the actions of man if

we look closely are not superior to those of a pig. The people who surge around them—brutalized by wine, heavy eating, and harlots—the noise, the heat prove beyond any doubt that Signor Lavaccara is right.

*

*　　*

THE OTHER SON

(*L'altro figlio*)

Here too we find picturesque Sicily with its young women wearing bright kerchiefs and its poor old women looking like bundles of dirty, black rags. Here are some of the women as Pirandello has sketched them: "Gialluzza, a small, thin woman in her thirties with hair once blond, now lifeless like tow, that she wears in a big knot at the back of her head; Marassunta, an old woman in her sixties, in mourning, wearing a discolored cotton dress, her black kerchief tied under her chin; Tuzza, in her forties, with her eyes always fixed on the ground and with a mournful voice; Marinese, red-headed and gaudy." The picture, significant in its dusky colors and one in which life seems to be caught and made immobile, is completed by "Jaco Spina, an old peasant with a black knitted cap and in shirt sleeves, who lies on his back, his head resting on a donkey's saddle, while he is listening [to the women], smoking his pipe. Some children, burned almost black by the sun, run here and there."

We are taken back to the early years of our century when emigration took away from Sicily all the young men, while old mothers were left behind, poor and broken-hearted. Maragrazia is one of them. Pirandello has caught her in all her miserable and almost revolting ugliness and poverty, insisting on the thick net of wrinkles that covers her face, on her eyes with turned-back eyelids, bloody with continuous weeping, on her sparse and disheveled hair. "She seems a heap of rags; rags greasy and heavy, always the same, winter and summer, torn and tattered, without any color, and smelling of all the filth of the streets." She is wretchedly poor and unhappy. Her two sons have gone to the Argentine, and they do not even write to her. On that day twenty-four men are leaving the village to seek their fortunes in America. One of these young men, Tino, passes by and takes leave of the women who, Italian-wise, were seated on their doorsteps. Maragrazia begs Ninfarosa, an intelligent young woman who knows how to write, to compose a letter to her children. Tino will take it to them.

The poor woman is considered a nuisance by everyone in the neighborhood. Ninfarosa deceives her and does not write down the heart-breaking message that the mother is sending to her sons. She just scribbles a few signs, folds the sheet, and gives it to her. The village physician happens to go by and Maragrazia asks him to read the letter to her. Ninfarosa's deceit is discovered. The physician is perplexed and indignant. In excusing her act, Ninfarosa tells him that this old woman has another son with whom she refuses to live, saying that he is not her son.

The explanation that the doctor hears from the old mother takes us back to the days when Sicily was overrun by bandits. In a night of terror her husband was killed by them, and one of them attacked her—and this child was born. With stubbornness and almost hatefulness she asks the doctor whether it can be said that he is her son. The doctor, more sympathetic than the women of the neighborhood, writes a long letter to her sons in the Argentine, a real letter.

In reading this short dramatic sketch entitled *The Other Son* our interest is attracted by the picturesque, narrow street in the little village of Farnia in Sicily. Pirandello gives us the name of the village, out of his respect for the scientific accuracy on which naturalism insisted. He objectively shows the cruel indifference of the women for the heartaches of the poor old mother. All the stage directions are given with meticulous care, rendering most accurately the clothes of the women, their postures, their names, and feelings that do not go beyond the realm of sensations. Life is presented in its unchanging monotony and in its quaint picturesqueness with a sudden plunge into a gruesome past very much stressed by way of contrast.

*

*   *

THE PATENT

(*La patente*)

The Patent is a dramatization of a short story that has a distinctly provincial and Sicilian flavor. It deals with a poor man, Chiarchiaro, whom human malice has goaded into a sort of frenzy that makes him hate all mankind. People have spread the rumor that he is a sorcerer. Everyone has refused work to him, as well as to his three daughters. Everyone shuns them. Now Chiarchiaro is suing two influential townspeople whom he surprised making conjuring signs as they passed by him.

A strange, truly Pirandellian judge who, in spite of his queer ways, has a lot of compassion for his fellow-men, sends for Chiarchiaro in order to make him withdraw his charges, because, as the matter stands now, he knows that he will have to convict Chiarchiaro. Judge D'Andrea enters the room carrying a small cage in which he has a goldfinch. It is his constant companion. It had belonged to his mother who had died the year before, the only person he held in affection in this world. He takes the goldfinch from the small cage and puts it into a larger one. "Hush now," he tells it, "and let me administer justice to these poor, fierce, little men."

His colleagues are constantly poking fun at him on account of his goldfinch. "What about you dressed up like that?" he retorts, referring to the funereal, judicial robes, and sending forth a vitriolic attack against those who take life too seriously. We are all funny, one way or the other. He and his colleagues are not so serious now as they were when, as children, they played the game of judge. "All the greatness was in the robe, and within we were children. Now it is the reverse. We have grown up, and the robe, having lost its

sacredness for us, has become the game of our childhood."
The implication is that, at best, life is august in its appearance, but once we lose respect for the stately appearance with
which man clothes himself, everything crumbles with it. His
colleagues chide him about the fact that he passes his leisure
time in talking to his little bird. The Judge admits it: "I talk
to him imitating his voice with my whistling as well as I can,
and he answers me. If he answers me it means that he finds
some sense in the sounds that I make. Just as we, my dear
friends, believe that nature talks to us with the poetry of
her flowers and with the stars of her heavens while perhaps
nature does not even know that we exist."

When Chiarchiaro arrives, the Judge is surprised at the
eloquence and logical arguments of the poor sorcerer. No,
Chiarchiaro will not withdraw his charges against the son of
the mayor and against the city alderman. He, Chiarchiaro,
is a sorcerer and hopes that the court will convict him, thereby
giving him a patent as sorcerer. Men with impunity have
called him a sorcerer until they have reduced him to the
point that he feels that with the hatred that he has accumulated
within him he can destroy a whole city. Now he must be
convicted, and thereby recognized by the law as a sorcerer.
That conviction will be his diploma, just as the Judge had
to take his diploma before he could practise law. Chiarchiaro
will have a profession!

The Judge asks, almost overcome with astonishment, what
he will do with it. With ill-controlled vehemence Chiarchiaro
answers: "What shall I do with it? Can't you really see
that much? I shall put it on my visiting cards as a title. Ah!
does that seem little to you? It is my patent! It will be my
profession! I have been stabbed, your Honor! I am an honest
man and a father. I used to work honestly. I have been
dismissed and thrown into the street because I was a sorcerer.
The only thing left to me is to begin to practise the profession
of sorcery."

He will put on a strange suit that he has made himself.
He will frighten people. He will let his beard grow; he will
put on awesome glasses. He will go in front of gambling

houses. The proprietor, the gamblers will pay him, not to
have him there in front of the place. He will go near various
shops, jewelry stores, factories, and they will all pay him
in order to send him in front of a rival shop. He will make
money as a sorcerer. "It will be a kind of tax that I shall
exact from now on," concludes Chiarchiaro. The Judge seriously says, "The tax of ignorance." Chiarchiaro does not
agree with him. It is the tax on everybody's health because he
could actually destroy everyone and everything through the
hatred that has filled him, because of men's malice.

As Chiarchiaro is insisting on the need of his being convicted, the window suddenly opens and strikes the cage,
knocking it down and killing the poor bird. At that noise the
other judges and the court employes rush in, asking what has
happened. In a broken voice Judge D'Andrea explains: "The
wind . . . the window . . . the goldfinch." Chiarchiaro
with a shout of triumph rejects that explanation: "The wind?
The window? It was I. He did not wish to believe and I have
given him proof." Turning to the astonished and frightened
spectators, he adds: "And you will die, one by one, just as
that goldfinch died." They all are awed, but his reputation
is made. They all beg him not to use his evil power on them.
Chiarchiaro imperiously shouts: "Then you pay here, immediately—pay the tax!— All of you!" They all pay and
Chiarchiaro, turning towards Judge D'Andrea in exultation,
cries: "Did you see? And I haven't got the patent yet! Start
the lawsuit! I am rich! I am rich!"

Chiarchiaro is the first character that gives evidences of
traits that, enriched and deepened, will blossom into more
complex personalities in later plays. He possesses that fixity
of thought and intensity of passion that become exaltation
and lead to conscious artificiality. Pirandello has fashioned
him by endowing him with a simple psychology such as only
a poor peasant can possess. In all his humble personality
he is a real character because he possesses an intensity in
his passion that colors every act of his life and every feeling
of his heart.

The play, a little jewel of its kind, is made by the philosophical judge, D'Andrea, and by the wretched and pitiful Chiarchiaro. The tragic element has stealthily penetrated into the humble theme, and it has permeated the structure of the play.

*

* *

THE JAR

(*La giara*)

The Jar is also taken from a short story. More than anything else it shows an attempt on the part of the dramatist to present an exasperated logic in primitive characters.

Zi Dima is a gruff mender of oil jars, those huge jars, taller than a man, in which in Sicily they keep their precious golden liquid, olive oil. Every day he takes his implements, and goes from town to town mending jars. There are two methods of doing it. One is by using a powerful glue that he has invented, another by sewing the broken pieces with a steel thread.

One day Zi Dima is called to fix a jar for Don Lolò, a wealthy farmer, known all over the countryside for his stubbornness and for his *penchant* for lawsuits. Zi Dima suggests his own method: to glue it with his marvelous glue. Don Lolò wants his jar sewed. Two stubborn, relentless wills are pitted against each other. Zi Dima must yield. It is Don Lolò's jar, after all. He enters the jar and sews it by first drilling holes and then passing fine wire through them. When he tries to come out of the jar, he can't. The neck is too narrow.

A legal question arises: Who will pay for the jar that will have to be broken? Zi Dima from the inside of the jar tells Don Lolò that it is his fault and asks Don Lolò to break it and let him out. Don Lolo naturally does not wish to break his precious jar. He argues very acutely against old Zi Dima and finds an indescribable pleasure in indulging in the legalistic subtleties which are his hobby. Zi Dima is very philosophical about his plight. He lights his pipe and peace-fully waits in his new shelter. Don Lolò, one of those gigantic men that one often saw in the fields, people always ready to use violence, gets madder and madder, and finally kicks the jar and sends it rolling down the hill. The jar breaks against a tree. "I win!" shouts Zi Dima, rising from the débris of the jar.

This is the elementary subject matter that Pirandello has dramatized without being able to wipe out the original flavor of a delightful short story. Pirandello is more interested in the delineation of characters and in their picturesque indi-vidualism than in the dramatic development of the slight event that he relates. One need only look at Don Lolò to be convinced of this: "He is a huge man in his forties, with the suspicious eyes of a wolf. He is extremely irascible. He wears an old white hat with a huge brim, and has golden rings in his ears." His language is not different from that which one hears in the country among laborers and farmers: "May St. Aloe help you to break your neck, you and your mules." So he greets a muleteer who wishes to know where he is to unload the manure that he has carried to Don Lolò's farm. In his love for lawsuits, Don Lolò carries a copy of the civil code in his pocket, and studies it so that no one may dare dispute what he says and does. His lawyer has given him that copy of the code because he has tired of seeing him in his office every day. Now he can study his own cases by himself.

The descriptive and therefore external character of the early plays is evidenced by the long and minute scene descriptions. The characters stand before us in a clear-cut contour, but they do not possess the depth of character that Pirandello has created in later plays. They are more pictur-esque than dramatic. Pirandello has kept the names of his characters in the original Sicilian form, another proof that in the beginning of his dramatic career he was a direct deriva-tion of Sicilian naturalism.

Don Lolò and Zi Dima are perfectly executed little etch-ings such as Pirandello has lavished upon his literary work, be it the short story or the drama. The author has skilfully presented also the temperaments of the contained and gruff Zi Dima and the quarrelsome and violent Don Lolò, both studied in the natural setting of old Sicily.

*

*   *

LIMES OF SICILY

(*Lumie di Sicilia*)

More complex, although woven on a very humble personage, is *Limes of Sicily*. Limes are fragrant fruit that grow in that island and which in the play are taken as the symbol of the purity and simplicity of Sicilian life as contrasted with the sensual and vulgar life of the continent.

Micuccio Bonavino, the hero, is a simple Sicilian peasant who has traveled from his little home town to a tumultuous city of northern Italy in order to see again his sweetheart, Teresina, who is now a celebrated singer. We meet Micuccio in her house as he arrives after the long journey, a jarring note in the luxury of the singer's home and in contrast to the sophisticated servants, with the "collar of his rough coat turned up to his ears, a dirty bag in one hand, and a little valise and a musical instrument case in the other." Micuccio had brought with him a bag of sweet limes to offer to Teresina, that they might bring to her the memories of the past when they loved each other through their common passion for music. Micuccio played the piccolo and Teresina sang. He was determined to make a great singer out of her. He sent her to a conservatory at Naples for four years with the money collected from the sale of a piece of land that his uncle, a priest, had bequeathed him. Teresina had had a marvelous career. She had sung in Milan, Rome, Spain, Russia.

Micuccio does not find Teresina at home. She is at the theatre. There will be a reception in her home that evening for her friends who by chance are all of the masculine sex. Micuccio can see only Zia Marta, Teresina's mother, who in spite of the worldly life of her daughter and in spite of her velvet dresses and hats has kept intact her simple soul and the sincerity of a good peasant woman. She stays with Micuccio while Teresina entertains her smart friends in the big and beautifully illuminated parlor. Marta reveals to Micuccio all the misery of that life: "Appearance, luxury, debts, money, then want, masked by tricks and subterfuges." They sit by themselves in a little room and dine together, served with foods that Micuccio has never before tasted. Micuccio has seen another world. He never knew that such beauty and luxury could exist. He is so overwhelmed that he can hardly eat.

Zia Marta and he go over the beautiful, even if not always happy days, spent in their village. In that house, dedicated to corruption under the name of art, there passes on the wings of memory the peaceful beauty of the field and there echoes the chirping of the swallows that made their nests in the ceiling of the garret where Zia Marta and Teresina lived, and where Micuccio cherished his modest dream of love for the girl with the beautiful voice. Zia Marta has not forgotten the little women with their modest virtues whom want had taught how to beg without seeming to do so: "Do you remember Annuzza with her little clove of garlic? She came with this excuse, a clove of garlic, just as we were about to eat something." Annuzza is dead now. Zia Marta envies those dead; at least they rest in the cemetery of their little village. Who knows where she will be buried? Her life is far from being happy, as she confides to Micuccio whom she loves as a son. Here she cannot even make the sign of the cross when she begins to eat.

As Micuccio talks, his words uncover patches of blue in the sky of far-away Sicily: marriages, children of people they know, the quiet, happy life, even if monotonous, of their town. A wave of laughter and high voices that bespeak the beast comes to them. Zia Marta is perturbed. Micuccio's face registers his emotions, from astonishment at the luxury of Teresina's house to joy in seeing Zia Marta again. There is longing in him, too—that of seeing Teresina. Teresina, in fact, comes. "She is dressed in silk, covered with magnificent jewels, her bosom bare in very low-cut gown, her back and arms bare. She enters hastily, and it seems that suddenly the little room is illuminated by a violent light." Micuccio is "dazzled and stupefied as if before a fantastic apparition." He can only utter the name "Teresina." She says a few words, indifferent and artificial, like many greetings that people exchange, and returns to her friends.

Micuccio sees the abyss that time has opened between them. Slowly the truth begins to penetrate his simple mind while anguish oppresses his poor heart. Now he understands fully the nature of that laughter and of the noise that comes from the room where the party is going on. He learns from Zia Marta that Teresina is no longer worthy of him. There is nothing to do but to leave the house and return disconsolately to Sicily. Before going out he remembers that he has his beautiful and fragrant limes with him. He pours them out of his bag on to a table. "Limes," cries Zia Marta, with tears in her eyes, "our beautiful limes!" They both look at them in silence. Micuccio has an idea. It seems to have slowly emerged from the nebulous distance of his mind: "What if I should begin to throw them on the heads of all those fine gentlemen?" As Zia Marta looks at him imploringly, he changes his mind and leaves with his valise and his piccolo.

Teresina enters the room and sees the limes. She is not moved by them. She gathers up as many as she can and invites her admirers to see and enjoy them, unmindful that their touch will contaminate them. The play ends with the wanton laughter and the loud and gay voices of Teresina and her friends; Micuccio is forgotten. Pirandello has left the two lovers to their destiny.

Micuccio is perfectly drawn, and he is as close to a dreamy peasant as the artistic rendering allows him to be. In his humility and simplicity he carries a deep, philosophical *motif* which is derived from the author's sad realization that change is an inevitable element of life and that it is useless to struggle against it. Micuccio, by remaining immobilized in his little village, had not changed. Teresina had. How could the two understand each other? The final separation was a logical consequence of the change that Micuccio had helped to bring about.

Pirandello does not bring Teresina back to the old and perfumed world of limes and orange groves. He is too sophisticated to do that, but he brings out in the conversation between Zia Marta and Micuccio all his attachment for his island which he relinquished, but which he could not forget, when he wanted to try his wings on the open spaces of the continent.

A bitter philosophy permeates the play and moves like a shifting and ominous light over its vicissitudes, seeming to say: If we do not change we are denied the stir of modern life, civilization; if we change we join lots with Teresina. The author is perplexed in choosing between the primitive but necessarily limited conditions of life in Sicilian villages and the life of capitals full of movement and splendor. It is hard to choose between being like Micuccio and being like Teresina, although Pirandello's sympathies are with the quaint peasant and with his beloved Sicily.

VI

Painful Mirth and Tragedy Make
Their Entrance

LIOLÀ

and Other Minor Dramatic Sketches

The naturalistic theme in the particular and well-defined characters that naturalism assumed especially with Verga, Pirandello's great master, appears also in *Liolà*. The setting and the characters of this play share in a distinct manner the most salient traits of Verga's art. Liolà is a happy-go-lucky young peasant, not different from Verga's primitive fishermen, with the difference that Verga reveals through his elementary and humble characters his thoughtful and tender temperament, while Pirandello lets his humorous mind bring into the play a deep note of painful mirth before the contradictions of life.

Before analyzing *Liolà* we shall briefly discuss three short plays in which the author has enclosed very dramatic, highly passionate, and tense moments.

*

* *

AT THE EXIT

(*All'uscita*)

At the Exit is, according to the author, a profane mystery play, having as a setting the exit, or entrance as we would call it, of a cemetery. Characters and events are suspended midway between life and death. The characters are the "vain appearances" of the Fat Man, of the Philosopher, of a Woman who was killed by her lover, of the Child with the pomegranate, while the solid aspects of tangible life are represented by a Peasant, his Wife, an old donkey, and a Child.

The drama is taken from a newspaper account of a crime committed by a lover who kills his mistress and then tries to commit suicide. Pirandello has given a fantastic treatment to the play, imagining that the husband of the woman, impersonated by the Fat Man, is already dead. He sits sadly at the exit of the cemetery thinking of his past life, regretting that he did not enjoy the fresh and pure beauty of flowers, the melody of a nightingale to which he could have listened in his garden. His life was harassed by his wife who possessed a "harrowing, torturing laughter that used to burst forth from that cruel red mouth of hers, between the cut of her lucid teeth." He confesses: "Every time I heard her laugh, it seemed that the earth trembled, the sky became cloudy, my little garden withered, bristling with thorny thistles. Laughter springs from her bowels like a frantic rage of destruction."

This woman had a lover, and she treated him just as she had treated her husband, while she had for the latter the "voluble affection, a little playful, a little biting, of the first days of their engagement." The lover could not stand that distressing and maddening laughter, and killed her. As the Fat Man sits there at the cemetery exit, his dead wife comes to him and relates how she was killed. She says: "A shot; I felt a sensation of cold here; I fell; he lifted me from the ground, put me on the bed, kissed me repeatedly, then wounded himself. I felt him slide to the ground, moaning at my feet. There endured to the very end on my lips the warmth of his kisses. But perhaps it was only blood." In fact, it was blood that she wiped away, her face twisted in spasmodic laughter. She comments: "It was blood. No kiss ever burned me. While the ceiling of my room seemed to lower itself closer to me and everything was becoming dark, I hoped that that last kiss would at last give me the warmth for which I had always longed from the very depth of my being. It was my blood, instead, the useless burning of my blood."

She confides the inner secret of her intimate life to the vain appearance of the Philosopher while her husband shakes his head bitterly. He fails to understand now the actions and feelings of this woman just as he had in life. At this moment a child is seen advancing on his rosy feet over the grass of the cemetery. A new being is awakened in the tragic woman. She becomes gentle and soft and walks towards the Child, who has died with a last unrealized desire in his little heart: the longing for a pomegranate. He has a pomegranate now in his tiny, chubby hands. The Woman breaks it and the Child eats the red, juicy grains, from the palms of her hands; then he disappears. She weeps bitterly over her unrealized desire for a child.

Pirandello has enclosed here, behind the passion of the Woman and the resigned patience of the husband, a drama of denied motherhood. The warmth of her blood (Pirandello treats this element very naturalistically) led her to profligacy and death because her motherhood was thwarted.

The husband points out to her a little peasant family that advances in the dusk behind a donkey that is carrying home a bundle of grass and a child. A sense of quiet peace, of rustic tranquillity, rises from the group and tantalizes those two beings for whom life had held tragedy and sorrow. Would it not have been better to live that quiet life, to have had a child from whom to learn the joy of laughter and the purity of life rather than to roam in the tragic desert of passion and hatred?

The vain appearances that evanescently move in the play seem to be the result of the detachment with which Pirandello views at times the outside world. Looked at from an impenetrable subjectivism, our fellow-men appear to the author like the impalpable appearances that we meet in this play. For years Pirandello moved among men like a shadow among shadows. However, he is opposed to those who complicate life and by so doing fail to live it with simplicity and candor. If the husband had lingered over the serene aspect of nature which he let pass unnoticed under his eyes; if the woman had had the joy of a child, their life would not have ended in tragedy and death. The longing for a child has taken here a physical, carnal, although deeply poignant form.

It is interesting to note this solid part of Pirandello's thought which he uses as a basis for his art, because, although it disappears in some of his plays, especially those written in the turmoil and chaos of post-war days, it finally reaffirms itself in his latest plays. Indeed, if we look beyond appearances, it is ever present in his dramatic production, even if hidden by his humor and at times by his gloomy pessimism. The happy peasant family, standing for the massive aspects of life, is presented with an idea of contrast with the unhappy and tormented couple whose tragedy endures even beyond the boundaries of this life.

*

*   *

THE VISE

(*La morsa*)

The Vise is another short play portraying an intensely dramatic moment as an expression of the author's tragic state of mind. There is a uniform, closed sky, as in an impending storm, which weighs heavily on the tense situation that has caught three human beings in a snare; then there comes a sudden flash that spells death.

Giulia in a moment of folly had run away with Andrea Fabbri, who had become her husband. He himself did not understand how he had done it. He was not made for frivolity. He was a man of steel, a hard worker. To atone for his irresponsible action he has begun to work like a madman, and in so doing has neglected the sentimental woman who has become the mistress of her husband's best friend, Antonio Serra. This is the situation that holds them as if in a deadly vise. Antonio fears that the husband suspects them; that he has seen them kissing each other goodbye the day that he and Andrea left on a business trip. The silence of the husband, prolonged for several days, hangs over them like a crushing weight. He tortures them, until, denying his wife the right to see her children again, he forces her to commit suicide.

She dies, redeeming herself by asking her husband to promise her never to reveal to her children the shame that led to her death.

This short play, similar to the small but strong sketches that a great master may have drawn in an interval between two great paintings, is interesting especially for the vividness with which Pirandello has rendered the tense and closed character of Andrea and the tormenting suspense of the guilty ones. Pirandello obeyed the dictates of naturalism in looking upon instinct as an overpowering force, but he reached the height of artistic greatness by lending to his characters his own intensity of feelings. Andrea is a figure sculptured as only Pirandello knows how to do it. A few touches of his strong fingers, and Andrea, crushing in his honesty, genius, and strength of character, destroys the ephemeral whim of another poor Madame Bovary.

*

* *

THE DUTY OF A PHYSICIAN

(*Il dovere del medico*)

Tommaso Corsi, the main character in *The Duty of a Physician*, like many of the individuals portrayed in plays of this period, has that hidden weakness that leads him to sin, not for love, not even for passion, but just by chance. Endowed with an impetuous character, he lives furiously, without reflecting. Anna, his wife, analyzes as follows his temperament and behavior: "He did not give time to his judgment as he did not give weight to his acts. It was useless to make him stop to consider his wrongdoing. A shrugging of his shoulders, a smile, and that was all." She has to confess, however, that no vice had ever clung to him. He had remained spontaneous, always joyous, the same friendly person to all.

One day he was discovered with the wife of a friend, the most fatuous woman one could imagine. The husband shot at him. Corsi, in self-defense, killed the husband. Realizing what he had done, he tried to commit suicide, but a physician, an intimate of the family, bandaged his wound and saved him. Anna, a long-suffering and superior woman who, knowing her husband's temperament, has been big enough to forgive him, passed sleepless nights and anxious days at his bedside as he wavered between life and death.

Pirandello has wished to stress the uncontrollable factor of passion in life by making Corsi an almost ideal man, so he says of him: "He is very tall and most handsome. His face is as pale as wax, and a little drawn, but his eyes shine almost in a childish way." The woman who led him to his downfall is portrayed as a worthless person, and her husband as a fit companion for her. Corsi is meant to have all our sympathy, although the author unflinchingly leads him towards his punishment.

As he is convalescing he is sincerely penitent and touched by his wife's goodness. He says to Anna, taking her face between his hands and drawing it near his with infinite tenderness: "You understand, you feel that it is true if I tell you that never, never in my heart, in my thought, have I betrayed you." It was infamous to be caught in that shameful moment of stupid idleness. His life was wrapped up in her and in his children as he saw and understood, more clearly than ever, the very moment that his rival fired at him. If Corsi fired back it was not only in self-defense, but also because he could not allow himself to be killed for that woman.

Now he is better, almost well, but a grave decision is impending on his wife and on his friends, a lawyer and the physician. He must be told that he is to be prosecuted and very likely will be sentenced to life imprisonment: "It will be terrible," says Anna to the doctor. "He is like a child. He is moved, weeps, laughs at anything at all. Just a moment ago he was saying as soon as he is fully recovered he wishes to go to the country for a month."

When Corsi hears of the possibility of his having to go to prison for life, he is distraught. The very fact that he tried to commit suicide is against him, since this action can be construed as a recognition of guilt. He sees now how cruel his friend has been in saving him. He asks the doctor by what right he has done so. He should never have done that, since he did not have any right to dispose of the life which he had given back to him. He vehemently tells his friend, the physician: "I had placed myself outside the law by inflicting on myself a punishment graver than that which the law can give."

It is too cruel for Corsi to have to face the possibility of going to prison for life, now that he knows how great and beautiful his wife's love is, how sweet his children are, what a pleasure it is to work for them. Corsi reopens his wounds. His friend the physician, realizing that he has no right to save him, murmurs: "No, no, I cannot. I must not." Corsi dies.

The approach of the humanity of the characters is still governed by the consideration of those sides of human life which naturalism claimed as its own, but the author has allowed his art, be it within the narrow boundary of a short dramatic sketch, to enrich itself with psychological depth and complexity.

There is nothing here of what is usually referred to as a Pirandellian complex. Tommaso Corsi is not at all tortuous or intellectual. The author views him, as well as the other characters, with great objectivity, and beyond them he feels the tragedy of human life. The play encloses a short, tense, and striking action centering on the despair of a man who wishes to touch his lips to a pure and cool water that suddenly recedes and intensifies his thirst, much in the manner of the mythical Tantalus.

*

*   *

LIOLÀ

(Liolà)

The setting of *Liolà* is in the "country around Agrigento, today." We find ourselves in a farmhouse with olive and almond trees in the background. There is no idyllic peace, however, in the little nook to which Pirandello leads us that we may witness the awakening of a dramatic action.

A few young peasant girls are singing while shelling almonds, and their joyousness is contrasted with the surly nature and grumbling of Zio Simone, an unpleasant old man who complains of everything: the scant harvest, the slowness of the girls at work, his childless marriage to Mita. He had married her only in the hope that, being young and strong, she might give him an heir. And she, poor Mita, had accepted her cross because she was poor and Zio Simone enormously rich.

There is in this comedy the open and objectively drawn sensuous atmosphere that one finds in the fields, where civilization does not cover the instinctive side of life with frills and conventions. The fact that Zio Simone wanted a child, and Mita, beautiful and healthy, had not given him one, is discussed quite openly. There are not any morbid innuendoes on the part of the women, although their conversation ripples with openly sensual amusement. Zio Simone vents his rage on poor Mita and rudely sends her home, calling her a good-for-nothing who serves only to make him the butt of everybody's ridicule.

There pass at that moment the three children of Liolà, a happy, handsome young peasant who knows only how to sing and enjoy life. Those three children are the fruit of his love affairs with young girls of the village who have not known how to resist the ardent lover. When the girls had presented him with the children, Liolà had been neither embarrassed nor disconcerted. He had taken them home to his old mother and he had worked for them very happily, because it did not cost much to feed and clothe children in agricultural sections, where children are a real asset in tilling the fields. The author contrasts the free and joyous life of Liolà with the torpid, narrow-minded, and hateful one of old Zio Simone. Liolà, who chances to pass, tells him: "Stop being like that, with your feathers all ruffled like a sick capon."

There is in the play an echo of the life that Verga depicted in *Cavalleria Rusticana*. We find in both the same country setting, the same primitive people and passions. As in *Cavalleria Rusticana* Lola and Santuzza are rivals, so are here Mita and Tuzza, a cousin of Zio Simone. Mita had been the sweetheart of Liolà, and since Liolà still seemed to think of her, even now that she was married to Zio Simone, Tuzza had wanted to take him away from her and she had fallen as others had fallen.

It was truly hard to resist a young man like Liolà. Here is his self-portrait: "I am no bird for a cage. I love to fly with unclipped wings. Today here, tomorrow there: in the sunshine, rain, or wind. I sing and I am intoxicated and I do not know whether more by my songs or by the sunlight." Wherever he appears he brings joy and life. Girls hasten to go to work where they know they will find Liolà. He takes his three children with him in his cart and they are growing like their father to love to sing and to dance. He is an extemporaneous poet of no mean ability, and on festival days one can hear him reciting his verse to an enthralled audience.

Tuzza and Zio Simone both find themselves in an unpleasant situation: Tuzza because of her impending motherhood and Zio Simone because of his offended masculine pride. Tuzza gives him the opportunity to save his face and to have an heir by her. She confesses to him that she is going to have a baby by Liolà. Her plan is that he should claim the child as his. Zio Simone accepts.

A man who is willing to do this deserves a lesson. His lot is not to be envied when his fate is in the hands of such a humorist as Pirandello. Zio Simone boasts before the world that he has a son by a woman other than his wife. He will have to pay dearly for the sorrow that he brings to Mita. The revolting satyr has gone home and has announced the fact to Mita that Tuzza is the other woman, and that if no child has come to their home it is Mita's fault. The poor girl has cried bitter tears in silence and humiliation. He has beaten her, has dragged her by the hair through the house.

Although accustomed to suffering, Mita cannot endure her life with Zio Simone, and she returns to her aunt's home. Zia

71

Gesa had brought her up and had been a mother to her. It had been she who had forced her to marry the old satyr. Poor Mita had accepted with grief and resignation Zio Simone's proposal of marriage, and life had been a blistering load on her poor shoulders.

Zia Gesa's house is next door to Liolà's. Is it to be wondered at if nature and dramatic logic take their course? Liolà goes to Mita's house, and the old love blossoms again. Now Zio Simone will have two children, one by Tuzza and another by his wife, two children that he will have to claim as his own while in reality they are Liolà's.

Mita yields because Liolà brings back to her the memory of their happy childhood when love had come with the same simplicity and beauty that clothe the flowers that grow by the wayside. Moreover, Liolà appears ready to vindicate her against Zio Simone, Tuzza, and Tuzza's mother. He relates to her the scheme that the three had conceived on the day that Liolà, obeying the pangs of conscience, had gone to Tuzza's home to ask for her hand in marriage. No longer jovial, but with strength and sentiment, he tells Mita: "Goodness only knows what I had to swallow, when I went there to do my duty, and under my very eyes that nasty mother made your husband go into the room where Tuzza was. I saw you, Mita, I understood the harm that would come to you, and I swore to myself that they would not go scot-free."

Pirandello sees to it that they do not go unpunished. Tuzza's offer to Zio Simone loses its weight and value after Mita tells her husband that she is going to have a baby. Placed by this change in the situation between Tuzza and Mita, Zio Simone, just as Liolà had thought, defends Mita, who is his real wife, against Tuzza who used him to cover her wrongdoing and shame. Tuzza and her mother, Zia Croce, cannot expect to have Zio Simone's money now that he is going to have a baby by his wife.

There is the morality of life and the morality of books. The two do not always dovetail. Pirandello claims justification by the morality of life in giving to his comedy the solution that he does. He lets Liolà and Mita triumph over the greed of Zia Croce and the deceitful scheme of Zio Simone and Tuzza. He vindicates, too, gentle and suffering Mita in that he allows her to belong to the man whom she had loved in her youth, the only glimmer of light in a sad and drab existence.

The solution that Pirandello gives to his play reminds one of Machiavelli's *Mandragola*. Here the cowardly, old, and repulsive Messer Nicia, the husband, is punished by being made the butt of ridicule, with love triumphant over the schemes and machinations of greed and ignorance. Pirandello, too, places a sentimental nucleus at the very heart of this somewhat salacious comedy: Love—even if it is free love—struggling against greed and deceit, with love triumphing at the expense of its two sordid enemies.

VII

A Humorist Looks at Virtue

MAN, BEAST, AND VIRTUE

and Other Minor Plays

We have repeatedly explained the relation of the dramatic sketches that we are studying to the naturalism of Verga and Capuana. No great artist has ever been a slave to a literary movement, and Pirandello is no exception. He naturally felt the influence of the artistic current that predominated in his youth, but his genius was never cramped by it. If Liolà is a child of Sicilian naturalism in his elementary simplicity and rustic grace, other characters appear in whom Pirandello is trying to enclose a more subtle and complex sense of human personality. His contacts with naturalism do not prevent him from leaving the imprints of his personality and the at times quixotic traits of his mind on the instinctive themes that he chooses. In fact, naturalism assumes an extremely humorous and even grotesque tone in *Man, Beast, and Virtue*. Before analyzing this play we shall briefly study three short sketches in which the study of the individual stands out in sharp contrast to the objective tendency that we have noticed in the dramatic works we have already reviewed.

*

* *

CECÈ

(Cecè)

Cecè is more interesting to the critic than to the lover of dramatic art. Pirandello has lent to a superficial individual utterances that are in sharp contrast to the levity of his temperament and the worldly character of his actions. The dramatic vicissitude presented in the play is very slight. Cecè, the protagonist, true to his character, only thinks of having a good time. He is one of a class of people living with perfect leisure and luxury in the hustle and bustle of our civilization, people the old civilization transmitted to us, who seem to thrive also in the midst of the feverish activity of the new one.

One day, as he is trying to kill time in a café with other men of his type, he sees pass by a beautiful woman whose bad reputation they all know: Nada. His friends scoffingly say: "She is too high for you." He wagers that she will be his. After a short time he announces to his friends that he has won the bet. It goes without saying that he soon tires of Nada, all the more that she is, like women of her sort, very extravagant and a drain on Cecè's pocketbook.

As Cecè is meditating on the best way of getting rid of her, Squadriglia, a one-eyed road builder and contractor, calls on him to thank him for using his good offices with the Minister of Public Works in Squadriglia's behalf. He wishes to show his gratitude to Cecè by offering him money. Cecè is surprised at the clumsy way the boorish contractor has chosen. He proposes a different way, as eccentric as can be any suggestion coming from Cecè: to tell all the possible and conceivable evil about him to a person that he would designate.

Squadriglia is half surprised and half indignant. Cecè explains that Nada has three three-thousand *lire* notes signed by him which he must have back at any cost. She is expected at his apartment at any moment. Squadriglia must receive her and tell her that Cecè is a scoundrel, a son who is taking his old parents to their grave. He must make his picture so exaggerated as to make the woman realize that the notes in her hands are worthless.

When Nada arrives, after the first surprise is over, she hears such ignominious charges and accusations against Cecè that she is easily persuaded to accept a small amount of money in return for the three notes. Since Squadriglia has to catch a train, he makes a hasty exit and leaves Nada in Cecè's apartment. The latter is not long in returning. He feigns surprise upon hearing that she has given the notes to

75

that man. With his histrionic ability he pictures vividly to the surprised Nada his plight now that that man, the worst usurer in the city, has the notes in his possession. For punishment, Nada must give Cecè enough kisses to make up to him the evil that will engulf him.

Pirandello has lent to Cecè both physical and mental characteristics that can be recognized in more complex and truly tragic characters. He is presented as follows: "Although showing in his face the signs of a life of debauchery, he is still full of vivacity and restlessness. He has the air, if not exactly of a lunatic, of an absent-minded person. He changes his expression rapidly at the darting of different images in his most mobile imagination. He is smoothly shaven, most attractive, and has shining eyes and red lips. He dresses with exquisite elegance." Cecè is made to express typically Pirandellian ideas about human personality, but this *motif* is only an external element in the play, since it is not developed and does not have any connection with the unfolding of the action. It is strange to hear on Cecè's lips such words as these: "Is it not tormenting to think that you live diffused into a hundred thousand individuals who know you and whom you do not know?" This *motif* is the central theme of one of Pirandello's greatest novels, *One, No One, a Hundred Thousand*, in which the plurality of the human personality has assumed an almost religious meaning merging with the annihilation that the mystics of all times sought through their being lost in the Deity. We also hear Cecè utter these deep and tormenting words: "I am sure that you agree with me that we are not always the same. According to our humor, moments, relations, we are now one way and then another; happy with one, sad with another, serious with this man, funny with that one." This is the theme that permeates the tragedy of the Father in *Six Characters in Search of an Author*, and it is accorded in various plays a deeper and always new treatment.

Cecè is as worthy of expressing these ideas as a rough contractor like Squadriglia is capable of understanding them. In fact, they jar on his lips to the same extent that the practical and uncouth Squadriglia finds them incomprehensible. Pirandello places them in the play as if gathering them from some distant obscure part of his mind. Their presence here, however, shows that the author needed the medium of a more subjective art to express feelings that the worldly and superficial Cecè could not logically utter.

Looking at the play in its minor details, one notices the evident concern of the author with describing characteristic traits of his characters. Squadriglia, for instance, is "a huge, rough man, a little ill at ease in his city clothes, used as he is to wear his working togs. He has only one eye and no trace of the other on his face because he had skin grafted over it when a mine burst and took it out."

The play is a short dramatic sketch that shows Pirandello's humorous side while hiding the tragic element that is placed on Cecè only as an external ornament.

*
*   *

THE IMBECILE

(*Imbecille*)

The Imbecile is projected against the party spirit which divided Italy at the beginning of the century into two hostile camps: the Republicans, or Leftists, and the Conservatives.

We are introduced into the office of a Republican newspaper which from all external appearances shows that Republicanism not only meant war on the king, the church, and capitalism, but that it stood for a heroic life deprived of capitalistic comfort. In fact, the office of the *Republican Sentinel* shows "disorder and filth on the old and worn-out furniture and even on the floor." Men with leonine heads and Mephisthophelean beards, and wearing vivid red neckties, emblem of revolution, move excitedly in the newspaper office.

A man, Luca Fazio, is seated in the vestibule waiting to see Leopoldo Paroni, editor of the newspaper. Fazio is desperately ill with consumption, as is evidenced by a violent cough that he tries to stifle by pressing his handkerchief against his mouth. To a man who is face to face with death the disputes of men of different parties, their hatreds and their clashes such as the one he hears is in progress in the streets of Costanova, seem unspeakably small and meaningless.

The clash, the clamor of which reaches him, is one into which personal animosities have been injected and in which personal gain is trying in vain to hide behind patriotism and humanity. Feelings run so high that the two factions are embroiled in the public square and come to blows in the midst of a wild confusion. Far from a struggle between contrasting ideals is the struggle between the Honorable Mazzarini who is in power and Paroni who would like to take his place.

While the last newspaper reporters are about to be sent into the fray by the courageous Paroni, who prefers to watch the battle from the window of his office, a woman arrives and announces that Pulino, a destitute and sickly man, has committed suicide. "What an imbecile!" shouts Paroni. "He should have first shot my enemy, Deputy Mazzarini, and then killed himself. I should have paid his fare to Rome." (Seat of the Deputies.)

Luca Fazio rebels at hearing the term "imbecile" applied to the poor, dead Pulino. He rises like a ghost from his corner and takes Paroni into a room. After ordering him to lock the door, he points a pistol at him and informs him that Deputy Mazzarini has paid his fare from Rome to Costanova with the understanding that he, Fazio, should shoot Paroni and then commit suicide. Paroni must admit that his political enemy has beaten him in the battle of wits. At the sight of the revolver, he falls on his knees, his Republican ardor and courage dampened.

Fazio looks at him with supreme disdain and scorn and does not carry out his threat to kill him. Instead, he compels Paroni to write under dictation the following words: "Luca Fazio, before committing suicide, came to my office, armed with a revolver and informed me that in order not to be called an imbecile by Mazzarini or anybody else he had to kill me like a rat. He could have done it, but he preferred not to because he felt loathing and pity for my cowardice. It has been enough for Luca Fazio that I have declared to him that I am the true imbecile." "Now sign," Luca orders him. After Paroni with a trembling hand has affixed his signature to the paper, Fazio takes it and walks out of Paroni's office. On the following day that document will be found on his dead body. He will stand immune from the charge of stupidity. Paroni will be indicted for his cowardice in offending the memory of poor Pulino. He has signed his own political death warrant and forfeited his human dignity by calling himself an imbecile.

The character that creates the play is Luca Fazio. There is in him true dramatic force, concentrated and powerful. He looks at the world from his observation tower where death is ready to hoist its victorious banner while he, unmindful, with cynical coldness looks at human cowardice. He is a giant near the boastful and verbose politician Paroni.

The play is grimly ironical. There rings through it Fazio's cold and desolate laughter that dwarfs into nothingness the political passions of man.

Pulino and the peasant woman who announces his death bring into the play the voices of the average daily existence. Luca Fazio stalks into it as a symbol of the tragic individualism that the author is trying to express.

*

* *

THE MAN WITH A FLOWER IN HIS MOUTH

(*L'uomo dal fiore in bocca*)

Who has not seen a man with a flower in his mouth? We may even have noticed one on cheap illustrated cards or in a photograph that a sailor has had taken of himself for his sweetheart—at least an Italian sailor—or a sergeant in the army of his Majesty the King. But imagine that instead of a flower, be it a rose or a pink, that man has in his mouth a red spot that proves to be a cancerous growth. What then? Then we shall have the genesis of this short play that bears the long and intriguing title of *The Man with a Flower in His Mouth*. We find in it a typical attitude of Pirandello: tragic laughter before a ghastly aspect of life.

The author calls this short play a dialogue. It is a dialogue between two men, one of whom looks at human life as a tragedy while the other accepts it, submitting in silence to its torturing monotony and to its cruel whims. They meet by chance after midnight at a café in a railroad station.

The peaceful man has just missed the train because of the innumerable purchases he has made for his wife and daughters who are summering away from the city. The poor man had been carrying so many packages that by the time he had arranged them, two on each finger of both hands, the train had left. While he is waiting for the next train, a strange individual sitting at the table next to his begins to talk to him and discusses his tragic philosophy.

He is a man who is forced to cling with his imagination to other people's lives like a climbing rose to the bar of an iron fence, that he may stand the tragic weight of his life. His great solace is in observing other people: "Not of the people I know. No, no. I could not! I experience a loathing, a distress. But I must adhere to the life of strangers; around them my imagination can work freely, not at random, however, but rather taking into account the slightest details discovered in this and that man." This is the only way by which the speaker can divert his thoughts from his own misfortune. Life, or death, has branded him by putting a flower in his mouth in the form of an epithelioma or cancer: "Death, do you understand, has passed; it has thrust this flower in my mouth, and has told me: Keep it, my friend. I shall be around in eight or ten months."

Can that man be other than he is? He is restless; he cannot stay one minute at home as his poor wife would like him to do. So he goes out and stands in front of show-windows admiring the cleverness with which shopgirls tie packages. He is afraid to stay in his own company, to penetrate into his own heart, to ponder over his life. Woe unto him if he did. He might even become murderous, as he confesses to his alarmed and trembling companion. The tragic man reassures him that he is not going to destroy him and asks a favor of him: "Tomorrow you will arrive at dawn at your home town that I imagine lies at some distance from the station. You can walk that distance. Count every blade of the first tuft of grass that you meet on the way. I shall live as many days as there are blades of grass. Good night, sir." He disappears, leaving his chance companion there frightened to death.

The play, short as it is, is a document of Pirandello's power of observation. He, too, has gone through the wide and narrow streets of towns, cities, and capitals, and has sought relief from the distressing thoughts that crushed him by letting his eyes wander from one aspect to the other of the life that stirred around him. The play affords an insight into the nature of the imagination that Pirandello lends to his characters. He does not allow human fancy to go in search of idyllic situations and dreamy landscapes, but he does allow his characters a detached feeling from the earthly reality when the weight of their lives becomes so crushing.

Here, too, there is grim humor, together with pity for the man whose days are numbered, whom death or life has treated with such an ironical cruelty. Pirandello has altogether left the objective element in his art and has become tragically subjective, portraying an individual whom a bitter misfortune has compelled to detach himself from life, from himself, to live in the contemplation of a life from which he is excluded.

*

*　　　*

MAN, BEAST, AND VIRTUE

(L'uomo, la bestia e la virtù)

The most naturalistic of Pirandello's plays is *Man, Beast, and Virtue,* in which the treatment of the theme of instinct has assumed an extremely ironical form. Rarely has the author indulged in such broad laughter and poked such malicious fun at man as in this play. The thoughtful look habitual to his eyes has disappeared, and a twinkle of malice darts from them.

The play involves Signor Paolino, a teacher who lives by giving private lessons, Signor Perrella, captain of a ship, who comes home only at long intervals, and the virtuous Signora Perrella. Pirandello, in a humorous vein, has presented in these characters three very odd individuals. Signor Paolino voices the opinions of the author in the same tense and excited manner as that in which Pirandello's typical characters do in most of his plays. Paolino shouts what he thinks and is vehement, blunt, and sanguine. He breaks forth into violent tirades against insincere people like one of his neighbors, Signor Totò, a druggist, the personification of a miser, who goes every morning to Signor Paolino's home to be offered a cup of coffee. He has a habit of "rubbing his hands together under his chin as if to wash them at the fountain of his saccharine, stupid graciousness." Paolino quite bluntly tells him: "Get a housekeeper." He is equally declamatory and violent with two pupils who go to him for a Latin lesson. "They have an indescribably beastly aspect. Giglio resembles a black billy-goat. Belli a big monkey with eyeglasses."

The only lesson taught that day is an outburst against human hypocrisy. He calls the pupils' attention to the fact that the Greeks called comedians *Upocrites*. Signor Paolino thinks that that is grossly unjust, since he doesn't see any harm if a poor man plays the rôle of king. It is just his profession, his duty. But when does evil appear? "When one is not a hypocrite by profession, for duty, on the stage, but out of pleasure, gain, wickedness, habit, as it is in life, because to be civilized means exactly this—within, as black as a crow, without as white as a dove; within as bitter as gall, on your lips honey."

At this point, Signora Perrella comes to see the high-strung, eloquent professor, accompanied by her son, Nonò. She is, judging from appearances, "virtue, modesty, reserve personified," but the unpleasant truth is that she is going to have a baby and that Signor Paolino, the private teacher of Nonò, is the father of that baby. On that very day Captain Perrella will arrive and everything will come to light. The poor woman has difficulty in controlling her nausea. She opens her mouth like a fish, and looks so ridiculous as to excite the laughter of her son Nonò. Only by using a beautiful book as a bait can Signor Paolino extract from the child the promise not to laugh, especially in the presence of his father.

Captain Perrella is a terrible husband, and in another city has a mistress with five children. He never even looks at his wife. He comes home, eats his dinner, locks himself in his room and sleeps until the next day when he leaves again for a long voyage.

Now the only thing that will save Signora Perrella will be virtue, virtue that will make of the terrible captain a good husband, thus avoiding shame and scandal.

Signor Totò, the druggist, with his brother Nino Pulejo, a physician, will have to combine their efforts and knowledge and prepare a love potion that will make the husband amorous. The strange concoction prepared by Totò is disguised in a cream cake that is placed by Paolino in the middle of the dinner table. If Captain Perrella will partake of that particular piece of cake in which the potion is concealed, virtue will be saved.

Paolino is the stage director of the whole affair. He orders Signora Perrella to get rid of her awkward and modest attire and to display all the beauty and charm that she possesses. His plans are somewhat in danger when Captain Perrella, upon seeing his wife all painted and in a very low-necked gown, breaks into laughter that forbodes no good. He refuses to have her sit in front of him for fear of having a sudden fit of laughter and choking. She meekly exchanges places with Paolino. After a long, anxious dinner, interrupted by the captain's fit of temper at Nonò's lack of manners, the medicated part of the cake disappears into the voracious mouth of the captain. On the following morning, Paolino discovers that the virtue of Signora Perrella has been saved.

As in other plays, morality is looked upon here by Signora Perrella and Paolino as a means of hiding a wrong situation and, therefore, is accorded a humorous treatment. Pirandello is moved to laughter when he sees that these people have recourse to morality only when they are in danger of being discovered. The play is a projection of that laughter, and it is the way that a humorist has chosen to proclaim the importance of morality.

The play is in the literary tradition of Machiavelli's *Mandragola*. As in Machiavelli's celebrated work, the husband is duped and held in ridicule because he is responsible for the illicit love affairs of his wife. It was due to Captain Perrella's immoral living that poor Signora Perrella was led to sin.

The comedy has the appearance of being highly immoral, yet these light, ludicrous, and obscene events assume a deeper note as they pass through Pirandello's personality, and what seemed a scoffing mockery ends in serious implications. As a result of this undertone of seriousness, the author is lenient with Paolino and especially with the neglected Signora Perrella, while he is very severe with the captain. Pirandello puts on Paolino's lips a lengthy discourse to show that the responsibility is the husband's.

Paolino is the character who is closest to Pirandello's heart in this play. Not that he is a hero, an exceptional individual, or a great personality, however. He is as close to the average person as any of Pirandello's characters, but he shares with other characters that repressed, livid resentment against man and even against life. He, too, has been exasperated by experience, and he is always ready to pour his hatred on everything and on all. "You are all lined with deceit," he shouts. "The patent side of passions, even the most agonizing, has the power, I know, of moving all to laughter. Of course, you have never experienced them or you are used to covering them."

Man, Beast, and Virtue is a strange fable with a startling morality. The morality is that the beast, inherent in all men, saved honesty and virtue that man was about to offend.

In spite of his somewhat philosophical utterances and his excited gestures, Paolino is not yet endowed with a tragic soul. He still is, to a certain degree, external, which shows that Pirandello was forcing himself into the elementary psychology of an individual like the irascible teacher who is still too enveloped in the net of sensuous life to possess the fixity that a tormenting idea, arising from a sad experience, gives to individuals that Pirandello portrays in his best plays.

From characters that we have here and there met in these rudimentary attempts at drama, we can see that the author was tending towards more complex personalities. Our attention has already been attracted by solitary individuals crouched in a dark nook and revealing through their suffering and sneering posture their tragic sense of life. Such is the hero of *The Man with a Flower in His Mouth*, and such is Luca Fazio, whom death is pitilessly stalking.

When such characters appear we are nearing the portals of the majestic and tragic structure that Pirandello has created with the agonizing dramas he has revealed in his art, and we can truly say: Here begins the true and significant drama of Luigi Pirandello.

Part Two

THE DRAMA OF BEING AND SEEMING

VIII

Introduction

After the objective attitude towards reality shown in varying degree in the plays that give evidence of inspiration from Sicilian naturalism, Pirandello appears in a mood that he qualifies as humorous or grotesque. He distinguishes very sharply between humor and irony. To him irony is a rhetorical figure of speech that means the opposite of what it says with the purpose of hurting. It does not possess the deep and tragic implications of humor. Humor is a peculiarly philosophical attitude that obliterates the dividing line between laughter and grief, and it presents man as harboring in his heart a strange feeling of exaltation and of scorn, of pity and of derision for himself. Humor is understanding and compassionate, and, if the humorist laughs, there is a vein of grief in his laughter.

Pirandello's æsthetic ideas are discussed in a book that he published in 1908 under the title of *Umorismo* (*Humor*) which shows the vastness and depth of his intellectual background and also the seriousness with which he prepared himself for his art. It is fortunate that his reflective attitude has not marred the spontaneity of his inspiration. In this book the author studies the nature of humor in European literatures, insisting especially on English, Spanish, and Italian humorists. He considers a typical expression of humor to be Giordano Bruno's attitude towards art and life inclosed in his saying, "Sad in mirth, mirthful in sadness." Pirandello also ponders admiringly over Machiavelli's profession of literary faith: "If at times I laugh or sing, I do it because this is the only way I have to provide an outlet for my painful tears."

Pirandello's ideas on the grotesque, which he believes to be the artistic expression of humor, have led many critics astray in that the latter have tried to interpret the whole of Pirandello's production through the æsthetic canons expressed in his book on humor. To apply these æsthetic beliefs to the whole of Pirandello's drama would be the same as to study Dante's *Divine Comedy* in the light of the æsthetic ideas of the *Convito*, or Tasso's *Jerusalem Delivered* in that of his discourse on the heroic poem. The critic and the poet do not necessarily harmonize in every writer, and often the poet sees distances and heights and depths that the vision of the critic can neither encompass nor fathom.

The ideas expressed in his *Humor*, however, dovetail with a section of his drama, the foreground of which is occupied by the ludicrous appearance of reality which hides or veils a ghastly anguish that torments the characters. Indeed, these ideas are the genesis of the drama of "being and seeming."

In this new field of artistic search and creation Pirandello's master is no longer, as in the days of his naturalism, Giovanni Verga. His place has been taken by the humorists of European literatures, and especially by Alessandro Manzoni [1] and a younger writer, Alfredo Cantoni, who had coined the phrase "Smiling in appearance, grieving in reality," and about whom Pirandello wrote a masterful critical essay.[2]

Humor detects contrasts and shadows, and reaches especially the fundamental clash in man—that of sentiment and of reason. It considers reason as an infernal mechanism that reduces life into concepts. When a situation is looked upon and lived as an abstract concept, we can move in it with the utmost ease because we can mold concepts to suit our taste and pleasure, since concepts do not possess the unwieldy and unbending solidity of actual facts. Concepts, however, being the result of intellect and reason, are the negation of life, which in its essence is fluid and spontaneous. We seek a refuge in them only when we have become so cerebral as to be deprived of spontaneity of feeling and of living.

For Pirandello good and simple people possess spontaneity of life (a characteristic also shared by plants and animals), but their life is necessarily limited, uneventful, and prosaic.

[1] See D. Vittorini, *The Modern Italian Novel*, Philadelphia, 1930.

[2] "L'opera di Alfredo Cantoni." In *L'illustrissimo—Nuova Antologia*. Rome 1906.

Over-intellectual people enlarge the boundary and scope of their life, but they fall prey to intellectual complications and to artificiality. Their inner life is a place that fears light, since terrible shames are hidden there. Since they are compelled to go among men and they want to appear decent and even heroic, they hide themselves behind a fictitious personality that expresses itself with exalted gestures and idealistic words.

Pirandello calls this process *"costruirsi"* or "to build up oneself." In its simplest forms this process refers to the social mask we wear when we go among our fellow-men and lavish smiles that hide grimaces, honeyed words that are spoken in order to conceal real feelings. In its essential character, however, this process portrays a conscious self-deception which we force on ourselves, because without it we could not stand the weight of a painful situation in which we are caught. There are moments in life—the author had experienced them —when it is not possible to appear to others as we actually are; to show our poor souls stripped of the many veils that we throw around them.

Pirandello has shown in his plays that there are cases when loathing for life and for ourselves is so great that it transforms us into madmen. The typical Pirandellian character of this stage of his drama is a man distressed, with mobile eyes, tense, and unable to relieve that tension, for fear that his whole being, moral and physical, may disintegrate. When all alone, he grits his teeth and clenches his fists, while within him disgust rises like a polluted tide. Who could then show himself as he is, not only to others but to himself? It is then that reason begins to function, and it covers with idealistic hues a situation which is inwardly putrid. Reason lends to Pirandello's characters beautiful masks which they press against their faces while they walk among their fellow-men, composed and stately. However, there is the face and there is the mask which never become one, and Pirandello's characters know it. They feel from time to time that the face wants to appear or that circumstances in life threaten to remove the mask. They desperately cling to it, and press it with agonizing strength over their faces, feeling the hurt, the bruise, the burn, yet ready to endure that suffering because it is more bearable than the one inflicted on them by what they know about themselves.

This process, which has given life to immortal characters in Pirandello's drama, presupposes a ghastly moral shame and an acute and tormented sensitiveness. It is also predicated on the assumption that all men are, to a varying degree, theatrical, especially if highly intellectual. An intellectual man acquires in reflection what he loses in spontaneity. It is a law of life, and the mask that man dons is a logical means of self-defense. Since Pirandello's drama begins when the voice of instinct has been silenced and his characters are stranded on the bleak shore of disillusionment, all their life centers in their intellectual raving. Pirandello listens to them, smiles at them, sometimes cruelly, sometimes pitifully, and he shows them that in reality there is no use gesticulating like energumens, shouting and protesting. They are face to face with life, and they must accept it as it is.

Pirandello is compassionate with his characters, but he is also aware that their exaltation is artificial. He knows that as soon as we become exalted, since exaltation appears in people who are not endowed with simplicity, it becomes artificial and conscious of itself. Sentiment is then absent from us, and we must make up for it with the cold power of reason. Then we exaggerate, we shout, and we try to persuade others and ourselves to something of which we are not convinced. As long as we endure in the tension of exaltation, we are not conscious of the extreme lack of sincerity in us, but, if we should happen to look into a mirror and see ourselves in it, we immediately realize the unbearable ugliness of our deception. Seeing ourselves live suspended in the revolting image of our falseness destroys our exaltation, and we appear in all the pity of our betrayed humanity.

The result of this intuition is that the plays of the "grotesque," which largely make up the section of the drama of "being and seeming," move from ridicule to pathos. This pre-

vents Pirandello's drama from being either low farce or an
evanescent dream.

It is well to point out that the process of self-deception does
not destroy the initial ego in Pirandello's characters. The
natural and normal self becomes temporarily obliterated by
hard and cruel necessity, and through the juxtaposition of
these two selves, the original and the artificial, there arises
the drama of "being and seeming," with the inevitable clash
between them. More than from his brain the drama derives
from the heart of Pirandello, and his work is a delicate and
passionate analysis of a humanity that suffers and tries to
appear at least calm; that inwardly bleeds through shame
and outwardly puts on the veneer of decency. It is not at all
necessary to think of the subconscious or of Freud, unless we
wish to appear erudite to make an impression on the unsophisticated. Let us see how pitiful are the characters of the
plays that we are going to study in this section: Ciampa,
Ersilia Drei, Elma, Henry IV. Under the masks there suffers
in them the human heart with an agonizing sorrow. It is unjust, therefore, to state that between "being and seeming"
there is no difference, and that in Pirandello there is not a
point at which the actual reality ends and the fantastic one
begins, a statement very dear to Pirandello's critics. Pirandello's characters wilfully and consciously try to destroy the
actual reality because it is unbearable for them, but they
cannot free themselves of it.

It is evident that Pirandello's characters have at least
temporarily the postures and mannerisms of supermen. It
must not be forgotten, however, that their author does not
take them seriously, and that the drama consists in dissecting
their artificiality. In this fashion the drama is urged towards
its climax, and after a moment of exaltation the characters
reënter their ordinary life, either like Ciampa with a loud
and jarring laughter, or tragically like Henry IV plunging
into a lucid madness that is the only solution life has left for
him.

From an æsthetic point of view the intuition of the grotesque transforms man into his own enemy, and the center of the play is transported into his very heart, affording to the author the opportunity of a searching and tormenting analysis.

The real genesis of these plays is in Pirandello's experience. With the secret of his painful and tragic domestic life hidden in his heart, he moved among men for years. Could he have revealed to them the truth of that condition? He learned then what it is to "build up oneself," and he discovered that most human beings had to seek in that process a screen for the cruel pranks that life had played on them. These plays reflect the most distressed period of Pirandello's inner life. This period begins with Ciampa's laughter in *Cap and Bells;* it develops through the cynical, but pain-giving utterances of Leone Gala in *Each in His Own Rôle;* it scoffs and jeers at everything human with Diego in *Each in His Own Way;* it softens before the calamities that befell Martino Lori and Ersilia Drei in *All for the Best* and *Naked;* it rises to a tragic height before the mental tortures of the emperor Henry IV; and finally it opens the haven of a peaceful and pure life before Elma in *As You Desire Me,* although the author does not allow her to find a shelter there for her harassed and tortured flesh and soul.

The immense surge of humanity that suffered in these plays cannot be the result of an abstract process. In the silence of long years of work Pirandello has created a galaxy of true and great characters, a crowd of poor, grieving creatures whose mouths are twisted in a grimace that tries to be a smile, whose eyes are staring and dull, and whose hearts are pierced by a long pin that they try to remove from their hearts to let it transfix their brains, for, though that may be more painful, at least it allows them to live.

IX

The Blinding Effects of Truth

CAP AND BELLS

(*Il berretto a sonagli*)

In *Cap and Bells* we are led back to the atmosphere of old Sicily in the days when, here as elsewhere, men were tyrants over women. As one character puts it: "They make of us soles for their shoes." That a wife should close one eye and perhaps both on her husband's escapades was a necessary corollary of the men's tyranny and the women's lack of economic freedom.

The household of Cavalier Fiorica is in a turmoil because Donna Beatrice knows what everybody in town suspects: that Cavalier Fiorica, her husband, has had for a long time an affair with a young woman who is married to Ciampa, an old man employed in a general store owned and run by the debonair Cavalier Fiorica. Fana, the old servant, who has seen Donna Beatrice come into this world, views the difficulty in the traditional attitude, "the Lord's will be done." Noble women of old had their lips sealed even if their hearts bled. Had not Donna Assunta, Donna Beatrice's mother, done so in her younger days? Even Fifì La Bella, her brother, thinks that Donna Beatrice is destined to end badly if she keeps harping on the theme of "Shameful men, infamous husbands." Fana never heard of "using violence with those who are stronger than we. Men are led back home quietly, with grace, and with gentle ways." Poor Fana's advice is wasted, for Donna Beatrice, in despair, has confided her trouble to La Saracena, a fearful and reckless woman of the lower classes, "an enormous, powerful woman in her forties, a veritable terror, boastful, with a large yellow silk handkerchief draped over her shoulders, and a blue shawl, also of silk, tied tightly around her waist." La Saracena is bodily detached from the setting of old provincial Italy; one of those women always ready to run errands of any kind, to take a hand on election days, to defend virtue and vice alike with a tongue that feared no word. Her ideas are entirely opposite from those of the quiet Fana. "There is no need of a tragedy," she tells Donna Beatrice. "You will just give him a good lesson. I kicked my husband out of the house four years ago. Now he follows me like a poodle. He shakes in his boots." But Donna Beatrice's husband was not one with whom such methods could be used. Physical strength played a large part in marital relations in those days, and sociologists might well remember that it has had and has a place even today, outside of the boundaries of the law.

The characters, as we can see, are ordinary individuals, and the atmosphere created by their thought and feelings closely follows that of everyday life. We are even more definitely convinced of this when quaint old Ciampa appears on the scene, sent for by Donna Beatrice, who wishes to send him to Palermo just before her husband returns. Ciampa is still the child of Sicilian naturalism: "In his fifties, with long, thick hair, unkempt, pushed back, without a mustache, his cheeks covered by two large whiskers that extend even under his hard, penetrating, and most mobile eyes like those of a madman, behind his heavy spectacles. He has a pen over his right ear and wears an old coat of a custom officer's uniform." He is odd in his appearance and still stranger in his elementary psychology, if we believe what Pirandello tells us. Ciampa appears before Donna Beatrice, using at first the mellifluous words that used to be customary in addressing the wife of the master who gave employment and almost had the right of life and death over his employes: "I kiss the hands of my lady. Always exposed to the orders of my mistress." His mobile eyes are riveted on Donna Beatrice, who speaks with insinuations that hurt. Her jealousy of Ciampa's wife makes it impossible for her to hide her feelings, that is, it makes her truthful. Often, however, the truth cannot be gazed upon. It blinds; it burns into one's eyes. Ciampa notices her strange way of speaking and tells her, "It seems that you have your mouth . . . well . . . as if you had eaten crab apples this morning." At this, as she attempts to hide behind the untruthful statement that everything is as it always has been, he informs her that "the instrument is out of tune." He explains to her and to us, too, that "we all have three switches in our heads: the serious, the civil, the mad one. We need the civil one above all others, since we have to live in society, and that's why it is in the middle of our foreheads. . . . We should devour each other like so many hungry dogs. . . . But that will not do. For example, I should devour Mr. Fifì. That would not do. What do I do then? I give a little turn to the civil switch and I go towards him with a smiling countenance, my hand stretched out: 'How glad I am to see you, my dear Mr. Fifì.' "

We here find ourselves before Pirandello's biting analysis of man as a social being. If we forget to turn on the civil switch, we utter strange words that are followed by stranger deeds. Donna Beatrice speaks as she does because she is oscillating between telling the truth and continuing to deceive her fellow-men. At this point Ciampa, a mixture of book-keeper and journalist (he is very proud of his literary leanings, so proud that he always carries a pen over his ear), waxes philosophical. He turns on for a moment the serious switch. "We are all puppets, Mr. Fifì," he exclaims. "The divine spirit enters into us and becomes dwarfed into a puppet. . . . It should be enough to be born puppets through divine will. No, we all add another puppet to that one: the puppet that each of us can be or believes himself to be. And then quarrels begin. Every puppet wishes to be respected, not so much on account of what he believes he is as for the rôle that he has to represent outside. Face to face with himself, no one is satisfied with his rôle: each if placed in front of his own puppet would spit in his face. But not others; others must respect that puppet." The inference is that we all try to save appearances. Donna Beatrice hates her husband, but when she goes out with him she takes his arm, and so they advance through the main street of the town, answering with smiles the greetings of those who take off their hats to them. Ciampa is no different. "How can you know, my lady, why one often steals; why one often kills; why one often—imagine him ugly, old, poor—for the love of a woman who keeps his heart as tightly as in a vise, but does not allow him to say 'ouch' without immediately stifling that complaint on his lips with a kiss, so that this poor old man is destroyed and intoxicated—how can you know, my lady, with what physical pain, with what torture, this old man can submit even to the point of sharing the love of that woman with another man—rich, young, handsome—especially if the woman gives him the satisfaction of saying that the other man is master and that things are so arranged that no one will become aware of it?" What can poor Ciampa do more than try to save his respectability? It is easy to say "Rebel, give up your job." It is easy to talk of rebellion. Rebellion is often lined with banknotes. Another idea has often crossed the threshold of Ciampa's brain: kill. But he who kills goes to prison. Blocked in his natural reaction, Ciampa has recourse to that life-saving process that Pirandello calls *"costruirsi"* (to build up oneself), forcing on himself the illusion that his dignity and name are safe as long as he saves appearances. So he locks his wife in his room when he goes out and shows everybody that he has the key. He offers to take his wife to Donna Beatrice's house, now that he has to go to Palermo, that no one may point the finger of suspicion at him.

Donna Beatrice refuses to keep Ciampa's wife as a prisoner during his absence. She has decided to burn her bridges behind her and to rebel. She will have her husband caught in the company of his ladylove. In fact, she swears out a warrant for him. Spanò, the head of police and a friend of Donna Beatrice's family and of the not less powerful one of Cavalier Fiorica, feels that he would be in a very serious plight if he should have to arrest Fiorica. He sends a colleague, Logatto, a stubborn, hot-headed Calabrian, to perform the unpleasant task. When Logatto finds Fiorica in Ciampa's quarters, he places him under arrest. One can imagine what happens. Spanò describes the scene: "As Fiorica felt the officer's hands on him, he became a fury of hell. If I had been there I should have endured everything; even if he had slapped me, I should have put up with it for the sake of our friendship. That mulish Calabrian, on the contrary, insisted on citing him for contempt and assault and arrested him."

Now it would seem that Fiorica and Nina Ciampa will be convicted, since they have been found together in Ciampa's apartment. But what of it? Does not the house belong to Fiorica and do not Ciampa and his wife work there in the store? Why so much ado about nothing? Their appearance did not afford any reason for a charge of immorality. Donna Beatrice is, nevertheless, jubilant. She has found a courage that she never suspected in herself. "I am free!" she shouts to the members of her family who have gone to her house after the scandal spread like wildfire all through the town. Her brother rejoins, "Free? You are crazy. Free to come to my house, now, without being able to put your nose out of the door! She calls herself free, forgetting that she is without a social status . . ." So declares Fifì, who does not particularly relish the idea of having at home a sister who is neither married nor single. "The shame is his," proclaims the elated Donna Beatrice. "It is yours, too," replies practical Fifì. The salient point of the situation is that Donna Beatrice has to return to her husband, and that was not easily done in the good Sicily of the nineties. That husband of hers had a devil in every hair, as they put it very graphically, and heaven help her if he ever laid hands on her. Spanò warns, "It would be prudent for the lady not to be found at home if I succeed in having him freed." This is all the more true since circumstantial evidence is in favor of the husband. In his suitcase they have found a prayer book and a box of sweet almonds for his wife. Fana always said that Donna Beatrice lived like a queen at home.

The one who is really crushed is Ciampa. He has gone to Donna Beatrice's house to hand her the jewels that she had pawned at Palermo to pay the latest of Fifì's gambling debts. Ciampa is as pale as a ghost; his face and clothes are covered with mud. He has broken his spectacles and, unable to see, has fallen and cut his forehead. His appearance is a pitiful symbol of the condition of his mind and heart. He is blind now. His painfully fabricated structure of respectability has been torn down by the alleged discovery. Now that the mask is removed there is only one thing to do: kill both Cavalier Fiorica and his wife.

Here we see the power of that fictitious belief that Ciampa accepted when he felt that to lock the front door of his home relieved him of responsibility. As soon as Donna Beatrice makes it impossible for him to believe that his respectability is saved, he becomes a potential murderer. He has been compelled to turn on the serious switch, and the serious switch leads to violence and death. Would it not have been better if he had been permitted to continue to use the civil switch, the one that forces us to utter sweet words when anger and hatred make our eyes look like those of a beast, when we are ready to cast aside all laws and conventions, stripping life of its cloak of decency? Truly that would have been better for Donna Beatrice, too. What will she do when her husband's rage is vented on her? Fifì and Spanò try in vain to console Ciampa and convince him that nothing incriminating has been found. Furthermore there is a legal document now that testifies to the innocence of his wife. Old Ciampa is not convinced. He feels that since the police, the town, the whole world know of his shame, there is no possibility for him to reënter the groove of his daily existence. His life has been destroyed, even if his life was his hidden shame. The carefully made puppet of himself has been broken by Donna Beatrice. He will kill and destroy. Everyone tries his best to convince him that to kill will be folly.

In the course of the conversation, Fifì happens to use the word "crazy," referring to Donna Beatrice. It is as if a sudden ray of light has penetrated into the dark night of Ciampa's life. That word affords him the possibility of restoring the poor and pitiful puppet of but yesterday by proclaiming Donna Beatrice mad, thereby destroying the validity of her testimony and actions. He seizes that word and repeats it with joy and exaltation. They all repeat it—Donna Assunta, Spanò, the people who gradually slip into the room. Crazy! Crazy! Donna Beatrice is crazy!

Ciampa suggests that she go for three months to a sanitarium so that everyone will believe that what has happened has been the result of her madness. Life will resume its course as before. They will all be wiser for the experience, but none the less tragically grieving and pretending. Crazy! If so her testimony is not valid. So much ado about nothing. Crazy! What is most astounding is that that word—a magic word—offers a way out for all of them. Donna Beatrice will be pardoned by her husband. He himself will be able to take his wife back. Donna Beatrice will have to pay. Is that too serious a punishment for her? Has she not branded three persons with shame before the whole town? And then, is it a punishment? For three months she can shout what howls in her heart. She can be herself by turning on the mad switch. To Ciampa, only madmen tell the whole truth. He instructs Donna Beatrice: "It does not take much to play the part of a mad woman. I shall teach you how to do it. All you have to do is shout the truth before everybody. No one believes you and everybody takes you to be crazy." Donna Beatrice, furious and convulsed with rage, asks: "Ah, so you know I am right and that I was right in doing this?" Ciampa does not agree with her. "Ah, no, no, turn the page, my dear lady. If you turn the page, you will read that there is no greater madman in the world than the one who thinks he is right!— Please, go! go! Have the pleasure of being mad for three months. Does that seem trifling to you?" He envies her: "I wish I could do it, as I would like to! To snatch completely open the mad switch, to put on, down to my ears, the cap and bells of madness and dart into the public square and spit the truth in people's faces. Begin! Begin to shout, Donna Beatrice." Donna Beatrice realizes that Ciampa's solution is the only solution. She sees that she must accept, but having the prerogative of being truthful, she begins to vent her resentment on Ciampa by imitating the voice of the he-goat, the animal that in old Europe is the symbol of a betrayed husband: "Bèèè! bèèè!" Ciampa is overjoyed. She is harmless now, so he laughs, "while the curious neighbors leave the scene, urged now by the chief of police, now by Fifì, commenting on Donna Beatrice's misfortune. Ciampa throws himself on a chair, in the middle of the stage, breaking forth into a horrible laughter of rage, of cruel pleasure, of desperation."

The underlying belief in the form of a bitter morality is that only the mad can be truthful, that the fate of the sane is infinitely sadder and more tragic than that of people who are demented. Think, in fact, what an unbearable pressure his curbed hatred exercised on poor Ciampa's breast. What a relief it is to be able to shout one's hatred. There is a living hell within him. There is no coolness that refreshes the burning of the flames, no hand that touches the hurt and soothes it; only that inner rage, that burning sensation, that sometimes breaks forth into violence, murder, revolution.

The fundamental tenet of Pirandello's artistic creed, "to build up oneself," has blossomed here into one of its strangest forms—the self-deception of Ciampa. Pirandello has enclosed a big problem in a small man, and out of him a giant has grown. Ciampa is a Prometheus of his own kind, less stately than the classic one, but closer to our humanity. His life is all in that mask that by constant pressure has become one with his face. There is no differentiation in him between face and mask, so that when his mask is removed, it uncovers tendons and nerves which hurt and bleed.

Here, too, we find traces, deep scars, of social satire, over the elementary environment that serves as a setting. There are men who have no scruples in calling a person like La Saracena a witch and then using her to run errands for them. One of these is Fifi La Bella, a good-for-nothing, given to gambling and women, who is always ready to ask favors of his sister, Donna Beatrice, but who sides with her husband instead of defending her against his profligacy. Deepening the satirical tone, Pirandello shows us that La Saracena and the chief of police, who are given the task of uncovering the guilty lovers, are themselves the negation of morality. Pirandello laughs and grieves as if saying: "See in whose hands lies the fate of honesty!" Both the central theme and the characters are light, even ludicrous, and close to life, but they are made to carry the weighty burden of a tragic sense, acquiring thereby a deep significance.

The play, under its apparent humor, has an undercurrent of unspeakable sadness revealed not only by the ulcerated wounds in poor old Ciampa's heart, but in the plight of Donna Beatrice as well. Pirandello tries his best to persuade her not to rebel against her life, and suggests that she resign herself to her fate. He wants her to share the stoic resignation of which he knew the bitterness but also the poignant comfort.

This play has often been interpreted and staged as a play of jealousy, Donna Beatrice's unfounded jealousy of poor Ciampa's wife. As such it is a maimed work, with all its deep, tragic sense cut off. Even a cursory reading should persuade us that we are before Pirandello's typical drama with light characters who acquire a deep and tragic meaning when they become the receptacle of the humanity of their creator. The old rhetoricians claimed that only the kings and princes were worthy of tragedy. Pirandello has shown that the tragedy of the everyday life and that of an ordinary mortal like Ciampa can be deep and true.

X

Illusion and Heroism

ALL FOR THE BEST

(Tutto per bene)

Pirandello, in his musing and searching attitude, has always stood inquiringly before life. He has looked upon reality as on a prism for him to observe, turn in his hands, and study in its many facets. In *All for the Best*, he shows how in the light of a sudden revelation even a sublime existence may appear ludicrous. We are confronted by a husband whose whole life has been absorbed by his cult of the memory of his dead wife and his love for his only daughter. One day he suddenly discovers that she is the daughter of another man. It is natural enough for us to look at other people's lives. The whole universe is a panorama at which we may look from our observation point. There are situations, however, in which we become the object of our own observation, and we are led to see ourselves suspended in the past in a posture which is ridiculous and shameful.

The central figure of the play is Martino Lori. After Silvia's death, he has lived like an automaton for sixteen years, mechanically performing certain duties all hinging on her memory. An intimate member of the household describes him thus: "He has eyes that cannot be described. You ought to see how he looks! How he listens! As if things, voices, the very voices best known to him, that of his daughter, of his friends, had an aspect, a sound, that he fails to recognize, as if life all around had—I don't know—lost its consistency." Every day he goes to the cemetery, no matter what the weather, to put flowers on his wife's grave. He is not interested at all in the world around him. In his passive attitude he has allowed his daughter Palma to look upon a friend of the family, Senator Manfroni, with the affection

104

and trust that are due only to a father. The very home where they live, although it bears the name of Lori, is actually dominated by the scientific and political personality of the illustrious Senator.

Lori is typically Pirandellian in that he is an outsider in life. He does not belong in the company of Ciampa, Henry IV, Delia Morello, Michele Rocca, the Father in *Six Characters in Search of an Author,* and of other characters in whom exaltation becomes conscious and leads them to "build up themselves." Lori, unlike these characters, has been relegated to a position outside of warm, fluid, joyous life, not by his sophisticated and over-developed intellect, but by a great misfortune. Pirandello places him near the realists, the practical, and contrasts him with them.

There is a galaxy of ultra-realists in the play. At the very beginning we make the acquaintance of La Barbetti, Silvia's mother, a woman who managed to have three husbands, one of them a great scientist, Silvia's father. She is almost illiterate, makes ridiculous blunders every time she speaks, but undaunted, she refuses to be confused or mortified. She has known how to be gay without losing her respectability, at least in society. Pirandello uses his placid but searing irony on this lady who comes to Lori's house on the day of Palma's wedding with the evident intent of a reconciliation. Silvia, in her love for her great father whom La Barbetti had abandoned, had always refused to have anything to do with her. She now brings a wedding gift to Palma and makes her understand that she will be heiress to her fortune if the Lori family will be cordial and decent. Indignation at La Barbetti's impudence almost overcomes Lori. Palma, however, does not see why she should refuse a nice gift from her grandmother on account of a past that does not exist at all for her. She lightly announces to the bridegroom: "I have discovered a brand new grandmother right here, in the vestibule."

Senator Manfroni, the chief realist in the play, is equally emphatic in condemning Lori's exaggerations. To his way of thinking, Lori is always exaggerating. The Senator is the perfect gentleman, who, for Pirandello, is a man of great distinction, accustomed to live in exquisite luxury, the master of others, but especially of himself. He is master of himself, however, not in the lofty meaning usually attributed to this expression, but in that he assumes a steel-like, cold attitude towards everything and everybody, a man capable of controlling every noble emotion, of checking every lofty feeling, replacing emotions and feeling with the lucid and shrewd workings of his mind. He is internationally known as a great physicist, but in reality he has stolen his discoveries from Bernardo Agliani, Silvia's father. He has taken notes that the master left unfinished at his sudden death and has published a book under his own name that made him famous. Near the Senator, other realists move and act, steeped in their normal life that affords them a goodly share of pleasure and joy. Palma, her bridegroom, Marquis Flavio Gualdi, their friends, are all individuals who live in a pleasant present while Martino Lori is lost in an evanescent, shadow-like past, the only reality life has left for him.

A clash is inevitable. To the practical minded, idealists are absurd and foolish. To the idealists, the practical are equally absurd and offensive. This contrast may even turn children against their parents. In fact, Palma treats her father with condescending patience, with coldness, almost with haughtiness. When she is about to start on her wedding trip with her aristocratic marquis, she does not want her father to accompany her to the station, insisting on taking leave of him there at the house. Lori is unspeakably hurt and goes to the cemetery to tell his pain to his dead wife, while Palma joyously goes towards life. All is just as it is in the world of reality where the majority of people cling to its tangible aspects while a few, when rejected by the living, turn towards the dead for comfort. After the marriage, in the whirlwind of new social duties and conquests, the distance between father and daughter becomes more accentuated. It compels Lori to ponder over his position in his home. He has to admit that it is truly strange, and moreover that it always

106

has been so. He begins to brood over it. Vividly and harrow-
ingly, there comes back to his memory what happened the
very day that Silvia died. Manfroni had sent him out of the
death-chamber, telling him that his little daughter wanted
him. When he had returned, he had found Manfroni sobbing
on the bed where Silvia lay in the glimmer of four candles.
Manfroni had gradually taken his place as a father to Palma
because he was Lori's intellectual superior, a wealthy man
with consequential friends who might be useful to Palma
in the future. That is how Palma had happened to marry a
rich marquis. Flavio would never have married her if she
had not been given to him by the Senator.

Lori cannot even go to the palace of the new Marchioness.
What would be the use of his going there with that long,
gloomy face of his, his unseeing eyes, his evanescent personality? One evening he masters his courage and goes to
Palma's house to discuss with her that situation which has
become unbearable to him. Palma does not even invite him
to dine with the family. Lori remains alone in the parlor,
heart-broken, while the others laugh and dine. They are the
practical ones. He is the idealist! Later that very evening,
Palma unwittingly calls Manfroni by the name of father in
Lori's presence. Lori is astonished and crushed when he
realizes that the name is not addressed to him, but to the
Senator. Palma, exasperated by both her mistake and the
fact that she believes that Lori has always pretended not
to know the truth, tells him that she called Manfroni father
because he is her father, as Lori well knows. There are two
crushing blows in that statement: one the offense to Silvia's
memory; the other a cutting accusation directed against him
by Palma who believes that he knows. His whole life is disturbed. The past is desecrated, made grotesque and hurting.
He sees himself going to the cemetery while people laugh,
thinking that that was a farce on his part. People have thought
that of him for sixteen long years. He sees men and women
nudging each other at his passing, telling each other that he
had accepted that situation because it meant advancement in

his career, money, comfort. Had not Manfroni succeeded in making Lori knight-commander and minister of state from a mere clerk?

What will happen now to the picture of perfection that he has embodied in his wife? Lori goes over the past, trying to mend it, trying to save whatever he can of it. Silvia must have sinned with the Senator before she married, while she was looking for a position after her father's death. It must have been a short-lived folly. Lori cannot lose hold of that picture of a perfect wife. Nothing will be left to him if that is destroyed, especially now that he knows that Palma is not his daughter. "When you were born," he cries to Palma, "she had already repented. She was mine, mine! She was mine from that moment, was mine, only mine, from your birth to her death, for years, mine as no other woman ever belonged to a man. For this reason, I have remained thus. . . . She wiped out with her great love every vestige of her betrayal." He remembers now and understands why Silvia, during these three years, had insisted that he keep Manfroni away, gradually but firmly. She had repented. She was only his, Lori's. What torments him most is that Palma thought that he knew: "How could you believe that I knew?" he says. "Ever since you were a child you have seen me go every day to her grave." Palma confesses that her coldness, her disdain were due to the very fact that she thought he knew. Lori feels lost and cries: "She dies for me in this moment, killed by her betrayal. Do you understand that now I have nothing at all that offers me any support? Where am I now? What am I here for? You are not my daughter . . . I am as if emptied. I have nothing left in me." In fact, the discovery of the truth has destroyed the memory of his wife that he has kept alive in his bleeding heart, renouncing life, and it has robbed him of his daughter. Feelingly he tells her: "You are nothing to me and I am nothing to you— nothing. If you only knew how fully I realize now that the years of this nothingness have been so many!" Here again Pirandello shows the power of an illusion. Everything crumbles when that illusion disappears.

Lori, however, cannot permit absolutely everything to vanish. Pirandello presents him as desperately trying to salvage something from the wreck of his life. Lori goes to visit Manfroni that very night. He waits three hours for him to come home. With directness, almost with violence, he requests the Senator to reveal to him when it was that Silvia had become his. Manfroni is disconcerted at first, but it does not take long for a man who has "complete mastery" over himself to regain his composure. Men like him are, to Pirandello, like those toys that always stand up no matter how you throw them. Manfroni has to confess that it was immediately after her marriage, when Silvia, accustomed to the intellectual and refined atmosphere of her father's home, grew tired of the narrow life that a little clerk afforded her. She wanted to go back to teaching and she went for help to Manfroni, her father's pupil. She wanted to run away with him but found that to Manfroni his career meant more than her love. She returned to her husband; her love for Manfroni turned to hatred. After three years she died. Their sin had given Manfroni a place in the household. "All for the best!" It was a consolation for a man like Lori, a humble heart, satisfied with the crumbs that fall from the table of those who are seated at the banquet of life, to know that his wife had returned to him, repentant.

This, however, does not destroy the ridicule and shame which surrounds Lori's past. He cannot live now; but before he destroys himself he will seek vengeance: he will unmask Manfroni before the whole world; he will tell that Manfroni stole his discovery from Agliani. He has the proof. He shouts: He can compare the original draft of the discovery and Manfroni's book. He wants Palma to know, in his desire to destroy the affection she has had for Manfroni, to make him appear before her what he is—a cold mechanism of perfidy.

Only Palma can calm him. She is touched by the pitiful condition of this man who, after all, had given her his name and protected her from shame. She tells him that she believes him, that he has all her esteem and affection. Her affection will give him the feeling that she is his daughter. He will live in the warmth of that affection. Lori picks up the broken pieces of his life, puts them together, makes for himself a little nook still warmed by the memory of his wife, by the remembrance of those three years of perfect and tender love. He cannot complain. He can also count on Palma's affection that is greater now than before, when she called him "father." Lori needs that little affection and he accepts it gratefully, murmuring, "All for the best."

The play is very compact, held together by the passion of Lori, around whom it is built. Had Pirandello lived at the time when playwrights were concerned with the dramatic unities of time, place, and action, he could easily have afforded to respect them, since the impetuosity of his characters naturally crowds the action into a very short time and a narrow place.

As usual Pirandello does not judge. He puts it up to us to decide whether the conduct of Lori, the idealist, after poor Silvia's death, is to be preferred to that of Manfroni and Palma; whether it is logical and normal to grieve and remember to the point of being crushed, or whether it is better to forget. Pirandello, thoughtfully and grievingly, places before us the spectacle of what happens in the alternate succession of life and death, although it is evident that his sympathy is with poor Lori.

There is nothing in Lori of the tortuous reasoning that Pirandello gives to others of his characters. The tortuous thinking belongs to the average person, who is Lori's antagonist.

The comedy has a strong undercurrent of social satire in that it shows the false renown of an unworthy scientist. Pirandello directs the darts of his ridicule toward Senator Manfroni. He flays him as a lover, as a father, as a friend, and as a scholar. "You never had any real passion," says Lori to Manfroni, and he makes him appear the slave of his own career. It is of no use to have published books, to have become a member of a foreign academy, to have had honors heaped on him from all sides, to be a rich and illustrious senator. His weakness is within. His greatness stands on a very weak basis. Lori can destroy it, if he wants to. In the end the man of sentiment, unhappy in the eyes of the world, fares better than the one who for a career has silenced every voice of sentiment. Lori acquires the affection of his daughter, while the Senator sees his own share in it diminished and almost destroyed. Perhaps Pirandello, the humorist, has stealthily intervened so as not to make the solution too lofty and bordering on sentimentality. Perhaps that mind of his that is always bent on seeing the humorous side in the most idealistic situations has suggested that Lori was very practical after all, that dreamy-eyed idealists always get something out of life in spite of appearing so desolate and lonely. They are, at least, sure to get our sympathy. Pirandello's humor is a mobile light that flickers here and there, but in the end it is obscured by his sympathy for the passionate resignation of Lori. It is this sympathy that has made of Martino Lori a figure that stands high above the proud marionettes of Pirandello's practical and worldly antagonists.

XI

The Tumult of Life and the Aloofness
of Concepts

EACH IN HIS OWN RÔLE

(*Il gioco delle parti*)

Each in His Own Rôle is a play in which the treatment accorded to the theme of "being and seeming" is humorous, at least on the surface. Pirandello has remained true to the æsthetic principles set forth in his *Umorismo:* ludicrous exterior, a tragic soul. The action centers around a very serious point of social etiquette: If the wife is offended the husband must defend her by challenging the offender to a duel. The husband, in fact, challenges the offender, makes arrangements for a deadly duel, and then compels his wife's lover to fight it, for had the lover not taken his place the night the wife was offended?

Leone Gala, the protagonist, lives in perfect accord with his wife by being separated from her. In appearance he is a well-dressed, distinguished-looking man who unobtrusively walks through the streets of a modern city, letting his eyes rest indifferently on the various aspects of life. He occupies an apartment by himself, and is waited on by one servant, Filippo, who has to listen to his master's deep, philosophical discussions. This exemplary husband and not less extraordinary man has reduced life to two functions: to eat and to think; cooking utensils and books; kitchen and library. He allows his wife perfect freedom. Once a day, he goes to her apartment, inquires after her health, stays half an hour, and on the dot he leaves to return to his philosophical musing. Then Filippo is the victim of long and abstruse discussions. Bergson is the chief target of his attacks. To Gala, the spokesman for Pirandello's ideas, it is useless to attempt to discuss the relation between reality and reason. Reality is a blind, overpowering current that carries everyone in its fury. The only way to cope with it is to put ourselves outside of it. Bergson tries to rationalize reality by stating that reason "can only consider the sides and character of reality which are identical and constant," while "what is fluid, living, mobile, obscure in reality, escapes to reason." Gala with amusement criticizes: "I do not know how it escapes to it, for the very fact that Mr. Bergson can say it. How has he managed to reach this conclusion except through reason? Then, it seems to me, it does not escape to it." This and numerous other discussions take place while Gala goes to the kitchen, dons a spotless white cap and apron and, aided by Filippo, prepares his daily food, while his mind tries to ward off the onslaught of reality upon his peaceful existence.

Outwardly, Leone Gala is ludicrous, but when we become acquainted with his intimate thoughts we find ourselves before a tragic individual. The cold indifference which characterizes every act, every word, even every motion of his body, is consciously assumed and tragically lived. Caught in the clash between reason and sentiment (sentiment is here instinct, the turmoil of being alive, life), he has, in order to survive, emptied his every act of the mysterious and disturbing fluid of sentiment. Now he lives according to "reason." Gala's reason is not that of the classical drama of Racine and Corneille, but a detached attitude that prevents whatever happens around him from reaching him. By means of this attitude he can live in a vacuum. He is a body without sensitivity, a pitiful phantom that goes through life without living it. Married to a woman who was totally irrational, he thought that his only solution was to live apart from her. Having found life as irrational as his wife, he experiments to discover to what extent he can detach himself from life also. He can truly say of himself: "I live in such a climate, my dear, that I can afford not to pay attention to anything at all; to be indifferent to death as well as to life." He has understood that life is a game, "a sad event, my dear, when one understands the game of life." The only remedy is to find a desperate defense against it: "the firmest, the most stable, because no hope urges you to yield in the slightest degree either to others or to yourself." It is a defense against all men, against ourselves, against life, "against the evil that life does to all inevitably."

For a man who has reached such a sublime and categorical pessimism, the only solution is to live in one's intellect, "not to live for ourselves, but to see others live from the outside, for that short time that we are compelled to live." The essential thing in Gala's mind "is to find a concept in which to fix ourselves so that we may revolve around it and live in it." He means by concept an act of his life, deprived of the impetuousness of instinct and of sentiment. He finds in this abstraction a method of conduct that makes him impervious to the tangible aspects of life, by making them exist only in his own mind. Not a flower and its exquisite perfume, but just the cold picture of a flower, such as a scientist would have; not man with his intricate mental processes, his contradictions, his changes, but just figures and statistics that do not set at play the disturbing element of our sentiment; not Silia, his wife, with her caprices and her feminine irrationality, but only the form of a wife, just as he, to her, is the form of a husband without any content: such as these are his concepts.

Silia, a pretty young woman, full of whims, is characterized by an extreme uncertainty of her acts and emotions, swiftly passing from love to hatred, from enthusiasm to indifference. She is fantastic, restless, and speaks of feeling the limitations of her body. She confesses that the only pleasure that she has derived from it has been that of tormenting men. She has taken Guido Venanzi as a lover, just for a diversion, perhaps just to be perverse. Now she is terribly bored with that superficial man. "Everything you say is a yawn," she tells him in an uncomplimentary way. Her torment is Leone Gala. He is the puppet master who makes her move by invisible threads. She feels his presence as an incubus. "I free?" she says to Guido as the latter is in her apartment late one evening. "I see him constantly. He gave me this liberty as something worthless, while he went to live by himself after having taught me for three years that liberty does not exist." Through his tortuous reasoning, Gala has taught her introspection; he has destroyed her instinctive spontaneity, and with it the joy that a gay, pretty woman can derive from life. She sees his eyes constantly ("Oh, so hateful, piercing like two needles, under the appearance of a blank expression"). She hears his voice in the prison of her liberty that he has built for her. She frantically cries, "I am crushed for hours by the thought that such a man can exist, almost outside of life and as a nightmare in the life of others!" She is so desperate that she decides to get rid of her husband at any cost. She is exasperated to the point of saying, "I would pay with my life if someone would kill him."

The opportunity arose one night when Gala made his daily visit. Her lover, Guido Venanzi, was entertaining Silia by boring her. Gala insisted as usual on his concept of reason and instinct, expressing delight at the degree of the rational isolation which he had attained. To be more convincing he brought forth an example derived from his experience as a cook. He taught no other than Guido Venanzi, who must have laughed up his sleeve while listening, that a concept of life is like an eggshell without the content. The content is instinct, turbulent instinct, and we must empty it if we wish to live according to the method of perfect life that he has found. "You pass a pin through the empty shell as a pivot and you amuse yourself in making the shell turn around it. It is very light now, and you play with it as you would with a celluloid ball, tossing it from one hand to the other, here, there, here, there; then, paf! you crush it between your hands and you throw it away." In its practical application this example referred to Silia, who was meant to represent the egg without its content of instinct and sentiment. He had taken it, perforated it, removed the content. Now Silia was only the concept of the wife. She was harmless. Silia was so angered that when Leone left the house she threw the empty shell of an egg at him from the window. Instead of hitting him, she hit a group of four tipsy gentlemen who happened to be passing.

115

They went upstairs, mistaking her for a young Spanish dancer who lived in that neighborhood and who was quite immoral. That was a serious insult, and among well-bred people an insult is paid for with a duel. Silia had a most brilliant idea: to have her husband (had he not remained her legal husband, at any rate?) avenge her honor in the hope that Miglioriti, one of the debonair gentlemen who had invaded the apartment and one of the best swordsmen in the city, might free her of him.

On the following morning, Silia herself brought the news to Leone. She thought that at least that news would shake him out of his indifference. Leone, who did not even know what a sword looked like, agreed to challenge Miglioriti. Upon doing so, he demanded terrible terms, a duel to the finish, with pistol and sword. The seconds were duly chosen, the place was decided on, the exact hour indicated. The calm of Leone was extraordinary. Silia, who at first had rejoiced, was greatly perplexed. The reason for Gala's calm appeared very vaguely in a conversation between him and the two lovers. Gala accepted his rôle as a challenger on the grounds that Guido Venanzi, who was in the apartment with Silia, had not come forward to defend her when the four intoxicated young men entered. Gala had done this because he was revolving around the pivot of the concept of a husband as he explained: "Be sure that I shall not move from my pivot no matter what happens. I see both myself and you playing —and I am amused. That's all."

It was a game of rôles. Strangely enough, there was a general feeling in social circles that it was the part of Guido rather than of Leone to defend Silia. Leone dominated all with his enigmatic calm. He prepared everything, ordered everything. He arranged that the duel be fought on the following morning in the garden adjoining his apartment. The fatal morning came. His apartment was filled with friends, his seconds, and the doctor. Leone still slept. Guido Venanzi, upon going to call him, was surprised to find that he was not ready. Ready? He had done his part when he had challenged Migliroti; now it was Guido's part, as a lover, to defend the woman in whose house he had been when she was insulted. Guido could not resist his arguments, fought the duel, and was killed. These are the jests of life and death.

Although Pirandello has treated with ill-concealed amusement Gala's cerebral way of dealing with life, he sympathetically realizes what that detachment means to poor Gala. For this reason he has allowed him to outwit his wife and to make a victim of her lover. Gala has foiled death because he has been able to keep away from the swift river of passion and instinct by reducing life to a series of cold concepts.

Leone Gala, although focused at a closer range, is as tragic as Henry IV, the Father in *Six Characters in Search of an Author*, or as any tragic character that Pirandello has given us. When he laughs one can detect under the froth of exasperation a longing in his heart for the freshness and richness of the life that he has renounced. He has an intellect as sharp and cutting as a Toledo sword. When he finds Guido in his wife's apartment he accepts the situation with the utmost calm, but looks in such a penetrating way at him that the latter is compelled to explain that he has gone there to drink a glass of chartreuse. "It it green or yellow?" queries the subtle Gala. "Green, I believe," answers the confused Guido. Whereupon Gala prophesies, "You will dream of crushing a lizard with your teeth." One can see Pirandello laughing gleefully at his diabolic humor. Gala, in whom Pirandello has disguised himself, is not an attractive character. The fact that he has been endowed with disconcerting and even unpleasant traits is a mark of the objectivity of the author's method. When we see Gala, an intellectual gentleman, incongruously attired as a cook, we realize the effect that the misfortunes of life can have on us. This is humor for Pirandello who never took his sorrows too tragically, but always bore them with a quizzical smile that wandered like a subdued light over his countenance. Had he not done so he might have been one of those individuals who bother their fellow-men with their laments. Pirandello always has a stoical

117

soul, and when the breaking point comes he relaxes into a smile or even laughter. Then out of that state of mind, a character like Leone Gala comes to life.

The author himself gives us the key to this play in *Six Characters in Search of an Author,* confiding to us that Leone Gala was reason and his wife was instinct. It is unjust to call Gala abstract or cerebral. He is conscious that he is unnatural. What counts more is that he knows that he cannot be natural. "Woe to me if I were," he says. If he had been, he would have gone back to Silia whenever her physical appeal overcame his studied indifference. He would have "degraded" himself for having yielded to instinct, and afterwards he would have felt all the lowness of his acts. He expresses this feeling to Silia, who acknowledges his superiority together with her defeat. He tells her: "Don't you think that sudden flares of emotion rise also in me? I don't allow them to cut loose: I seize them; I tame them. I nail them." Emotions are to him wild beasts, and he is the tamer: "I swear to you that sometimes I feel inclined to be devoured by one of these beasts . . . even by you—now that you look at me so tranquilly and repentantly. But no! because believe me: it is all a game. And this would be the last and would destroy the pleasure of all others. No, no, . . . Go, go." He is another character whose destiny is to live in desolate isolation and exasperated loneliness.

As is his custom, Pirandello is more occupied with the complications that instinct can create than with the power of instinct itself. The undercurrent of the play is forced renunciation of instinct and of life. One should not be misled by the salacious events that are here portrayed. A violent asserter of the freedom of instinct is on the same footing as one who denies the right of instinct. They are both equally preoccupied with it. In the development of Gala's character and under the ludicrous events which he creates, we detect the incertitude of one who is perplexed by the strange powers of instinctive life.

In spite of Gala's tortuous and elusive "concepts," there is a very practical side in the method of life which he evolves and which he imposes on himself. Pirandello has afforded him in that method a way of finding life livable. It gives him a superiority over all. He is inaccessible, since no one can hurt him. He has disposed of his rival in a clever manner and he can still continue to pass from one hand to the other the lucent, empty eggshell, playing with it as with a celluloid ball, light, so light.

XII

The Many Faceted Prism of Truth

RIGHT YOU ARE IF YOU THINK YOU ARE
(Così 'è [se vi pare])

Pirandellian humor also runs through *Right You Are if You Think You Are.* Humor, however, colors only the external side of the play, because the pathetic element affirms itself, and becomes larger and deeper as the play develops, till finally it culminates in the last scene, one of the most dramatic that Pirandello has created.

The play is constructed on clear-cut lines dividing a group of the *élite* of a provincial town, who are curious to the point of being cruel, from three individuals who are the victims of their morbid curiosity. There is a typical Pirandellian character between the two groups: Lamberto Laudisi.

In his looks, in his intellectual traits, he bears the marks of one of those characters in whom the author has embodied his wisdom of life. Laudisi stands on the boundary line of instinctive life and reflective intellect. He has reached the conclusion that the only solution for the tragic snares in which humans are caught is a complete categorical subjectivism. What Laudisi claims is that truth is not a bare, brutal, and clumsy fact, but the feeling which animates that fact. He concludes that feelings are so personal, subjective, and elusive as to defy our cold apprehension. He is a pitiless observer of "human stupidity" and he characterizes with this uncomplimentary epithet the cult of the absolute certitude that his sister's family and her friends want to reach concerning a situation which cannot be expressed in rational terms. Laudisi is described to us by his author as follows: "Slender, elegant, without foppishness, in his forties, he wears a bluish purple smoking-jacket with cuffs and black embroidery. Endowed with a subtle, witty intellect, he becomes quickly irritated, but then he laughs and lets people do and say whatever they please, finding delight in the spectacle of human stupidity." Laudisi claims that each human being is an unbreakable unit and that each one of us is unable to penetrate into the mystery of another: "What can we *really* know of other people? Who they are . . . how they are . . . what they do . . . why they do it . . ." Each of us can only feel the outside world, men and things, in a subjective way—which is real to each one of us, but stands in sharp contrast to the results of other people's contacts with the same reality. This actually means that reality, in certain cases, does not have an identity of its own, but that it acquires as many aspects as there are individuals in whom it mirrors itself. Laudisi is very practical in his categorical subjectivism. He does not mean that we "must no longer believe even what we see and touch." What he wants is that we shall believe what we feel and see but also "respect what others see and touch, even if it is the opposite." This belief is a particle of Christian charity seen by a philosophical and somewhat paradoxical mind.

As is evident from the aforesaid, Pirandello does not generalize. He is directing our attention to a specific situation in which a logical approach, based on actual data, does not help at all. Three persons—Signora Frola, Signor Ponza, and Signora Ponza—are involved in one of those situations that make the appeal to the irrational acceptable to human beings, and give to the observer a feeling that life stands on the brink of the abyss of nothingness. Signor Ponza claims that his present wife is his second wife, whom he married after the death of his first wife Lina, the daughter of Signora Frola. Signora Frola claims that Lina is not dead, and that the Signor is demented in believing her his second wife. Signor Ponza has just arrived in town as a secretary in the prefect's office, and lives with his wife on the top floor of a tall, lonely building in the outskirts of the town, while Signora Frola lives alone in an apartment. Every day she goes to see her daughter, but is not allowed to go upstairs to her apartment. She stays down in the courtyard, her mother-love satisfied with a glimpse of her child and with receiving loving messages from her by means of a basket she lowers with a string as is the custom in Italy. The strange thing is that Signor Ponza is deeply devoted to his mother-in-law. He is as tender with her as if he were her own child. He looks after her, goes to visit her every day and passes with her as much of his time as possible.

The whole town is agog over this irrational behavior. Who ever heard of a mother, especially in Italy, who was not allowed to see her daughter? Whoever heard of a son-in-law who spent all his leisure time with his mother-in-law? A flame of curiosity rises and sweeps over the town. Everyone wants to know definitely what the mystery is. The most curious gather at the Agazzi home to map out a campaign. Signor Agazzi is a counselor to the prefect and, therefore, a superior of Signor Ponza.

When the play opens Signora Agazzi is discussing with her brother, Lamberto Laudisi, the unheard-of rudeness of Signor Ponza, who refused to receive her and her daughter Dina when they went to call on Signora Ponza. They had called there before and, after waiting for fifteen minutes at the door, had to leave somewhat embarrassed. Under Laudisi's questioning they have to confess that they went there out of curiosity, but that, at any rate, it is customary to pay a visit to a newcomer, especially when she lives next door. They emphatically state that it was certainly due to Signor Ponza's influence that the dear old lady, Signora Frola, had not come to let them in.

They went to call again and Ponza himself came to the door. "It is his countenance that disconcerts the whole town," says the horrified Signora Agazzi. Ponza had made a little bow and had stood silently before them, his terrible eyes riveted on the two confused ladies. He had finally spoken, saying that his mother-in-law was ill, and that she thanked them for their kindness. With these words he had stood there waiting for them to go. Signora Agazzi and her daughter, mortified, had hastened to leave.

Now Signor Agazzi, as Ponza's superior, is protesting to the prefect and asking for an apology. There is a conclave in the Agazzi home concerning this deplorable episode. A group of other scandalmongers arrive: Signora Sirelli, red-headed, plump, complacent, bedecked with rings, and burning with curiosity; her husband, the object of her biting sarcasm, a man about forty, "bald, fat, with pretenses to being elegant," and Signora Cini, a friend of theirs, "an awkward old lady, full of eager malice, covered by an air of naïveté." All that these people know is that Signor Ponza, his wife, and his mother-in-law are in deep mourning because they come from a town in Marsica which has been destroyed by an earthquake; that they have lost all their relatives in that disaster. Signor Ponza has a tragic face with the eyes "of a wild beast and not of a man," as young Dina informs her friends, who are eager to receive any information to assuage the burning curiosity that devours them.

They are all determined to know the truth. Signor Agazzi has brought pressure to bear on the prefect, and Signora Frola will have to apologize for the rudeness of her son-in-law in not allowing two ladies, the wife and daughter of his superior, to call on her. In fact, Signora Frola comes to call in the midst of all this hubbub. She is "a neat, modest, most affable little old lady, with a great sadness in her eyes, but constantly softened by a gentle smile on her lips." Signora Frola tells them that she and Signor Ponza live in a sort of isolated world which they themselves have closed with their own hands with the result that their harmony is perfect and they live quietly in it. Her explanation has the effect of only whetting more the desire to uncover what is behind the strange conduct of Signor Ponza. They cannot believe that it is due to "a sort of malady, a fullness of love—but closed —that's all! . . . An overpowering fullness of love, in which his wife must live, without ever coming out of it, and which no one must enter." They all qualify Ponza's behavior as pure "egotism." Gently Signora Frola, in her compassionate understanding, agrees that perhaps it is, but "an egotism which gives itself entirely, as a complete world of its own, to his wife." When she leaves, the words "mystery," "violence," "barbarism," echo in the room.

Signora Frola has hardly left the house when Signor Ponza arrives. He is "thickset, dark—with an almost fierce look, with bushy black hair, low forehead, heavy black mustache like a policeman. He clenches his fists continuously and speaks with difficulty, with ill-contained violence. While he is speaking, his eyes remain hard, fixed, gloomy." He announces that Signora Frola is crazy and that her madness consists exactly in believing that he does not want her to see her daughter. "What daughter, in God's name, if her daughter has been dead four years?" exclaims, almost shouts Signor Ponza. He informs his listeners that two years before, he had remarried, but Signora Frola still believes that his second wife is her daughter. Tenderly he refers to the beneficial effect of this belief: "It has been lucky for her because she had fallen into a sort of gloomy desperation at her daughter's death, while her lucid madness makes her happy in the belief that her daughter is alive." As soon as Signor Ponza leaves, the gentle Signora Frola quietly returns.

As readily as they had accepted Signor Ponza's version of the mother-in-law's madness, they accepted Signora Frola's explanation that he, Ponza, is in an unbalanced state of mind. He has come to believe that this is his second wife after his first wife, Lina, was sent to a sanitarium for a year. Upon her return, he had claimed that she was no longer Lina. He called her Giulia, and he was so assertive in his belief that they were forced to perform a second wedding, a mock ceremony. Would a mother speak so calmly of the situation if her daughter were dead?

The two speak with so much plausibility that it is hard not to believe them both. One oscillated between the two explanations, unable to take sides, and almost excusing the cruel curiosity of the Agazzi family and of their friends. The fatuous, bald-headed, and round-bellied Signor Sirelli, much to the surprise of his red-headed wife, has a practical idea: let us put Signor Ponza and Signora Frola together; let us put them face to face, then we can be sure that the truth will be discovered.

Sirelli's suggestion is followed: the two confront each other.

Signora Frola, who beforehand has expressed her belief in Ponza's madness, when the latter appears and furiously inveighs against her for having left her apartment, sweetly agrees with him as to the identity of his wife. Everyone gloats over the fact that now the truth has been discovered. If Signora Frola treats Ponza like a spoiled child and pretends to agree with him, it is evident that Ponza is crazy. But Ponza, after acting so violently, as soon as his mother-in-law leaves the room, reacquires his composure and says: "I beg your pardon, ladies and gentlemen, for being compelled to offer such a spectacle to you in order to remedy the harm that you unwittingly do to this poor woman." Then he has been feigning; not he, but Signora Frola is crazy! How swiftly our opinion changes before a reality which is inconstant and variable because it is colored by the sentiment of those who participate in it! In order to help Signora Frola endure the sorrow of her daughter's death, a sorrow that normally would have killed her, Signor Ponza, according to what he says, shouts the truth to her as if it were his own madness. It is the only way to keep her illusion alive. What a madman believes cannot be the truth—then, Lina, her Lina, is alive. The disappointed spectators of the strange scene between Signor Ponza and Signora Frola ask of him: "What? Did you pretend?" Ponza, in the fixity of his pitiful exaltation, answers: "I was compelled to. Don't you understand that this was the only means by which I could let her live in her illusion, that of shouting to her the truth in this fashion as if it were my madness?" Of course they do not understand. How could they, normal and happy people, understand this pitiful contrivance, indispensable to two persons who are helping each other bear the burden of their sorrow by not accepting, each for the sake of the other, the naked and crushing truth that would make life unendurable for at least one of them? Laudisi ironically laughs: "There you are, ladies and gentlemen, the truth is discovered."

The only solution is to hear the person herself about whose identity there is doubt—Signora Ponza. If they ask her who she is; whether she is the first or second wife of Signor Ponza, they will certainly get the correct answer. The truth will undoubtedly be disclosed.

They do so. The prefect compels Ponza to bring his wife to Agazzi's house. Signora Ponza advances rigidly, in deep mourning, her face hidden by a dark, thick veil, impenetrable. She has lost the distinctness of human features that make human individuality. Her tragedy has blurred all that constitutes her personal identity. As soon as Signora Frola sees her, she calls her: "Lina, Lina!" rushing towards her and clinging to the veiled woman with the thirst for love of a mother who has not for years held her daughter in her arms. But at the same time is heard the voice of Ponza who dashes on the stage shouting: "Giulia, Giulia!"

At his shouts the veiled woman stiffens in the arms of Signora Frola. She begs both of them to leave. Signor Ponza and Signora Frola go out clasped in each other's arms, caressing each other, in tears. The veiled woman speaks: "What else can you wish from me? As you see, there is here a misfortune that must be respected, because only in this way can the remedy prevail that compassion has lent it. The truth is only this: I am both Signora Frola's daughter and Signor Ponza's second wife; yes, and for me, no one, no one!" The prefect insists: "Oh, no, for you, my dear lady, you must be one or the other." "No," she replies, "for myself I am the one that people believe me to be."

There follows a stony silence in which are merged the disappointment of the curious, the quickened wound of the three victims, and the tragic laughter of Laudisi. There is also our reverence before the tragedy of three human beings who had to clothe truth with illusion to bear its terrifying countenance. Beauty of symbol is blended perfectly in harmony with depth of sentiment!

The central idea of the play is the belief that we are absolutely subjective and that the only way to live and to let other people live is to accept this point of view. Lamberto Laudisi does so, and he respects the odd situation existing in the Ponza household. The others, totalitarian logicians, apply to this specific case a generic idea, and by so doing they create their own discomfort and destroy the peace which, even if based on illusion, allows three persons to live peacefully. The gentle, merciful, and human power of illusion has taken life in a situation of unspeakable sorrow and tragedy and has given Signor Ponza and Signora Frola the calm that they have reached by forcing on themselves a belief that did not correspond to the truth, but was more endurable than the truth. Truth was their own grief and tragedy.

Let us not laugh at Pirandello's claim of the power of illusion! Illusion is empty when it is sought by idle dreamers and by seekers of idyls. Then it is sentimentality. But when illusion is a bitter necessity, it is sublime and pitiful, and such is the one that unfolds before us in this play.

The true heroine of the play is Signora Ponza. Pirandello has embodied in her the symbol of reality, which is veiled, nonexistent, until we give a meaning to it by letting our sentiment infuse life into it. Pirandello predicates the subjective value of truth, and the play pivots on this query: Is truth, objective and categorical truth, always possible? Laudisi reveals to us Pirandello's point of view when he states that he is not interested in the actual data about the Ponza family: "Reality for me does not consist in the facts, but in the sentiment of those two, where I cannot penetrate except through what they reveal to me." The facts concerning them "have been annulled, not by an external accident—a fire, an earthquake; but by themselves in their hearts . . . creating, he to her, or she to him, a phantasm which has the same consistency of reality, in which they live perfectly, in full accord." They "breathe in that reality, they see it, feel it, touch it." Why shouldn't we respect it?

Sirelli and the others wish to "explain," assuming an attitude coldly scientific and selfish: The truth is one, either Signor Ponza is right or Signora Frola. They lack the gift of sympathy and understanding. At this point, Pirandello's thought merges with the teachings of great religious leaders who in their exalted individualism glorified "holy madness" which was nothing but their sentiment in contrast with the objective and instinctive reaction of the average man. Pirandello has put in challenging form and somewhat intellectualized what we usually find in the form of a religious precept. The admonition "be charitable" is very close to the subjectivism of Lamberto Laudisi. When we are charitable we give up our own point of view, which is our interpretation of the outside reality, and accept the other man's point of view which contains his interpretation of the same reality.

If we allow our minds to ponder over the author's doubt of the benefit of a categorical but unbending, even heartless concept of truth, we see that a gentle though sad vein of human sympathy runs through his attitude. What can absolute knowledge do when we find ourselves face to face with the death of a person dear to us? It does not help us to bear our grief to think that to die is the common lot of humanity; nor to know the nature of the disease, and to follow its progress step by step on the doctor's chart. What good did it do Pirandello himself to know that his wife was demented? Did that knowledge destroy the reality he had to face for so many years?

It would be futile to speculate upon whether Signora Frola or Ponza is right. The play hinges on the fact that the identity of the wife remains a mystery. The author has been able to lead us through three long acts, balancing with perfect ease between humor and pathos, without satisfying the curiosity not only of the Agazzi family, their friends, and the town, but also our own. We should act against the desire of the author if we attempted to tear aside the veil from Signora Ponza's face. If we did, we should imitate the critics of Dante who attempt to identify a sinner among those that Dante condemned to the loss of their physical and personal identity. It is immaterial to know who Signora Ponza, veiled and grieving, actually is. We must accept her heart-rending confession, and grieve with her.

XIII

Changing Character of Human Opinions

EACH IN HIS OWN WAY

(*Ciascuno a suo modo*)

Pirandello has projected in *Each in His Own Way* one of his most tormented and pessimistic moods, although his pessimism is the direct reaction of the belief that only humility and stoic silence can help man in the tragedy of being human.

The setting is laid in a more aristocratic atmosphere than in his earlier plays. His characters here are also more intellectual and, therefore, more tormented and complicated, since life for Pirandello becomes more tormented and complicated as it departs from a presupposed idyllic beginning where goodness and happiness reign. "I, too, have learned to do my acrobatic stunts, by myself, coming from the country to the city—here—in all this falsity and unreality, which becomes more false and unreal from day to day," says the tragic heroine, adding that there is no way to revert to the original simplicity, and that "to try to recreate this simplicity in us and around us appears—is, indeed, false."

At the outset we find ourselves in the aristocratic home of Donna Livia Palegari. The Subtle Youth and the Old Gentleman, guests at a formal tea—one eager, the other cautious to the point of hypocrisy—discuss the question of forming and reaching opinions, and whether or not we have opinions. Diego, another guest and Pirandello's spokesman, denies that we have real opinions since we change them according to circumstances and persons involved. He denies also the validity of what we call conscience, which is nothing but "others" in us, that is, what others think reflected in us: public opinion that determines our acts.

"Everything is mobile, fleeting, without weight. I turn here, there. I laugh. I hide myself in a nook and weep. What

129

torment! What anguish! Continually I hide my face from myself, so ashamed am I at seeing myself change." So, disconsolately speaks another guest, and these words reveal the state of mind of the author which in turn colors the thoughts and actions of the characters. Everything is spasmodic, tortuous, torturing, because there is no basis for the thinking and the acting of these beings who are deprived of opinions, of beliefs, of conscience.

Pirandello is not making here a generic case. The generic and average man is for him, as we have repeatedly stated, an abstraction. He is concerned with individuals only, his characters. Granted their inability to form a definite opinion, their irrational behavior is a logical consequence. It is also the negative reflection of a positive side: If an individual were capable of a clear and deeply and sincerely felt opinion, rational behavior would follow. Pirandello, however, goaded by his life-experience, has seen around him and in himself largely the negative side. It is easier to see the positive one in the quiet chamber of our imagination.

The inspiration of the play came to the author supposedly from a newspaper clipping, telling of an actress from Turin for whom a promising young sculptor, Giacomo La Vela, committed suicide. Almost on the eve of their wedding she had given herself to the *fiancé* of La Vela's sister, Baron Nuti. Pirandello realizes very well why that has happened: instinct, a tragedy of instinct. But what will those characters say if he asks them? Will they confess humbly and contritely what they have done? He knows that they will not. Thereupon he places them in his comedy with a slight change in the name of the actress, but replacing the sculptor, La Vela, with a painter, Giorgio Salvi, and Baron Nuti with Michele Rocca.

Delia Morello is one of those celebrated and glorified harlots who were very popular in Italy in the beginning of the century, women of singular beauty, moving in the best of masculine society. Artists and writers sought their company because these women were interested in the arts, too, since a little smattering of culture was good bait for intellectual people. They had inherited the place of prominence that Imperia occupied in the sixteenth century, in the very city and in the very court of the Popes. Delia was not intellectual. Pirandello does not like intellectual women. She was full of the sensitiveness that tragedy develops in human beings.

The value of men's opinions was quickly tested that afternoon in the palatial home of Donna Livia Palegari, who was very much concerned over the report that her young son Doro had, the previous evening, taken the part of the actress Delia Morello. Referring to the suicide of Giorgio Salvi, Francesco Savio, an intimate friend of Doro, had accused the actress of having perfidiously contributed to the death of the promising painter. Doro had risen furiously to defend her, defying the ridicule and indignation of all. He had given an idealistic explanation of what had happened. He had maintained that it could not be said that Delia Morello had "wilfully planned Salvi's ruin by giving herself to the other man, almost on the eve of the wedding; because the true ruin of Salvi would have been, after all, his marriage to her." When his mother, both scandalized and fearful of a duel, reproaches him, he tells her that he is sincerely ready to acknowledge that he has been wrong in taking Delia Morello's part against his friend Francesco Savio. The mother is overjoyed.

At that very moment there arrives Francesco Savio who confesses that he too has seen the foolishness of his own position, and has come to tell his old friend how sorry he is. The strange thing is that a new dispute arises when Francesco repeats the arguments that Doro has advanced in Delia's defense. To Pirandello that is quite natural. In the first place, they have merely changed positions; so that they are as far apart now as they were the previous evening. Besides, when we hear another person repeating something that we have said and know to be false, we naturally resent it. That falseness becomes galling, irritating beyond endurance. Translated into terms of everyday life, Doro's reaction is parallel to our resentment when we hear another person saying to us, "You fool," an epithet that we have numberless times applied to ourselves. Through Francesco's words Doro had seen himself in a mirror that distorted his features and made grimaces at him. His arguments were hollow, annoyingly hollow, as he well knew. Why should that idiotic Francesco have come there to repeat them to him? That is why he called Francesco "buffoon" five times in a fit of rage, and the latter, offended, left the house.

As soon as the two friends separate with the certainty of a duel, Delia Morello comes to thank Doro for believing her innocent. She has "recognized" herself in the arguments advanced by him. He has expressed what she has never been able to understand about herself. Doro, who has just acknowledged the weakness of his own reasoning, under the sway of Delia's beauty, believes again that she is innocent. He is ready again to defy public opinion and ridicule, and even to go against his mother. "See," grievingly laughs Pirandello, "that is the value of man's opinions and actions!"

These rapid changes and most unforeseen reactions are not easily understood unless we picture Doro and his friends as persons yielding one moment to the sincere impulse of instinct (instinct is always sincere), and at another moment to the complicating force of reason or "conscience," as Pirandello calls it here. Conscience is identified in the play with the process that we well know by now, and that Pirandello calls *costruirsi* or "to build up oneself." These characters are not telling the truth (how could they tell the truth?) and therefore they transform the hideous reality into a network of clever explanations, which make the original situation both ludicrous and sad. For this reason Pirandello has projected on the screen of his art a crowd of grotesque figures, puppets, as he calls them, shouting, gesticulating figures with staring eyes, tense, as if possessed by evil spirits like young trees furiously tossed by the wind. The most tormented of all is Delia Morello.

Pirandello has not made of Delia a monster of iniquity as did Donna Livia Palegari and her aristocratic friends. She is sincere in all her complicated falseness. She is "one of those women born by chance—always outside of themselves —wanderers who will never know where they are going to end. And yet, so many times, she seems to be a little frightened child imploring help." Pirandello is not cruel to his characters. He is too sophisticated not to see the truth, but he is sorry to see what he sees. Tears and mourning are not the only means of showing sadness. There is also laughter, the tolerant laughter peculiar to him that shows his sympathetic sorrow. Diego, who laughs with that tolerance, tells us, "That's my way of laughing and my laughter hurts me more than anyone else." Delia lived tragically under the weight of her shame when she heard the explanation that Doro first gave to her actions. She is in a state of exaltation now. Doro by his defense has created an artificial atmosphere in which she can see her past in a light which is not maddening and unbearable. She has been able "to build up herself" through the idealized image created by Doro. That image is her salvation, and she clings to it with the same desperate passion with which one clings to life.

Delia is not concerned with what people will think of her. She tells Doro, "My gratitude is for what you have thought, felt—and not because you have shouted it to everybody else." He has revealed a new being in her, a being that before she had tried in vain to find. "I struggle, I suffer—I don't know—as if beyond myself, as if I must always pursue the person that I really am, in order to stop her and ask her what she wants, what she suffers, what she would like me to do to calm her, to give her peace." Now that a new self has been revealed to her, she hates all the artificiality with which she has covered her face and destroyed her soul. She has discovered—or did she know it before this?—that she hated the adoration that men had for her body, neglecting "her." She is sincere as she speaks of the neglect of her soul by men, but she adds: "And I punish them exactly where their longings converge. I excite those desires that nauseate me, in order to avenge myself better—and I avenge myself by offering this body to one whom they least suspect!" There are in her, sincerity and fraud, innocence and malice, as she at times catches, as if on the wing, a fluttering dream; again, at times, she shows the tricks of a prostitute. The subconscious merges with the fantastic as she tries to excuse her wrong to Giorgio

133

Salvi, whose beautiful intellect and soul perished because of her.

They had met at Capri. He had asked her to sit for a portrait, then to be his model. She had consented. He looked at her with the eyes of an artist, though, like all others, only at her body. Sentiments were colors to him. The ideal pleasure that he took in her beauty made her frantic, because she could not avenge herself as she did with other men. What Doro had said was so true: "To a woman an angel is more irritating than a beast." Hatred for Giorgio, handsome and intellectual, grew in her in a slow, veiled, tortuous manner. The moment to avenge herself had come. She let her body shine before him in all its sensuous splendor. He, too, became intoxicated with it. She denied herself to him. She gave herself to Michele Rocca, his sister's *fiancé*. But when she did (it was so, just as Doro had imagined) it was that they might be surprised together, making her marriage with Salvi impossible, for his own sake and in his interest.

Doro happens to mention Francesco's arguments which interpret Delia's conduct in quite a different manner. He does it to contrast the brilliancy of his defense with the drabness of Francesco's attack. Delia, in the version of Doro, appears to have dissuaded Salvi from marrying her. For this reason she had denied herself to him and, believing he would refuse, had imposed upon him terrible conditions; such as introducing her to his lovely mother and to his exquisite sister, of whose loftiness and purity he was both proud and jealous.

In Francesco's version, her refusal to marry Salvi, and her declining to give herself to him, were perfidious means of obtaining more and more concessions, so that she might become the absolute mistress of his life. Only in this fashion had she succeeded in having Giorgio introduce her to his family, and she had gone there, victorious, before society, near the purity of his little sister—she, "the spurned, the contaminated one." In Francesco's opinion, Delia had given herself to Rocca because she knew that Rocca had been opposed to her being taken into the family. To avenge herself, Delia had decided to allure, to attract him into the whirl of her sensuality "only for the pleasure of showing to that sister the timbre of the pride and honesty of such spotless paladins of morality." What depths of stupidity Francesco had reached in his senseless explanations! Much to Doro's amazement, Delia says, "Who knows that I have not done it for that reason?" The actions of these human beings are not to be considered in the light of rationality. There is in them obscure thinking and, therefore, obscure behavior. Doro is not different from Delia. He is going to fight a duel with Francesco, and admits that he does not know why.

The one who pricks the iridescent soap bubbles of all these people is Diego. He is not different from the others in excitement and tension, but he knows the game and acknowledges it, while the others seem unable to see their own artificiality. He knows how to read himself clearly, fearlessly; and Pirandello has assigned to him the rôle of representing him. Therefore Diego performs the unpleasant task of taking these characters apart, piece by piece, and showing them that there is no other alternative for them and for himself: either they must be tragic with reality or ludicrous with fiction. Pirandello has lent him his own tormented soul and intellect, while Diego describes the tragic grief that torments him by saying, "I have reduced my soul, by constantly burrowing into it, to a mole-hole." Two years before, he had lost his mother after a long illness that had made her unrecognizable. He had spent nine sleepless nights near her as she moaned, almost unconscious, disfigured, on her deathbed. He had known the agony of counting by the striking of the clock the last hours of a dying person. He had discovered that no affection is strong enough to stand the neglect of the most elementary needs of life. Sleep and hunger conquer even our deepest love, love for our mother. In a fit of futile revolt, he had caught himself wishing his mother dead. Once he had seen himself in the mirror of his wardrobe, bending over his moaning mother, and he had seen on his own face "the expression with which he was stealthily anticipating his own freedom with an almost joyous fright."

Diego has fathomed the human heart down to those mys-

135

terious and terrifying depths. He has reached a tragic nihil-
ism about life. Life wavers between a ghastly nothingness for
those who think, and the stupid monotonous certitude of the
everyday existence with its solid but limited and cramping
reality, for those who cling to the tangible and concrete side
of life. Life is to him "a continuous destruction which not
even the strongest affections escape." One can easily imagine
how fluid and fleeting are "the opinions, the fictions that we
create for ourselves, and all the ideas that in the ruinous
flight of life we succeed in perceiving. We learn something
contrary to what we knew, we experience a sudden change in
our impressions, we hear a word uttered in a different tone,
and Mr. So-and-So who was white becomes black. Images
of numberless things flash continuously through our mind and
change our mood without our realizing it." How can he believe in conscience and opinions? How can he take seriously
the words of these characters, puppets of passion and illusion? He tells Doro that it is his love for Delia that makes
him take her part and declare her innocent. Doro denies it
and Diego reveals his crushing pessimism. Woe unto us if we
look into our own hearts!—"Conscience is an elastic network
whence—if it should loosen a little—escapes madness, which
nestles and hides within each of us. Then there wander before
you, disconnectedly, images accumulated in so many years,
ambiguous acts, shameful lies, ferocious hatreds, crimes
meditated in the shadow of your thoughts, even in their slightest details, unrevealed desires."

There is another man whom Diego has to dissect, whom
he has to bring before the pitiless light of his inquiry—
Michele Rocca. Rocca has come from Naples upon hearing
of the incident between Doro and Francesco in which he was
involved. He has come to challenge Doro to a duel for insult-
ing him while defending Delia. He, too, has his idealistic
interpretation of his actions. The mere fact that he can talk
relieves him of the tension that has oppressed him since the
day of the tragedy. Excitedly, but also theatrically, he states
that he did not wish to steal Giorgio's *fiancée*, as he has been
accused of doing. He had been urged by Giorgio's mother, his

sister, and even by Giorgio himself to prove his contention that Delia Morello was dishonest. His relations with her were prompted only by his desire to afford Giorgio the proof of her perfidy. Refusing to face the truth, Giorgio committed suicide. Diego gives an entirely different explanation of Rocca's actions: "He does not wish to have to confess that he has been a plaything in the hands of a woman—a little puppet that Delia Morello has broken by throwing it into a corner, after amusing herself by making him open and close his arms as in an act of prayer, by pressing with her finger on his chest the spring of passion. Now the little puppet is up again; his little face without a nose, all cracked, chipped. . . . The little puppet shouts that it is not true that the woman made him open and close his arms in order to laugh at him, and that, after laughing at him, she broke him. He says 'No, no.' I ask you if there is any spectacle more touching than this!"

Diego has gone to Francesco's house to tell him of Rocca's arrival. Francesco is busy training for his duel, practising with his fencing master and seconds. Both Delia and Rocca arrive. Delia has come to beg Francesco not to fight the duel with Doro. She begs him for her sake not to do it. She succeeds in enveloping Francesco too in her charm. Upon seeing Rocca, Francesco attacks him, insults him, defies him. He thinks that Delia is his, but he is wrong. Pirandello brutally uncovers the truth. As soon as Delia and Rocca see each other, they throw off the mask of their interest in Giorgio Salvi. The truth is that their blind passion has overpowered them since first they met. Placed face to face, they are unable to resist it, and they fall into each other's arms, while Francesco cries, "It is absurd, it is monstrous! There is between you the corpse of a man." Rocca acknowledges it. "It is monstrous, yes, but she must stay with me! She must suffer with me, with me." It is the logic of instinct, which is stronger than reason, and which uncovers and destroys all the false constructions of the intellect, leading these characters from the ridicule of self-illusion to the tragedy of reality.

In this play the æsthete and the moralist have come to the

help of the dramatist in order to project on the screen of art pitiful and tragic events. The æsthetic considerations and the moral concern, however, do not destroy the dramatic character and the pathos of the vicissitudes that we witness. Pirandello in building up the play has been very much concerned with the relation between art and life. He has introduced in two intermezzi the real persons from whose life he took the idea of the comedy: Delia Morello and Baron Nuti, who are in the audience, mingle with the spectators, and witness their lives reënacted on the stage. They represent life as it is in its actuality, while the Delia of the play and Michele Rocca represent the way in which man interprets idealistically his shameful acts. The former are tragic and crushed by their tragedy; the latter gesticulate and find solace in their bubbling, excited chatter, until they are compelled to return to the plane of reality, whence a social incident had removed them. When Delia and Nuti see themselves in the fixity of art, in which is reflected all the ugliness of their deeds, they become outraged and violent. Delia Morello leaps on the stage and slaps the actress who is impersonating her. None the less violent is Baron Nuti, with the result that a confusion arises in the theatre and an imaginary third act, so Pirandello informs us, is not played. The public, after either admiring or condemning the play, goes home.

Outwardly the play seems involved, gloomy, and pessimistic. When we single out the various strands that Pirandello has woven into it and look at the intimate texture of the work, it becomes clear and faintly illuminated by the light of his idealistic philosophy of humility. All those tortuous constructions are due to the fact that Delia Morello and Michele Rocca do not possess resignation—the gift of the humble of spirit. When we find ourselves in a world the only sure reality of which is death, where we are not sure of our own acts and of their reasons, of our opinions, of our conscience, when we know so little about ourselves, when we are one today and another tomorrow, when the only absolute certainty is that of the "little certitude of today," of our material possessions, of the fleeting existence of our bodies, when life is a continuous erosion of the most precious things we have, what armor will protect us other than humility? Do not ask for conclusions and solutions. Life is a conclusion and a solution unto itself. We are lost between the elusive and maddening fluidity of our ideas and the consoling gift of a gentle dream: "We advance sadly along a road already invaded by the shadows of the evening. It is enough to raise our eyes to a little loggia still illuminated by the setting sun, with a red geranium that glows in that light—and suddenly a distant dream touches our hearts." This sudden pure emotion is a true consolation for us humans. Pirandello is against pride and deceit: "Detach from yourself the little puppet that you create with the fictitious interpretation of your acts and your sentiments—and you will immediately see that it has nothing to do with what you are, or what you may truly be—with what is in you that you are not conscious of, and which is a terrible god, understand, if you oppose him, but which becomes immediately compassionate for every guilt if you abandon yourself to him and do not wish to find excuses."

There is a scene which reveals the intimate sentiment of Pirandello. As Francesco is preparing for his duel with Doro, and his friends are discussing the elusive meaning of all this ado between the two friends, Francesco is reminded of the countryside where he was supposed to go to visit his sister and his little niece when the unfortunate incident occurred. The beauty of the country and the charm of the little girl are made to float invitingly before the man who soon will either face or give death. Real life was there in that beauty, in that affection, in that charm!

The keynote of the play is given by the very title, *Each in His Own Way*, which refers to the duty that each has in creating his own reality. Reality is not a convention; it is not an object that everybody calls by a given name. Reality is something that we must create with our own souls, out of our own lives, in humility and candor: "Here we teach that you have to build the road on which you walk, singly, for every step that you wish to take, battering down what does not belong to you, because you have not built it yourself, and you have walked on it as a parasite." The only logical consequence of human volubility, of the ludicrous changes to which man abandons himself with wanton madness, is "the tragedy of a deranged and a convulsed soul that has lost its bearings." Delia Morello and the people who move around her in the play had not succeeded in creating their own reality, and for this reason they could only act as poor marionettes, guided by the arbitrary and violent hand of instinct and by the volubility of their minds.

XIV

The Beauty of a Lie

NAKED

(*Vestire gli ignudi*)

This play might be called the comedy of the unmasking of a lie if we did not feel that the false statement made by the heroine was so naïve and touching as to make us rebel at qualifying it with a term that bespeaks base deception. Since Ersilia Drei paid with her life for trying to die surrounded by an imaginary, romantic halo, it befits us to be kind to her and sympathetic with her experiences. She had always had an aspiration towards the beautiful, but life had constantly conspired against her. Her longing was for a modest sort of beauty, such as even an average person is wont to desire. Hers was, in fact, a common species of sentimentality, but it held for her the promise of beautifying a life made up of commonplace events, of vain aspirations, and, alas, of shame.

Ersilia Drei, sick and wan, is presented to us by a comparison that Pirandello derives from his observation of the immediate reality: "It is as when a poor little beast in the street happens to fall into the midst of a group of nasty big dogs, and the gentler the small one is, the more they attack it and bite it and tear it apart." In desolate dejection, "shaking her head and slightly opening her hands that she holds in her lap" Ersilia Drei confesses, "I have never succeeded in being anything at all." She was a nurse, one of those continental nurses, girls of good family, refined, sensitive, and accustomed to move like shadows in wealthy households. "I was but a nurse's uniform, frayed, that is hung every night on a nail in the wall," she characterizes herself. She had charge of an exquisite little girl, Mimmetta, the daughter of Grotti, the Italian consul at Smyrna. One day a fine-looking naval officer arrived from Italy. There is an oriental background to the story: the sea, the sun, the oriental night full of palm trees and perfumes. Love sings for the first time in her heart. She becomes engaged to the naval officer, but it is a short parenthesis of happiness for her. Tragedy falls like a pall over the household. The little girl entrusted to her care falls from the terrace down to the street and is killed. Ersilia hastens back to Italy and finds that her *fiancé* is going to be married to another girl. She goes to a public park and takes poison. She wants everyone to know that she has died for love, a betrayed sweetheart.

Failing to die, however, she tells her story to a newspaper reporter when she is recovering in a hospital. Men have been cruel to her: by saving her they have proved the horrid truth about her and her life. They have torn the nice little dress that she made to cover her pitiful nakedness. Now that everyone has discovered the truth she will be taken around the town to be shown to the curious mob; the fiction with which she has given a look of decency and romance to her death will be heartlessly destroyed. The pitiful and romantic story of Ersilia Drei has filled the newspapers, and all of Rome has been stirred by it. A novelist, Ludovico Nota, becomes interested in the case of the poor young woman and writes a novel about her. When Ersilia leaves the hospital, he invites her to go to live in his apartment. His housekeeper, at first furious, upon learning that Ersilia is the romantic victim whose story covered the front page of the newspapers, becomes very maternal and puts herself at her disposal. Franco Laspiga, who jilted her, upon hearing that she has attempted suicide because of him, suddenly develops a feeling of responsibility and wishes to atone by marrying her. The subtle quality of Pirandello's mind reveals itself, here as elsewhere, by calling attention to the fact that in every dramatic event there is always an element of cool, planned, opportunistic consideration. Ersilia Drei did not try to die for love. She simply could not bear the heavy burden of her life any longer. Franco does not wish to marry Ersilia merely because she is a heroine. He has been jilted by his *fiancée*. Ludovico Nota is not prompted to be kind to Ersilia by a feeling of compassion. He has

142

dreamt of a gay romance, as he reveals to the poor girl who is still frightened from having gazed upon death.

Franco, twenty-seven years old, tall, blond, slender, and elegant, rushes to Ludovico's apartment in order to throw himself at Ersilia's feet and ask her pardon. He is thankful to Ludovico for giving her shelter. Ludovico, who is very much irritated by all the publicity that he is receiving, answers sharply, "Are you grateful to me because I am no longer a young man?" This query reminds us of Pirandello's habit of portraying even out-of-the-ordinary events in an atmosphere where the common and ordinary sounds and modes of life are never absent. Franco is obsessed by his guilt: "How much harm I have done to everyone! It seems as if the whole world is full of the evil I have perpetrated. I am crushed by it."

The solution seems to be very close at hand. An optimist might say, Well, Ersilia Drei has succeeded. Now Franco will marry her and they will live happily ever after. This optimism, however, does not tally with Ersilia Drei's feelings. She refuses to have anything to do with Franco. She writhes in her bed and threatens to throw herself out of the window if he enters the room. She is frightened as she cries, "Is it my fault if they have saved me?" Indeed, she has to face a difficult situation when Franco goes to see her on the following day, speeded by idealistic ardor and zeal for redemption for himself and for her that is in sharp contrast to the reception accorded him by Ersilia. "Do not touch me, do not touch me!" she cries with fervor, as Franco tries to take her in his arms. She tells him that the situation has changed now, that it is not true that she has tried to commit suicide for him. She looks at him and states, "I have difficulty in even recognizing you."

Pirandello at this point stresses the change that even a brief time has wrought in Ersilia. How can she say that she hardly recognizes a man whom she has loved, to whom she has given herself, and for whom she has declared that she even attempted to commit suicide? The sharp contrast between the present and the past is determined by contradictory emotional states unrelated to each other and representing two distinct moments in the life of the character. The life of a machine is the best coördinated; that of man lacks coördination in an inverted ratio to its richer emotional span. Ersilia Drei sees Franco in a light that is totally different from the one by which he was enveloped at Smyrna. That light was created by the sentimental effervescence of her soul and imagination. Now she sees him with the detached objectiveness of one who is tied to this life against her will. Franco is most insistent in his generous impulse and, in being so, he is cruel because he forces poor Ersilia to destroy the beautiful iridescent shell that hides a terrible truth—the life that she lived after the young officer, having awakened love in her, left her in the consul's house.

To persuade him that she will refuse any offer from him of love, marriage, help or protection, she hurls at him the ghastly spectacle of what happened the night before she attempted to commit suicide. "You must know that I offered myself to the first man that passed," she says. Ludovico Nota comments, "In desperation! On the eve of her suicide! Do you understand?" This makes Franco more eager to atone for his wrongdoing, since the greater Ersilia's misfortune, the greater is the sense of responsibility that is awakened in him. Ersilia is compelled to admit to Franco that after his departure she yielded to the consul and was his mistress until by their neglect they caused the death of Mimmetta. The consul, who has come to the apartment to demand an explanation of what had been published in the papers, finds himself face to face with Ersilia in what the author makes a very poignant scene. Each accuses the other of responsibility for their wrong relationship. In what Ersilia calls her revolt at being contaminated, Grotti sees scheming means of exciting him. She says: "You caught me by surprise when I still felt the fire that he [Franco] had kindled in my flesh . . . and, deny, if you can, that I bit you. Deny that I scratched your neck, your arms, your hands." Grotti answers, "You coward, you were exciting me." They go over the days of lust and romance that caught them in a deadly net, and they see unspeakable miseries in them. Acts that once might have loomed in the light of sentiment now exude filth and generate disgust. Grotti, like the Father in *Six Characters in Search of an Author*, rebels at Ersilia's attempt to summarize all his life in that stupid episode of his existence. He wishes to return to the fullness of his daily life that "you, cursed woman, have held in your sway for a moment, by confusing me. What! Do you believe that my whole self is contained in that moment of stupid idleness and of lust that I spent with you, for which I had to pay so dearly? With the unhappiness of my whole life: the death of my child." As many of Pirandello's characters do, Grotti tries to excuse his profligacy on the ground that he was unhappy with his wife. He had been as a father to Ersilia for a long time, and he was glad when Franco Laspiga gave evidence of an interest in her that culminated in their engagement. When he understood that she had given herself to Franco, his first reaction was a feeling of pity and sympathy. Then Grotti felt his attitude tinged with the sensuality that arose from the thought that she was no longer pure. Once, in days subsequent to Franco's departure, she had seemed to look at him in a way that betrayed her doubt as to his paternal feelings towards her. That glance marked their downfall.

Both Ersilia and Grotti are emphatic in their accusations. Pirandello does not accuse. He looks with eyes that flash with understanding, malice, and compassion, and says it was the blind force of instinct. Now that they are no longer bewitched by the enchantment of passion, now that passion is dead, they find only ugliness in it, and experience a revolt that leads to hatred and to nausea. It is especially so for Ersilia, who sees herself torn between the spirit and the flesh in expressing her complex detachment from the past that attracted her with its promise of happiness and gave her tragedy. "My flesh obeyed, but not my heart—never—I felt hatred for you, as my own shame! I never consented with my heart that bled because I had betrayed it like a shameless thief. I looked at my naked arms and I bit them! I yielded, yes, I always yielded; but I felt within me that my heart did not surrender!—Ah, infamous person that you are! You destroyed through vice the

only joy of my life—which I could hardly believe possible—
the joy of being betrothed." Passion has for Pirandello tentacles rather than soft, caressing hands. His characters throw
themselves into its fire, more out of desperation than because
passion lures them with its attractiveness.

Sudden changes take place when the truth is known. Franco
calls her a bad woman. Onoria, the housekeeper, who had
developed a great love for her, labels her an impostor.
Pirandello is amused at these sudden changes of sentiment;
particularly at Franco who now denounces the immorality
of Ersilia's action when he himself has been guilty of the
same wrong towards her. Has he not been engaged to a girl in
Rome and has he not proposed to Ersilia while at Smyrna?
Would he not have married the other girl had the wedding
not been postponed by the news of Ersilia's attempted suicide? However, Franco is right on one ground—in being
resentful at Ersilia's lie that she tried to kill herself for love
of him. She has no right to say that after her relations with
the consul. Even Ludovico Nota is puzzled by this strange lie:
"To be frank I fail to understand why she lied when she was
at death's door. Certain lies can be useful in life, but not
in death."

No one sees her real reason for the lie. Desolate and alone,
she takes poison again, and announces that she has lied not in
order to live but in order to die. She finds in her approaching
death calm and sweetness. She smiles and says, "If I had not
done this, no one would have believed me when I said that I
did not lie to live but to die." As she speaks "she makes a
gesture of disconsolate pity, hardly opening her hands, a
gesture that says without words the reason why martyred
humanity feels the need of lying." They have all lied, Franco,
Grotti, Ersilia. "It is," as Ersilia explains, "because we all
wish to appear at our best.—The more one is . . . the more
one is . . . [*she means "revolting" but she feels at the same
time loathing and so much pity that she is hardly able to say
it.*] the more beautiful we wish to appear. [*She smiles.*]
Well, yes, to cover ourselves with a decent dress. . . . I tried
to make a decent little garment for myself, at least, for my

death. That's why I lied. I swear it to you. I had never been able to have one in my life without having it torn by the many dogs that have always attacked me in every street; without having it soiled by the basest and vilest miseries. So I attempted to make myself one—a beautiful one—to die in— that of a betrothed, in order to die in it with a little sympathy and pity from everyone. Well, I have not been able to have even this! It has been torn from me, cast into the gutter and spurned. . . . Now go. Let me die in silence: stark naked. Go. Go and tell, you to your wife, you to your *fiancée*, that this poor girl has died naked." Pirandello has clothed her with his sympathy and with the beauty of his art. Now, Consul Grotti will return to his career; Franco will marry his *fiancée;* Ersilia lies dead. At least her desire is fulfilled. She is in our hearts clothed with the sympathy and pity that her creator has won for her.

The plot is very short and uneventful. The interest centers above all in the halo of human pathos that surrounds the gentle figure of Ersilia Drei and in the keen analysis that allows Pirandello to disclose the hidden motives, shades of unthwarted intentions, and deeds of the various characters. This appears in a vivid light in the analysis of the relation between Ersilia and Consul Grotti. Probing, but probing with a compassionate heart and a gentle hand into the diseased wound, Pirandello discovers that Grotti's paternal feelings were not less real and true than his infatuation and profligacy. Grotti says to Ersilia, "If you had believed in my disinterestedness in you, in my goodness which was indeed real, the beast would not have awakened in me, suddenly with all its desperate hunger." But all of Pirandello's sympathy goes out to Ersilia Drei. He is aware that her pitiful life, seen from the point of view of Grotti, of Franco, of the family of his *fiancée*, is horrible. It precipitated "the scandal, it snatched from people a pity that was undeserved, a universal commiseration," yet he insists that we must look at it from the point of view of poor Ersilia Drei who lied because she aspired to a life of decency. The contention of Consul Grotti that the Smyrna episode was a meaningless interlude in his life is even truer in the case of Ersilia. As she and her former lover stand face to face, passion is rekindled in the veins of the man, but Ersilia disdainfully rejects him because, to her, the dead child stands between them.

Pessimism forms a gloomy background to this play. Since the characters are morally hideous, they are compelled to clothe themselves with dignity while inwardly they are conscious of their misery. It is not a case of hyprocrisy. Nothing would offend poor Ersilia Drei more than this word. She was lying to adorn herself for death just as people are washed and dressed before burial. She did not lie to and for others. She lied to and for herself. She was conscious of her lie, but thought that if she paid for it with the modest token of her life, she would make enough amends. Indeed, the main *motif* that runs through the play with consoling effect is the power of a lie even though thwarted. What would life be without the ornaments and trappings of imagination? Why do we try to keep the natural color of our hair and the freshness of our complexion, fighting against the destructive power of time and of death? Are these not deceptions? Is not the whole of civilization a compassionate lie, when one realizes that at the end there stands the gigantic and gaunt specter of Death?

Pirandello feels unspeakably sorry for mankind, sorry for himself, sorry for the poor characters that have been brought before the public and have been made to reveal a truth that burns and destroys. He seems to say with sadness: What we have portrayed is life, and the only thing for these characters to do was to cover the shame into which they had fallen when instinct ruled them in the oriental, intoxicating beauty of Smyrna. Woe unto us if we did not call to our aid pitiful deception! When the shame of these characters is uncovered in broad and glaring light, despair and death follow. Had Ersilia died, enveloped in the romantic halo of a suicide for love, she would have added a sentimental, beautiful page to the many that have been recorded, even if only in the ephemeral life of a newspaper. But men insisted on discovering the truth, and tragedy made its entrance.

When we look in retrospect at the events of the drama,

they seem to be covered with a minute web in which the ironical is faintly visible in a predominating, pathetic tone. Irony takes here the form of the query: Who can determine the precise boundaries between goodness and hypocrisy, between heroism and necessity? They seem to merge into each other when one considers that Franco, Onoria, and even Ludovico Nota pass so readily from exaltation to condemnation of Ersilia. Pirandello pleads for human compassion. Is it necessary, after all, to imitate these characters in their sudden changes of attitude? Is it not better to refrain from passing judgment on poor dead Ersilia, and to let her sleep in peace, enshrouded in the veils of human sympathy that Pirandello has awakened in our hearts?

XV

Madness as the Only Refuge

HENRY THE FOURTH

(*Enrico Quarto*)

H*enry the Fourth* is pure tragedy and one of the greatest plays that Pirandello has written. Under the grandeur of history he has disguised an intensely touching human drama. When the Emperor Henry IV disappears and the man looms in all the agony that tortures him, his humanity is as complex and deep as the figure of the emperor was stately.

We find ourselves in the majestic throne room of Henry IV. The valets and private counselors of the German emperor are around the throne waiting for the monarch to enter. Historical names echo: Goslar, Worms, Saxony, Lombardy, the Rhine. A naïve reader or spectator might at first believe that this is an historical play. Pirandello, however, in the realistic trend of his art, has always focused his attention on life close at hand, on man as he lives on this planet of ours with his complications and tragedies. At the very outset, therefore, the author takes care to call us back from the lofty and stately region where our romantic minds may have wandered. We hear words that destroy the spell of our historical dream:

—"Give me a match."—

—"Well, you can't smoke a pipe in here."—

Men dressed in the costumes of the eleventh century are poking fun at a new courtier who, dressed as a man of the time of Henry IV of France, has come there, having confused the two Henrys. The confusion is truly a calamity because Bertoldo, the new courtier, has perused an entire library in order to prepare himself for the part of being a member of Henry IV's entourage. The great emperor asks questions of these noblemen of his court, and woe unto them if they do not give him the logical and proper answers! The intrigues of

the time, wars, men, dynasties, prelates, popes, kings, rebellious princes, all live again as the life of Henry IV and
his times is daily reënacted. But this is only the form of the
life that surged in and around the emperor. The content is
absent. There are, to be sure, the clothes, the throne, and the
valets with halberds, but these men are playing their parts
because they are paid to do so by a wealthy relative of the
present Henry IV. For these men the tragedy that they represent is pure though lucrative comedy. They stand for the
common lot of man with nerves well protected against being
unduly sensitive, ready to react with broad laughter to any
situation that may stir, and, therefore, disturb their contented apathy.

The only one for whom the dualism between form and
content is destroyed by a tragic misfortune is Henry IV. One
day, twenty years previously, during a masquerade in which
he was disguised as the German emperor, he fell from his
horse, struck the back of his head on the pavement, lost consciousness, and, upon coming to, he believed that he was
Henry IV. His wealthy sister had him placed in a magnificent old castle where everything was arranged so as to make
his pitiful illusion possible. He lives exactly as Henry IV
did. He receives his ambassadors and the ambassadors of
foreign countries; he rants against Peter Damian whom he
blames for the tense situation existing between him and Pope
Gregory the Great; he asks Countess Matilda to intercede for
him. Very discreetly Pirandello confides to us that the extraordinary situation would be easier to understand if we
knew certain details about the man. For months previous to
the pageant Henry IV had prepared himself to play the rôle
of the German emperor by reading the history of the time
and by becoming saturated with its spirit, as do imaginative
people who readily identify themselves with the man that they
study. He had always been a great, genuine actor, and he
used to transform the life and feelings of the characters that
he portrayed into his own life and feelings. It had been easier
for such a man to feel that he was Henry IV than it would
have been for a matter-of-fact individual. To help make the

illusion perfect there is an entire wardrobe full of the costumes of that period, perfectly executed by competent theatrical supply houses. It is an expensive scheme, but there is an
enormous patrimony, that of Marquis Nolli, his sister's son,
at the disposal of the mad emperor. Valets and courtiers are
thoroughly instructed in their rôles. They know that the
Emperor's wife is Bertha of Sousa, a sister of Amedeo II of
Savoy, and that the emperor wishes to repudiate her. They
are versed even in the details of the life of the emperor and
of the historical personages that mingled with him.

The only jarring notes in the midst of so much venerable
antiquity are two modern oil paintings, one representing
him as Henry IV, and the other the Countess Matilda. To
Henry IV they are images reflected by a clear mirror from
an indefinitely vague past where his life, after the fall, ceased
to possess the flow of living things and became frozen in the
idea that he was Henry IV. His likeness represents him as he
was twenty years before. A servant, Giovanni, in a cutaway
coat, enters and breaks even more the illusion that we are
back in the eleventh century. The courtiers jokingly tease,
"Man of the twentieth century, away! You demon, evoked
by the magician of Rome!" Giovanni shouts to them to put
an end to their nonsense since he has come to tell them that
Marquis Nolli has arrived with a group of ladies and gentlemen. They come from the world of life where people move,
love and hate, grow old and die, while others are born. They
do not know what it is to be immobilized as is Henry IV, for
whom time ceased to flow twenty years ago and who now believes himself to be still a youth of twenty-six. A sad plight
this is, to be sure, but one that promises eternal youth, and,
if the illusion be complete, blinds one to the flesh that withers,
the hair that grows gray, the strength which ebbs away, in a
word, to the inescapable and fatal disintegration of life which
goes on for all and for everything. These visitors are old
friends of Henry IV: Donna Matilda, her daughter Frida and
her *fiancé*, together with a physician and a middle-aged
gentleman, Belcredi.

Their conversation better informs us about the masquerade

and the queer individuals who took part in it. We are taken back to the time when youth and gallantry blossomed around the beauty and charm of Donna Matilda. She had two ardent suitors, the present Henry IV and Belcredi, who now enjoys her favors. Belcredi is a scoffing, cynical cerebralist, "slender, prematurely gray, a little younger than she; he has a curious head similar to that of a bird. He would be most vivacious if his agility (that makes of him a formidable swordsman) were not as if sheathed in a sluggish, oriental laziness that reveals itself in his strange voice, a little nasal and with a drawl." It is not correct to state that Belcredi and Matilda are lovers. There is hatred intermingled in their relation. Belcredi is a past master in antagonizing everyone with his insinuating remarks that reveal his perversity and the acuteness of his intellect. Donna Matilda is still beautiful, although she has to wage a gallant fight against ravaging time. Her mouth, "most perfect with a hint of sorrow," reveals in her a tragic person who has never found herself since that masquerade twenty years ago cut out of her life the man who is now fixed in the illusion of being Henry IV. He was a little odd, Donna Matilda confesses, but because he was full of life, temperamental. She had made the mistake of treating him as she treated all her admirers: "Among the many misfortunes that befall us women there is that of seeing before us, from time to time, two eyes that look at us with a restrained, intense promise of a lasting affection. [*She bursts out laughing, but her laughter is strident.*] Nothing is funnier than that! If men were to see themselves with that lasting promise in their eyes!" However, she did not laugh at her genial and temperamental admirer as she laughed at others, as she laughs at Belcredi. "When I laughed at him it was also for fear. Perhaps his was a promise in which one could believe. But it would have been most dangerous." He had impersonated Henry IV because she was disguised as Countess Matilda. Happiness had stood before her, but she had not seized it and made it hers. She had married another man, had had a daughter, Frida, the living image of her. Her husband had died. Belcredi had taken her body while her soul hated him.

Donna Matilda has come to the castle for the first time. Here she is now in this hall, a place of grandeur and of mockery and, therefore, of tragedy, where the man who had possessed the key to her rebellious soul has lived twenty years a living death, softened by illusion. She, the doctor, and Belcredi enter, disguised as personages of the eleventh century—Donna Matilda as Adelaide, Bertha's mother, the doctor as Hugo, Bishop of Cluny, and Belcredi, since he insisted on coming, as a monk of Cluny. He looks like "an ostrich dressed as a monk," according to Donna Matilda. When Henry IV enters, a broken man, a wreck of magnificent manhood, we are seized with the feeling of the tragedy of his life and perhaps of all life. He, as is to be expected, is typically Pirandellian in that his temperament bears all the marks of that mental state that the author calls "a sincere exaltation." Even Belcredi, his rival, is compelled to admit it: "Not that he simulated his exaltation. On the contrary, he became sincerely exalted, but immediately he saw himself, and that ended it." He saw himself and at once the warmth of sentiment vanished to be replaced by the cold process of reason that led him to exasperation and despair. Then he tried to distract his mind by doing strange things. He organized pageants, dances, and charity balls. He now confides to his visitors: "Life flows away from us and the man of yesterday stands before us men of today immobilized in such a hideous form that we cannot bear to look at it." He asks Donna Matilda: "Has that ever occurred to you, Madame? Do you really remember being always the same? Do you recollect that day? How could you have perpetrated that deed?" [*He stares so fixedly into her eyes that she almost faints.*] In Belcredi, he sees with hatred Peter Damian, his enemy. The courtiers try in vain to convince him that he is only a monk of Cluny.

Is it possible for a true madman to feel intuitively the presence of a mortal enemy and be sensitive to the atmosphere created by people who have played such a great part in his life when they come before him disguised as historical personages? Can a madman speak as poignantly of life, of its swift passing, and of its destructive quality as Henry IV does, addressing himself to Donna Matilda? Why does he speak so much of the need of a mask and implore that he be allowed "to live in its entirety this life from which he has been excluded"? Is he conscious of playing a game of tragic duplicity? The doctor, in his dogmatic, scientific certitude, believes that Henry IV is a genuine madman, while Donna Matilda, with feminine intuition, feels that he has recognized her and that he is pretending. She tells the doctor: "His words have appeared to be full of a sad longing for my youth and for his own, on account of this horrible thing that has happened to him and that fixed him there in that mask which he cannot remove from his face and of which he wishes to be freed."

As soon as the visitors leave, the astonished courtiers and valets hear words that show that Henry IV is conscious of his madness, and, therefore, in at least the current understanding of the word, he is no longer mad. Henry IV rebels when Landolfo, one of the courtiers, says: "I wish I had known that it was not true." Henry IV asks in a voice that betrays his inner anguish: "Does it seem to you that it is not true?" He tells them that his fiction is true because he lives it as true, and concludes: "Only so, truth is no longer a jest."

The doctor, persuaded of the normal madness of Henry IV, has a plan: To suddenly confront him with Frida dressed as Countess Matilda was on the fatal day. Frida is placed in the niche whence the portrait of Donna Matilda has been removed. Donna Matilda as she is today is to stand before Henry IV at the same time. The doctor thinks that the shock determined by the clash of two different stages of life will bring to Henry IV the realization that twenty years have elapsed, and will break off the threads that bind him to the fictitious image of himself. He will be cured; he will be a normal individual again. When Henry IV suddenly sees Frida, the past surges back to him, overpowering him. He stands there staring at Frida, the symbol of his destroyed youth. Emotion and terror make his whole body quiver. Belcredi, to whom the courtiers have revealed Henry IV's

155

confession, ironically and cuttingly mocks the whole performance. Vehemently Henry IV remonstrates and relates the story
of the tragic years that he has lived entombed in that castle.
For twelve years he had lived in a state of true madness which
had come upon him when he fell from his horse that Belcredi,
in his jealousy, had made rear by pricking him.

What was he to do when he knew that his madness had
left him and he was, once more, sane? Should he have told
himself: "Away with these trappings. Away with this empty
fiction. Let us go out. Where? To do what? To be pointed out
stealthily by everyone as Henry IV, no longer in the present
attire and setting, but arm in arm with you, [Belcredi] among
the dear friends of life? I should have arrived with the hunger
of a wolf to a banquet already over. I preferred to stay mad,
to live my madness with the most lucid consciousness and thus
avenge myself of the brutality of a stone that struck my
head. . . . I filled this solitude, squalid and empty as it
appeared to me when I opened my eyes, with the color and
splendor of that distant day of carnival."

As he goes over his solitary and lonely life, the only fact
of the past full of significance for him is his love for Donna
Matilda. There she stands now in Frida as true and real as
she was in that far-off day of dream and gloom, of beauty and
desolation—the day of the masquerade. He is swept away by
the poignant force of his vivid recollection. He rushes towards
Frida and tells her: "You have been frightened, my child,
by the joke that they have persuaded you to play on me—
without understanding that for me it could not be the jest
they intended, but this awesome wonder: dream that becomes
alive in you more than ever. There [in the picture] you were
an image. They have made of you a living person. You are
mine, mine, mine by right." [*He embraces her, laughing like
a madman, while all shout with terror.*] Belcredi dashes forward to take Frida away from him. Henry IV draws his sword
and wounds him mortally. Henry IV, "with his eyes wide
open, frightened by the life of his own fiction that suddenly
has forced him to commit a crime," surrounded by his
courtiers, cries out, clinging to his madness: "Now, indeed,

there is no other remedy. [*He calls them around him as if to protect himself.*] Here, all together—all together, and forever." Madness is his only refuge.

Pirandello has projected in Henry IV the desperate passiveness to which he resigned himself when haunted by the inescapable but crushing event of his poor wife's madness. In the words of Henry IV, there echoes Pirandello's feeling of powerlessness in his despair. "I believe that phantasms are nothing but a little unbalanced condition of our mind: images that we fail to hold within the boundaries of the kingdom of sleep. They appear even in the daytime; and they terrify. I am greatly frightened when at night time I see them before me—disorderly images that, having dismounted from their horses, laugh. I am sometimes afraid, even of my blood that throbs in my veins like the thud of steps resounding in distant rooms in the silence of the night."

The drama is a subtle study of the interplay of the conscious and the subconscious, the rational and the irrational, as they may be observed in human actions. To what extent are our acts conscious? If we, without being seen, should look at the valets as they stand around the throne of Henry IV, we should believe, judging by their actions and words, that they were true and real. What difference is there between seeing them and seeing ordinary persons moving in the realm of actual life? As with grave mien they discuss matters of state with the emperor, we have no proof that they are acting. Conversely, we cannot ascertain that they are not acting when they speak and act in their capacity of men of today. We can be led in a most convincing manner to these paradoxical extremes by a process of logical and complete subjectiveness. Pirandello goes more deeply into the question of the reality of human personality. For twenty years, these valets have lived as men of the eleventh century. It is highly improbable that they have not merged to some extent with that superimposed rôle, even so far as to have their identity obliterated for hours at a time at least.

This play makes us realize more than any other how unjust is the accusation of abstract and cerebral so often applied to

Pirandello. One feels constantly the author's reaction against those who lack spontaneity in life. He focuses his attention both on the worldly people of whom Henry IV, Donna Matilda, and Belcredi are the exponents and on the scientists, represented by the doctor. Pirandello finds himself at odds with both of them. The exaltation with which Henry IV lived before the tragedy speaks of a lack of real emotion and simplicity which led him to complicate life and to rationalize it. The doctor's stand is pure abstraction, and Pirandello ridicules him. The man of science is sure that the madman will react just as he expects and prescribes. It seems very peculiar to the author that the doctor, in his scientific dogmatism, has the courage to classify as demented one from whom he expects such a logical and certain reaction. Reasoning for Pirandello is a useless encumbrance that bespeaks man's inability to seize life in its essential points. The fantastic ravings of Henry IV before the accident were more cerebral and useless than his illusion centering around the belief that he was an historical character who lived eight hundred and eighty years before.

The power of the living reality is one of the strongest *motifs* in the play. What compelled Henry IV to leave the artificial groove into which he had gathered whatever débris of his life was left to him, was the call of the living life that reached him through the youth and charm of Frida. There was a violent clash between the desolate coldness of his solitude and the warm breath of the world that he had forsaken. That clash made it impossible for him to cling to his illusion and, therefore, it revealed the tragedy of his lucid madness. But it also made him feel that he was unfit to reënter the swift current of life that goes on and on, leaving behind all those who cannot keep pace with it. Tragedy stalks in, superinduced by this harrowing contrast. Critics are apt to put abstraction in Pirandello where it does not exist. If, upon seeing Donna Matilda as she is in the picture and as she is today, we should state that Pirandello conceives reality as existing on two planes, we might succeed in displaying brilliancy, but we should fail to feel what the author meant to be seen. The predominating element is the author's feeling of the swift passing of time with its transforming and ravaging power. The doctor thought and spoke of the two planes, but he is the butt of Pirandello's ridicule, and critics who follow him will share the same fate.

All the characters in the play are molded with that vividness and clear-cut contour that Pirandello lends to the creatures of his imagination. Henry IV, however, towers above them all. His madness is a case of lucid madness, a madness that is kinder than sanity; a madness to which one goes for shelter when life becomes crushing and unbearable. Were we to view Henry IV as an ordinary man, feigning madness, he would arouse indignation in us for his prolonged pretending. If we accept his conscious madness, we stand before him appalled by the greatness of the sorrowful and tragic existence of one who has willfully cut himself off from life because he knew that life held no promise for him. We see him as a tragic figure, enmeshed in the contradictions of life, immobilized in the merciless fate of his madness, but surrounded by the warm sympathy and pity of the author. He stands unforgettable before us as one for whom a conscious, planned madness is more tragic, harrowing, and devastating than one of which an ordinary individual is unaware. The madman as illuminated by the poet has eclipsed the one diagnosed by the physician.

XVI

Dualism of Personality

AS YOU DESIRE ME

(*Come tu mi vuoi*)

We have seen it repeatedly stated that Pirandello does not express the dualism of personality in the scientific and pathological sense. He deals with the tragic need of having to force upon ourselves a personality that we know with the utmost clearness is not ours. In the earlier plays this process was conceived with more objectivity and less sympathy. The author could laugh as he related the adventures of his characters, even if laughter was painful to him. As his feeling of sympathy has increased, the element of laughter has gradually diminished until, in the latest plays, it has disappeared altogether. The absence of laughter has elevated the tone of his drama, lending to it the grandeur of tragedy in the expression of all the pity that the author feels for life and man. This is especially true of *As You Desire Me*. In it the idealistic elements, which existed in the form of broken threads at times hardly visible in the earlier plays, appear now in a clearer form.

As You Desire Me is a play of absolute, exasperated, irrational idealism, indicting modern life with its ambiguity, its lust, its commercialized sensuality, and placing the sense of true reality in the beauty of the soul. In the avowed intention of the author, it is the story of the soul that has tried to live on this earth and could not. The soul that has been embodied in Cia, the beautiful wife of Bruno Pieri, one of those rare women whom Pirandello has placed high above the average— a luminous expression and a glimpse of an unattainable dream. Sharing the nature of a dream, she has illuminated the life of people around her and then has swiftly disappeared. She lives only in the memory of those who have known and loved her, and in a portrait by Boffi, a friend who caught and immortalized her in the cold but merciful mold of his art. In the portrait she appears as the bride of Bruno Pieri in the days that were happy for them, before the last war submerged the world in blood and grief.

Ten years have elapsed. Between the dreary present and the beautiful past there is the invasion of Northern Italy during the War when the brutal invaders overran the Villa Pieri, violated Cia, and carried her away with them. Everyone has believed her dead: her husband, their friend Boffi the painter, Uncle Salesio, and Aunt Lena who, following the untimely death of Cia's mother, had brought her up as her own daughter. After years of fruitless search they have all resigned themselves to the belief that Cia is dead. Uncle Salesio and Aunt Lena have deeded their property from Cia to her sister, which act displeased Bruno very much.

This is the background, tragic, but truthful, when we think of what happened during the last war in the invaded regions. After ten years, life has resumed its normal rhythm in the villa. Time has added its unkind touches to all its dwellers, but Cia's villa, restored, is again beautiful with the house nestled in a restful, green, serene landscape. Man has temporarily won against the destruction and the victorious greed and lust of other men. Uncle Salesio is again busy attending to his flowers, and he has filled a large basket to arrange in exquisite vases in the house. He is, we are told, "a little thin old man, who would still be spry if his shoulders and the back of his head were not glued together." Aunt Lena, supervising what he does, and finding fault with it as of old, is a "stout and solid lady in her sixties, with a large masculine head all covered with strange, gray curls." She is direct, with an abrupt way of speaking, just as Uncle Salesio is timid, meticulous in what he does and says. These characteristics of the solid tangible reality serve the purpose of keeping the play on the plane of everyday reality. If the idealism of Pirandello is similar in its origin to that of the past, it is truly modern in that it places, side by side, both the negative aspects of life whence it originates and the luminous goal to which it aspires.

161

Cia, after ten years, has been found. Boffi, the artist, has discovered her in Berlin. He has never forgotten her. He was in Berlin when he saw a cabaret dancer who resembled Cia. He wired her husband and followed her home several nights, calling her by name while she turned and laughed at this new admirer with a strange, Mephistophelean look on his face, with a twitch that made him raise his head "as if not to drown." He feels disgust for the filth of life. The dancer, whose name is Elma, is in her thirties, most beautiful. There is a sort of scowl on her face as if to impose her will, in order not to yield and to let herself go to the very depth of abandonment, "where her soul, devastated by the storms of life, would almost be dissolved." Under a very elegant mantilla she wears one of the splendid and strange costumes of the character dances that she invents. She is the mistress of Carl Salter, a sensual and revolting German writer.

He and his daughter, Mop, are waiting for her to return. As is usual in Pirandello's love entanglements, only hatred feeds the passion of Salter and Elma. She is independent, reckless, impudent to him. She flaunts her scorn at him, discloses his weaknesses, the misery of his literary fame. That very evening Elma arrives in the company of four youths drunk with liquor and lust. They appear to Pirandello thus: "In the subdued light and confusion, those youths, one fat and pink, another bald, another with bleached hair, effeminate to an unbelievable degree, seem agitated marionettes with wanton, exaggerated, meaningless gestures." Boffi has defended her against them until they reached the apartment.

The richly furnished apartment and its occupants are the extreme embodiment of Pirandello's sense of revolt against the sensuality and inanity of modern life. Mop, in silk pajamas, crouched in a large armchair, is silently crying. Her father is angrily commenting on Elma's companions. There is rivalry between father and daughter, for both love Elma. Here is Salter's daughter as seen by Pirandello: "Her face is marked by something ambiguous which moves one to nausea, and at the same time with something tragic which perturbs one deeply." Here is Salter: "His face is puffed, pale, with clear eyes, almost white in the circle of dark pouches around them, clean-shaven, his thick lips standing out in sensuous prominence." He has a revolver in his pocket, determined to put an end to a life that is unbearable to all.

Elma is a little drunk, too, but one feels in her a superior person, a person who is not steeped in the lust that surrounds her; indeed, one who shrinks from a lust that exudes shame and awakens revolt in her. Her soul is not dead, since she is conscious of her own shame and she lives in torment. She affirms her right "to lie with the life that I live." She shouts: "There are no longer secrets today, nor modesty." Human beings are like beasts "with the difference that beasts at least are natural, endowed with the wisdom of instinct, while in man, to be natural is a sad, destructive, and also filthy folly. Woe unto us if reason did not serve as a strait-jacket." Pirandello has placed in Elma his tragic idealism. She turns to Boffi and says: "My name is Elma, did you hear, an Arabian name which means water." [*In so saying, she moves all her fingers, spreading her hands to signify the forced lack of consistency of her life.*] Life has passed through her fingers like water, a symbol of her bitter tears. That is the deep side of Elma, but she has been compelled to repress that side by being gay: "They made me drink so much wine! Oh! And five cocktails, champagne." She has thrown herself into the whirlwind of disgusting sensuality which for Pirandello forms the most salient characteristic of modern civilization. Elma bears the name of the "Unknown" in the play. There is a symbolic meaning in that name. She had been made unknown even to herself by the moral misery of her life.

The higher Pirandello's idealism rises, the greater relief lust takes in his play. This explains why he has embodied his idealism in a lost woman. Some might express astonishment at this combination and attribute it to Pirandello's humor. This is not humor. It is knowledge of the human heart. In order to see the serene countenance of good it is often necessary to know the ugliness of evil.

Boffi reiterates to Elma that she is Cia, Donna Lucia. She laughs. Boffi believes that she is feigning. What proof can he have that she is not? He insists frantically. She denies, then affirms, to tantalize Salter, who shoots himself in her presence. She agrees to leave with Boffi on the strange adventure. She has but one alternative: either be the soul of Cia and go to Bruno, or be Elma, the Unknown, and stay with Salter. She chooses to be Cia. To a person like Elma, who is in the depths of despair, Boffi's offer is the only way of escape. She does it, as she says, "to flee from myself; not to have any remembrance of anything, of anything—to empty myself of all my life—here, look: just body—to be only this body. You say that it is hers? that it resembles hers? I don't feel myself any longer. . . . My heart beats and I don't know it, I breathe and I don't know it, I don't know any longer whether I am alive. I am only a body, a body in the expectation that someone may take it. There—if he can take me—if he can give a soul to this body that is Cia's body—let him take it and put his memories into it, his own; a beautiful life, a new life. I am desperate. . . ." She will live again now, reincarnating the soul of Cia. She sees in that possibility her own freedom, freedom of herself, freedom from Salter and Mop, freedom from the night life of Berlin. She will reach the unity of her life through her soul—through the soul of Cia.

Pirandello takes every care to show the possibility of this transformation. Our knowledge of the identity of a person rests on a very weak basis. I say that I am "X" and you believe me. If tomorrow a person comes and says that I am "Z" what logical grounds have you for refuting it? It is useless to say: After all, we know ourselves; we know who we are. Pirandello's aim here is to arouse our sympathy and understanding for cases in which the clearness of the identity is not possible, and in that lies the great pathos which rings through the play. We are before a person who is compelled to disavow herself in order to bear the weight of life. The greatest punishment for Dante's sinners was to have their human features obliterated or distorted. Their tragedy was forced on them. Pirandello makes his characters obliterate their own personality, leading them to a deeper and more pitiful tragedy. The author is entirely conscious of the new fate that he has decreed for his characters. He does not laugh any longer. He is tragic now.

So Elma, the Unknown, becomes Cia. She goes to the villa, as beautiful as the Cia of ten years ago, although now distracted, dismayed, and apparently unable to take complete hold of herself in her old environment. She is still the same Elma intimately, half ready to reform, half ready to reenter the inferno of life.

The difficulty on the part of her relatives to accept the physical Cia has not been great. The fertile imagination of Pirandello has succeeded in making the acceptance quite plausible by asserting that people seldom agree on the physical traits of a person. The same person will appear to one as the perfect image of the father, to another as the perfect image of the mother. Cia's eyes, for instance, are green to Aunt Lena, blue to Uncle Salesio, and gray to her husband. Why should they have difficulty in believing that she is their Cia after the changes that ten years make? The natural goodness that abides in every human being, in every woman, appears again in the Unknown, although at times the scowl of the old self suddenly reappears; then she speaks with uncontrollable vehemence, with excitement. She has found a diary written by Cia during the first year of her marriage. It is the diary of a noble person. She reads it passionately and with longing; she imbues herself with the soul of Cia, as she lives in that diary; Cia, a creature of exquisite beauty, purity, and goodness. The beauty of the Unknown acquires again the serenity that it had lost.

But the Unknown finds it infinitely difficult to have her identity, as existing in the soul of Cia, recognized. It is easier to make the body of Cia live again in her than it is her soul. From the very beginning she has had to struggle with all the human miseries that surround our bodily existence. She has had to hear stupid recriminations about the property which had been transferred to her sister on the assumption that Cia was dead, and that now must be returned to Cia. She cries out: "I did not want any of this, from the very beginning— nothing of all this." With harrowing insistence the doubt

comes to her whether Bruno is interested only in her or in the
property that now will return to him: the villa, the fertile
lands that he had reclaimed from the devastation of war,
only to see them given to Cia's sister. She is perplexed by the
fact that it is hard to draw a straight and narrow line between pure love and interest. She has to admit likewise that
Bruno is more interested in her body than in her soul. There
was a mark on Cia's body that the Unknown does not have.
He is confused by that absence. The mark means more to
him than the beauty of Cia's spiritual qualities. Who can
draw the line between where love ends and passion begins?

The final test comes when Salter, who has not died of the
self-inflicted wound, brings from a Vienna sanitarium to the
villa the actual Cia, a wreck of humanity, both pitiful and
revolting to look at. She is the Demented One in the play.
The Unknown surprises Aunt Lena in an attempt to ascertain
whether or not the Demented One is Cia. Aunt Lena "with a
sudden resolution, conquering her own distaste, while all
present are shuddering with horror, takes the face of the
Demented One in her own hands and calls: 'Cia, Cia.' The
Demented One remains passive with her mute, meaningless
smile." The Unknown meanwhile, unnoticed, has come downstairs followed by her husband. She has the proof that they
doubted. They did not have faith in her, the faith that she
wanted. She is hurt. Her old self asserts itself again. She is
defiant, haughty. She strikes back at those who have destroyed the possibility of her new life, who have made her
realize the futility of her noble attempt. She has wanted true
love and she has not found it. She says to the confused members of the family who have gathered in the house: "Many
an unfortunate one, after years, has returned just like that
[*she points to the Demented One*], with features obliterated,
unrecognizable, without any memory, and sisters, wives,
mothers, have fought to have the unfortunate one with them.
Not because they have recognized him, no (cannot the son
of one resemble that of another?), but because they have believed him to be their own, they have forced themselves to
believe him to be their own. And there is no contrary proof

that may be valid when one wishes to believe!—It isn't he? But for that mother, it is he; yes, it is he! What does it matter if it isn't he if a mother keeps him and makes him hers with all her love? Against every proof she believes him to be hers. Against any proof she believes him to be hers. Did you not believe me even without proofs?" Elma could only be the soul of Cia with Bruno, or her own body, her tortured and profaned body, with Salter. The end comes when, obeying the cruel logic of the premises, Elma returns to Berlin with Carl Salter.

No ascetic writer—not Saint Augustine in his *Confessions,* nor the author of the *Imitation of Christ*—has expressed the revolt against the flesh as violently as does Pirandello in this play. He has portrayed it in the Unknown with an exasperation that approaches frenzy. Modern civilization is reduced here to a brutal phenomenon incompatible with the need of the human soul. Pirandello's idealism is irreconcilable with the practical and material aspects of life. He is as unbending as the monks of old who believed life possible only in their little cells, or as the mystics who dreamed of a perfect life in the communion with Christ or with the Deity. Their upward flight was based on renunciation. Pirandello, like them, seems to be unwilling to recognize the necessity of the practical elements of daily life. On this ground the play embodies not only the tragedy of Elma, but it also tends to attract one into a gloomy circle where there is the feeling of the hopeless tragedy of all: the soul cannot live on this earth unless it accepts the limitations of actual life, limitations that are harrowing and dwarfing. Below the lofty level to which Elma tried to make Bruno and his family rise, there lies the stifling plane of petty considerations and concerns. Only the exasperated, irrational, idealistic mood of the author can explain such an attitude. It is irrational, to be sure, if looked at from the point of view of Bruno and the mediocre lot that compose Cia's family; but quite in accord with Pirandello's philosophy that life is only in the sentiment that permeates human acts.

Pirandello has now openly asserted his faith in sentiment

to which he has given positive connotations. He is very far from his initial position, where he identified sentiment with the cold construction of the intellect. Sentiment is no longer misguiding subjectivism. It is a luminous force that alone may redeem Elma's life. At an earlier stage of his thought Pirandello was placed between sentiment and reason, and mistrusted both. In a more serious mood, with a consciousness of life enriched by experience, he recognizes that sentiment is the only solution. If Elma's sentiment pointed to a height that defied what is grossly natural in man, it also afforded satisfactions and it held promises that were unknown to those who lived on the plane of everyday life. From this point of view Pirandello's idealism is quite rational and constructive.

The basic cause that made it impossible for Elma to transfuse herself into Cia's soul, to be Cia, was that both Bruno and his relations tried to recognize Cia by her body while she was only soul. The issue arises quite limpidly and poignantly in the play, whether the "real" part of the human personality rests on the physical characteristics of man or on the deeper qualities of his mind and soul.

There is not the slightest doubt in the Italian original as to which of the two women is Cia; that is, who is the pitiful body of Cia and who is the soul of Cia. The doubt concerning the identity, however, is ever present in the play; indeed, the whole play centers around this identity, which is kept a secret for Elma's antagonists but not for the spectators, who are given the opportunity to admire the cleverness of the playwright in mastering the situation with his subtle technique. Anyone in the play can with equal logic claim that Elma is Cia or the contrary. This actually happens with Salter and Bruno disputing with each other the material identity of the Unknown. The spectator, however, clearly sees the intentions of the author when he sees the Demented One stand near Elma, the Unknown. Cia, living only in her soul, is searching in vain for a shelter, for a new, pure body. The tragedy that has befallen Cia ten years before doomed her to an irreparable destruction. For this reason Cia is represented by the pitiful figure of the Demented One and by the

Unknown who tries in vain to make her soul live again in herself. The soul of Cia can live only in the memory of her dear ones and in the cold, distant life that Boffi's art gave to her when he saw her in all her beauty and loftiness.

The solution, leading to Elma's return to Salter, is befitting real tragedy. In the classical tragedy the solution was death. Our ancestors must have known less the torture of the soul if death, physical death, was to them the greatest calamity. Pirandello, a spokesman, in this, of the modern man who is more accustomed to death than were his ancestors, views the torment of the mind, the anguish of the heart, as being more fearful than the physical death. That is the reason why in his plays, as in many other modern plays, the climax keeps the characters in the living death of the torment of the mind. The ancients were more merciful and practical. Death ended it all. In modern tragedy there is no solution. Elma is left on the rack of having to go back to Salter after trying in vain to be as pure and lofty as Cia. There is no hope for her, and so she is reëngulfed by the nauseating and revolting life of the flesh, chained to the white-eyed man she loathes.

XVII

In the Realm of Mystery

ONE DOES NOT KNOW HOW

(*Non si sa come*)

One Does Not Know How [1] is the latest of Pirandello's plays. Its author looks upon it as one of his best dramatic works. It is derived from one of his most fundamental beliefs: his belief in the realm of mystery. Man moves in an impalpable atmosphere of dreams, whether he is conscious of it or not. Because of this he walks over the bleak planet of the earth as a bewildered stranger and a grieving vagabond. Beyond the boundaries of time and space, above the arched blue curve of the sky, there is life unformed and unfettered, life out of which a strange god has carved the earth and the universe. No laws, no limitations, no boundaries exist there. Life is a ruinous stream that roars into dazzling white stretches of infinite space. Woe to us if we have a glimpse of that primeval life! We become both terrified and deified by it. We cease to be human and our contact with the average man becomes impossible while there is born in us the irresistible urge to reënter the stream of universal life. This belief was implied in preceding plays but here it appears in a clearer form, and it affords the main *motif* of the work.

In *One Does Not Know How* the urge of the infinite and the presence of mystery are revealed under the form of the uncontrollable character of our emotions and acts. There are moments in life when something frightful and horrible happens and *one does not know how* it has happened. After the act which was brought about by the tragic absence of our will and consciousness, we are confronted by a brutal and clumsy truth and we are stranded on the desolate shore of

---

[1] This play has not yet been published in the Italian edition. The author most kindly gave me the German translation by Stefan Zweig, which I have used.

grief. Then we feel suspended halfway between our own world and that of primeval life, unfit for the former, unable to attain the latter. This is the form that the sense of personal isolation has taken in Pirandello, creating one of his most powerful and tragic characters in Count Romeo Daddi, the central figure of the play.

The drama unfolds in the beautiful villa of Giorgio Vanzi, a naval officer married to Ginevra. Intimate friends of theirs, Count Romeo Daddi and his exquisite wife Bice, are their guests. There is also another guest in the villa, Marquis Nicola Respi. The atmosphere is charged with uneasiness as if laboring under an impending storm. They all talk of the strange conduct of Romeo Daddi, who acts as if he were not master of his own acts. He stares with a tragic fixity which suddenly relaxes into a wan smile that makes one shudder. He utters strange words as he moves like a ghost in the Vanzi home. He keeps mumbling to himself: "What? Nothing. Everything is buried! Everything is sunk!" It seems that his whole inner world has been destroyed by a violent earthquake.

Romeo's unstable mental condition disturbs Bice, his wife, and Ginevra, the hostess. Bice confesses to Ginevra that at times one can see insanity in his eyes, but "he says things that frighten you because they seem to be taken out of your own soul, as if they were the thoughts that flashed through your mind a moment before." This fact makes it impossible or at least very hard to consider him insane, since logically one must infer that we are all insane if he gives expression to our own thoughts. He wonders why "so many seek in wine and drugs a refuge into an artificial paradise when actually we live so little in complete consciousness, when we are constantly snatched from ourselves through the indefinite element of our impressions, through the sun-induced drunkenness in the spring, through the awe of mysterious silence, when we get a glimpse of the sky and of the sea or of swallows darting in flight." Romeo has lost hold on himself through the realization of the uncontrollable character of his emotions, of his perceptions, and of his thoughts. Staring with eyes that seem to come back from infinite distances, he says to his friends: "See, now it seems that I am looking at you, but who knows how you appear to me? I hear you, I answer you, I am with you, but deep within me I am at the same time elsewhere, in the wave-like play of impressions and perceptions that I could not represent to you without really appearing insane."

Less affected by Romeo's condition are the two men, Giorgio Vanzi and Marquis Respi. They are individuals who seek their goodly share of pleasure in life and have learned the ways of the world that teaches how to snatch forbidden fruit and to put the stone of forgetfulness over the act. The only price that life seems to exact from them is that of discretion, of stealthy steps, and then silence and oblivion.

Not so with Romeo Daddi, whom two tragic circumstances have robbed of the easy philosophy and limited sensitiveness of the average man. Once, when in his teens, by sheer accident he killed a peasant boy in a fight. As was his wont, he had gone into the fields where the free expanse of the country awoke the sense of similar endless distances within him. Suddenly he noticed that a peasant boy had caught a lizard in a sort of noose that he had made with a long stem of rye. As Romeo leaped forward shouting: "No, do not kill it!" the boy had crushed the poor creature against a stone. It was shortly after sunset. Romeo still remembers "the ghost-like shape of the moon that was beginning to be tinged with a pale gold against the gray of the sky that softened into the dying twilight." With unspeakable horror Romeo saw the eyes of the poor animal contract in pain; he saw its tender body quiver before it stiffened in the rigidity of death. He struck the stupid and brutal killer. There ensued a battle with heavy, moist clods of earth. Romeo, who was about to have the worst of the encounter, suddenly snatched a stone and struck the boy on his head. Dead! Romeo, still panting, his heart beating to the point of suffocating him, leaned against the wall and gazed with terror at the silent immobility of the fields under the moon, at the boy who lay there, his face half hidden in the earth. An increasing sensation of a formidable, eternal solitude swept over him: "It was not I. I did not mean to do that. I knew nothing about it."

From that day he had learned that there are acts which are beyond our control, acts the contour of which is blurred, fading into death and deceptions. Experiences of this sort are not easily blotted out from one's life. They do not pass like perfumed breaths of wind in a moonlit night. They are stones that weigh heavily on us, buried in the mysterious depths of our hearts; they are blows that make us open terrified eyes into the infinite. For thirty years that tragic secret had made an automaton out of him. And now, just a few days ago, Romeo had soiled his soul with another crime, the betrayal of his best friend, of Giorgio Vanzi, the man he loved like a brother. He had sinned with Ginevra, Giorgio's wife, a woman at whom he had never looked with covetous eyes. One morning Bice was about to leave the villa, and Romeo and Ginevra had gone to see her off at the end of the drive where an automobile was waiting for her. When Bice had kissed Romeo it had seemed to Ginevra that that kiss had touched her lips. After Bice drove away, Romeo and Ginevra walked towards the villa in the midst of the intoxicating perfume of flowers. They had gone into the house, they had been compelled to sit near each other. A mysterious force had thrown the woman into the arms of the man. The whole universe had been blotted out. Inhibitions, the social barriers that hold together our being, had fallen like dead dust, like nothing at all, and the two had felt the roaring torrent of life envelop them. They were snatched outside of the laws of man, outside of themselves, primeval beings again, unfettered and free.

But the awakening had come. Romeo had seen himself before a deeper and more tragic abyss: betrayal of his best friend. Ginevra had resumed control of herself more readily since, like most of Pirandello's women, she was very instinctive. She did not wish to speak of their fall. It had happened and that was all. She had very little remorse. She loved her husband too much to feel remorse. If she had yielded to Romeo, she had done so when she was too full of love for her husband. She was absent, at least her consciousness and her will were absent, when they sinned. Now she has no regrets and she wants to forget.

This reaction is quite in keeping with Pirandello's concept of womanhood. Women are more instinctive than men, in that love absorbs all of their being and they yield to it with a complete abandonment. Desire is born to women on the wings of dreams. Not so with men, in whom the more acute power of "reason" makes the experience of love more complicated and turbulent, even more theatrical.

Romeo cannot stem his remorse and his repentance. He has to talk about their sin; he must reveal it to his wife, goaded by a mysterious force before which his inhibitions are of no avail. The more he talks to Bice and to Ginevra about it, the more he feels unable to live on the same planet near care-free, happy, and instinctive beings like Respi and Giorgio. Only those who are practical can live.

Romeo feels the urge towards disintegration. He knows that he deserves a punishment, but his punishment must not be the one that the law of man metes out to offenders: prison. No. If, after the crimes that he has committed, he has felt face to face with the mystery and the infinite, his punishment should be freedom: "Away, away, where there is nothing firm, established, no houses, no relationship, no cause and effects, no contacts, no laws, no customs, nothing. Freedom as punishment! Banishment into dream, as saints go into the wilderness." He realizes with increasing and more harrowing clearness that we have lost touch with cosmic forces through our being "human," through the fact that we have become civilized and have encumbered the earth with houses and theatres, skyscrapers and churches. We have "built up ourselves" to the extent that we live as a world within a world, the "human" world separated from and hostile to the divine realms of life. This realization comes over Romeo and frightens him, especially after his experience with Ginevra. Had Ginevra and he yielded to instinct in the immense distances where life is unhampered by laws and customs, outside the artificial mold that man has imposed on it, all the complications and the tragic consequences of their sin would not have come in the wake of the lapse of their consciousness. He would not be confronted now by the brutal fact that he has betrayed his best friend. He would not hear within him the echo of a terrifying voice that calls him adulterer and traitor. But he has sinned in a man-made world where he has followed the call of the cosmic voice of instinct, and for this reason he is now lost and desolate.

A great problem looms before him, the problem of human responsibility: how and to what extent are we responsible for certain acts from which our sense of consciousness is absent? Near him lives a flower of perfect femininity, Bice, his wife. He is curious to know whether she too may be subject to these lapses of consciousness so that nature may also play on her its strange pranks. He pries into her soul, torments her until one day he wrenches from her the confession that once in a dream she had belonged to Giorgio. This seems monstrous to Romeo. Even Bice, the purest woman he had ever known, the one around whom everyone saw the halo of dream, was prey to the mysterious forces of instinct. She had sinned just as he had.

Romeo's torment is boundless. He is gradually drawn towards his fate by the irresistible force of his subconscious or unfettered self. He knows that Giorgio will kill him should he learn of his betrayal, but he has to confess just as he had to kill the peasant boy and just as he had to sin with Ginevra. He has become an automaton in the hands of Destiny. As he sees that Giorgio is about to go away with Ginevra without having become aware of what has happened, he cannot resist the impelling force that harasses him and urges him towards his doom. He unfalteringly tells. Giorgio does not understand and does not forgive. He draws his revolver and kills him.

Romeo, by telling, places himself outside the boundaries of practical life. It is logical that Giorgio, the practical man, should kill him. Romeo's last words are: "That was done in the human way," thus conveying what the author meant to emphasize: the victory of the average man over the individual who is doomed to isolation and even to destruction.

Pirandello never loses his sense of balance between the divine afflatus of his cosmic aspiration and his grasp on the limited and concrete daily reality. Even in his seeming paradoxes there are fragments of truth that glitter and at times dazzle. His searching mind has discovered bitter and perplexing truths in the darkness and depth of the human soul. The author has not made of Romeo an abstract embodiment of the divine in man. Like all Pirandellian characters, Romeo possesses the tortuous element that their creator finds nestled in the dark folds of the human intellect. He can explore Bice's heart as a diver explores the mysterious depths of the sea. He even surreptitiously intimates that something deceitful and underhanded exists between Bice and Marquis Respi, who had been one of her admirers.

Although Pirandello places the theme of the uncontrollable character of our actions in the very center of the play, he is careful to contrast Romeo with the instinctive quality of Ginevra's temperament and with average men like Giorgio and Marquis Respi. Romeo had always felt the urge towards a life unfettered of all the restrictions to which men have subjected it. Often, as he walked along a country road, he would kick a stone, telling it as he did so: "Have a good time and fly wherever you desire." As a child, as he wandered in the fields, he used to envy his dog, Fox, who always knew what to do: to follow his master faithfully. Fox was pure instinct. Romeo was the prey of unknown forces that held an unbreakable sway over him and made a restless vagabond out of him. The boundless expanse of the country attracted him because his soul was thirsty for the infinite. When he had killed the young boy he had felt that he was outside the precincts of the everyday life. An unspeakable loneliness had seized him and poignantly a strange realization had come over him: "It was not I. I did not do it. It happened in a region that lay beyond my consciousness."

The solitude of Romeo is now increased a thousandfold by his sin with Ginevra and because of her attitude towards him and towards their fall. She does not understand why he torments himself so insistently and pitilessly. She frankly tells him: "All my desire was for Giorgio. I had never been like that before. All my blood was aflame in my veins." She vividly recollects that intoxicating morning as if to find an excuse for her weakness in the bewitching charm of nature and, therefore, to disclaim responsibility and to remove a personal character from her surrender. More practical than Romeo, she points out to him the way that one must follow if one wishes to continue to live: forgetfulness. The boundary line between virtue and deceit is not very clear-cut. In order to carry on one has to be like Ginevra who shouts: "I do not know you. I have loved only him, Giorgio." And she buries the past by obscuring it in her consciousness.

More striking and harrowing is the contrast between Romeo, sensitive and self-tormenting, and Count Respi, a debonair libertine who knows with scientific accuracy how far he can go with ladies even if they happen to be as lofty as Bice. Respi is an irritatingly happy average man. Romeo tells him: "I envy you, Respi. I don't praise you, but I envy you. Nothing has ever happened to you outside of your will. Because you don't look into yourself, you have perfect control over yourself. You *know* all your escapades, you fortunate man. You can be satisfied with or repentant of what you do, and for that reason you are to be envied." Romeo had never known the joy of satisfaction or of repentance, because his acts had always been beyond the range of his full consciousness. There was no merit nor demerit in all he did, and he was completely detached from his own acts.

Romeo analyzes also the average qualities of Giorgio's personality. Giorgio, too, is a "fine specimen of the man who *knows*, who is conscious of all he does, even of short-lived escapades which are no crime during such long absences." He refers to Giorgio's life on his cruises and to his love affairs in his short visits to various ports.

Romeo envies both these men because they possess full mastery of themselves, albeit, it is within the narrow boundary of their sensual life. They are creatures of the senses and they live happily in that realm, unmindful of the call of the infinite which torments Romeo. But is their life truly to be envied? Is it not dwarfed by the narrow range of their emotions, by all that cramps and limits the spirit of man that has been banished from the realm of things eternal?

The author has lent to Romeo Daddi the *cupio dissolvi*, the longing for disintegration, of the mystics. Pirandello does not like the present trend in Italian criticism represented especially by Pietro Mignosi, a professor at the University of Palermo, which tends to make a mystic, indeed a Catholic, out of him. Yet, unquestionably there is, particularly in the present play, a strong undercurrent of mystic thought, if by mysticism we mean the attempt to gaze on universal life through the trelliswork of the tangible world. In *One Does Not Know How* one is ever conscious of the author's concern over the boundless spaces that stretch "beyond the horizon," to use a phrase of Eugene O'Neill's, who resembles Pirandello in hearkening to voices that come to him from unknown distances. There is in Romeo a complete detachment from all earthly possessions, from all that man calls conquest and progress. He says: "Truth and reality abide in God alone. All that pertains to us is perishable and destined to die. Our will, our wisdom, our knowledge, all this is nothing." His vision enlarges as the end approaches. The divine overpowers the human in him, and we feel the ethereal quality of a pure spirit as he atones for his guilt.

At the same time we should not lose sight of the fact that Pirandello returns here to his meaning of reality which, to him, is based not on the crude apprehension of the outside world but must be vivified by our sentiment, and made alive by our faith and passion. It is not enough to know that the moon is in the sky and the forest is on earth. As such the moon and the forest are mere abstract concepts. We must let our "sentiment" envelop them, since only by our so doing "they acquire a full reality." This full reality is our possession when we are carried away, down the swift current of the sea of being, unaware of the ties that hamper us, one with the infinite.

Pirandello has humanized the drama of Romeo by allowing the complicating force of "reason" to have a certain hold on him. Romeo wavers at first and does not openly tell Giorgio of his sin. With the cunning of despair he tries to lead Giorgio into the intricate net of his reasoning: "Imagine that my wife had told me that she had dreamt of you and had been untrue to me in her dream." He tries to prepare him for the stark truth by asking him what he would do if his wife should tell him that she had sinned with another man in a dream. Giorgio, the average man whose practical sense always works towards making his life comfortable, states that a woman should not tell her husband of such a dream. In vain Ginevra deftly seeks to help and suggests that guilt is absent from what is done in a dream. (Romeo's wrong and hers had been a dream too.) Giorgio, with the inexorable logic of the average man, does not understand and, upon learning the truth, he kills.

The humanity of Romeo is also enhanced by the fact that we see him trying in vain to cling to the pleasurable aspects of life. He longingly says: "If we could only cling to the knowable things!" His failure makes us realize how great a misfortune and tragedy Pirandello has embodied in his character. Poor Romeo is carried to his doom by the same blind forces that the Greek dramatists felt in the obscure fate of man. There is nothing that he can do against his destiny. He must go on and on carrying the burning load of his guilt till death opens for him the portals of the infinite.

Pirandello has never revealed the tragedy of being human more powerfully than in this play. To be human is to know how to cope with the tricks of nature, of man, and of the daily existence. If successful, we are thus led to the dwarfing and satisfied happiness of the beast, leaving untouched the world of mystery that slumbers in the depth of our being. So we must choose: Either we must be satisfied brutes or unhappy spirits thirsty and hungry for a precious liquid and food that most human beings neglect. To the pure spirit in us, the whole of life, even nature is an artificial construction.

This play has a marked tendency towards pure lyricism in

179

that action is reduced to a minimum and the whole drama centers about the harrowing inner experience and mental anguish of Romeo Daddi who towers above the other four characters that the author has placed near him. Two short stories, *Cinci* ("Cinci") [2] and *Nel Gorgo* ("In the Whirlwind") [3] are the material source of the play. In the play, Pirandello has attributed to Romeo the experiences of two different characters that form the warp of the two stories.

If we look in retrospect at the plays contained in this section and which correspond to Pirandello's intuition of the "grotesque," we see that the drama is first created by the artificiality of the characters. As a result, the events that unfold before us are comedy, that is they are permeated by laughter, the laughter of Pirandello who notices and unmasks the complex artificiality of the characters. As time has enriched and deepened his thoughtful observation of life, a sense of tragedy viewed as one with life and permeating the very texture of human life has appeared in his drama. The complications and the isolation of man are not superimposed by lack of sincerity. They are there because they are part of life. There is no escape. It is the common fate of us all. If we were to ask Pirandello to what or to whom the process of "building up oneself" is applied in this play, he would answer that the average man and the average life have undergone this process. Laws, customs, inhibitions, nature, cities, churches, and statues are all prisons in which universal life is caught and suffers. The hero here is Romeo because he has freed himself of the artificial barriers of earthly life. He has joined the mystics of all religions and of all times who sought and attained their communion with the deity and were lost in it. Perhaps he has laid the foundation of the religion of a distant tomorrow.

In this fashion Pirandello has left the lowlands of mockery and has risen to the sublime and lonely heights of pure tragedy.

[2] *Novelle per un anno*, XIV, 199–212.
[3] *Ibid.*, VIII, 193–207.

Part Three

SOCIAL PLAYS

XVIII

Introduction

The social theme was implied in Pirandello's attitude of observer and critic of human acts. In analyzing man's actions he was logically and necessarily led to the consideration of the social environment.

Pirandello's social drama has distinct antisocial leanings. Influenced by his unhappy experience of life, he always viewed modern civilization in the light of corruption and profligacy. His exasperated idealism created an abyss between actuality and dream that never gave him the hope of a better condition. Even in the early play, *Limes of Sicily*, we have seen that the drama of Micuccio Bonavino, the symbol of good and old Sicily, rises from the contrast between a mythical perfection as embodied in country life in Sicily, and the corruption of modern civilization. The author accuses progress of having shattered the dream of the poor young peasant who looms gigantic in all his simplicity against the laughing and coarse, though elegantly dressed, friends of Teresina.

Pirandello's irreconcilable attitude towards modern civilization, and his antisocial outbursts are found as an undercurrent in many of the plays considered in other sections. His antisocial attitude forms the background of *As You Desire Me*, just as it assumes a sad note in *The New Colony*, where the author reaches the gloomy conclusion that an ideal society is possible only in the dreams of men like Plato and Tommaso Companella, who liked self-deception. In reality the restless and struggling instincts of men make a perfect civilization impossible.

Social implications are scattered in most of Pirandello's plays, although we are including in this section only the four in which the social element is in marked evidence. This social attitude takes the form of a pondering, at times humorous and at times idealistic, over the problems of marriage, the fate of human society, and the meaning of immortality, which themes are developed in the plays herein contained: *The Pleasure of Honesty; Think It Over, Giacomino; The New Colony;* and *Lazarus.*

These plays show the more solid part of Pirandello's thought, although the presence of serious ideas does not bear any relation to the æsthetic value of the works. This is particularly true of *The New Colony* and *Lazarus,* where Pirandello's idealism reveals itself in an evanescent form, failing to become embodied in strong personalities. On the other hand, *The Pleasure of Honesty* and *Think It Over, Giacomino,* are very solid and significant works, and can be ranked with the best that Pirandello has produced.

A social play has necessarily a moral intimation. Pirandello is a modern moralist who approaches moral problems with a smile rather than with a solemn countenance. Anyone who sets out to write a play about matrimony dealing with the validity and social significance of marriage takes upon himself a very hard task. It is easy to degenerate into senseless and vulgar recrimination, or into idealistic and sentimental exaltations. Pirandello has had the good taste to hide his moralistic tone behind a deceptive screen of humor and laughter, with the result that we are suddenly and greatly surprised when in the end we find ourselves before the serious countenance of moral life. The idea that morality is an integral part of the very texture of life acquires a deeper meaning when it comes to us from the original and brilliant paradoxes of a humorist. Morality is rendered palatable and artistic by making it lose its solemn and forbidding aspect.

The element that stands out in Pirandello's social plays and in the social implications of his drama is the moral inferiority of man, and, by way of a logical contrast, the superiority of woman. Pirandello, like most modern playwrights, has been very chivalrous with women and he contrasts the superficiality and fickleness of man's affections to the deeper feelings of woman. This attitude is the result of Pirandello's approach to the theme of instinct. He has never succeeded in overcoming a sense of loathing and revolt for sensuality. As people tie to a dog's neck the chicken it has killed in order to cure it of the habit, so Pirandello has never been able to free himself from the thought of the lowness of sexual instinct. He is not like Dante, who read in the book of experience that there are worse sins than lust, and consequently assigned in his Inferno a worse punishment to the traitors than to the lustful ones. Pirandello is constantly harassed by the presence of instinct in his characters. He seeks a refuge in the concept of purity that he has lent to women. In his social drama he shows that the loftiness of woman could make life different for his characters, but that these are made blind by the violence of their lust to the loftier life that is projected before them. This is the social implication that is found in *Diana and Tuda,* in *She Wanted to Find Herself,* in *Grafting,* and even in the tormented *As Well as Before, Better than Before.*

In his earnest and passionate attitude towards life, Pirandello insists that formality is not enough to give a meaning and rhythm to our actions. If he often presents characters who enshroud their deeds in the pomp of conventionality and formalism, he leads them to their doom when they refuse to heed his pleading that life is not an abstract concept nor a moral appearance, and that our acts are not meaningless, mechanical motions. His strong individualism has always led him towards a deeply felt mode of feeling and living, even if to do so was painful to the point that he had to call on humor and laughter to relieve the tension.

In many of Pirandello's plays there is a strong undertone of satire before the spectacle of social life. It would be wrong to characterize such a spectacle with the epithet of "miserable" or "sad," a natural characterization that social satire is inclined to give to human actions. Pirandello is too full of human compassion to justify such adjectives in reference to human events. Man advances to the best of his ability on the path of life, and if he falls we should not excuse him, but should feel pity for him. Pirandello reveals his attitude in words that are uttered by one of his most perfect characters, Baldovino, in *The Pleasure of Honesty:* "We are not alone. There are two of us: we and the beast. The beast that carries us. There is no use to whip it; you can never compel it to act according to reason. Try to persuade a donkey not to walk near a precipice. The donkey will take blows, flogging, hard pulls at the halter, but it will go there because it cannot help it. And after you have beaten it soundly, look at the grieving eyes of that poor beast—tell me, don't you pity it? I say pity it—and not excuse it. Intelligence that excuses the beast descends to the lowness of the beast. But to pity it is a different matter. Don't you think so?" (*The Pleasure of Honesty*, p. 227.)

Pirandello is not the rigid moralist who formulates moral laws in his cold brain, stifling the voices and claims of his heart. Such a moralist carries a book in his hands, keeps his eyes fastened on it, and passes judgment based on the letter of the law that has no spirit for him. History has registered many unbending figures of stern reformers. One recalls in this connection Calvin and the judges of the Spanish Inquisition. Pirandello has never failed to be compassionate.

The analysis of social life that he affords in his plays is of the nature that is found in playwrights whose power of observation was greater than their gift of fancy. He is closer to Molière than to Racine, closer to Goldoni than to Metastasio or D'Annunzio. What he lacks in external fantasy is compensated for in him by a deep sense of human sympathy for the foibles of his fellow-men.

XIX

The Strange Adventures of Lady Honesty

THE PLEASURE OF HONESTY
(*Il piacere dell'onestà*)

In this play we find ourselves before a strange, quixotic treatment of the theme of honesty. Pirandello, following the spirit of his times, when morality is more practised than preached, does not give us a treatise nor an oration about it. Rather he approaches the problem with his usual quizzical smile. He seems to be at first uncertain whether honesty is an impelling force of life or just an empty word. As events develop, he and his readers are led to the conclusion that something powerful abides in honesty, something that man can momentarily cast aside, but to which he must eventually turn to give consistency and support to his life.

The moral problem which constitutes the very texture of the play arises from an immoral situation. Agata Renni, a young woman who is approaching the age when the possibility of marriage becomes rather doubtful, has had a love affair with Marquis Fabio Colli, a man in his forties who is separated from his profligate wife. Agata's mother, to prevent a scandal, decides to marry her to Baldovino, member of a noble family in dire financial straits.

Pirandello has looked with ironic and indulgent eyes on the mother who, in making arrangements for the marriage contract with Maurizio Setti, a cousin of the Marquis and a former school chum of Baldovino's, admits that she has played her part in the fall of her daughter. Grievingly and feelingly she confesses to Setti, "You cannot understand what torture it is for a mother to see her daughter advance in years . . . begin to lose the first flower of her youth. One does not have the courage to use the rigor that prudence suggests. Ah, honesty! What a mockery at times, my dear Setti! When the eyes of a daughter turn to you almost imploringly for a little love, the lips of the mother cannot utter a word, since she has known the world and had her big or little share of love." Agata's mother had actually steeled herself against interfering with Agata and Colli while they were in the garden on a starry night filled with the intoxicating perfume of flowers. "Outside, flowers and stars; within, anguish and the most heart-rending tenderness. And the mother cries within herself: 'Let all the stars and all the flowers for once be for my daughter,' and there, in the darkness, she stands, watching over a crime to which all nature invites, that tomorrow men and her own conscience will condemn. I cannot be excused, dear Setti, but I deserve sympathy."

The sin arises from this background of a mother's grief and from a wave of sentiment on the part of Agata Renni who felt unspeakably sorry for Colli whom she knew to be "unhappy, separated from his unworthy wife." "And you see," insists the mother, "this reason which should have prevented Agata from going to such a point has been the one that has led her there. When a woman has waited so many years for a companion without finding him, and at last meets a man who deserves all her love, and she knows this man to be ill treated, embittered, offended by another woman—believe me, she cannot resist the spontaneous impulse to show him that not all women are like that one; that there are some who know how to answer love with love and appreciate the luck that the other has spurned." Pirandello's characters do not sin for profligacy. Sentiment is their worst enemy. There is not in Pirandello the strong, elementary naturalism of Verga in his Sicilian stories. Agata sins because of sentiment, and because of sentiment her mother has relaxed the close watch that mothers once exercised over their daughters. But the problem is there, cruel and terrible in its stark reality: Agata is going to have a baby. So greatly ashamed is the mother that she even goes so far as to wish death for herself. "One ought to die afterwards, but death does not come. Life continues, life that to be and to endure needs all those things that in a moment we have thrown away." Woe unto Agata if the world should know that she, unwed, is going to become a mother!

Ridicule and shame would be heaped on her. There is only one thing to do: procure a husband for her in order to save appearances; to rectify the situation; to make it moral by draping over it the cloak of honesty. Here is the first lance that the serious ironist, Pirandello, breaks in favor of an old chatelaine, Honesty. Agata cannot reappear in the world without at least the appearance of honesty. Honesty that we cast aside when the voice of instinct and sentiment sings in our hearts is our indispensable possession, painful as its acquisition may be. Its acquisition is truly painful for Agata. She has to marry a man whom she does not know, Baldovino. But "sentiment must be restrained; it must recede in order to make place for reason."

Here is the drama. We are at its very portals where we meet Baldovino, a strange individual who, with his quixotic temperament, dwarfs everyone around him, although he was meant to enter the Renni household in the rôle of a humble understudy. A man like Baldovino cannot remain in the shadows of mediocrity. He has been tossed by the stormy waves of life; he has reached high towards the stars with his intellect, while he has known the mire of the very depths, dragged down by his instincts and passions. Setti has gone to interview him at his dilapidated villa in the town of Macerata. Following is the impression that Setti received from their conference. "It seemed to me that I was not on this earth any longer—but in a strange, fantastic land, lugubrious, mysterious, where he moved freely in the fashion of a master and where the most bizarre and impossible things could happen and seem natural and customary."

It is easy for Baldovino to accept the strange request of his old school chum, Maurizio, who proposes that he become the *pro forma* husband of Agata Renni. To a man constantly balancing on the seesaw of fantasy, the more absurd the adventure, the more acceptable. Baldovino, incapable of living a normal life, has found in his lucid abstraction resembling madness a means of compromising with life which helped him to bear his lonely and drab existence. In his daily suffering, condemned to a distracting solitude in that sluggish and somnolent provincial town, reduced to poverty, desperately alone, he cannot touch earth, so heavy in mental and almost physical pain is the price exacted by that contact. If one be allowed to describe it so, he has reached a sort of strange pragmatic wisdom, based on detachment from the aspects of a normal reality, which permits him to abandon himself to sudden wild flights into the realm of fancy where possibilities are endless.

It is necessary to have clearly in mind the tragically fantastic character of Baldovino's mode of thinking and living in order to understand the play. He has renounced all that side of life that we may call material and concrete and which centers about instinct and obeys the dictates of sentiment. Baldovino is only "intellect," not because he delights in floating on the fleecy clouds of the irrational, but because the circumstances of his life have forced him to take refuge in the lonely castle of his imagination. Imagination, so the idealists of all times say, is the last refuge of those whom a happy and joyous life has rejected. Under these circumstances Baldovino's intellectual wanderings into the realm of the absolute are tinged with grief and resentment, with hatred and longing for destruction, yet he holds them in abeyance by the purifying force of his idealism. In the fortress of his lucid imagination he can re-create the harrowing conditions of his existence, and contemplate them with a detached feeling, since his heart is absent and only his intellect functions.

The life of Baldovino must be envisaged through the absolute preponderance of his intellect and the exclusion of his heart. As long as we are ruled by the heart we are not capable of a detached attitude. Heart is to Pirandello instinct and sentiment, and to listen to its dictates is to live in the warmth and in the blind violence of living things. To be dominated by instinct means to Baldovino to cling to the pleasurable gifts of a natural life. How can he in his lonely superiority and his ghastly isolation entrust himself to the flow of a natural and instinctive life? He has become the perfect embodiment of a man living only through his intellect. He transforms facts into concepts, thereby depriving them of their power to hurt him. The concept of sorrow is not so destructive as sorrow itself, nor is the concept of joy as delectable as joy itself. He knows that, but he also knows that sorrow in his life far outweighs joy. Consciously he has to still his heart that claims its share of joy, and cling to his intellect that creates for him a world of formulas and concepts. He is penniless, for instance, but by the quick opening of the shutter of his mind, he can see endless figures galloping towards the infinite, giving him the sensation of the possession of millions, billions, trillions. Society has stupidly called him dishonest for not paying back to a few thickheaded but tenacious *bourgeois* the money that they had lent him. He has been denied credit, condemned to penury. The mobile flight of those figures is his vengeance. Setti's proposal is rather odd, indeed, unique; but it does not shock a man accustomed to roam in the world of the irrational. So he accepts.

What strikes Baldovino most is the fact that he whom society has always branded as dishonest, is now called upon to save the honesty and good name of Agata Renni, of her mother, of her lover, and of her unborn child. Following the lucid sword of his logical mind, he becomes a sort of categorical imperative, a stern defender of honesty. Once a husband, he decrees that there will not be any compromise nor half measures. He will be an unbending dictator. Since all concerned must rally around honesty, they will have to be honest, literally and intrinsically. This uncompromising form of honesty is the easier since they all are assuming an artificial rôle before the eyes of society. Artificiality, according to Baldovino, presupposes the absence of sentiment, making it possible for us to measure our words and deeds, to "build up" ourselves, as the stage director of this drama tells Colli. Baldovino insists, however, that they be sincere among themselves by laying bare the facts, no matter how bitter. Colli's sensibilities are shocked by the blunt: "Agata has been your mistress." He rebels at that crude way of putting it, but Baldovino has the cold logic of facts in his favor.

The scene between Colli and Baldovino is a powerful one. Face to face, the two men are trying to stake their lives on a

191

situation that, when the fog of uncertainty and social hypocrisy is removed from it, gapes before them in all its shame
and ugliness. The one who removes the fog is Baldovino. He
asks Colli to speak "openly," but adds that openly means not
only to talk frankly with others but to act sincerely with one's
self. Baldovino is pitiless in his sincerity. "When I enter this
house," he says, "I present myself to you in a form adapted
to the relation that I must assume with you. You, in receiving
me, must do the same. But, ultimately, behind our masks
which are facing each other, behind the Venetian blinds and
curtains of hypocrisy, are hidden our most secret thoughts,
our most intimate sentiments, all that we really are for ourselves, aside from the relations that we wish to establish with
one another." Baldovino hates these "constructions," the
superimposed personality that he has to force on his intimate
self. "I experience within me an unspeakable nausea for the
self that I am compelled to build up and display in the relations that I must assume with my fellow-men."

This sense of "nausea" redeems Pirandello's characters
from the charge of moral turpitude and from that of abstraction. In discussing the situation with Colli, Baldovino insists
that their respective positions be clearly defined before he
consents to play the rôle of formal husband. Colli must not
think that he can continue to enjoy his dream of love with
Agata. Everyone will have to be honest. All will live in
celibacy. "I must become a tyrant," announces Baldovino to
Colli, "and you must respect me, not so much me personally,
but the form which I represent: that of an honest husband
of an honest woman." Baldovino accepts the rôle of being
only the "form," the "mold" of a husband. He will move like
a concept among people who have known for years the richness of the gifts of life and nature. He will be as abstract as
a concept, but he will possess by virtue of that form, its elusive, intangible, yet undeniable power.

The marriage ceremony of Agata and Baldovino creates
a situation laden with grave possibilities. It seals a mask on
Baldovino's face, a mask which burns and sears. Now, more
than ever, to exist means to Baldovino to renounce senti-

ment, to replace it with cold reason. Here is a man living near a woman, a lovely woman like Agata, compelled to repress every feeling, every sentiment, condemning himself to an unnatural passiveness. From the outset, two distinct points of view clash in violent contrast: that of Colli and of Agata's mother, both of whom want to use Baldovino as a screen for the prolonged happiness that Agata finds in Colli's love, and that of Baldovino who accepts his rôle of defender of honesty with the enthusiasm of a crusader and the rigor of a logician. A problem arises: To what extent can the form be and remain a pure form, that is, a construction of reason, resisting the efforts of sentiment to break into it, to fill it with its turbulent strength? Baldovino's life is an abstract and cold form only on the surface. He knows that on that form depends his whole present existence, the respite from financial worries, and the petty material fetters with which life strangles the best part of an intellectual man. If he repudiates that form he will lose every contact with Agata and with the fictitious structure of life that he has erected which, painful as it is, possesses enough consistency to give a purpose to his existence.

For ten months under the apparent calm of the situation a great struggle goes on. Colli and Agata's mother have been planning to get rid of Baldovino as soon as the child is born. Colli, much to the astonishment of all, has founded a banking firm at the head of which he has placed Baldovino, who has displayed a real genius for organization and administration. Under him the firm has flourished beyond expectation. He has ruled with an iron hand. He has truly become a categorical imperative, and, reasoning as he does according to absolute principles, he provides a pattern of perfect life for all. He confesses, "Suspended in the air, I float as if resting on a cloud. I experience the pleasure of saints in the frescoes of churches." His pattern of perfect life applies both to the bank and to his home. If honesty in business is a logical necessity, then everyone has to be honest, and the same honesty must guide the actions of all the members of his household. His logic is so penetrating and convincing that no argument can resist its thrusts. Agata's mother, Colli, and the directors are all crushed by the power of his reasoning. This is so because he reasons as a categorical imperative, and he can do so because he lives in and thinks and orders from the lofty tower where he has enclosed himself.

Baldovino is aware of the effect of his rule on the people around him. "They complain, don't they? Tell me," he asks of Setti. "They shout—they champ the bit. . . . Well, I know it! I stifle them. I stifle anyone who comes near me. But you see; I cannot help it. For ten months I have not been a man . . . I am almost a deity. You should easily understand that. I have a body only for the sake of appearances. I am steeped in figures, in speculations, but they are for other people. There is not in them the gain of one *centime* for me, and I don't want there to be. I am here in this beautiful house, and I almost do not see, hear, nor touch anything. At times I marvel at hearing the sound of my own voice or the noise of my footsteps. I am living—do you understand?—de-li-ci-ous-ly in the absolute of a pure, abstract form." This is why Baldovino can be all that he is, honest even in handling millions. Everyone sees in him a mirror of perfection in which none dares look at himself. To listen to his order is to obey the cold and unchanging voice of righteousness. The strange fact is that Agata submits to his orders with respect and finds logical whatever he commands.

The situation becomes graver for Colli when a child is born to Agata and motherhood destroys the lover in her. Now Baldovino stands between her and Colli and acquires a deeper significance when she realizes that her son will bear his name. Colli is justified in remonstrating with Mr. Setti for choosing a man out of the ordinary. Baldovino is distinguished, even good-looking. His intellect is such as to dwarf into nothingness a placid and commonplace man like Colli.

Baldovino's rôle appears more and more important as time passes. He becomes conscious of the value of his presence in the Renni household as he realizes that Agata's mother and Colli are still determined to get rid of him. He ponders over the possibility of gratifying their wish by committing an un-worthy action and thus affording them an excuse. He is forced to admit that that would be a perfect solution to the problem of eliminating him as a husband. Once the child is born he is no longer needed. But as a father he cannot so leave it. He has accepted the rôle in order to save the child too. "If as a husband I can go away without doing any harm to my wife, who will drop my name and resume hers; as a father my dis-honesty would damage my son who bears my name. The lower I shall fall, the greater the damage that will be done him."

The crisis is precipitated by various formalities in con-nection with the child's christening. Baldovino has decided to give him the name of Sigismondo. He knows it is a burden-some name and that "the poor child runs the risk of being crushed by it," but he is adamant against the protests of Colli and Agata's mother. Sigismondo has been the name of his father and of his grandfather. It is absolutely necessary for a child who will bear the cognomen of Baldovino to be named after his ancestors. "It is not for me," says the logical Baldo-vino, "it is for form, and for form, since I must give him a name, I cannot give him any name other than this one." How strong is the form assumed by Baldovino! Pirandello is like a scientist who comes by chance across a new fact, a new formula, and marvels before the magnitude of his sud-den discovery. Of greater moment is the question whether the child will be baptized in church or privately at home. The grandmother contends that the child should be baptized at home to lend more dignity to the ceremony. Baldovino coun-ters with the argument that no rite can be more austere and meaningful than when performed in church. Even the curate who comes to the house ready to perform the ceremony has to admit that this is true "at least in principle." Agata, upon being called upon to decide, sides with Baldovino. This shows that she has been won over to him and has detached herself from Colli, ruled only by a mother's instinct.

Colli fights his last battle by attempting to set a trap for Baldovino whereby he will appear to have misappropriated

half a million *lire*. Baldovino shows Agata the proofs of his
innocence. Agata stands by him. His innocence is the innocence and honor of her son. This fact plunges Baldovino into
a frenzy. If Agata stands by him, then he can no longer play
the rôle of a *pro forma* husband. He, by that very interest on
the part of Agata, cannot continue to abide in the region of
abstractions. He decides to leave Agata. Dressed as he was
when he first went to her house, he is ready to go. He stands
between the pure form into which he has walled himself and
the old self of the days spent in his dilapidated villa at
Macerata. That self is there, held in subjection by the new
rôle he has imposed on himself. "You know," he says, "I have
in me a horrible beast of which I have tried to free myself
by chaining it to these conditions which were offered to me."
He discovers that his greatest enemy is hidden in him: his
own sentiment. It has been possible for him to be purely a
form as long as sentiment was absent. Now sentiment has
gradually flowed back into the artificial mold of the husband
of Agata Renni. Baldovino has felt interest and love appear
and grow in him: he has repressed and stifled them. When
Agata sides with him, he must flee. He must be true to his
promise to be only a form, an abstract concept. He gives
Colli the proofs of his innocence. Let Colli accuse and ruin
him. He can begin again the life of an intellectual rover, of
a sentimental vagabond.

Contrary to their hopes, the plotters discover that the elimi-
nation of Baldovino will be a common disaster. The son's
future, in which they are all interested, is so closely depend-
ent on him as to make a continuation of the existing situation
an impelling necessity. They all beg him to remain, the
mother, Colli, Mr. Setti. Baldovino, however, has resolved to
leave Agata. He thinks that his wife is clinging not to him
but to the pure form that he promised he would be. Agata
has learned to appreciate and even love Baldovino. She announces that he can leave if he wishes, but she will follow
him. He is her husband. Baldovino capitulates when he feels
that Agata's esteem for and interest in him have opened a
new horizon to his desolate soul. Under the mask of husband

and father his real features have so asserted themselves that the nobility of the human profile has taken the place of the grotesque and painful mask.

There is an undertone of social satire in the very events that form the warp of the play. Pirandello views with grieving mockery the attempt to hide the illegitimacy of the child under the cloak of a marriage ceremony. The clear-eyed Baldovino saw very well that the mother and Colli wanted to use honesty as a means of perpetuating a wrong situation. They wanted to use him as a soulless tool and then cast him aside. The author, half ironically and half thoughtfully, makes Baldovino don the armor of honesty and fight gallantly for it against the machinations of his enemies.

Defending the pitiful and yet glorious plight of intellectual life, Pirandello chooses Baldovino, a man out of the boundaries of society and civilization, and contrasts him with the exponents of the more fortunate class, individuals to whom society has granted wealth, social status, and respect. The man who has been renounced by society is superior to his antagonists in everything, especially in honesty. He has an ethical concept of business, and his honest practices are resented by civilized individuals like Colli and the directors. When Maurizio Setti comments on the success of the concern of which Baldovino is the head, the latter calls his attention to the fact that he does not steal as many bankers do. He rejoices in the feeling of perfect aloofness from the miserable slavery of money. He says: "To see hundreds of thousands of *lire* pass through your hands, to be able to consider them just as cheap paper, not to feel the slightest need of them, is a divine pleasure." It is the pleasure of honesty realized to a perfect degree by one who is accustomed to roam in the realm of the absolute. To him, a perfect logician, it is equally absurd that wealthy people should have religious ceremonies performed at home. Baldovino informs the curate that rich and poor are alike in the eyes of the Lord. The curate agrees in principle with Baldovino that the child should be baptized in church, but sides with the family in agreeing that out of regard for custom the ceremony could and should be performed at home. This is the reason why life is as we see it around us, and why civilization often appears to be only a mocking name.

To Baldovino civilization does not mean order or progress based on the ending of the struggle waged by our ancestors in the jungle. Indeed it marks an intensification of it. He shows his fingernails to Maurizio and says, "Do you see to what a point we have arrived? We do not cut our fingernails to disarm ourselves. On the contrary we do it that our hands may appear more civilized, that is, more adapted to a struggle fiercer than the one that our ancestors in a primitive stage fought only with their nails."

This play, like many of Pirandello's works, could be and, indeed, has been attacked as being abstract and cerebral. The truth is that Pirandello has shown the defeat of the abstract and cerebral Baldovino before Baldovino the man, who finds a meaning to his life in the promise of Agata's love. Even in the mental aloofness of the days spent at Macerata and when he lived in the pure form of the concept of a husband, Baldovino is too conscious of his mask to be abstract. Abstraction is rhetoric, and Pirandello's characters feel too vividly and passionately the weight of their grief and tragedy to be rhetorical.

Pirandello is here a brilliant and ironical asserter of the power of honesty. As a genial and quixotic knight of Lady Honesty, he breaks his lance against those who preach of her in hollow voices and with solemn faces, while he attacks those who are inclined to think that honesty is just a prejudice of narrow-minded people. Pirandello the humorist begins by placing honesty in a man who lives outside the normal boundaries of life and by claiming that to be absolutely honest we must live as abstract formulas. Eventually he shows that honesty is imbedded in the very texture of social life to the extent that even when assumed as only a form it becomes a powerful reality and leads to the fullness that it is meant to afford to men.

XX

Where the Law Cannot Reach

THINK IT OVER, GIACOMINO

(*Pensaci, Giacomino*)

This play is built around old Professor Toti, who is the negation of a schoolmaster and the glorification of a compassionate man. He is old and tired, and his high-school pupils make all sorts of noises and play all kinds of pranks as he teaches them the sciences. One day a youth leaps through the first-floor window, much to the uproarious amusement of the pupils to whom the professor is trying to teach the various families of monkeys. The school principal, who has come to investigate the cause of the commotion, is furious. He tells Toti that he should retire, and that he will then receive a pension. Toti takes him at his word. He will not retire from teaching, but he will marry, and marry a young girl, just for spite, so that at his death his pension will cost the government dear. Toti is one of those old gentlemen who laugh because they possess a greater wisdom than so many who go around with a solemn mien, all filled with their importance. He enters upon marriage with a perfect understanding of the step that he is taking. Whimsically explaining to the principal the reason for marrying, he says: "A wife? What wife are you talking about? Just an act of charity. You, then, are like everybody else. You see the professor and do not see the man. You hear that I wish to get married, and you imagine a wife near me as a husband, and you begin to laugh. A wife at my age? That would be funny. I a husband? Just a profession, an appearance. In reality, nothing at all. I am and shall remain a poor old man who will have the company for two or three years of a person who will be grateful for the good I do her at the expense of the government."

The ridicule is turned on the principal as well as on all

those who wish to laugh at the old professor. Ridicule cannot touch him, for he knows the world and is intelligent enough to shield himself even against the ridicule that usually is cast on an old man when he is betrayed by his wife. "I count on that," he says. "That will touch my profession as a husband, but not me. Indeed, I shall see to it that the husband, as a husband, shall be betrayed. Of course. Otherwise, how could I, poor old man that I am, have any peace? But how could I be offended—if I am not a husband—nor can I be one—nor desire to be one? A charitable deed, that's all—and if all the imbeciles of the town wish to laugh about it—let them laugh. It will not worry me."

Toti marries Lillina, the young daughter of the school janitor, an arrogant, disrespectful fellow who hated Professor Toti and was in the habit of reporting him to the principal for the lack of discipline that he noticed in the science class. Lillina has been having an affair with Giacomino, the young man who leaped through the window of Professor Toti's classroom. Lillina has revealed to Toti the distressing fact that she is going to have a baby, and the old professor, touched by her tears and by the sadness of the situation, has married her with the one stipulation—that Giacomino, for whom he has a great fondness, continues to be her lover. Lillina is the ideal girl for Toti. She has a lover and she is very young, so the government will have to pay a pension for a long time. She will look after Toti. She will look after him, give him a home, and when the baby comes he will find great joy in the little child: "A little child whose hand I shall hold and with whom I shall take a walk. For an old man there is no better company to learn the way to the grave."

Two years have passed since Toti's marriage to Lillina. They live very happily in a home cheered by the little boy, Ninì, whom Toti loves as if he were his own. The old professor has had the luck of receiving quite unexpectedly a considerable amount of money, 140,000 *lire*, from his brother who died in Roumania without leaving a will. The professor has invested his money in a city bank where he is the strongest stockholder. Thanks to him, Giacomino occupies a nice position in the bank. Toti still teaches, with no better discipline in his classes than before.

One day he receives a call from the school principal, who has come to tell him that he must resign because all the parents are protesting against having a man like Toti instruct their children. Toti rebels: "I expect to have someone, since you are not willing to do so, come to discuss with me not what seems but what is. I mean my conscience." Lillina, meanwhile, has become very morose; she cries constantly, is nervous, indifferent, and impatient with her little Ninì. Toti believes that it is due to the fact that people are protesting. "Well," he says paternally to Lillina, "that should not concern us at all, because you and I know that we don't do anything wrong and must think only of keeping together, waiting for time to show that I am in the right.—Not now, but at my death, when I shall leave you well provided for and without worry."

That is Toti's dream—to leave Lillina and Ninì all he possesses and have Giacomino marry her, rectifying a wrong situation. Giacomino, however, is thwarting his plans. For three days he has not come to the house nor has he gone to the bank. This is due to the intrigues of Rosaria, Giacomino's sister, and Father Landolina, who are trying to break up the relation between the two lovers.

Father Landolina, anxious and subtle, goes to see Toti. He intervenes because Giacomino's sister has appealed to him. "It is a question, my dear Professor, of a poor Christian soul who, whether rightly or wrongly I don't know, is hurt, offended by incriminating rumors that have spread over the town about her brother." Rosaria, who is a very pious woman and has been a mother to Giacomino, wishes him to marry. A girl has already been chosen for him. Giacomino has promised his sister that he will never see Lillina again. It is very convenient to have a logical and moral excuse for the instability of one's feelings. Father Landolina begs Toti to give him a written statement to the effect that all gossip about Giacomino and Lillina has no basis whatever. He and Rosaria want to show this document to the parents of the girl in order to calm their apprehensions about Giacomino's moral character. Toti is furious, but restrains himself and courteously sees Landolina to the door.

He decides that the only thing to do is for him to take Ninì to Giacomino and remind him of his duty towards his child and towards the mother. Old Toti, with his half sophisticated, half jovial laughter on his lips, is met by the cold politeness of Rosaria. He is told by her that Giacomino is not at home. He brushes aside her statement with his subtle laughter, and enters the house. That laughter is the worst weapon that she has ever encountered. She is powerless before it and goes to inform Giacomino of the professor's visit. In the meantime, Toti takes Ninì on his knees and sweetly talks to him: "Do you know who will come here now? Giami. You love him, don't you? He, too, brings you sweets and toys. But you must love me more, my child, because I am about to leave you. You cannot understand these things yet, and you will never understand them, because when you do you will have forgotten me—this man who has held you in his arms—clasped you so—so, and has shed tears for you."

Giacomino enters as old Toti is speaking so tenderly to his child. He is ashamed of himself; but he has promised his sister, he has been engaged a month to the girl that he is going to marry. Toti is very angry with the moral indignation of an old man who, having treated Giacomino and Lillina as his own children, has defied ridicule and now sees the fruitlessness of his effort. He pleads, but as Giacomino refuses to yield he threatens that he will go with the child to his *fiancée* and expose the whole truth to her. Then he pleads again: "Is it right to so ruin a home, a family, to break the heart of a poor old man, of a poor mother, and to leave without help and guidance a poor little innocent child, like this one, Giacomino, like this one! Don't you see? Have you no heart? Don't you see your child here? It is yours, yours." Giacomino is touched and clasps his little boy in his arms. Lillina is saved in spite of the protests of Father Landolina and of the sister. Giacomino returns with Toti and Ninì to his home, another example of the old saying that "the home is where the child is."

The play corresponds perfectly to Pirandello's concept of humor: it contains a situation that is ludicrous if looked at from the outside, and pathetic if the inner feelings are known.

The comedy has been characterized by Adriano Tilgher as the comedy of a husband who does not wish the lover to leave his wife.[1] It sounds like one of those characterizations meant to whet the appetite for immorality. *Think It Over, Giacomino* is a comedy built on elements that are illogical and immoral for those people to whom morality is only appearances. To Pirandello morality is the substance of life; it abides in the very grain of life, and as such it has to react on what is basic in human needs, and it encompasses the physical and spiritual sides of man. Toti finds the immoral situation, and since he is compassionate he tries to save Lillina from shame. The wrong situation is not created by him. It is brought about by the neglect of Lillina's parents and by nature.

There are bitter reflections on morality as it is usually interpreted by people like Lillina's parents and Giacomino's sister. Often morality is nothing but our own interests. We appeal to moral principles when they can strengthen our positions. We neglect them, we reject them when they oppose our desires. Pirandello unmercifully flays the bombastic arrogance of the janitor, Lillina's father, that hid a mean and despicable nature. He is equally unmerciful with the hypocrisy of Father Landolina and Giacomino's sister. Cinquemani, the janitor, had no scruples in prostituting his sixteen-year-old daughter by marrying her to a man in his sixties, yet he was ready to kill Giacomino and to turn Lillina out of his home when he discovered their love affair. Toti, in a voice that expresses the moral indignation of the author, shouts: "Where do you expect her to go, you old fool? You accuse her when the responsibility is yours, because you did

[1] *Studi sul teatro contemporaneo*, p. 139.

not watch over her and have kept her here among all the filth that pupils write on the walls and on the benches."

When the janitor and his worthy wife discover that by agreement of all concerned Giacomino has continued to be Lillina's lover, their moral sense rebels. They resent Giacomino's presence only because their plan was to enjoy a comfortable old age on Toti's money, with a widowed daughter. That is the value of their morality. Rosaria's moral sense is not loftier. She wants Giacomino to give up Lillina, but she hopes that he will be able to keep his position in the bank with Toti's protection. A written statement from Toti would have meant that the situation would have been quietly remedied by eliminating the elements that she did not wish while keeping those that were remunerative. Father Landolina represents the cold, moral law, and as such he is the target of Pirandello's thrusts. The law solves through marriage the problem of the relation between a man and a woman. But what of cases like that of Lillina's and Giacomino's? Had the matter taken the course that Lillina's parents had meant it to take, the girl would have become a prostitute and Giacomino a shifty, irresponsible man. Father Landolina stands for the categorical, unbending spirit of the law as is evidenced when he wishes the written statement from Toti. To him that document would be enough to destroy the wrong situation existing between Lillina and Giacomino. His action and attitude show the lack of reality of the law whenever it relies only on appearance, ignoring the truth and the substance of a situation.

The play carries also a feeling, a rebellion, on the part of one who believes in the pragmatic values of life against the formalized ones. It is not enough to go before the law in order to be husband and wife. Here the humorist comes to the fore. Toti and Lillina had gone before the law, yet they were not husband and wife. The humorist with glee shows that in this case the reverse is true. Those who had not asked the sanction of the law were actually husband and wife. At this point the humorist disappears, as Pirandello discovers that the real bond that binds them is a child.

The figure that stands out in constant relief is that of Toti. Since the moral question is continuously present, Pirandello makes him the arbiter of the morals of the characters and the one who, in his own erratic fashion, is willing to be a martyr in order to rectify the immoral situation between Lillina and Giacomino. He expects to die in peace in the belief that they will become legally married. In answer to the urge of his compassionate heart he had created a solution that benefited all concerned, even if he had to bear the brunt of ridicule. Toti, however, had the saving grace of laughter that became a formidable weapon against his enemies. It was laughter that led him to win his battle in favor of little Nini, whose soft hands had warmed his cold hands before death, obeying the law of nature of which he had an infinite understanding.

XXI

Impossibility of a Perfect Human Society

THE NEW COLONY

(*La nuova colonia*)

We are in a maritime town of southern Italy, in a wine shop where sailors, smugglers, and harlots have their rendezvous. The atmosphere is one of grimy poverty, of social injustice, and of powerless revolt. The chief characters are people who live by smuggling, and therefore have the police always at their heels. Among them stand out Spera, a poor lost woman, and Currao, a handsome youth, strong, daring, and rebellious.

These people have been brutalized by want and by the struggle that they have had to wage for the bare necessities of life. Their strong, bony features and ungainly limbs testify to the physical struggle, while in their words there is the echo of an internal hatred that partakes of frenzy. "Good—evil: you who have time and leisure can busy yourselves with the consideration of such things." So says old Tobba in whose coat there are more "patches than there were wounds on the flesh of Christ." Life is so unbearable for them that their only escape is to go to live on an island where penal prisoners used to be kept and which is now deserted because it is slowly, insensibly sinking. These people, rough and ill clad, are like broken molecules in the social body, ready to fly in every direction, goaded by the loathing for their life. Spera voices their sentiments: "Loathing, yes, loathing, you of your life, I of mine. I am quivering all over. I feel my bowels twisted like a rope."

Spera is a grotesque mask of womanhood, but she wants a different life because of the baby that she has borne to Currao. Currao, too, wants to live honestly, but he is helpless. When he goes out to sell fish that he received for help that he had given two fishermen, two guards arrest him, believing that he has stolen them. There is only one thing to do: to go away, to go to the island even if it sinks into the sea. Are they not sunk there, as Spera says? "And here, where you are; are you not sunk? You could not sink more deeply than you have here. At least there it will be God who will make you sink—not men more wicked than you! More wicked if they refuse to let you come up to the surface just to breathe. [*She presses her hands on her breast.*] An irresistible desire to breathe from the depths of my lungs has entered into me."

The situation in which these people are placed is such that moral desperation takes hold of their being, even physical being, and makes them writhe and sneer while a sudden thirst for a new life is born in them. Thirst is the word that expresses the parched feeling in their throats and in their withered souls, and the desire of their lips to touch something soothing, pure, and fresh. They will work. Spera "will serve them, mend their clothes, take care of them if sick, and she will work with them: new life, new life, and ours—made by us."

They rig Tobba's old boat and sail for the island. Spera will have her child with her, and as she goes to get him from his nurse now, after five months, her breast feels a sweet, warm flow of milk: milk for her baby. They all cry "Miracle! Miracle!" because in the beginning of a new life what is extraordinary has a powerful hold on man.

Life is at first very happy on the island. They find shelter in an old house, half battered down. Currao is their recognized leader. They set up a tribunal, since they have discovered the need of having to organize themselves under a law; they who have fled from the law of the land. Spera is a sort of queen and saint for them. She has become beautiful again, "so natural," so ennobled by the love of her baby and by the purity of life on the island.

Until now Pirandello has abandoned himself to the feeling of hope, of goodness, and of the idyllic in the crude form that it can take in the smuggler's heart; but now his penetrating and sophisticated mind sets to work Instinct looms again like a terrible and devastating god. All the men on the island desire Spera, the only woman in the place, but she is Currao's because she has had a baby by him. There arise violent questions of ownership as to whom this or that belongs, as to who is to occupy this or that room. One of them has left the group and has gone to live by himself in a corner of the island. Spera tries in vain to instill in them the beauty of her faith: "There is a way of being all for all; and do you know which it is? That of being nothing for ourselves."

Crocco, a despicable scoundrel, represents the forces that are for disintegration and destruction. He resents Currao's position, thinking it easy for him to be on the island. "It is easy for you to occupy your position," he remarks. "What does it cost you? You have her [*he points out Spera*]. You are the leader and you rule." It is of no use for Currao to tell him that he is "the servant of all, the first in giving, the last in taking"; that there must be a law, only "now, here, there isn't any longer the law of others; there is your own." To Crocco that is nonsense. It is the law of Currao, and for that reason Currao stands for it. Crocco is unfit to be social. Someone accuses him of being wicked, of having been born wicked. Spera quietly and understandingly suggests: "We are not born wicked. It is only that he no longer finds the way of being good to anyone—and no one helps him to find that way." In fact, everyone on the island is against Crocco. One day he rushes to the old boat that is moored in the bay and sails back to the land to avenge himself.

Crocco goes to see Padron Nocio, a rich fisherman, owner of many fishing boats, whose young son Dorò has gone to the island because he loves Spera. Padron Nocio sails with four boats to fetch his son. Crocco leads the expedition. They take with them wine and women, the symbols of the old civilization that will destroy the new one that Currao has attempted to build. The inhabitants of the island at first want to prevent their landing, and they threaten them with long poles and stones. Padron Nocio informs them that he has come for his son, and Crocco shouts, "Mita is here! Women are here! Women!" Mita is the beautiful daughter of Padron Nocio. Women were the bait for the hungry males. The old smugglers throw their weapons away, and run to the beach, shouting in exaltation "Women! Women! Women!"

Currao sees himself lost. He is attacked and menaced. To keep his power he agrees to marry Mita, but he would also like to keep his son, Spera's baby. How could she allow him to have her whole life? She seizes her child and flees. She flees to the rocky heights of the island and shouts that if Currao touches her son the earth will tremble and the sea will engulf them all.

The earth obeys the wrath of a mother. It quakes and the waters submerge all the island except a last high spot where mother and son have taken refuge. The love of a mother is the only thing which is saved in the wreck wrought by human passions. One sees here the wistful eyes of Pirandello focused on the spectacle of human society with the same half amused, half grieving expression as when he looked at the vicissitudes of but one individual.

There is in this play a deep vein of philosophy and antisocial sentiment. Life as it is lived today, with its amusements, ambitions, envy, and intrigues, is evil, while there is another life which glows in children's eyes: a life of which men have a glimpse for a fleeting moment, but which they forsake and crush. The aspiration of Spera and of the persecuted smugglers has been a reflection of the divine life which abides in the form of a faded remembrance in the soul of man. Inevitably, actual life has come and has reached out with its tentacles and has overpowered it. This has been the fate of the colony on the island. Evil personified in modern civilization has reached out there, too. The antisocial strain is derived from Pirandello's belief in life as a primitive entity, with candor, beauty, and original purity violated by civilization. It is fatal that the everyday life should deface us and leave us a prey to instincts.

Pirandello places his concept of pure life in the island which represents nature. Spera finds her beauty and serenity as soon as she is removed from the filth of the city and plunged into the pure bosom of nature. She is the embodiment of Pirandello's idealism. Her philosophy is like that of the great saints and mystics who spoke of complete annihilation.

The play reminds one of the adventurous flight back to nature of Robinson Crusoe; only Pirandello looks at life with more searching and disillusioned eyes. *Robinson Crusoe* was written when the world was about to make one of those titanic efforts in the creation of our industrial civilization. Pirandello wrote after the World War—the last chapter of industrial civilization in its extreme forms. He has no faith in our present civilization. The tragic thing is, however, that in this play—even Currao's civilization proved to be not better than the one he had fled. The only figure that is constructive is that of Spera, but her idealism is so lofty that it is a closed book to the average person and does not offer a pattern for the conduct of an average life. Life offers no solution. Disillusion and discouragement hold our temples as in a vise, while a gray, stormy sky hangs overhead. Only in the distance a faint light quivers. It is the dreamy idealism of Spera.

XXII

Resurrection and Immortality

LAZARUS

(*Lazzaro*)

L*azarus* is a religious play with social implications. The author has expressed in it his religious beliefs, which start with a departure from the stereotyped idea of a theological God and end in a passionate, personal, and rather vague Christianity. In it Pirandello identifies God with the soul of man and looks upon the soul as merged with him, both during life and at our bodily death.

The question of life after death constantly occupies the mind of the author. Religions have variously and poetically depicted life in the hereafter. Pirandello sets this problem before himself: What would happen if a man should die and upon being called back to life by the help of science should realize that his eyes had gazed upon an empty and dark beyond? Science affords such a possibility, since it has discovered that an injection of adrenalin into the heart will cause life to ebb back into the body.

There are two distinct sets of characters in the play: one drawn with heavy black lines carries the author's dislike for theological religions; the other enveloped in idealistic veils and sympathetically treated gives us the dreamy concept of life that vibrates beyond the gloomy spectacle of human existence that Pirandello usually transports upon the stage. Here is Diego Spina, his chief antagonist and one of the central figures in the play: he is "a little over forty, tall, thin, with a pale, gaunt face, with hard, mobile eyes, always aglow like those of an excited maniac." Here is a monsignor: "Monsignor Lelli, mellow in appearance, not always succeeding in hiding with his glances and smiles all the bitterness that he has within him."

Against these figures Pirandello has projected those who

embody his own sense of religion and of an ideal of life: Sara, Diego Spina's wife, who has left him because their ideas on life and on bringing up children are so different as to make their living together impossible; Arcadipane, a child of nature, a strong, healthy, handsome, benevolent, and serene peasant with whom Sara has gone to live on a farm as his common law wife after having left her husband; Lucio, Diego Spina's son who refuses at first to become a priest, only to offer himself to Christ when a new sense of Christianity is born within him. On the fringe of the play there are minor characters, drawn in accord with that sympathy for characteristic persons of the lower classes for whom Pirandello has always had a particular and justified liking. There is a sturdy old servant, Deodata, who takes care of little Lia, Diego's crippled daughter, and who does not approve of the excesses of her master. She is religious, but possesses the practical and spontaneous feelings of women of her class for whom religion is a safe investment for a moment of sorrow. To her, Diego Spina's harsh religion is pure madness. Near her there is Cico, a queer beggar, "a slender man, old, bizarre, with small blue eyes lucid as crystal, penetrating, cheerful, and very expressive." He very much resembles Ciampa of *Cap and Bells*. Instead of Ciampa's switch of madness that compels men to make a clean breast of unpleasant and hateful thoughts, Cico is endowed with a little black devil that lives within him and, according to him, says things that should not be said.

Pirandello guides Diego Spina through the experience of being brought back to life. He is a man whose religious beliefs are strictly orthodox, and is imbued with the indifference for the gifts of material life that has been the basis of theological religions. Christ is to him the symbol of a suffering which is unmerciful, harsh, and cruel.

As the scene opens we see on the wall that runs around the courtyard of Spina's house "a large, black cross with the likeness of a squalid Christ all covered with blood." The religious beliefs of Diego Spina are not abstract propositions. They are a guide for the conduct of his life. He believes in sacrifices; not only the sacrifices that the Lord requires of us, but those which we must seek in order to offer them to him. This spirit of sacrifice—almost a reflection of the spirit that prompted man to sacrifice victims to the Deity—has brought conflict between him and his wife. "She loved her children with too passionate a love—as many mothers do," he tells Monsignor Lelli.

Diego Spina has had two children by Sara—Lucio and Lia. They were delicate and neurotic like their father. Diego sent Lucio to a seminary to prepare for the priesthood, and he put Lia in a convent where the child, her health neglected, was taken ill and ended by her legs becoming paralyzed. She is about fifteen, but looks like a child. Diego is sincere in his almost brutal belief that if we suffer we acquire merit before God. He refused to comply with Sara's wish that the two children live on their farm in the country where life would be more wholesome. Sara had recourse to the law; human justice decreed that the husband was right.

She left him, and went to live on one of their farms. It was not until two years later that she became the common law wife of Arcadipane, to whom she bore two children. She has cast away her expensive clothes and is now dressed like a peasant woman. Country life has kept her young and lovely, and she is beautiful in her simple attire. "Beautiful, yes, beautiful: she seems to be still in her twenties! As she passes by, radiant as the sun, everybody turns to look at her! A miracle!" So Cico expresses his admiration for her.

Sara's life on the farm has been very happy. She and Arcadipane live on the soil in a truly Franciscan fashion. They have cultivated every inch of Diego's farm and have made it wonderfully productive. They love the springs that bring fertility to their land and quench their thirst; they know suffering and joy through the travails and joy of the earth. Their two children, handsome and healthy, children of love and of nature, work with them. They live on the products of the land, and they send whatever part of the harvest they do not need to the town hospital, since Diego has refused to accept anything from them.

This is the situation when Diego suddenly decides to found a retreat for indigent people on the farm where his wife and her companion have lived for years. We learn of this plan through Cico, who comes to Spina's house saying that the devil must have told Diego to build that retreat. Cico, who calls himself "the Lord's tax collector," feels that his profession will now be ruined forever. He has been in the habit of going to wealthy people and asking them to pay to him the rent in advance for their home in the other world. He has been very successful as he has gone from door to door, reciting a long and monotonous poem, half religious and half humorous, in which his own poverty is contrasted to the wealth of the rich. As things are he will have to go to Diego Spina's retreat and people will say: "Now you, too, have a home. Why should we give you money?"

Cico voices in his queer, simple way Pirandello's perplexity over the problem of evil. In a theologically constructed universe, evil should have no place. Cico asks: "O Lord, but why? You give us teeth, and one by one you remove them; you give us eyesight, and you take it away from us; you give us strength and you take it away. Look, O Lord, how you have reduced me! Must we not bring back to you even one of the many beautiful things that you have given us? It will be a fine thing, a hundred years from now, to see before you figures like mine." Cico has been saying this in front of a mirror of a show window, giving utterance to the words of the little devil within him. Monsignor Lelli, who happens to pass, gives him the right answer: "You foolish one, God reduces you so that death may not be so hard for you to meet." But Cico retorts: "God could take away also our desire to eat when he takes our teeth away, and yet he doesn't!" Everybody laughs. Monsignor does not answer. This is Pirandello's way of putting a big problem in a small form.

The theme of resurrection and immortality is introduced in the play by the fact that Dr. Gionni brings back to life a white rabbit that belonged to little Lia. Diego, upon learning this, takes the animal away from her, in spite of her protests and tears, because it was evidence of something that clashed with his religious beliefs. Only God can give life or miraculously call us back from death to life. Dr. Gionni disclaims any power to perform a miracle, nor is he sacrilegious, for he says: "I can also consider science as an instrument of God. It is all a question of understanding each other."

That day Sara goes to Diego's house for the first time since they were separated. He still loves her. Only his stubborn nature and his unbending faith keep him away from her. Her serenity is in deep contrast with his excitement. The feeling of immensity that she had known through her contact with nature makes everything in that house appear dwarfed and old. The purpose of her visit is to tell Diego that their son Lucio has come back to her on the farm, determined not to become a priest. She begs Diego to relent. She too believes in Christ, but a Christ who gives life and not death and pain. She knows her children. Physically, they are like their father, but they have her temperament. They have been endowed with her spontaneous sense of life. When they lived closeted in the old, severe schools where Diego had sent them, they felt that they were being robbed of freedom and life, of sunshine and health. They are instinctive. Lucio has told his mother: "My life, when I was there in the seminary, was . . . smell, taste of incense, of wax, the taste of the holy wafer, and a fear of the steps that echoed inside the empty church."

Lucio's crisis is very scantily presented. It is clear, however, that the author wishes to bring out that a new faith has been born in Lucio's heart, which has urged him to go out into life and, following his mother's example, to earn his living by tilling the soil.

When Diego hears that Lucio has decided to give up the priesthood, he rushes out of the house to find him, is hit by an automobile, and dies. He has lain dead for three-quarters of an hour. Two doctors have certified to his death. Even an official death certificate has been issued. Dr. Gionni succeeds in resuscitating him with an injection of adrenalin.

Lucio, confronted by this portentous event, feels his faith grow stronger. The chief tenet of his new faith is his belief in immortality, but not in his father's sense. To Lucio, when the body dies it is only a bit of dust that returns to dust, but the spirit continues to live because spirit is eternal, and infinite, and it lives as such in us. The mistake that we make is to believe that the spirit may become ours during our existence. To Lucio God is "the eternal present of life."

Dr. Gionni wishes Diego Spina to be kept in ignorance of his death and consequent resurrection. He fears that the shock may be too great for him. Unfortunately, on the day that Diego Spina, Monsignor Lelli, and the notary go to the farm to dispossess Arcadipane and to deed it over to the new institution for the needy, the truth is revealed to the new Lazarus, quite accidentally. The notary jokingly asks Diego if his death certificate has been revoked. The whole truth comes out.

The effects of the sudden discovery of that truth are very serious. Cico is very severely jolted. If Diego does not know of his death, it means that beyond life there is nothing at all. So reasons the grotesque beggar, who throws his red cap on the ground and shouts: "Enough of your God, Monsignor. I'll keep my devil from now on. No one will fool my devil." As is to be expected, losing the idea of the traditional God makes him lose every sense of moral responsibility. Honesty, the law, the sacraments, everything falls with it. Even gentle Lia, with a wistful smile, as if talking to herself, says to her old servant: "What about the little wings, Deodata, that I was supposed to have in compensation for the feet of which I have been deprived down here? That's the end of my flight up there now."

In the town there is a great deal of commotion, and everybody looks upon the doctor as on a sorcerer. As to Diego, his reaction is stronger than that of the others because his faith was stronger. His whole world has crumbled and he finds himself standing angry and desolate on the brim of an abyss of nothingness. His neurotic temperament, formerly held in check by his religious beliefs and now a prey to murderous frenzy, leads him to attempt to kill Arcadipane, who is about to leave the farm. He and his little family were going to move to another place where they would find shelter and peace as before. Diego is half demented, and it requires the efforts of all to quiet him. It is only the personal, warm, deep religion of Lucio, together with the fact that he has again decided to become a priest, that changes Diego from violence to calm reasoning, and from reasoning leads him back to faith. "Where was my soul while I was dead?" asks the father. "In God, Father," answers the son. "Your soul is God, Father; and you call it yours; it is God, you see." Lucio explains that it is a miracle of science that Diego has been brought back to life again, but since "our soul is God in us, what do you expect a miracle of science to be except God's miracle when He wishes it to be performed?"

Lucio grows exalted as if a divine spirit has passed over him. He restores peace in the heart of his father. His mother continues to live with her companion and her new family. Little Lia is healed and she can move her paralyzed legs while they all stand in wonder before the manifestation of the new faith.

Lazarus is not a great play, although it is interesting as a document of the idealistic background of Pirandello's concept of life. There are two main themes in the play: one tortuous and torturing, represented by Diego Spina; the other calm and serene, represented by Sara. Had Pirandello stressed unduly the over-intellectualistic traits of Diego, he would have eclipsed or minimized the serenity of Sara, with the result that the play would have fallen short of the goal that the author, in a rare peaceful mood, had assigned to it. So Diego, who seemed destined to be an outstanding figure in the drama, remains half drawn and obscured by his antagonist, Lucio, when the author expresses through him his religious and idealistic feelings. Lucio, however, is an evanescent character, because the ideas he represents have a greater relief than his humanity.

The weakness of the play is in the flimsy theology with which Pirandello has replaced the old one. Lucio's beliefs are couched in terms not different from the many vague terminologies that are used to express the unthinkable. Fortunately for man, for religion, and, to a certain extent, for the play, he veers towards a practical content of faith which merges with what is basic in every religious teaching: the pragmatic value of faith. It might seem at first that the author has given expression here to the usual clash between faith and science—faith represented by Diego Spina; science by Doctor Gionni. Knowing Pirandello's attitude towards the power of sentiment, which, even if illusory, is a great force in life, we cannot expect a glorification of science by a man to whom a simple faith is of paramount importance. The play steers away from any intellectual interpretation of religion, and points towards the ideal life that Sara had found in the simplicity of the fields and in her love for Arcadipane. As the play develops, Sara is differentiated from both the abstract idealism of Lucio and the cruel theology of Diego Spina. In the serenity with which Pirandello clothes the life of Sara and Arcadipane there is the halo of a rustic idyl that bespeaks pure dream.

Inherently the play carries with it Pirandello's indictment of modern civilization as represented by the townspeople, by Diego Spina, and, in its religious aspect, by Monsignor Lelli. Sara had to break its laws to find her happiness. She had to leave her husband in order to find the Franciscan peace and simplicity for which her heart longed. Sara stands between civilized and primitive life; between capitalism and a vague form of communism; between Diego and Arcadipane, and she experiences loathing for civilization, for capitalism, and for Diego, while she finds a measure and rhythm of a happy existence in the normal and loving life that Arcadipane has given her.

The keynote of the drama is this natural life, the ideal of which the author presents to his characters as a goal. In leading them there, he does not hesitate to break the law of man, proclaiming the law of nature and of God. For this reason Sara and Arcadipane are revolutionary souls in their elementary simplicity. Near the torment and complications of Diego Spina's mind and life, Sara and Arcadipane rise before us as the symbol of a pure and noble life that the author dreams for the few who have the courage to break the barriers of convention when convention is tainted by insincerity and denies us joy in the gifts of the earth.

Part Four

THE DRAMA OF WOMANHOOD

XXIII

Introduction

There logically arises at this point the question whether in the drama of Luigi Pirandello there are elements that interrupt his predominating pessimism, his tragic tension, his gloom, and the bitterness that transforms some of his characters into exalted marionettes.

Childhood is one of the fresh and fragrant flowers he has woven into the crown of thorns which he has placed over the brow of the mock king that is man. The voice of a child occasionally brings a soft and refreshing note into the din made by the excited words that echo in the plays; a soft hand steals into the tense hand of Pirandello's heroes, trying in vain to lead them to dewy meadows of asphodel where life is good and joyous. At times a child is presented in the light of an unfulfilled desire of a woman's life, and he opens a tantalizing vista before the person who longs to touch the velvety flesh of a baby or to hear the sound of a little voice that would have drowned all the harsh noises of life had her desire been realized. More often childhood is brutally crushed, as in *Six Characters in Search of an Author* or in *Tonight We Improvise*.

The theme of childhood naturally blends with that of womanhood, and they both belong to the constructive and positive stage of Pirandello's thought and drama. The naturalistic sketches present the author in the predominating rôle of a painter; the plays of "being and seeming" and the social plays emphasize Pirandello the humorist, as do some of the works considered in the section on "Art and Life." One notices, however, in some of these plays, that the author veers towards a more thoughtful and constructive outlook on life.

The aspirations of the heroines in most of the plays included in the present section are towards a life of purity which experience has denied them. It would be hard to prove that his earlier characters, the naturalistic Liolà and Micuccio, for instance, or the grotesquely exalted Father in *Six Characters in Search of an Author,* or the tragic emperor in *Henry IV,* aspired to a life different from the one which was assigned to them. The naturalistically conceived characters are not capable of imagining any state other than the one that nature and life have prescribed for them, while the characters treated with Pirandello's tragic sense of humor know only conscious exasperation of feelings, and to live in the inferno of their painful exaltation is the sole way by which life is made possible for them. Deprived of that exaltation, they are æsthetically maimed. In the plays of womanhood characters are no longer deformed by ludricrous postures and traits. The *motif* of building up oneself disappears, while illusion is given an idealistic and religious meaning.

This tendency is a direct derivation of the idealistic strain which we see encircling the gloomy and bleak waste of life, as Pirandello conceives it. There is in Pirandello's heart a hidden and repressed surge of sincere emotion and pathos, a longing towards peace and goodness, which he has succeeded in channeling into these plays. It is a natural reaction for a man who aspires—and a sensitive man aspires when he finds himself in a situation that oppresses him—to think of a life different from the one in which he is a tragic actor. If a man is deprived of imagination, he submits sheepishly to any abuse from life; if he is a highly sensitive and imaginative man like Pirandello, he reacts either by abandoning himself to bitter and broad laughter, or by giving himself to deep thinking. The result of this concentrated thought is the themes of womanhood and motherhood that have given life to the plays enclosed in this section: *As Well as Before, Better than Before; It Is Only in Jest; Either of One or of No One; Other People's Point of View; The Wives' Friend; Mrs. Morli, One and Two; Grafting;* and *The Life that I Gave You.* With the exception of Fulvia in the first of the above-mentioned plays, we find ourselves before constructive and positive personalities which mirror a less tormented state of mind than that we have noticed in previous plays.

The theme of womanhood centers predominatingly on

motherhood, the chord that has never lost its resonance in Pirandello's plays. No matter how perverted his women have become, how low they have descended, they have always kept in their hearts a little nook of purity and softness where abides the love for a child.

XXIV

The Turmoil of the Irrational

AS WELL AS BEFORE, BETTER THAN BEFORE

(*Come prima, meglio di prima*)

The play revolves around a husband who believed he could regain his wife's heart without appealing to the instinct of motherhood. The play takes us to a small town in Valdichiana, Tuscany, where one night a woman tries to commit suicide. Her husband, a celebrated surgeon from whom she has been estranged for thirteen years, is notified by the priest and arrives to find her near death. He also finds there a romantic lover who remonstrates at having an operation performed on her because he fears he will lose her if she is saved. The husband, using his rights as a husband and as a surgeon, operates on her and saves her life. Here a problem arises: Will she go back to her husband, or will she resume the irrational life that she has been living for thirteen years by passing from one lover to another?

The play is constructed on the interplay of rationality and irrationality in the life of Fulvia, the tragic woman whom we find convalescing in the Penzione Zonchi, her beauty ravaged by time and experience, her soul tortured and embittered.

Let us notice at the outset that Pirandello has built his play on very solid lines. He lays a great deal of stress on the accurate and detailed description of the setting with the suggestion of the Tuscan landscape with its stern fir trees, its peaceful green valley, and a winding road that leads to the boarding house at the summit of the hill. He also describes with a painstaking minuteness its interior, the furniture, its odd proprietor, Don Camillo, who at the same time is a priest, a school teacher, and the owner of the establishment; Roghi, a big, calm, well-to-do farmer, who has gone there to consult the famous surgeon about his sick little daughter; Don Camillo's sister-in-law and her daughter Giuditta. These people,

representing just the average humanity, are set in sharp contrast to the striking individuals who are the characters enacting the strange drama that is to unfold before us. Fulvia and
Mauri, the lover, are individuals who have left the quiet shore
of an ordinary, monotonous life, and have gone on the open
high seas, led there by passion, while tragedy swelled the
sails and the roar of the storm echoed in their hearts.

Fulvia, tired of being tossed and bruised, had tried to find
peace and oblivion in death. Her last lover has been Mauri,
a magistrate in a little town in Umbria, to whom she had
meant a new life, a sense of relief from the living death of
his existence with his peasant wife, nine years older than he,
and with his no less uncouth children, who called him not
"daddy" but "your honor" in homage to the title of magistrate that meant so much to their mother. Mauri appears at
the *pension* to claim Fulvia as his own, disputing her husband's right to renew possession of her. Mauri believes that
Fulvia has attempted suicide for his sake. Now he has given
up his position, his wife, and his children. He is ready to
dedicate himself to music, the unrealized dream of his life,
and Fulvia will be his forever. The whole presents a very
romantic combination: music, love, and a hopeless, blurred
future ahead.

Fulvia is partly amused and partly interested in the prospect of this sort of life for her. In sober moments she feels
detached from Mauri. Actually, he has been just one of the
many lovers she has had. When he enters the *pension* and
violently clasps her in his arms, telling her that she is his
forever, she looks at him, first with indifference, then with
surprise, finally with scorn, and says, pushing him away:
"Are you still here bothering me? . . . Why, I hardly know
you. . . . Oh, stop talking like that." Mauri has just said
that he has given her all his life. All his life when there has
been only a short erotic interlude between them! In her lucid
intervals he is to her nothing but an exalted sentimentalist,
not different from the numerous lovers who had uttered those
very words, leaving her uncertain whether they were deified
by her guiles or she was duped by their sincere folly. In this

case we cannot say that Fulvia is another woman now, and then draw a sharp line between the Flora as she was known when she lived as a prostitute, and Fulvia the redeemed woman.

Critics have played too high a stake on the element of double personality where Pirandello is concerned. Fulvia is tired of life, and she is disgusted with the filth that rises like a contaminating tide towards her and tries to stifle her. She has closed herself in a cynical coldness and aloofness. She is a pitiful and tragic human character. As such, she is very complicated, and Mauri has for her the appeal of the irrational, standing before her as the embodiment of the thirteen long years of wandering, gypsy-like life that she has lived since she left her husband. Therefore she is interested in Mauri too, since he stands in contrast with her husband who represents the rational life of a wife and mother to which she has to return if she forsakes Mauri.

Fulvia is presented as one "who has a visible disdain, and a true and deep hatred for her beautiful body, as if it has not belonged to her for a long time . . . not having ever shared, except with a fierce nausea, the joy that others have found in it." Her body has been the source of her tragedy. Her husband awoke in her perverted desires and made her feel unworthy of living in the purity of a home as a mother to a little daughter, Livia. She left him and wandered from city to city, passing from one lover to another, gradually lowering herself to the point of living with a mosaic worker who drank and beat her. Then she had known Mauri.

Here is Mauri: ". . . in his forties, dark, thin, with lucid and mobile eyes like those of a lunatic; almost joyous even in the deepest agitation, expressive. He speaks and gesticulates with that theatricality that is characteristic of an exalted passion, a theatricality warm and sincere, but which, at times, is conscious of itself to the point of almost seeing itself."

Life has also left deep marks and scars on Silvio, the husband: ". . . tall, in his fifties, bony, solidly built, wears gold-rimmed spectacles. He is smooth-shaven. The top of his head is almost bald, but long locks of blondish hair, discolored, fall in disorderly fashion on forehead and temples. He pushes them back from time to time and then holds his hands on his head, as if meditating. He has the air both distracted and turbid of a man who is going through a violent crisis of conscience, but wishes to hide it, so he stands there almost overcome by a deadly inertia, with a cold, empty, and resigned smile on his lips, and by an uncontrollable expression of mockery, a reflection of old, malignant passions not yet extinguished, although long subdued."

The background of the play is a tumult of passions that left these three human beings strewn on the bleak shore of disappointment and tragedy. Here again we find Pirandello's nausea for lust, a feeling that is reflected by the physical shuddering of poor Fulvia and the psychological incertitude of Silvio.

Fulvia is now forced to select either her husband or her lover. Her resolution to choose between them depends upon whether her husband can appeal to something noble and pure which still lingers in her soul, left unsoiled by all the filth that has contaminated her. In their masculine blindness both Silvio and Mauri advance only the arguments of responsibility and remorse, which are of no value to Fulvia because she does not recognize the validity either of Mauri's responsibility or of Silvio's remorse. She exclaims: "I am between a duty which I do not recognize and a remorse that I declare imaginary." She does not wish to be taken back by Silvio through pity. She spurns that pity. For thirteen years she has known what it means to be alone and unprotected against the onslaught of life. "I have lived for years day by day. I have lacked the most necessary things, and a tomorrow without certainty does not frighten me any longer. Destiny can try all its whims on me." There is only one feeling that links her to her past—her mother love for the little baby that she left when her revolt against her husband made her desert him and plunge into the whirlwind of a desperate life.

Pirandello at this point displays all the subtle quality of his art in presenting to us a Fulvia who inwardly is tender and delicate and passionately waiting for her husband to speak to her about her daughter, and outwardly appears insolent, daring, mocking, and cruel. She keeps flitting from her husband to her lover, at times being ruthless with one, at times with the other, flinging at Silvio's face his own shame, and mocking the sentimentality of Mauri, until finally Silvio mentions her daughter to her. Then she breaks down, with an overwhelming outburst of love and pity. She cries with a new voice, with desperate sincerity, almost dejectedly: "Alas! I have been here so many days with him like the woman that I used to be, with all my heart of long ago suspended there in my home, my heart of a mother, all these days waiting for him to talk to me about my daughter, saying to myself . . . Stay here so . . . stay here . . . now he is good! He has come, now he will speak of her to you. Now he will tell you of her." But Silvio sees in her only the woman of his desire and in his masculine blindness does not take hold of the only link that might have joined again the present and the past: Fulvia as a mother.

Following the dictates of his cold and calculating nature, he suggests to Fulvia that the only way by which she can return home is to go back as his second wife. She cannot go back as Livia's mother. He has told Livia that her mother died when she was a baby; that her mother was a saintly woman. The child has grown up worshipping the memory of a dead, saintly mother, her childhood overshadowed by that grief, in a home where celebrity and wealth did not bring the warmth that a mother gives to her child.

Fulvia returns home to her husband, but not to her daughter as the logic of her sentiment would require. Her hypocritical husband has been blind to this important point. Her tragedy begins as soon as she goes back under an assumed name, as an intruder, a hated intruder to her very daughter who worships the memory of her mother. The delicate poetry of the anguish of a mother constitutes the central part of the play. She cannot reveal herself to her daughter; she cannot go over to her child and clasp her in her arms, lost in the happiness of having found her again.

Livia is "serious, stiff. Her face clouds over every time she makes an effort to look at Fulvia. She is a little over sixteen."

We see her dressed in the deepest mourning because that day is the anniversary of her mother's death.

Fulvia's situation in her home and before her daughter is relieved of its tragic character by ironical happenings such as the anniversary of her death. She has to see Livia in deep mourning and hear that three masses will be said for the soul of the departed Fulvia. She is told that her husband, out of consideration for his present wife, is unwilling to go to church. This cruel irony ripples over the play and makes suffering deeper and more human.

In all this tragedy and anguish Fulvia is not the redeemed, angelic person that a sentimental writer might have imagined. A woman who has gone through what she has endured for thirteen years of contaminated soul and flesh could not have suddenly assumed virtuous qualities. At every moment the old self, held in subjection, attempts to reappear. How can it be otherwise when Livia hates and despises her? Her hostility gives Fulvia the sensation of being dead. She has dreamt of a beautiful and perfect life, and now her life is more irrational than when folly held her in its sway. She has had to give to Livia the old furniture which the latter has claimed because it had belonged to her mother. She has had to give her even the layette that she had made for her with her own hands, and she tells us: "To find it together with my clothes of that time, was for me . . . well, I cannot tell you. I plunged my face in it; I breathed in it the purity of the past; I felt it tangibly in me, here, in my throat—as a taste—I wept in it, and those tears washed my whole soul."

But she reacts from this state of deep and pure emotion with a sudden, strange, and mocking laughter: "My name was Flora. An ugly name, to tell the truth! The name of a dog. He [Silvio] calls me Francesca, by my middle name." As Fulvia's existence becomes harder and harder she reproaches her husband for the imposture and lie under which he has brought her home. That lie has solved Silvio's difficulties to perfection, but has made Fulvia's life unbearable. She cries: "We must kill this lie because I am alive, alive, alive. I have reached the point of believing that she is the daughter of the other one, of the dead one. It is fearful! A shadow that has become a reality, and what a reality! It has truly killed in me my maternal instinct for her."

The situation becomes more complicated when Fulvia discovers that she is going to be a mother again. This means a new life for Fulvia whose heart is starving for her child's love. Should, however, anything at all wound her in the love of her new baby, a gust of folly would seize her again. She soon finds out that Livia not only hates her but does not respect her as the mother of the unborn infant, upon whom she looks as an illegitimate child, the baby of a woman not legally married to her father. There had not been any need of a marriage ceremony when Fulvia had returned to her husband, so Livia, upon investigating the matter, through her faithful servant Betta, finds no record of her father's marriage. She conceives the greatest scorn for Fulvia, her own mother. When the latter returns home with her baby, Livia is more haughty, flippant, defiant, unconquerable than ever.

The appeal of the irrational comes on the scene again with Mauri, a wreck of humanity, nervous and dreamy, who has come to tell Fulvia that he cannot live without her. After a year of aimless wandering, feverish, almost near collapse, he has returned to the woman who has given him an unforgettable glimpse of what true love is, who has burned her memory into his flesh and soul. Mauri is determined to have Fulvia go back to him. He counts on her mother instinct that Silvio, the husband, had failed to take into consideration. His hopes are not in vain. When Livia, sure that Fulvia is nothing but a bold adventuress, bursts into a fit of rage and offends not only her, her own mother, but the little baby, Fulvia rebels and strikes at the one who has been responsible for that situation—Silvio. Fulvia leaves him.

The only tie between Silvio and Fulvia was Livia, but Silvio's fraud had destroyed the daughter in her. Having broken the formula that made Fulvia's presence in that house possible—her being unknown to her daughter—her life with Silvio comes to an end. Folly sweeps over her and carries her towards the open spaces where life is free and tragic.

When she is compelled to reveal to Livia that she is really her mother, she realizes that logically she has no place in that home any longer. She breaks away from the unnatural situation that her husband has created for her, and lets the irrational take her back into a life that she hopes will give her full possession of her motherhood: her newly born child. This time she will leave Silvio, but she will take her child with her. It will be "as well as before, better than before." She turns to Mauri and cries: "My baby! Go! In the other room! My baby!" And then she announces to Silvio: "I shall take Livia with me this time! Tell her!—Yes, I shall take her alive—and mine!—With me, alive!—We shall go towards life!—Defying fate!" The real Livia is the new child. The other was dead.

Had Pirandello allowed Fulvia, after revealing her identity to Livia, to continue to live with Silvio, the play would have fallen into the depths of commonplace. The inner logic of the situation compels Fulvia to abandon her husband and Livia, the puppet he had engendered, in order to punish Silvio for ignoring the tie that existed between mother and daughter.

As in many of Pirandello's plays we find here a strong element of social satire determined by the author's rebellion against anyone who attempts to establish a relation without sentiment and feeling. The villain of the play is Silvio, the husband, and not Mauri. Mauri had been capable of finding in Fulvia's love a source of nobler feelings than had the tortuous Silvio. The rebellion against cold, ironclad forms of life is voiced by Mauri when he wishes to unmask the stately composure of his rival: "You could teach me that all depends on the first time we take off before everyone's eyes the dress that society has forced on us." That dress stands for the veneer of civilization, for customs, habits, laws, that do not sink very deeply into man's consciousness. The playwright flays here the large part in our social behavior that is pure form with no adherence to our soul.

Pirandello calls this play a comedy, but it is a deep and stirring example of a tragedy on the theme of motherhood.

XXV

The Form and Substance of Matrimony

IT IS ONLY IN JEST

(*Ma non è una cosa seria*)

This play which is one of the most spontaneous and charming that Pirandello has written, takes us to a *pension* run by a self-sacrificing and self-effacing young woman named Gasparina. She is a gentle figure drawn from life. The dramatist has embodied in her the silent sacrifices of countless women who in running a boarding house follow their womanly instinct in making a home for the men who live in it. She is "very thin, a little worn, neglected. She would be most vivacious if suffering, anguish, and the sadness resulting from what she has gone through did not repress the spontaneity and liveliness of her temperament and personality, and did not give her a humility, smiling and resigned."

Pirandello has woven a lovely and touching story around her, enclosing it in the frame of a drama. Her youth and beauty have been painfully obscured by drudgery. There are devotions that wither, affections that enslave and destroy. She graphically but truthfully describes herself when she says: "I am an old donkey accustomed by now to whippings and to all the jerks of the halter." Some of the guests have taken advantage of her goodness, as they often do with submissive people, and she has often been in despair, not knowing how to meet expenses. Her life at the *pension* has been very difficult. Not that her lodgers ever tried to make improper advances to her, for no one had ever thought of her as a woman. She was only the person who prepared the meals with the cook, supervised the serving, attended to the bedrooms, bought food, and received the payments when they were made. Her youth—she is only twenty-seven—is vanishing, fading away like a useless gift, and she is no more preoccupied with it than are the bachelors around her. She says to one of the guests, a woman school teacher: "Do you think that I am a woman? I am a mop. Everyone can, if you will excuse the comparison, clean his shoes with it."

One of the guests, the irascible, gesticulating, and shouting Grizzoffi, even calls her "Gasparona" with the derogatory connotation that the suffix "-ona" gives to a person's name. She was too busy to mind that! Grizzoffi was always punctual in paying, anyhow! The one who resented any insult to Gasparina was Signor Barranco, "a middle-aged man still in his prime, wealthy, with a big nose, very devout, usually silent, rather gloomy, yet with shy and timid eyes." He protects Gasparina and has often paid out of his well-garnished pocket what other people owed the poor girl. His wife died a few months before and left him all alone. Who knows that he might not have some intentions concerning Gasparina, that model of perfection and virtue? For a wife of a man of his age she might do, after all.

The inhabitants of the *pension* are rather striking, and the author has made the most of their peculiarities, putting them into comic relief. There is a professor of pedagogy, who, believing that nicotine is harmful, delights in inhaling the perfume of an excellent cigar that is being smoked by another guest, the irascible Signor Grizzoffi. Curious and witty repartee is heard between the old professor and Grizzoffi, as well as between Grizzoffi the woman-hater, and Gasparina's defender, the dignified Signor Barranco.

On this day there is unusual activity in the boarding house. Flowers have arrived and have been beautifully disposed in the dining room. Several bottles of champagne are ready to contribute to the feast. The most important of Gasparina's guests, Memmo Speranza, is returning from the hospital after having been wounded in a duel by the brother of a girl that he jilted. Memmo, the life of the place, is happy, young, handsome, always in love, and always changing partners. Girls are his weakness; he sees them and he cannot resist them. What is worse, he takes them seriously, proposes, and becomes engaged. From the time that he was nineteen up to now, when he is thirty, he has been engaged twelve times. "They surround you," he confides to us, "envelop you, inebriate you, make you lose your head. . . . They make you swear that you will love them *forever*. They even force you to swear it before father and mother." That is very dangerous for a man like debonair Memmo. "I am like straw," he says. "I catch fire immediately, I am a big flame, then I am drowned in smoke. Marriage is not for me. Love, yes. Marriage, no." He has been thinking very seriously of the sad plight of man, who falls in love, thinks that he will love a woman forever, and then is not allowed to change his mind when he realizes that his love is dead. With the mortality rate of his love affairs, after the danger he had gone through, he has to find some method of preventing the recurrence of a situation as serious as the one the escape from which they are celebrating today in the *pension*.

The banquet is offered by him (to whom money does not matter at all) to announce that he has found a radical remedy. Since he has been at death's door because of his impetuosity in proposing to girls, he wants to put himself in the situation of not being able to do so again. His plan is to marry a woman to whom marriage will only be a formality. In the midst of the hilarity of the guests, Memmo announces that this woman is Gasparina. At first Gasparina laughs, and so do the guests. One of them wagers Memmo a thousand *lire* and a wedding party that he will not marry her. Signor Barranco, in his moral susceptibility, is highly indignant. So is Grizzoffi, but this is a natural reaction in a man who is separated from his wife and hates marriage. Memmo, after accepting the wager, declares, "I know that one cannot fool with marriage. I have risked my life to escape it and I marry Gasparina exactly for this: to guard against the danger of getting married in earnest." Memmo will mortgage his name so that he will not be able to dispose of it by offering it to women with whom he might fall in love in the future.

After all, why not enter this novel scheme of marriage? Gasparina will be taken away from the inferno of the boarding house. She will have a small home of her own, a little rustic villa outside of the city walls, a nice garden, vegetable patch and chicken yard, the little dream that consoles the heart of every city dweller. "You will live there very happily, with a nice allowance and entirely free to do as you wish," promises Memmo to Gasparina.

Barranco and Grizzoffi, indignant at this awful jest and mockery, leave the table. The others celebrate with champagne the promise of this strange marriage. After a final toast to the bride and bridegroom, Memmo and his friends go to the city hall to arrange for a legal marriage. Gasparina in her usual submissive way has yielded, but she knows that it is a joke, for she says to her faithful maid, Rosa: "It is only in jest, Rosa."

Two months have passed, and Gasparina, in her rustic abode, with rest and tranquillity, seems another person. The fresh country air and the warm sun have given her color. She dresses well with modest taste. She still has her humble air, but one feels that her natural vivacity begins to reappear, although still suffused with sadness. She goes to visit Memmo in his apartment in the city for the first time. She wants to tell him that he is free to break the contract if he wishes. She has heard that he is still in love with the woman whose brother wounded him. Indeed Memmo, having been told that the girl had taken his part against her brother and left her house as a protest against her family, has felt the old love rekindled. Sentiment, his congenital weakness, has flowed back into the empty shell in which he had enclosed himself and is disturbing him. As far as Gasparina is concerned, he can break that shell, be free if he wants to. Gasparina also tells him that Signor Barranco, the middle-aged guest of her former *pension*, who looked after her so carefully, has something to tell him. The tender-hearted, ready-to-weep Signor Barranco has decided to marry her. He studied the girl while in the boarding house and admired her honesty, her sweetness, and sacrifice. He is growing old. Who will look after him in his old age?

Gasparina is now divided between a prosaic marriage with Signor Barranco, which will save her dignity, and the continuation of this mock marriage which begins to weigh on her

because the youth, the looks, and the temperament of Memmo
have wakened love in her humble heart.

After three months when the bonfire of Memmo's love for
his ex-*fiancée* has died out, Gasparina sends for him. He arrives at the villa and is struck by the charm and beauty of
Gasparina. That day she is truly beautiful. It is a June day.
"Her face is flushed. She wears a large straw hat and is holding three beautiful roses and a pink in her hand; she is truly
a flower." When Memmo suddenly realizes how beautiful his
wife is and hears that Signor Barranco wants to marry her,
he proclaims his love for Gasparina, and thereby the pure
form of marriage becomes a full reality.

In its structure the play pivots on the idea of substance and
form in marriage, but the soul of it, what gives beauty and
life to it, is the gentle figure of Gasparina on whom the author
has lavished his sympathy. Under the sadness of the vol-
untary beast of burden, he has found the woman, the grieving poetry of femininity. There is much pathos in her words:
"Yes, I'm getting married, but it is only in jest."

Memmo Speranza's marriage, viewed in the light of what
Pirandello calls logical, is a triumph of logic. What is human
is voluble, changing, chaotic, and therefore illogical. What
is logical is the result of abstraction from life, reducing life
to a pure "case" in which you can arrange everything without the interference of sentiment, just as on the chess-board
men and kings are arranged for a game. Pirandello humorously hints that from the standpoint of logic the perfect marriage is the one from which every emotional element has been
removed. Such a marriage would come the nearest to the institution as it exists in the books of the law or of sociology.

Before the charm and goodness, even the beauty, gently
veiled with melancholy, of Gasparina, the clever humorist
disappears and the man with the gift of human sympathy
takes his place. Then we see that Pirandello is fully conscious of the futility of abstractions because if we indulge
in abstractions, we do not live. He knows that the great tragedy of man consists in the fact that he plans his existence according to logic, while he must live his life as sentiment. With

a woman like Gasparina there is no need of abstraction. Memmo does not need to close himself in the chilly mold that he has artificially thrown around himself. Gasparina's charm and gentleness will teach him the way to the fullness of life. So the author lets Gasparina and Memmo be happy in the sway of sentiment, perhaps smiling like a father on his daughter's wedding day when the smile is not always entirely joyous.

XXVI

The Purifying Force of Motherhood

EITHER OF ONE OR OF NO ONE

(*O di uno o di nessuno*)

The *motif* that has often appeared in Pirandello's plays —that of conceiving motherhood as a purifying element in a woman's life—is deliberately and clearly resumed in *Either of One or of No One*, a comedy presenting an exquisite study of the soul of a poor prostitute. Apparently humorous, the play hides Pirandello's customary depth of mind and sympathy of heart for human misfortunes.

The play revolves around Melina, a poor young prostitute whom two young clerks, Carlino and Tito, invite to go from Padua, their home town, to Rome. They rent a room for her and gradually she becomes a sort of housekeeper and wife to them both. Having a little room of her own, being provided with food, with no worries, she blossoms again like a rose. She is like a mother to the two boys, darning their socks and keeping their clothes pressed. For four months the three have been very happy, quietly happy, because Melina has a halo of sentiment for them. But something has suddenly happened that has disturbed the rhythm of their existence.

Carlino, in his calmer temperament, and Tito, always ready to fly off the handle, have spent the whole night discussing this perplexing matter, and they are still doing so late in the morning. Their landlady, at one time very affable, is furious now that the hopes of marrying her daughter to one of the two young men have been shattered by the new development. That morning she takes the opportunity offered by the fact that the electric light is still lit in their room to express her resentment against them. It is a bad morning to start a quarrel, since the two young men are facing a situation unprecedented in their lives. They are expecting Merletti, a lawyer friend, to help them out of their difficulty.

240

The play hints that we should always go beyond appearances before we pass judgment on our fellow-men. Upon hearing that two young men have called a prostitute to Rome, our morals would be outraged. Pirandello, following the continental point of view that most young men have such contacts, wishes us to feel that those two have been prompted to call Melina to Rome not only by lust but also by a feeling of affection that redeems to a certain extent their passion. Sentiment, however, is what brings trouble to Carlino and Tito.

Merletti, the lawyer, represents opinion as formed from judging by appearances, which opinion, as such, has a generic character. He does not know what has prompted Carlino and Tito to act as they have, nor does he know anything about Melina, and yet he calls their action foolish. He has a theory of his own about matters of love; there is safety in numbers: "Four, eight, ten, if you wish. Why not? But not one, as you had," he states. Merletti, however, discovers very soon that those two poor boys had felt the need of a little affection, and that had prompted them to make their unusual arrangement. Merletti, a large man, healthy, boisterous, and jovial, coldly analyzes them: "Touch little birds under their wing; they keep there the warmth of the nest where they found shelter before they learned how to fly. You have not been able to detach yourself from your distant home town. That's why you live together, still bound by your memories of the intimacy of your homes up there. You are ashamed of those memories, as of a weakness that, once revealed, may make you ridiculous—so you put on a serious air."

Although the boys do not like to hear that, it is the truth. Carlino, the more spontaneous of the two, confesses that one night when they were all alone in Rome and very sad, the name and image of Melina floated before his mind. Why not have her come down from Padua? She was so good, so humble, so sweet. They wrote to her and the girl had come. She was very thankful to them for taking her out of her horrible and sordid life.

Merletti has to adjust a very grave case of conscience. Melina has confessed to Carlino that she is going to become a mother. Merletti breaks forth into an uproarious laughter upon seeing the two boys caught in that difficult and really unsolvable situation. He laughs at "the buffoonery of nature, for the thing in itself," while Tito is furious and threatens him with violence. Merletti tries to appease the menacing Tito by explaining his mirth: "Don't you see? You thought that you had fixed everything perfectly, wisely, but nature came along and turned everything upside down. You believed that you had thought of everything and, as if from a wonder-box, nature suddenly springs up with a baby in its arms and sneers in your face. Ha! Ha! Ha! You had not thought of this."

After the irresistible but sympathetic laughter of Merletti subsides, the serious implications in the play begin to loom: What are they going to do with that baby? Will they resort to an illegal operation? Will they allow Melina to keep her baby? And who is the father?

The latter question assumes an amusing tone when Carlino and Tito attempt to solve the riddle on the biological basis that the stronger of the two is the father. Carlino goes in front of the mirror, looks energetic, feels his muscle, puts on a scowl, puffs out his chest. Both he and Tito go out without any overcoat, although it is winter, in order to prove which is the stronger. The test costs Carlino a serious cold that keeps him in bed for nine days.

Melina, not having seen him for such a long time, goes to visit him. She is motherly and sweet. She has gone out to buy something for the baby. She wants to buy everything herself. She feels proud that she can provide for the child with the money that she earns sewing for rich ladies. In her spare time she has learned how to read and write, and she has bought a sewing machine. It is a new life for her, full of intimate satisfaction and contentment. Carlino is loath to destroy her newfound happiness, but he feels compelled to tell her that, since the paternity cannot be established, the only solution is to send the infant to an institution. Poor Melina rebels at that idea: "But it belongs to me!" she cries. "That is out of the question! The child will be born and I shall bring him up—

keep him with me—he is my child." Since neither Carlino nor
Tito can assume the responsibility of the child, she will take
the responsibility herself, completely. She cries desperately:
"Don't you understand that now that I have learned how to
live so, I cannot go back to my former life?"

In her tenderness for the child, who is her redemption, the
girl stands higher than the two men, who are touched neither
by the pathos nor by the moral force of the situation. They are
only preoccupied with the responsibility of the child, responsibility they feel they cannot assume until it is known who is
the father. As far as they are concerned, the child will have
to go to an orphan asylum. Melina rises in defense of her
baby: "Then in order not to feel that responsibility, to free
yourself of it, what do you want to do? Throw him away?
When I am here, his mother, who wishes to keep him for herself? Would you assume such a responsibility—which is a
crime, a true crime towards a child who is yet to be born—
merely because you want to take into consideration another
responsibility that you do not have and that you cannot have,
since it is impossible to know to which of you the child really
belongs?"

Melina tries to make them realize that to condemn an innocent child to be the child of nobody is unjust and selfish. Their
philosophy, cruel and unbending, stands out against the nobility and spirit of sacrifice of the mother: "I came to tell you
that I ask nothing of you, that I do not wish anything at all."
But the two men insist, appealing to the common practice of
society, and demand for Melina's baby the penalty that society inflicts on innocent infants for the guilt of their parents.
The title of the play echoes, fraught with an ominous meaning: *Either of One or of No One.* If it cannot be determined
who the father is, then the child will have no father and will
have to go where men herd the innocent victims of their lust.

To Melina the responsibility of the baby is a sweet burden; to them it is a punishment. Their punishment consists
exactly in this: that they do not have a baby although each is
tormented by the desire of calling Melina's baby his own. It
is punishment meted out by a just and modern judge.

Meanwhile hostility arises between the two friends, occasioned by the jealousy centering about the natural pride of wishing to be the father of the unborn child. They end by separating and hating each other. They never see Melina, although they offer to pay for her maintenance.

Melina is all alone when her baby arrives. She accepts her fate, happy in the sweet right of her motherhood. Often one life in unfolding exacts the price of another life. Melina is near death. She does not have any milk for her little one. She gets up, as pale as a ghost, sustained only by prodigious nervous strength, goes to the cupboard, takes a little piece of bread and, after wetting it at the sink, covers it with a cloth, making a sort of nipple, and gives it to her hungry three-day-old baby to suck.

Merletti comes to see her. She has begged him to find Tito and Carlino whom she has not seen since the time she discovered that her baby was coming. She wants to entrust the baby to them: to make them swear before God that they will not send him to an orphan asylum. Death is good to Melina's baby and to her. She dies in peace, knowing that her child will be cared for.

In a neighboring villa, in order to save the life of a mother, it has been necessary to sacrifice the child. That bereft mother will have Melina's bereft baby. He will be happy with the happiness that Melina provided for him with her life. Tito and Carlino will go on, and they will not forget, it is to be hoped, the pale girl who had found in motherhood a source of the elevation that society had denied her. Melina had given her son her family name: Nini Franco. Now he will have Signor Franzoni's name. So nature unfeelingly gives and takes, and is not concerned with the heart that rejoices nor with that which writhes in pain.

This play to some extent illustrates that undercurrent of moral sensitiveness which is one of Pirandello's most distinct characteristics. Pirandello shows the immorality of the situation existing between Melina and the two men by forcing us to ponder over the fact that a child has been born out of that lax way of living. The impelling moral sense is quickly wakened in the girl. Neither of the two men can continue to consider Melina an instrument of pleasure now that she has been made holy by motherhood.

Pirandello has entrusted Merletti with the task of representing him. Tito says of him: "It is no use talking. He absolutely dissects me! He absolutely dissects me! I, who within myself feel sure of my judgment, of my sentiments, cannot communicate with him." Merletti does not possess the reserve that characterizes Pirandello, but he is as sympathetic with the two boys as Pirandello is with his characters. He understands perfectly their plight, although he is moved to laughter upon seeing them caught by nature in a trap that promises no freedom. Merletti's laughter is his salvation: "It may be that I am a buffoon—yes—but since I am one, and nature is one also, I burst out laughing at myself—of my own accord. You, so serious, get hurt and make people laugh at you."

There are two points of view contrasted in the play: that of Merletti and that of Tito and Carlino. Merletti is a crude and heartless fellow with his theory of safety in number where women are concerned. The other two strive very hard to clothe their deeds with sentiment and to appear loftier than Merletti. Yet, in a situation which was *ex-lege*, the method advocated by the carefree lawyer was saner and less harmful to all concerned. In the end we find Merletti near the dying Melina, and Pirandello makes him appear in a better light than do the two sentimental young men who had not the moral strength to solve the situation which they had created.

It would seem that at first the author is going to let events be shaped by Merletti's proposed solution of sending the child to an orphan asylum, but as the play progresses the ruthless law set by Merletti softens into the more human treatment that is accorded to Melina's baby by the sympathy that her author has felt for her.

XXVII

The Power of Passive Resistance

OTHER PEOPLE'S POINT OF VIEW

(*La ragione degli altri*)

This is the touching story of a woman condemned to barrenness, who bears in silence her husband's relations with a former sweetheart, of whose baby he is the father. For years Livia Arciani has known that her husband Leonardo has had another home with Elena and their daughter Dina, but she has refrained from any protest because she felt that she had no right to deprive him of being a father. The play pivots around the sentiment of motherhood which has been denied Livia and which spells tragedy for Elena when circumstances compel her to give up her child.

Leonardo is a superficial man with literary aspirations that are made possible by his wife's wealth and long-suffering nature. He is an art critic for a paper financed by a deputy who expects a political victory in the parliament. Leonardo has been engaged, not for his literary merits, but merely because he, as Livia's husband, is the son-in-law of a man whose help the deputy sought.

There had been quiet, happy days in the life of Livia and Leonardo until one day there came a letter addressed to him. They read it together. "He had no secrets from me," Livia tells her father, remembering those days with regret and longing. The letter was from Leonardo's cousin, Elena Orgera, to whom he had been engaged and who just for a whim had refused to marry him. Now she is a widow and, being in need, she has turned to him for financial help. "I myself insistently urged Leonardo to send it to her. How could I suspect? But not even he, not even he, suspected then what was to happen."

Pirandello gives a dismal picture of the events that led Leonardo and Elena to their wrongdoing; of the cold attitude with which their relationship began; of the feeling of reciprocal indifference that enveloped their lives as soon as the inevitable monotony set in.

Elena, in looking back over the past, realizes that she should not have asked Leonardo to help her. She herself does not understand how they have become lovers: "What joy can be found in what has been dead for so long, crushed under the weight of dejection, need, detachment? Everything is almost over before it begins." This is the attitude towards passion that Pirandello lends to many of his characters. It is a disillusioned coldness. The misfortune of Elena and Leonardo was due to the fact that a child came to them. Naturally that established between the lovers a strong bond of necessity and resignation. Even Livia, the wife, recognized this bond, and bore in silence the wound to her feminine pride. The situation had been accepted by all three, just as one has to accept certain inevitable conditions in life: deformity, misfortune, death. It was not a happy situation, but it offered at least an appearance behind which Livia, as a wife, could bear her existence without losing her dignity. The true substance of family life was absent from her home, but that was her punishment for her barrenness.

All three, however, suffered. Livia had a husband only nominally and, as difficulties had increased, Elena and Leonardo had grown indifferent towards each other. Leonardo supported his mistress and his child with the money that he made at the newspaper, but that was not enough, and he had deteriorated mentally and physically. He had reached the point of looking on Elena as his punishment. Even his little daughter was a punishment and, cruel as that was, he had to admit it.

One day Livia's father, an old gentleman with very clear-cut ideas of right and wrong, and with the utmost respect for the letter of the law, goes to visit his daughter for a brief stay. Livia is determined to keep her unhappiness from her father. She does not do it for the sake of her pride, for the false pride of appearing contented when she was not. She is convinced of the futility of any attempt to remedy a situation that, to her, is incapable of solution.

She and Leonardo have moved for years in their aristocratic home without saying a word to each other, without mentioning the other woman, because they both have accepted the situation passively. The verdict of their lives is sealed.

Livia's father refuses to understand this when he becomes cognizant of the real situation. He blames Livia for her behavior from the very beginning, for her lack of suspicion of Elena Orgera, for having acquiesced so calmly, indeed supinely. He is likewise unable to understand Leonardo. Does he not have any conception of right and wrong? Does he not know that there is a remedy for everything except death? He, Guglielmo Groa, is ready to help him to rectify the situation—to give money to the other woman and make her disappear with her child, so that Leonardo and Livia can live together again.

There is in Guglielmo Groa the solid, unsophisticated, somewhat unfeeling type of the older generation—people with a clear-cut concept of a perfect universe created by God and, what counts more, guided by God. Death is their only unconquered enemy, and since they usually are long-lived they comfort themselves with the thought that they have even fooled death. They have established the independence of their country, they have improved it greatly economically, they have built roads and railroads. What is there that could stand in the way of a successful man? Guglielmo Groa finds himself for the first time before two human beings with an entirely different psychology and with a point of view that he simply cannot fathom. He concludes: "I must say that you are both crazy."

Here is the situation as it appears to Livia: "The wrong is over, paid for, and only its consequences are a punishment for him." Livia inwardly feels sorry for her husband. She has seen him slowly disintegrate. She cannot condemn him for not leaving his daughter to return to her: "If he had abandoned his daughter because convinced of not being able to keep her, and had returned to me, to the comfort of this home, he would have inspired in me loathing, horror. Do you understand now?" To her Leonardo went into that trap unwittingly, as a man falls prey to the tricks that nature plays on him.

She only feels sorry for him and she calls herself partly to blame for what has happened. Leonardo wanted a child. She could not give him one. That was why he had gone to Elena. Livia's reasoning is determined by her own longing for a child. The great tragedy of her life is not to have had a baby. All through the play she makes it clear to Elena, to Leonardo, to her father that when she married it was not for a husband, but for a baby. She lent her own feelings to Leonardo. It was not a stupid policy. She did not destroy that sentimental thread which at times is stronger than love and hatred.

Leonardo is utterly passive. He has reached the point of having to admit that it is useless to investigate human actions: "Right? I tell you quite frankly that for me there isn't any, that it is useless to accuse myself or excuse myself. I recognize my wrong, and since I have been punished I recognize that my punishment is just and I don't complain." He says this with cold sadness, convinced and resigned. Leonardo is tied to Livia by the tie of marriage, as a husband. He is tied even more strongly to Elena because of the child. Livia's father is the only one who refuses to admit that the situation is hopeless. Leonardo's conclusion as they discuss the matter is this: "Nothing, nothing. You can do nothing. It is entirely hopeless, believe me."

Livia's father still cannot understand. He gets a glimpse of the truth when Livia cries to him: "He has a daughter, father. He cannot listen to reason." Only then does the old gentleman realize that there are situations in which to reason or to follow the dictates of reasoning is perfectly useless, and he goes over to the point of view of Pirandello to whom reasoning is an element that normally precedes our actions. It is entirely useless to reason after the situation has come into existence. Right and wrong are splendid elements, but they are truly decorative and external when you face a situation that holds you in its deadly grip and does not let go.

Neither Livia nor Leonardo can see those elements in the surge of the events in which they are caught. It is no help to think that they are married, that Leonardo should not have left Livia to go with Elena. "Words, Father, words! I neither defend him nor accuse him. I see myself, Father, what I have lacked. Where children are, there is the home. And he, here, does not have any children!" She is helpless towards her husband because of this belief. She cannot desire to have him abandon his daughter.

The visit of the father has had only the effect of precipitating the crisis. It has been put up to Leonardo to choose between his wife and his daughter. Leonardo, as is to be expected, has gone with his child. The father's visit was responsible for another situation—Leonardo's dismissal from the newspaper. Now Leonardo is penniless, without any love for his wife or for his mistress, alone with his little daughter whom he adores but cannot support.

Leonardo goes home to fetch some papers and finds his father-in-law ready to leave, alone. Livia has remained loyal to her husband, faithful far beyond what he deserved. To her a wife is always a wife. Leonardo, touched, tells her that his gratitude to her is all that he possesses now. Livia stands before him not as a crushing and bruising embodiment of perfection, but as a gentle, though firm, woman who is full of understanding. "I know that you understand. You can spurn me, but you understand why I am so." Elena has shown him the door: "You are free to go whenever you wish—why not? Let us put an end to this. There is the door." A mistress is always a mistress, and when support is lacking, she will always turn the man out. There is no tie to keep them together.

Livia looms nobler and nobler before him. She has never lost her dignity. Her silence under the blow that had crushed her is a splendid display of courage. When she sees the plight of Leonardo, especially of Leonardo as a father with a daughter he is unable to support, she decides to go to see Elena and tell her that the only way out of the situation is to let her have the child. The scene between the two women is a beautiful one, for Pirandello has uncovered all the love and anguish that nestles in the heart of a mother and has revealed how deep is a woman's longing for a child.

Livia finds Elena and her daughter together in a poor, shabby room. Little Dina wants to play "country" and her father has gone to buy her toys; trees and sheep and a shepherd and his dogs. When, after a painful, tortuous introduction, Livia tells Elena the reason for her visit, the mother rebels: "What do you want? My child? I shall shout for help." Livia makes her realize that until now she has been the one who has taken into consideration other people's points of view—Elena's point of view. For that very child, for Dina, Elena's child, she had given up her rights in her husband: "I know too well that there is something stronger than any right of mine." She now appeals to the mother to give up her right as a mother. Livia speaks not only of right but also of duty, of necessity: "There is now a necessity that forces itself on everyone and denies the right of all: mine, the one that he may have to his child, your own right; to make us face only duty, his duty towards the child and your own, and the sacrifice that it imposes on all of us: including me, for the very reason that I have recognized it."

The solution is a terrible one, but it is the only possible one: she, the mother, must give up her little one, blonde and rosy, that the child may legally have her father's name and live in happiness, even luxury.

It is poor Elena's punishment. "Don't you understand that this is the wrong, the true and only wrong that you have done, not to me—leave me out—but to your very child, born here, in your sin? This wrong, with him the father, you the mother, this requires now a sacrifice that neither of you wishes to make."

Elena is skeptical as to the great interest that Livia takes in her child. She is resentful, even scornful. Livia then allows her to peer into her agonized heart. She has suffered the most cruel pain that a woman can suffer, the humiliation of barrenness. She has longed in vain for all that a child means to a mother. "I should be not a mother, but a slave to your child. Don't you understand that I am here before you, conquered, and that you win if you make the sacrifice? I should worship your child because she is the only thing I lack, and I should give her all of myself." Elena cannot understand, cannot see. It is her child: "I have given her life, my blood; I have given

251

her my own breasts. Why don't you think of this? She has come out of my womb. She is mine, mine." It is a cruel folly, but Livia insists that she has borne all those years of silence and repressed grief only because she knew that he, Leonardo, was a father. Now Elena must give back to her, not the husband, as she wishes to do (she does not want a husband in him), but the father, and to do so, the child must go with the father.

Leonardo returns with Dina's toys. He sides with the mother. Livia leaves. She will remain alone. Leonardo will have to stay with his daughter. Elena is uncertain. There is a life of struggle, of cold darkness for the pretty Dina, and Elena's own heart is uprooted. She wavers. The idea tempts and frightens her. Finally she yields. She goes to fetch a pretty hat for Dina, for she wants her to look pretty when she goes to her new mother. Leonardo seizes the child and flees. Elena comes back into the empty room. She understands. "Then she runs to the window and tarries there for a long time, gazing. Finally she draws back silently as if bereft of her senses. She looks with astonished, blank eyes at the child's toys on the table, sits near the table, realizes that she has the child's little hat in her hand, looks at it, and breaks into desperate sobs."

The play stresses the victory of virtue and silence—Livia's victory. She is one of those rare and truly virtuous persons who can sympathetically transform silence into a mighty force that works for right.

The antisocial strain is clearly in evidence in the play. However, only apparently is Pirandello against society and marriage. He is opposed to them only when they clash with certain fundamental human needs, such as, in this case, longing for a child. Pirandello is not against right and wrong. He is against a specific right and wrong. Here he is opposed to Livia's father because he failed to see that the key to the situation was the little Dina. For the sake of the recognized form of marriage and for the sake of his own daughter, he would have brushed the little girl aside unmercifully. To Pirandello the situation should be unraveled through the little daughter who had been born outside of the home and had to be brought into the home, even if the mother had to be sacrificed.

As the play develops we witness a conflict between the forces of nature and the laws of man. Leonardo in following blind instinct has exposed his child to the brand with which society marks illegitimate children. Pirandello, although he has to sacrifice that bit of commonplace, Elena, solves the problem by taking the child to the father's home, to the legal wife, thereby making the forces of nature subservient to the laws of man.

The play is projected against the background of modern life, rendered through the intrigues of a newspaper director who supports a deputy and keeps Leonardo on its payroll only because the father-in-law is a friend of the successful candidate. Modern life is envisaged through city life as revealed by the words of Livia's old-fashioned father: "But what is the matter? Hush here, hush there. May a person not say a word? One can do anything at all. Actions do not offend here. But as soon as one opens one's mouth—hush, hush, hush. Do words offend you? It seems that in the city only your ears become sensitive."

The strongest *motif* that detaches itself from the play is that only a child can keep two people together. The saying: "Where children are, there is the home," is a sort of proverb in Italy, and it returns more than once in Pirandello's plays. The home of Leonardo and Livia was unhappy because no child had come to them. They become reunited only when little Dina, even if born of another woman, comes to make their married life perfect. Pirandello states without any shade of doubt that Leonardo belongs where Dina is. He vindicates Livia as a reward for her understanding soul, for the long, agonizing silence with which she concealed her unhappiness. She had considered the points of view of others, and that resignation had been her strength and had vindicated her.

There is no feeling of exaltation in Livia's victory since it must be envisaged through the misery of poor Elena. Livia's victory is a victory without the blare of trumpets and the roar of an applauding crowd. It is rather a victory reached by the author's intellect even against his heart that is full of human sympathy for Elena, the only real victim, who pays the wages of sin with the sacrifice of her child.

XXVIII

The Loneliness of the Lofty

THE WIVES' FRIEND

(*L'amica delle mogli*)

Italo Siciliano [1] has called *The Wives' Friend* a comedy of modern corruption. Pirandello's sense of perspective applied to immorality does not react differently when focused upon present day or upon historically ascertained past. He has faith only in a mythical age of purity which in its indefinite contour makes that faith possible, although it escapes analysis. Purity is, to him, only an aspiration of the soul, of some mysterious particle of our being. Around it there is the terror and storm of instinct. That is true today as it was yesterday. *The Wives' Friend* is not, therefore, a play of modern corruption.

On the contrary, it is a play dealing with the tragedy of one who has been doomed to loneliness by the loftiness of her nature. It is dedicated to Marta Abba, the great actress, friend of Pirandello. One feels that the author has wished to express his admiration of the actress by lending her name to the heroine, the woman who has conquered the hearts of all the wives, and whom at the same time the husbands love also: Marta, tall and stately, veiled in the seriousness that her virtue casts over her lovely countenance. Her nobility and beauty strike us from the very first scene when she appears with a large bouquet of flowers in her arms: "She is most beautiful, with auburn hair, deep, sea-blue eyes, liquid, full of life. She is twenty-four years old. Her manner, not stiff, but most reserved, does not interfere with the pure expression of the noblest feminine grace. She dresses with exquisite taste."

The setting is in the Rome of today, among a group of friends of the upper middle class. Those who contribute to the action are four young married couples who are, men and

[1] *Luigi Pirandello*, p. 10.

women alike, dominated by the beauty and charm of Marta.
Her serenity is contrasted with the petty quarrels of husbands and wives who whirl around her, restless and dissatis-
fied.

Marta tries to keep peace among them. She had been the
confidante of her male friends when they fell in love with
their present wives; she had read their letters, often suggest-
ing the answers. When they got married, she prepared their
new homes for them while they were on their wedding trips,
and after they had settled down she tried to compose their
differences. Marta is the life of that circle of friends. Only
she keeps them together, as peaceful as couples can be.

They all live in the light that emanates from her. Away
from her, they quarrel, they are mean to each other, petty,
even cruel. As soon as they draw near her they fall under the
spell of her serenity. She is to look at; to worship also, but
this feeling abides only in a little nook in the husbands' hearts
that is unknown even to them. She is the one towards whom
longing goes in the form of an elusive regret for not having
married her. Most of the quarrels of these married couples
are the result of the fact that they all look upon Marta as an
ideal for the women to copy, for the men to compare with
their wives. How could they copy a woman like Marta? They
want to dress like her, to move like her, to act like her, and
they fail pitifully. The husbands, placed before the beautiful original and the dismal and grotesque copies, laugh, criti-
cize, make mean and cutting remarks. It is natural. One of
the husbands tells her: "You believe that you make our wives
more acceptable to us by inducing them to think, to act, to be-
have like you. They try to resemblé you and they reveal themselves unworthy of their model, awkward, stupid, clumsy,
miserable."

Why none of those men had not asked Marta in marriage is
a mystery and a cause of secret regret to all of them. Their
wives know it, and they all agree that the men showed very
poor judgment in letting the charm of Marta's beauty and
gentleness pass unheeded by them. Perhaps she had had no
time to think of herself and of her youth, absorbed as she had

been by her sincere and fervid concern for her friends' happiness.

The perfection of Marta is not of the stereotyped kind. She had reached the conclusion, very quietly within herself, that men and husbands do not seek what is noble and lofty in a woman, for she says: "I see very well how you want a woman to be! Well: just as you have dwarfed her—a monstrous shame. Your own vice and nothing else! Do not be surprised to hear me speak so. I am not one of those saintly persons who feign not to know anything at all. I am as I am, exactly because I know." She rebels at the fact that men see in a woman only the giver of sensual pleasure, blind to her deeper self: "Shouldn't this be a reward for you men, to have near you a woman, a real woman? The prize that no one must know, that is not revealed; that suffers, in the secret of her heart, of the joy that she gives, and in this suffering of hers is also a joy, a joy truly suffered from which life is born anew? The sweetheart and the mother, the sweetheart who becomes the mother, and who says, after patting the man's shoulder as one would a child: 'Enough now; be a man; do not see, in me and in you, only this.' "

That was the real reason why those men had never dared to propose to her. Marta was too lofty for them. Her reserve chilled their words on their lips. Each of the four husbands had found another mate, ridiculously inferior to Marta, and now they all bask in the lukewarm sentiment that bore resemblance to a flower that had not been allowed to blossom. Sometimes, this sentiment became tormenting because irreparable, and then there floated before them the picture of the life that might have been and had not been.

As is to be expected, Marta's four friends are differently affected. Two of them were resigned with the stupid composure of normal men in whom a wound of that kind is not constantly reopened by a vivid imagination. But one of them, Venzi, who is violent, restless, rather coarse, with a turbulent soul, loves Marta, and is as jealous of her as a person can be who can expect nothing.

Venzi, because of his irrepressible love for Marta, torments his wife and makes her very unhappy. Only Marta can place on the little heart of Anna Venzi the balm of her sympathy. Often Venzi tells his wife to put a new cosmetic on her eyelashes in order to enhance her eyes, and it hurts her so that she has to cry for pain. He laughs diabolically with laughter that shakes his huge frame, while in his eyes there is a dull light of desperation and hatred. He tells her to cut her hair short, only to laugh cruelly at her when she does so. Venzi is "about forty, of powerful build, especially in his chest, high shoulders, with a big curly head, a little gray at the temples, dark complexioned, clean shaven, still good looking, although too fat. He often grasps the lapels of his coat while dangling his head and rolling his turbid eyes almost in a childish way like a peevish or surly child. He dresses in black, carelessly."

Venzi is particularly upset now because Fausto Viani, a handsome, wealthy, distinguished, and amiable friend of Marta has just married, and while he was on his honeymoon she has prepared his home, revealing in every detail not only her exquisite taste but a personal sentiment for Viani that Venzi senses and resents.

Marta is very happy about the little nest that she has been able to prepare for her friend and his bride. A party is to be given in the new home to welcome back the newlyweds. Quite unexpectedly, Venzi goes to see Marta and disturbs the serene joy of her friendship for Viani.

Venzi in his usual diabolical manner makes the remark that the real mistress of the home is the one who has arranged everything with such perfect taste—Marta. They all agree that it is so and that it should have been so. Viani should have married Marta. There is a tense moment of uneasiness in the room, just as when a phrase or a word makes a deep impression on a person and may definitely influence his conduct, because it brings out into the clear light something that that person did not wish to confess.

It seems, in fact, that Viani had wavered between Marta and his bride for a long time; but then, like the others, had been too timid to propose to Marta. Marta laughs, blushes, denies, and resents the inference made by Venzi. She is happy only when they are happy, although, to be sincere, her rôle is not always without difficulties. It makes her happy, but there is also a tinge of sadness in her heart. Venzi has raised a little the veil that surrounds her soul.

Viani and his bride arrive. They are in quite a different mood from that to be expected of two young people returning from a honeymoon. Elena, the bride, is sick, terribly sick. She enters the home that Marta has prepared and refuses to see any of her husband's friends. She is nervous, upset, abrupt. She goes directly to her room. Marta is the only one who goes upstairs to her. As soon as Elena sees her she feels for her what all the other wives had felt—complete trust and faith. She is another addition to the choir of admiring wives that surround Marta.

Elena's illness is very serious. She is operated on, but her life is in danger since the removal of a tumor has not cured her. Her friends are worried. Her husband is distracted; Venzi is tormented.

Jealousy torments him. Suppose that she should die, then Viani would marry Marta. His jealousy suggests a diabolical plan to him: to make them all conscious of such a possibility. He sows a seed of suspicion in Elena's heart by making her consider what might happen in case she died. The house is ready, the house that Marta has prepared. Elena has to recognize that there is such a possibility. Her life becomes a torture because she has found herself capable of thinking such a monstrous thing of Marta and her husband; yet, she cannot remove that thought from her brain. Everything that Marta does for her, her attentions, her solicitude, her care, all is destroyed.

Venzi's is a novel way of vengeance and of torture: to transform into active forces the inner thoughts that everyone has at times when the irrational passes by us: black fluttering wings that touch our brains and leave a sense of cold in them. Venzi wants to take hold of the feeling of pure and noble friendship that exists between Marta and Viani and transform it into a conscious love, to make jealousy rise in Elena, to torment her and force Marta away from Viani.

Now that both Marta and Elena have been made alive to the possibility of an uncontrollable event that will take place after Elena's death, Venzi poisons Viani's mind, too, by making him see that deep in his heart he has thought of the possibility of marrying Marta, should his wife die. Why not? Marta is young, beautiful, exquisite. Now all three know. The stage is set for the tragedy of which his hopeless love for Marta makes Venzi the cruel stage director.

As Elena's sickness becomes more acute her torment increases too. She goes so far as to have Marta promise her that she will marry Guido Migliori, a handsome but uninteresting young man who has just asked Marta to marry him. She pleads: "Not for me! I believe you, I believe you! It is to remove from the head of that despicable man the thought that he has put here like a nail and which is driving me mad, killing me."

A few hours later she is at death's door. Pirandello places the husband before his dying wife and searches into his heart, and next to his grief for her agony, he discovers the nebulous, unrevealed thought entertaining without revolt the possibility of her death. It is a parallel case to the one already noted in *Each in His Own Way*, where a son confesses that after nine sleepless nights he has been led by exhaustion to desire that his mother were dead. In the case of Viani, it is not a question of his desiring Elena's death. He does not know whether her death would bring him a heartrending grief or the sense of freedom. As a matter of fact, he is distracted before the suffering of poor Elena. But a black wing, vampire-like, often beats in the endless abyss of human consciousness.

As long as Elena lives, Venzi hopes and waits, watchfully. If she dies, he will never allow Viani to marry Marta, never. As death is stealthily approaching, Marta and Viani are in a room adjacent to Elena's. Even their grief for the death of a human being so dear to them has been poisoned. Venzi enters the room unseen to witness his work of destruction. He moves like a thief. He is ready for anything. A few minutes pass. Elena is dead. Venzi shoots Viani and pretends that the latter has committed suicide. Marta goes over and a glance at Venzi reveals to her what has happened. She does not have any proofs. She can only weep and grieve over the only love of her life, a love that she would never have revealed to anyone, a secret sealed in her noble heart.

Venzi, with the intuitive power of jealousy, had surmised the truth. Marta loved Viani, but she would never have married him. A great confusion reigns in the house. The wives of her friends are determined to stay there with her, but Marta is a different person now. She turns to them and orders them to go out of the room: "I wish to remain alone. Leave me. I wish to remain alone, alone, alone." Such is the destiny of women like Marta, perhaps like Marta Abba, who are too lofty to be within the reach of man.

Pirandello's sympathy for Marta has led him to view the situation of modern women as a sad plight. They have to please men to get married. If they do not, even if they are as beautiful as Marta, they are doomed to loneliness. In this sense, Marta stands as an ideal of which her friends' wives are the ludicrous embodiment. It is natural that she should end as she did, sharing the lot of all ideals. Had she married Migliori, she would have been dwarfed into a placid nonentity.

This leads to another strong *motif* of the play: What will happen when something which might have been, that should have been, has not been? Tragedy can be the only result. Pirandello has made it arise from a natural, almost commonplace environment, in which Marta stands out very much as Beatrice, a dream of beauty and virtue, stood out among the women that Dante knew. Pirandello has here taken the place of Dante. May it be that Marta stands in the place of Beatrice?

XXIX

Where the Children Are, There Is the Home

MRS. MORLI, ONE AND TWO

(*La Signora Morli una e due*)

Mrs. *Morli, One and Two* is a comedy in which a woman, divided between the egotism of two men, finds again the unity of her life in her love for the little girl she had by her second mate.

The comedy is based on the idea that we are different with different persons. We are light hearted with some people, and as solemn as owls with others. This was the case with Evelina Morli who had only been joyous and carefree with her husband, Ferrante, while she had always been serious, silent, and subdued with her lover, Lello Carpani. Pirandello humorously and somewhat devilishly has inverted the rôles usually given to husbands and lovers. He has imagined Ferrante, the husband, full of life and mischief, always ready to take pleasure wherever he finds it, while he has fashioned in Carpani, the lover, a cold, stilted, and formal individual.

It may be accidental, however, since Evelina had married Ferrante when very young, and had been abandoned by him, leaving her with a little boy after five years of happy and almost irrational life. She had gone to a well-known lawyer, Lello Carpani, who saved her dowry and then made her his mistress. After the first stir of scandal, the best society of Florence had accepted Evelina because of her reserve, her gentleness, her seriousness. Lello had composed her as he had composed himself; he had made her over; he had taught her the correct etiquette, and thereby Evelina had won the respect of society.

Lello was one of those individuals who always assume a dignified air before the world for the sake of their profession. He had had the somewhat romantic youth usual in people who have literary leanings. Then the profession had come, and it had covered youth and poetry with the dignified robe of the law; not altogether, however, since because of Evelina he had defied the conventions of society. We are told that his almost conquered sentimentalism can "still be perceived through a peculiar little smile of his, and from the manner with which he passes his hand over his hair, which used to be very abundant and now is very scanty, but well arranged, with a part on one side and a little tuft on his forehead. His position! So many appearances that one has to put on and respect!" That is how a man becomes dwarfed by experience: "Alas! What are you going to do about it? This great seriousness of ours is necessary after all, although it contains so much hidden melancholy!" But what had Ferrante accomplished with all his good looks, his romantic outbursts, and his unbridled youth? He had left Evelina, had fled to America, and had not concerned himself at all with her fate nor with the fate of her son.

And yet it seems that it does not pay to be like Lello. Now Ferrante has reappeared upon the scene, has come to see Lello, and the perfect structure that the latter has erected around himself and his family life seems likely to totter and fall. It is true that Ferrante, although under an assumed name, has revealed that he has the best intentions in the world, but his very presence in Florence is an unbearable threat. Lello tells us that everything is confused and mixed up, for Ferrante who had disappeared and was as blotted out of his memory as if he were dead, now has reappeared. Pirandello seems to say to Lello: "Well, these things happen, my dear fellow. We plan our lives very carefully and the slightest change disturbs our beautifully laid plans."

Ferrante's return will most assuredly interfere with the quiet life of Lello Carpani. Now everyone will be reminded that Evelina is not his legal wife. Lello will no longer be clothed with the dignity of a husband. He will be looked upon as Evelina's lover. Everyone will say: "This woman has a husband and lives with her lover." Ferrante comments:

"That's correct, but it seems to me that as between you and the husband, this situation should be more upsetting to the husband."

The scene between the two rivals is a jewel of dramatic perfection and subtle humor. Lello, like people bent on appearing to be always perfect, reviews to Ferrante all his usefulness to Evelina from the time that she was abandoned by him. He wishes to cover with the glamour of the exceptional what is common decency and even self-interest. When he saved Evelina's dowry and legalized her husband's position, according to him he did so to make Evelina "entirely free of herself, not only without the preoccupation of every material difficulty, but free to rejoin her husband, if she wanted." Pirandello does not like people who want to appear perfect. He searchingly tells him: "You—forgive me for saying it—perhaps did not feel so much the need of honesty, as you did the need of appearing before her love adorned with honesty; as if to defy it by the comparison between the cowardliness of the husband who had fled, and your own abnegation." Lello boasts that he did not have the marriage annulled. Could it not be—so argues Pirandello through Ferrante—that he did not do so in order not to give to Ferrante the satisfaction of having it annulled in case he returned?

Now Ferrante and Evelina will meet again. To what extent has Lello been able to destroy the joyous nature of young and vivacious Evelina? Has he only concealed it under the composure that Evelina naturally assumed with him from the first day they met, he a famous lawyer, she a downcast and crushed woman of twenty-three with the care of a little boy, with her heart wounded by her husband's flight to America and by his lack of concern about her fate and his son's future? Has she forgotten the life of amusements, whims, and follies that she lived with Ferrante when first married? What has happened to the feelings that envelop those acts and keep them alive? It seems that almost nothing remains of the old Evelina. There is "a languor in her eyes, in her voice, in her smile," she is composed and dignified. In Evelina the fervor with which she and Ferrante have lived has gone into her love for her boy, Aldo.

Her first reaction towards Ferrante is one of open and violent hostility. She does not want Ferrante even to see Aldo. Aldo is hers. Ferrante has no right to him. She is the mother who wishes to have all for herself the son she has brought up. She cries: "Aldo is mine, only mine [*turning like a wild beast towards Ferrante*]. If you returned for this, you can go, because you have no right to him."

But Aldo interferes. He tells his mother that he is not a child, that he wishes to hear his father's side and know what reason he has to offer for his indifferent behavior. Ferrante has an excellent defense lawyer in Pirandello. After the financial crash that was brought about by others and in which his responsibility did not go beyond keeping the books in great disorder, Ferrante fled because, had he remained, he would have done a greater harm to his wife and child. By disappearing he took all the responsibility on himself, all the more that he knew the mother had enough money of her own on which to live comfortably.

Aldo sees that since his father is there, his situation is entirely changed. He must no longer remain with Lello where he feels like an outsider, crowded out by the seven-year-old half sister, Titti. Lello Carpani agrees with him. Aldo's presence in his house is absurd now that the father is back. As usual, logic was the handmaid of what suited him to perfection.

The mother is mortally wounded. She cannot let her child go. "Turning towards Aldo and embracing him and clasping him tightly with the fury of desperation, she cries: 'It is impossible. I shall not let you go. I could not live without you, my son. How can you think of abandoning me, abandoning your mother?'" Ferrante is calm. He tells her that he wants Aldo to decide. Aldo, obeying his own inclinations, and forced by circumstances, decides to go with his father. The mother may visit her son any time she so desires. Ferrante's strength is Aldo's presence. Evelina sees that the destiny of

265

Aldo is inextricably woven with that of Ferrante. If she gives up Ferrante altogether, she will lose her son. She has to compromise by allowing Aldo to go to live with his father, reserving to herself the right of visiting him.

Aldo and Ferrante are birds of the same feather. Aldo has his father's vivacity and love for life. They go to Rome as on a lark. They settle there. American money can do a great deal in Italy, and Ferrante lives in a princely fashion in a villa, and possesses servants and horses. There is only one thing missing—the mother, Evelina. Through a ruse, they succeed in having her go to Rome. They wire that Aldo is desperately ill. She arrives, is at first indignant, then threatens to return to Florence, and then to stay in a hotel. In reality she stays a week with them.

Events show that the past is not dead. Ferrante had thought that it was, years ago, when he had crossed the ocean and burned his bridges behind him, believing that he could start life over again. It had been impossible. He had to come back, urged by a force greater than his will. The life they had lived together had never lost its hold on him. He reminds Evelina of the happy days spent together and calls her again by the endearing name he used in their intimacy: Iviù. He calls her again, aloud, as he used to, with the same intonation of voice, and the whole past lives anew in the life that glows in that name. After her fright at being in the house of a man that she must forget, Evelina laughs. Ferrante later confesses: "I felt that laughter lacerate my inner self. Then our eyes met, and we were dismayed. No, the past was not dead."

In the atmosphere created by being together, just as once in a distant, yet vivid past, Evelina finds delight again in the most simple and almost childish pastimes. With little cries of fright and laughter she even goes on the seesaw while Ferrante and Aldo push her. She is young again, she is joyous, spontaneous, vivacious, happy. Father, mother, and son go on horseback; they laugh. It is happiness, such as none of them had thought could exist on this earth.

Pirandello seems to tantalize Ferrante by telling him how happy life would have been if he had not interrupted that happiness by fleeing to America! That is Ferrante's torment and punishment. As he sees Evelina as she used to be, the idea that she is his and no one else's rises in him, makes him hate Lello Carpani and revolt against the situation existing between him and Evelina. He knows that she is his. Why should she go back to Florence to be Lina (as she is called there) and not Evelina; Lina "the fierce little mother that she has become"; Lina serious and cold. How could she go back now?

Evelina has remained honest, in spite of the fact that the past has vividly risen before her and has tried to envelop her in its magic circle of slumbering, happy memories. But she has been strong because she "wanted to be able to return there again." With her renunciation she has bought the right to go back to Ferrante's house again in the only guise in which she could go back—as Aldo's mother. This is the argument that she advances against Ferrante who does not understand her in his rekindled love for her—the love of their youth.

In his masculine self-centeredness, Ferrante wants her to go there for him and not for Aldo. She gently tells him: "You cannot understand it, you cannot understand it, because only a woman can understand this." She is frank, open: "I feel that you are in him, in my love for him, while the love that I feel for my daughter, there in Florence, is for her alone." She had lived with Lello all those years, deriving strength from the life that Ferrante had always given her and that she found in Aldo. The reflection of that life had infused warmth into her existence. It had been a life of quiet duty to her son, to Titti, to Lello who had been good to all of them.

At the end of Evelina's week of happiness with her family, Armelli, a respectable law partner of Lello Carpani, arrives in Rome and discovers the truth. He wires to Florence the situation that he has found. He also brings the news to Evelina that Titti is constantly asking for her and that in Florence there is an epidemic of a children's disease. Titti has had a slight fever. That is sufficient to make Evelina strong enough to face reality and duty. She leaves for Florence immediately with Armelli. Ferrante and Aldo feel lost without her. They do not know what to do or what to say. Their silence in the sadness of the twilight shows that violence has been done to life and they are suffering for it.

We can easily imagine the scandal in Florence. Signora Armelli in her moral indignation calls Evelina's action "revolting." Miss Wright, the governess, leaves as a protest. In her innocence, Evelina cannot understand all this indignation. After all she has been with her son and in her husband's house. It is extremely hard to batter down the strength of an argument based on what is obvious to narrow-minded people. A lucid, sharp, and powerful argument appeals only to a few. A commonplace argument based on a usually accepted belief will rally the support of the many. In discussing the matter with Lello, Evelina had to face a man who was following the logic of the average person and using arguments based on those grounds. Such were the assumptions of Lello, and they were all the more irritating to him since he was powerless. Ferrante was Lina's legal husband. The ties of matrimony are strong; they remain so even after fourteen years.

The scene between Lello and Evelina after her return home conveys Pirandello's understanding of a woman's heart and of masculine blindness. Lello, in the rôle of a resentful and offended husband, thinks Evelina has betrayed him: "Ah, there! You admit it [that you have been in his house]. But like a brother, wasn't he? A brother who calls you Eva. Oh no, who calls you . . . what does he call you? . . . something like 'Ju,' the name of a mare." Evelina is perturbed by this sudden recollection of her life with Ferrante. She is offended by the crude and vulgar reference to the name by which Ferrante called her. Lello does not see this. He does not understand the delicate play of emotion that goes on in the exquisite soul of Evelina.

Evelina sincerely and firmly makes him understand that a woman like her knows how to protect her dignity, her honesty, and that "if I have returned it means that you may rest assured that I have felt that I could return." Had she yielded to Ferrante, as Lello in his frantic rage insinuates, she would not have returned to him and to Titti, her child. He is trying to go beyond the portals of her conscience, to investigate the natural and spontaneous feelings of Evelina over which she has no control and he no right of investigation. Lello's blindness and lack of understanding compel Evelina to tell him calmly and firmly: "If I have returned you must not believe that to return has not cost me anything." She has paid a high price for the right to return to him and to her daughter.

That might satisfy Lello's personal feelings, but what about the people and his reputation when everyone knows the scandal? It is a disaster. He is irritated by the idea of sacrifice, of what it cost Evelina to return to him. Her faithfulness becomes an insult. Evelina is compelled to reveal to him that the great factor in that moment of trial was her daughter. She had resisted temptation for her daughter's sake; for the right of holding her in her arms without blushing. Lello, blind with rage, counters: "What do you think I care about my daughter in such a case?" Evelina remembers that Ferrante had made the same remark: "He, too, there said to me: 'What do you think I care for my son if you come for him?'" She sees in a crude light the masculine aggressiveness and predatory attitude of the two men, and before it she affirms her right to lead her own life. She announces: "It is time that you both put an end to this, for my children matter to me if they don't to you. After all, you have Titti here; he has taken Aldo there. Each of you can be by himself in the fullness of his life, but not I, because Aldo there is his and mine. Titti here is yours and mine. He wants me for himself, you want me for yourself. I cannot divide myself, half there, half here. I am there and here, one, only one." In the name of this unity found in her children she is ready to break with Lello if he expects her not to see Aldo again, since she had repulsed Ferrante's advances in order to acquire the right to see her Titti again: "You are men, only men. I am a mother."

Titti appears. Pirandello advises: "From this point on, with a clear-cut differentiation, the scene must give the feeling of a life which resumes its rhythm on its natural basis." Evelina madly clasps her child in her arms: "You are right, my Titti. There is so much useless talk here, stupid and barren, and you have been left there alone." She looks at her, caresses her, and kisses her hair. Titti seems taller now, almost up to Evelina's shoulders. She takes Titti in her arms and sways her very gently, while Lello looks at them both, serene and smiling. Evelina continues to hold her in her arms and says: "But I don't want you to become a little lady too soon, no, no, my little one."

Steering away from any sentimentality, Pirandello gives the play a solution required by the inner logic of the situation. Ferrante had offended life by fleeing to America. He had forfeited his right to have Evelina. Rather unwillingly, the author is compelled to be good to Lello Carpani by making Evelina go back to him and continue to be his accepted, if not legal, wife. He had to force himself a little to do so, but he has done so in the end. Certainly Ferrante was the more attractive man. Lello was too artificial to inspire any liking, but, after all, he had protected Evelina and the boy.

The usual undercurrent of serious and solid thought is found here as in most of Pirandello's plays. In a case in which a marriage has been broken, the author makes the one who has done so pay for it. Marriage is not to be trifled with. The author also stresses very cleverly the belief that morality does not lie in appearances. Evelina is pure in spite of the belief of the average person. Signora Armelli is guilty of a shameful entanglement with Aldo under her dignified appearance and behind the mask of her social position.

There are no intellectual complications in the comedy, only normal characters and events, and Pirandello's scintillating dialogue never lags but gives a deep insight into the human heart. If one should be so ill advised as to stress unduly the element of double personality, one would miss the central point of the play: the unity of personality that Evelina found in her mother love.

XXX

A Mystic Interpretation of Parenthood

GRAFTING

(*L'innesto*)

In *Grafting*, Pirandello is still steeped in that fantastic
naturalism that can be recognized in so many of his plays.
He has never forgotten the analysis of the instinctive
forces of life, but his analysis has gradually become a philosophical, interpretative, or even mystic, musing.

In this play he ponders over love, and while being fully
conscious of the power of instinct, he reaches a mystic interpretation given to love by a woman who has been brutally
attacked and whose child, therefore, is not her husband's.
To Laura Banti who loves her husband deeply and sincerely,
the child who is to be born is his, his in her love, because she
loves only him. It is the same thing that happens in the process
of grafting trees.

In her villa where she goes after the frightful experience
in order to recuperate and to regain a sense of moral and
physical balance, she sees the old gardener Filippo grafting
plants in the garden. He skilfully makes a deep cut in the
plant, inserts the scion, and closes the wound. In the spring
a new fruit will come. "But the plant," explains the old
gardener, "must be in love, that is, it must desire to have the
fruit that it cannot have by itself."

There is such an analogy between her case and that of the
grafted plants. They, too, have been violated, cut, but they
will bear fruit because God has wakened love in them. The
plant through its own love makes the new bud its own, without knowing whence it has come. Her baby, too, will be made
theirs by her love. She is sure of herself. She sees as never
before the mystery which embraces all beings and things in
the universe. Cold reason is not adequate to explain to her
mother what she feels, but she says: "Nature knows it, my

271

body knows it, a plant, any of these plants knows it. It knows that it could not have happened unless there were love. It has been explained to me just now. I know this, that in me, in this poor body of mine, when the thing happened, in this tortured flesh of mine, there must have been love, and for whom? If there was love, it could not have been but for him, for my husband."

Laura had gone to the Villa Giulia in Rome to paint. She was working on a landscape and she wanted to catch in it the effect of light in the early morning. She had left the house very early for three days in succession. She had been attacked in the park by an unknown brute.

What will her husband feel? Giorgio had made a sort of mistress out of her, so Laura's mother confides to us. He did not want children. He was jealous of children. He wanted Laura only for himself. His first reaction upon learning of the attack is not one of concern about Laura, but a maddening desire to learn the details of the occurrence. Who was he? He wants to kill him. Nelli, his lawyer and friend, tries to persuade him that there is nothing to do. The unfortunate thing has happened and that is all. If the man is apprehended, he will get two or three years in prison. If Giorgio brings the matter to court there will be a terrible scandal, since it will get into the papers.

Giorgio sees his life enveloped by a dark circle. "Everything is over," he confesses. If he were to listen to his own true impulse, he "would go there, to her bed, and he would kill her, although innocent, for the very love that he feels for her." A desperate jealousy stifles in him every feeling of compassion for Laura. He refuses to see her, while she, in her anguish, calls for him. He calls for his automobile in order to go all alone to his country place. The only natural feeling that he experiences is one of cruelty, cruelty to all, to his wife, to himself. Just then Laura appears, a broken woman, appealing to him, telling him that she wants to be near him. Giorgio relents. "She raises her head in the tragic expectation that he may cancel her unbearable shame either through death or through love. As he, overpowered by the intoxicating feeling that emanates from her, always sobbing, seeks with his lips the wounds in her neck, she passionately places her cheek over his head." Will that passionate love of Giorgio give him enough understanding and sympathy when he learns that she is going to be a mother? Will he accept as theirs the baby that she is carrying under her heart?

Now she is alone at the villa of her husband's family, in the place where Giorgio has spent his youth and his adolescence. Giorgio was one of those young lords who used to think it quite proper to amuse themselves with young peasant girls at a time, not much removed from ours, when the world was free, just, and good, and the Golden Age reigned on earth, Italy included. Laura knows of an illegitimate child, the son of a peasant woman, of whom it was rumored that Giorgio was the father. Laura has sent for Zena, the peasant who had been her husband's plaything and nothing else. Zena comes to see her. She has quickly aged, and is already ugly and ungainly at twenty-five. She has had five children, and she works in the fields like a beast of burden. Laura wants to know from Zena the details of that gossip.

Zena is reluctant to recall a part of her life that is dead for her, but Laura is so gentle and kind that she overcomes Zena's shame and reserve. Zena was pretty, strong, and healthy then, and was engaged to her present husband. "Did he [Giorgio] know that you were engaged?" questions Laura.

"Yes, of course, but he, too, was very young," answers Zena.

What Laura wants to know is whether or not Zena surmised who was the father of her baby, Giorgio or her *fiancé*. Zena, with the candor of peasant folk, tells her that she was sure it was her husband's. She adds: "We peasants are sly. I see that you would like your husband to have had a baby by me. Well, I tell you this, that I, a peasant, gave the son to him who was his real father."

Giorgio arrives at that moment and hardly sees Zena. That episode of nine years ago did not mean much to him. He expresses surprise at Zena's presence there.

Laura, in the crisis that has gripped her whole life, feels

273

that she has never belonged to Giorgio as much as now: "If I belonged to you more, I should die. And yet death would be acceptable to me." She belongs to that man with a force and purity of which only a superior woman is capable. She cries to him: "I have only you! That's all: you, and nothing else which does not come from you counts. If I rejoice, if I suffer, if I die, it is for you. Because I am only as you desire me, as I desire myself: yours." She hopes that her husband will feel as she does about her baby, but she is bitterly disappointed.

Giorgio believes that he has been very generous in overlooking the misfortune of the attack upon her. But now it is the question of a child. He asks the doctor to tell Laura that he cannot accept a child that is not his with certainty. He requires that the child be eliminated through a surgical operation.

Laura firmly asserts her right of motherhood. She tries to make him see that. There is no guilt on her part, no wrong. She has given herself to him as no woman ever has, hoping that her love would wipe out the spot. Giorgio, in his lack of understanding, asks whether she did not "surround him with her love, envelop him in her caresses, to make him accept the situation." Laura is terribly hurt. She strikes back at him. After all there is as much doubt as to who is the father of her child as there was in the case of Zena's son. Giorgio is unbending.

Laura had hoped to lift him up to her. She wanted to save their love, to blot out a cruel misfortune, not brutally, as he had suggested, but with love and understanding. She cries to him: "I want you to see in your son all of me: he's yours because he's proof of all my love for you." Laura's passionate and noble love does not convince Giorgio. He is concerned about giving his name to a child that might not be his. Laura counters: "Do not be afraid of that. I shall have the courage that Zena had. It is a shame that, after the deceit, I cannot give him to his true father." Laura declares herself no longer his wife.

Giorgio realizes that he has opened an abyss between Laura and himself. Confronted by the certainty of losing her, he yields and love registers another of its victories. It is the victory of love over a purely physiological passion.

A very strong antisocial strain, as is to be expected, appears here too. Pirandello takes up again the defense of women and attacks the double standard that has been practised so long everywhere. Man, behind the stately appearance of the civilization that he has put up, has remained a brute. He has put on clothes, hats, fine shoes, and showy garments, but under it all there lurks the brute. Life "is still the forest! Still the forest! It is always the original forest!"

The play moves on the concrete and solid ground of everyday life. This permits Pirandello to prove convincingly his most idealistic and romantic thesis. Had he given a lyrical and fantastic treatment to the play, we would wander in the midst of evanescent characters. Laura is presented with traits that have at no time been exaggerated. She is a gentle, superior young woman, too lofty for her husband. Giorgio is a society gentleman who has never gone very deeply into the understanding of his wife and of life. He has not changed much from his love for Zena to that for Laura. Filippo, the gardener, and Zena stand for that directness and simplicity of instinctive life that is possible only in primitive beings such as are found in peasant life.

The drama sets a lofty goal before Giorgio: that of seeing the beauty of Laura's love and of lifting his own to a higher plane, rising above the intoxication of the senses. Here, as elsewhere, Pirandello qualifies this feeling that men share with lower animals as "sentiment." Giorgio says: "I am required to be generous, while here my sentiment roars like a wild beast." In later plays, the author gives a positive and constructive sense to sentiment.

Pirandello ridicules our individualism as fathers. We look at the child only as our own, as a proof of our personal value. We never think that we are either vehicles or tools and sometimes even puppets in the hands of nature. This is the real morality of the play: the power of nature and the universality of love. This feeling, in its unpretentious simplicity, lends to the play a cosmic sense of life.

XXXI

Only Illusion Can Conquer Death

THE LIFE THAT I GAVE YOU
(*La vita che ti diedi*)

This play appeared at the time when the author was interested in analyzing the value and proclaiming the necessity of the irrational as a means of escape.

We find here the tragedy of a mother who has to force on herself the belief that her son is not dead in order to stand the shock of that tragedy. Pirandello leads us to an understanding of the mother's grief and subsequent illusory process by calling our attention to the fact that in reality life is a constant death. As soon as life enters into us death beats the tempo of a silent funeral march with the same regularity as that with which the hands of a clock go on and on, while the time they mark never comes back. Is not that time, those minutes, hours, weeks, months, years, centuries, the road on which death has made its stealthy and inexorable advance? If you will look back into the centuries you will see death strangling life. In a collective sense life always rises again, but in an individual sense—and we live as individuals —it is death that ultimately overpowers life.

As her son lies in the death chamber, Donn'Anna Luna refuses to believe that he is dead. She talks to him softly with the composure with which mothers wait for their children to return when the latter have left them and have gone roaming over the world. She quietly says: "He has left. He will return." Had he not left their home when a youth and for seven years wandered after the woman whom he loved without hope of making her his? The corpse that is there before her is not he. She wants that body removed that she may live with her child as he lives in her memory, her real child. The man who came back to her, withered by life, disillusioned, sick, almost moribund, was not the child that she wanted.

Illusion is the last conquest of determination, and she must force herself to cling to the beautiful image that floats before her eyes on which was indelibly impressed the countenance of Fulvio as a child.

Her son had left her when very young and had gone to Florence to study. Here he had met an Italian girl who later married a Frenchman, Monsieur Maubel. The two went first to Liège, then to Nice. For seven years Fulvio followed her. She had two children by her husband, and for those children Fulvio and the woman, in spite of their great love, had restrained themselves and kept their love pure. For years the mother had remained shut up in her villa always thinking, gradually becoming detached from everything.

We have here the typical Pirandellian complex: a person given to absorbing and concentrated thinking, with thought acting as an acid on her material life, but affording solace to her mind and peace to her soul. The situation that confronts us in the play must be looked at through the mother's past, lonely life. Only so can we understand that her feelings are not arguments but real emotions. She had lived for long years in the solitude of her villa where "silence frightens one as he goes through the large, deserted halls. It seems that time falls precipitously into them." In this rarefied atmosphere Donn'Anna had waited while her thoughts followed her son, sympathizing with his great love, sacrificing herself for that beautiful passion.

It is natural that the average people who surround Donn'Anna fail to understand her. Don Giorgio, a complacent, fat country priest, not entirely uneducated, voices the belief that real life is in the beyond, and therefore the mother is not right in insisting that her son is alive. Donn'Anna retorts with an argument derived from the vague idealistic religion of the author: "I know that God cannot die when everyone of his creatures dies. . . . Not even you can tell me that my child is dead. You say only that God took him back with him. . . . Don't you feel that God is not there as long as he wishes to abide here, in me, in us; not only for ourselves but also that all those who have gone away may continue to live?" Without realizing how cruel they are, they strive to persuade her to see the truth that her son is dead, "and that if he lives in her he can only live in her memory." The curate, Donn'Anna's sister, the villagers, in their want of sensitiveness, insist on the actual truth as if the mother did not know it and as if she could accept it. She tells the curate: "I have never lived on anything else but memories. I have no other life but this one; the only one that I can touch— precise and present. But you utter the word 'remembrance' and immediately you make it recede from me, destroy it for me." The curate, by mentioning the words "memory" and "remembrance," destroys momentarily the perfect illusion in which the mother's heart and soul have found solace. She is perfectly aware that the physical life of her son is over, but she also knows that he can have another life, that he can be reborn through her love. She tells the curate: "God wants my son to continue to live. Not, of course, the life that he gave him here, but that which I have always given him! This cannot be taken away from him as long as life endures in me."

As the mother reënters the glow and flame of her illusion she forgets the actual and hurting truth and views the people around her as blind and powerless. She turns to Donna Fiorina, her sister, and gently tells her, as one mother to another, that for mothers the life of their children is only dream. They touch the tender flesh of their babies and they almost see it change under their hands. The images of their children are nothing but memories of dreams. Only a mother like Donn'Anna can understand that fully: "It takes seven years, I know, seven years passed in thinking of a son who does not return, and of suffering what I have suffered, in order to understand this truth that goes beyond every sorrow while there looms here a light which cannot be extinguished." She presses her temples with both hands. Had Donna Fiorina not noticed how her children, after one year's absence at the university, had changed? "They were young country shepherds a year ago, and now they seem two young lords," in the poetical but apt comment of Elisabetta, the maid.

Donna Fiorina is compelled to acknowledge the fearful truth uncovered by Donn'Anna. It was true. Her children had changed so as to be hardly recognizable; they look different and their ideas are no longer the same.

Donn'Anna lives quietly in the little closed world of her illusion, in a light that is artificial but consoling. The light that surrounds her is of her own creation, and she has to keep it burning with the oil of her human compassion and mother love. Only at times the tragic truth seizes her and overpowers her. She confesses to her sister: "What do you know of what I do when, upstairs, I abandon my head on the pillow and feel him, feel him in the silence and emptiness of these rooms where no memory suffices to animate and fill that silence, because I am tired? Then I too *know,* and a fearful shudder creeps over me. The only refuge, the last comfort, is in her, in the one who is to come and does not know yet."

The one who is to come is Lucia Maubel, the woman whom Fulvio has loved more than his youth and life. His death will be a test for Lucia's love. Will she continue to love him after she knows that he is dead? She comes to tell Fulvio that she is going to have a baby, his baby. She confesses to the mother: "Our love that had endured pure for so many years, conquered us in the end, stealthily." Upset and frightened, Lucia forced him to leave: "I could not meet my children's eyes," she says. Lucia is one of those women whom Pirandello has surrounded with the halo of nobility that every man sees around the quiet countenance of his mother. Pirandello does not need to make women erotic nor to complicate their eroticism to make them live in his art. Love, even if it breaks the barriers of the law, has a purifying effect on Pirandello's women, and rarely mortifies or offends their motherhood.

At first Lucia is hurt at Fulvio's absence. She does not understand the mother's words that he has left on a long journey. As she confesses the whole truth of their relation to the mother, she grows excited, almost distracted. She cannot go back to her husband now. Horror fills her at the mere

thought of having to live with him again. She has suffered
agonies that cannot be told while married to him. He is a
profligate man, "fatuous and cold. He looks at life to laugh
at it, at women to take them, at men to deceive them." Only
Fulvio's love has given her courage and strength: "I have
been able to stand living with him [her husband] only because I had someone to sustain me, to give me pure air to
breathe, outside of that filth." Fulvio has made her feel that
even the children she had borne to her husband were his:
"Those children (it is true) are not love that has become
flesh: they belong to that man—flesh—but the love that I
had infused into them—I, I with my heart full of him—had
transformed those two almost into Fulvio's children. Love is
one." She regrets that their weakness had led them to sin
after many years of brave renunciation: "We should not
have soiled ourselves!" she cries to Fulvio's mother. The
consciousness of having done wrong destroys even the pure
joy of motherhood in her. She has come to Fulvio to see
whether he could change that feeling and create in her the
joy of being a mother.

Lucia is tired, excited, almost frantic. Sweetly Donn'Anna
tells her: "I will teach you how not to go crazy, as I did for
such a long time, as long as he was there with you. I used
to feel him near me because I held him in my heart. He is
there." [*She indicates his room.*] She admonishes Lucia,
putting into words the bitter subjectivism that life had taught
her: "Never seek anything that does not come from within
you." Her strength must come from her heart, from her
sentiment, that will conquer any obstacle, even death. Lucia
insists on sleeping in Fulvio's room. She will be closer to him
thus. "Yes," says the mother to her, "in your heart. Yes, in
your heart." Lucia has been won over by the mother. Fulvio
is alive.

On the following day Lucia's mother arrives. She is a
perfectly normal and prosaic person. To her, Fulvio is dead
and Lucia has compromised herself by going to his home.
Donn'Anna pleads with her that Fulvio is not dead as long
as he lives in the child that Lucia is bearing him. Francesca,

Lucia's mother, shouts: "Do you want to keep my daughter tied to a corpse?" The brutal question wounds Donn'Anna, but she finds in the very facts of the situation the strength to answer: "A corpse? Death for her is there, near the man to whom you have tied her: *he* is a corpse."

Lucia appears as the two mothers are talking, and discovers the truth: Fulvio is dead. As Lucia tragically cries her love and despair, the truth of the situation appears to Donn'Anna in all its cruel and ghastly light. Bitter tears fall upon her defeated effort to keep alive her illusion: "Oh my child!—here on your flesh—now indeed—I see him die—I feel his cold corpse here, in the warmth of your tears." Lucia is very close to her heart, as close as ever a daughter was to a mother. She is touched by Donn'Anna's anguish and tells her that her love for Fulvio is undiminished by his death and that she feels that he lives in the little life that is about to unfold through their love. She wants to stay with her. They will live together in this new joy as they have been together under the hand of grief.

Lucia's mother thwarts their plan. Lucia must go back to her home and to her two children. Donn'Anna sees the cruel logic of that thought, and resigns herself to be alone in the empty house no longer illuminated by illusion. She is truly dead now: "This is truly death, my child—things we have to do, whether we want to or not—and things we have to say . . . now a time-table to consult—then the coach to go to the station—to journey on . . . we are the poor, busy dead.—To torture ourselves—to console ourselves—to quiet ourselves —this is truly death." She is dead when the idealism of the author fails to keep her illusion alive.

The theme, as we have already noticed, is still that of illusion, but no longer a tortuous illusion, usually a consequence of wrongdoing. It is the illusion that we are forced to impose upon ourselves if we want to bear our human fate. In the face of a pessimism that has become complete, Pirandello's idealism has assumed a definite and pragmatic value.

The play is in a logical line of derivation from the author's tragic idealism. It is a passionate pleading for this idealism because it has been his own solace for many long years of torment. As is his fashion, having advanced the idea that life is a constant death as the basis of his play, he attempts to prove that actually it is so. What men call change is only death. It is the illusory comfort that words give us. Before the transformation of the boy into the man, only self-deception makes us speak of change: "Does that not mean that he is another than the one that he used to be? And if the one who was before is now no longer, what does that *change* mean?" It may seem strange that Donn'Anna should utter this categorical pessimism, she, the one who later soars to a dizzy idealism. Yet this explains the very nature of her illusion which is tragic and human.

At first we hesitate to agree with Pirandello's disconsolate philosophy. However, in the ultimate analysis, his thought is consoling, and his arguments are so pointed and so vivified by the real tragedy of the mother that we are carried away by his passionate logic. Pirandello convinces your intellect at the same time that he touches your heart. If life abides in our thought and higher emotions, is it not a mistake to give physical death such a great importance? Why should the mother have seen her son in the bald-headed, bent, used-up body that came back to her rather than in the gentle and exquisite boy who had left her seven years before? Closed in her impenetrable subjectivism she could call life only what she had known, what had been the flame of her eyes and soul before he departed, the flame of her lonely life after his departure.

The author is perfectly conscious of the desolate subjectivism of Donn'Anna, and feels compelled to distinguish between the common lot and the individual. To the average unfeeling mob "life has always put a stone on the dead in order to continue its march over them. But it must be our life, not that of those who have died. We want our dead really dead to live our life in peace. That's why we justify ourselves when we pass over the dead."

Pirandello has conquered an insurmountable difficulty in

making plausible a thesis that at first seems irrational and absurd. He has done so by embodying the mother in a woman who is above the normal and average person in sensitiveness and nobility. By so doing he places the problem on a personal basis that silences the recriminations of those who might deny the possibility of the psychological reaction that forms the very woof of the play. As Donna Fiorina tells us: "She has always been like that! She seems to be listening to what others tell her, and suddenly she comes forth—as if from a fantastic distance—with words that no one expected." Pirandello's contention is that if others fail to understand her, it is because they have not had her heart-rending experience nor have they been endowed with her sensitiveness.

With extreme skill Pirandello takes the problem from the height of a lofty, even ethereal idealism, and leads it to the ground of practical life. Only through sentiment was the mother saved; only through sentiment could Lucia endure her grief at not finding Fulvio; only through that sentiment could life resume for her in her husband's home, near her children, illuminated by reminiscences of Fulvio's beautiful and perfect love.

Part Five

ART AND LIFE

XXXII

Introduction

In this section are included the plays that have a distinctly intellectual genesis. The author contrasts here life and art in its diverse manifestations: dramatic art, sculpture, and poetry. The plays herein considered deal with the experience of a dramatist, sculptor, and poet as they place themselves before life and muse over the central character of art looked upon as life caught in the immutable eternity of form. As the result of this attitude, Pirandello has given us *Six Characters in Search of an Author*, *Tonight We Improvise*, *Diana and Tuda*, *She Wanted to Find Herself*, and *When One Is Somebody*.

In their inherent character these plays are the expression of Pirandello's experience as a man and as an artist. Although the two experiences may meet, they are often in sharp contrast, and from this clash arises the drama that Pirandello portrays in his plays. The author realizes that before him there are two alternatives: either to choose the life immobilized in the concept of his own unhappiness, or to abandon himself to the life of instinct that clamors for its rights against duty and sacrifice. This practical concern prevents the plays from being treatises on art in the disguise of drama, and infuses them with a deep note of human feeling.

One of the considerations that, as we shall see, affords to Pirandello a nucleus around which he builds his play, is whether or not life is more powerful than art; whether we enhance or stunt our emotions and feelings when we transform them into art. In the earlier years of his dramatic career he leaned towards life, life alluring and warm, strong in joy and strong in grief, a tide that carries us on the crest of its waves and fills us with the feeling of a power that nothing can equal. The power of life, however, was not conceived in the light of the orgies of the senses. As he lived in stoical resignation, broken by the outbursts of rebellion that he voiced through his characters, Pirandello realized with increasing clearness how much more powerful was the tragedy he lived than the tragedy he portrayed. What he sought was the reality of his inner pain reflected in his work. Every reflection of it was pale and inadequate when compared with the anguish that lacerated his heart. It was natural that he should proclaim life to be more powerful than art.

This state of mind is projected in *Six Characters in Search of an Author* and in *Tonight We Improvise* as well as in *Diana and Tuda.* Here art is looked upon as an inadequate means of expression which dwarfs life and robs it of its fire and glow. This longing for the pulsing throb of life originates in the thirst and hunger for life that nature has infused in every creature, animate and inanimate. Through this longing Pirandello reveals the torment of the artist as he is confronted by problems of dramatic technique. He rebels against the fact that there is a vast difference between actors and characters: actors as they are engaged by a stage director; characters as they have been created by the playwright. He also resents dramatic art's being laden down with conventional tricks of all kinds—division into acts, light effects, make-up—all elements that life in its actuality does not need in order to be dramatic.

It is but natural that a man who seeks the actual as passionately as does Pirandello, and who rebels with violence at any attempt to sentimentalize life or to cover it with rhetorical veils, should feel attracted by the *Commedia dell'arte.* One must not call the author's attention to the fact that the *Commedia dell'arte* also had its conventions and formalisms. We cannot call an artist from the region of poetry before the tribunal of logic.

The *Commedia dell'arte*, or improvised comedy in which only the plot was outlined and in which the actors filled in the dialogue, has had a marked influence on Pirandello. It was the closest approximation of art to life, and conventionalities of drama and stagecraft had no meaning for the actors of the *Cinquecento* who felt the passion of life and art with equal intensity. Pirandello found another bond of sympathy with them. They too knew the power of laughter, and they rendered life through it in all its power and violence.

Pirandello, however, pictures in other plays also contained in this section a state of mind of an opposite nature which was forced on him by the realization that art actually gave him a solace that he vainly sought in life. He turned to art with the same impetuosity with which he had aspired to life, and he saw that art gives stateliness and immortality to it. The keynote of these plays is the realization that a feeling if left in its own fluid state is truly alive, but doomed to change and eventually to death, while if given artistic representation at the cost of losing its vehemence, it can attain immortal existence.

Here Pirandello the naturalist has turned into the tragic idealist who assigns a solitary peak to the creatures of his imagination, where they abide in a suffering cheered by the cold light of art. If the true essence of life lies in reflection, then art outdoes actual life in that we can reach through it a fullness and a height unknown to those who entrust themselves to the chaotic and stormy violence of instinct.

The two antithetical moods are not created by the desire of changing technique for the benefit of entertaining the public as would a cheap juggler. Like all true thought and art, they come from within, and they are generated by the realization that life in its primeval attribute flows unattainable in the infinite distances that only our soul can picture. Life needs form in order to exist in the world of actual realities, and it becomes dwarfed by it. Pirandello approaches life when his senses urge him to reach out for its gifts, but his intellect has already withered the fruit that his lips long to suck. Then pessimism looms, and it stretches its destructive tentacles over the whole universe. For a man who had reached such a state of mind, to turn to art becomes a logical and deeply felt need. In the uncontaminated molds of art, life can be kept in all its purity and beauty. For a man who had so copiously drunk at the bitter spring of sorrow, it was natural to reach this point of detachment and of objectivity.

The need of rising towards the blissful heaven of perfect

forms is also derived from the identity that Pirandello discovers between the clear-cut contour of a statue and that of
certain individuals who are so absorbed by a given painful
or shameful thought as to become identified with it. He knew
how clear and lucid, how terrible and agonizing was the
fixity of one's body and soul. The fixity of his individuals
and of all art bridged the distance between the drama of life
that he always sought and that of art that opened a new
avenue to his creative instinct. From portraying the fixity
resulting from a moral wrong, he passed to portraying that
due to the isolation to which all superior beings are condemned. Donata Genzi, in *She Wanted to Find Herself*, perfect embodiment of feminine grace and lofty womanhood,
expresses this new mood of the author. We find in her a
person who can look at herself in the mirror without ex-
periencing the feeling of loathing and disgust that Pirandello
has lent to earlier characters. The light of a higher ethical
life also animates one of his latest plays, *When One Is Somebody*. Here Somebody is strong enough to keep his love for
beautiful Veroccia on a high plane even when the voice of
instinct sings for him the song with which the mermaids
bewitched Ulysses' companions.

These plays, like those found in other sections, present a
decided change in the inspiration and state of mind of the
author. Pirandello has freed himself from the preoccupation
of instinct, and his eyes have limpidly gazed on a higher
life. As youth has forsaken him, he has seen more clearly
behind the veil of material and instinctive life, and he has
turned to art to express this new aspect of his drama. He
sought a lofty region, the presence of which his soul had
constantly felt even when gloom* and pessimism weighed
heavily on his outlook on life, and he found that region on
the summit where abide the divine and luminous forms of art.

XXXIII

Art Does But Dwarf a Tragic Life

SIX CHARACTERS IN SEARCH OF AN AUTHOR
(*Sei personaggi in cerca d'autore*)

In *Six Characters in Search of an Author,* one of the most complex and baffling of Pirandello's plays, a stirring dramatic action is so closely woven with keen and almost erudite discussions of art that one is at first uncertain as to the central idea of the work. The fact is that the motivation of the play is essentially literary, since there run through it various æsthetic considerations such as: Is life stronger than art? What happens when we attempt to enclose life in the mold of art? Is its reality increased or diminished? Does not the artist owe the reality of his art to the torment and anguish which have gnawed into the soul and the very flesh of the man?

In a material sense the genesis of the play is found in a short story entitled *The Tragedy of a Character* (*La tragedia di un personaggio*) [1] in which Pirandello in an imaginary conversation listens to the plaint of a character who laments the rôle that has been assigned to him by the author of a book that Pirandello has just read. There is a page taken bodily from this short story and inserted in the play. In a more subtle and psychological sense the play is the projection of Pirandello's long-tormented life into the life and torment of the Six Characters.

As the title suggests, this is a play of characters. It is pertinent at this point to inquire who is a character in Pirandello's mind and in what way he differs from a normal man and an actor. We know Hamlet, Don Quixote, Don Abbondio, Sancho Panza. They are characters in that they represent a feeling, an idea, a supreme overpowering emotion. They have lived in the flame of this idea or emotion all

[1] *Novelle per un anno.* Vol. IV, pp. 237–46. Bemporad, Florence, 1922.

through the centuries and they still live in it, immortal in their impassioned immobility. As we look at them they are alive in spite of their fixity. "When a character is born," Pirandello informs us, "he acquires immediately such an independence from his author that we can all imagine him in situations in which the author never thought of placing him, and he assumes of his own initiative a significance that his author never dreamt of lending him." There are cases in life, Pirandello claims, in which man acquires the fixity of a character. Under the pressure of the unmerciful hand of misfortune and grief, man often reaches a point where he becomes so closely identified with that misfortune and grief as to be the embodiment of a passionate state of mind which crowds out, to an absolute exclusion, every other feeling and sentiment. Then he is a character.

Looked at in this light the Six Characters are the projection of that fixity in mental agony and pain which is a typical state of mind of the central figures that Pirandello has made live in his drama. The play is, intrinsically and ultimately, a keen study of human personality to which Pirandello has accorded a most brilliant treatment. He has called to his help his own anguish, his own experience as an author, his original intuition of the human side of art and the procedure of the *Commedia dell'arte*. The Six Characters oscillate with perfect balance between the artificial life of glorified marionettes and the moving, stirring existence of tragic human beings.

Pirandello's fatherly attitude towards the children of his imagination is reflected in these new Six Characters who clamor to be made to live. They are so overpowered by the passion that stirs them that they beg a troupe of professional actors to allow them to reënact their tragedy. They claim with emphasis and passion that, living their tragedy and pain, they are real characters. They are completely absorbed in their grief. In this they resemble the immortal characters to whom truly great artists have given life, a life which is immortal. "Man will die, the writer, an instrument of creation, will die; but his creatures will never die, and in order

292

to live eternally they need not possess extraordinary qualities nor perform prodigies. Who was Sancho Panza? Who
was Don Abbondio? And yet they live because, living germs,
they had the fortune to find a fecund matrix, a fantasy that
could nurture them, make them live through eternity." The
Six Characters, too, are immortal in the fixity of their pain.
Pirandello stresses their fantastic reality as well as their
physical traits which they share with all humanity. "A
strange, most feeble, hardly perceptible light is around them
as if radiating from them: a light breath of their fantastic
reality." They possess "a certain dreamlike lightness in
which they appear as if suspended, but which must not de-
tract at all from the essential reality of their forms and expressions." They are true human beings, but they do not
represent a heavy, solid, unwieldy humanity impervious to
deep feelings. Indeed, they are suspended in the effervescence
of the passionate desire to communicate to others the burning
truth which torments them within.

The Father has that uncertain and vague smile of those whom
life has baffled and disappointed. Outwardly he may be any
one of the many people we know, "rather fat, pale, especially
his wide forehead, with round blue eyes, most lucid and
penetrating; wearing light trousers and a dark coat; speaking
at times in a mellifluous tone, at times abruptly and harshly."
The Mother, as pale as wax, with downcast eyes, and dressed
in deep mourning, appears "crushed by an intolerable weight
of shame and dejection." The Stepdaughter, eighteen years
of age, is haughty, almost impudent. "Very beautiful, she
too wears mourning, but with showy elegance." Near her
are two other victims of the tragedy: the wan Adolescent,
timid, distressed, moving like a ghost among them; and the
Son, twenty-two years old, who is tall and stiff, and looks
disdainfully at them all. There is also a child of about four,
the only fresh, delicate note in so much gloom and hatred.

The Six Characters, representing life at its highest pitch
of intensity and depth, arrive on the stage at the moment
when a troupe of professional actors are about to rehearse
a play by Pirandello, *Each in His Own Rôle* (*Il gioco delle*

parti). As they appear, there is in them the afflatus of theatrical personality which urges them to go to the actors and make the strange request of being allowed to reënact a scene in which, as they say, their whole life has become crystallized. Pirandello brings into relief the prosaic traits of the actors as contrasted with the impetuous Six Characters. Everything is in disorder in the theatre; some actors are smoking cigarettes, some are reading a newspaper, others are going over their parts. Not so with the Characters. They are all tense, in a perpetually high and feverish tension. They have no need to rehearse their parts. They know them, all summed up in one tragic scene. They insist, above all, on their reality, which they contemptuously compare with that of the actors and that of the average man. Man thinks that he possesses an unchanging unity, while in him are intertwined infinite personalities which are in constant state of change. His illusions of today prove to have been the truths of but yesterday, and the truths of today will be the illusions of tomorrow. Not so with a character who is fixed in a definite mold, all through eternity, if a genius has made him live in the eternity of art. "A character can always ask of a man who he is, because a character has truly a life of his own marked with definite traits so that he always is a somebody, while a man generally speaking can be a nobody." As to actors, the reality of their lives is separated from the content of their art. They act; they do not live.

The story that the Six Characters relate is truly heartrending. A strange mixture of pathos and shame envelops it. On the surface, it seems to be a drama of a divided family which includes a woman who has first lived with her husband by whom she had a son, and then with another man by whom she had three more children. There is nothing extraordinary in this, especially in modern times when divorces create even stranger situations. But our curiosity is aroused when we learn that all the misfortunes have been superinduced by the tortuous mental process of the Father. The Father is in fact an hyper-intellectual man who lacks that fluidity of feelings and sincerity of purpose that bring about a serene and quiet life. He speaks of the "complicated torments of my spirit." He himself informs us that he has always had an "aspiration for a certain moral character of life." This moral aspiration causes him to marry a woman of the people to counteract his own intellectuality. She is goodness and simplicity personified and lives only for her home and her child. Her husband, obeying his customary moral aspiration, takes the child from her and sends him to the country to be nursed by a sturdy peasant so that he may be in close contact with mother earth. There is in their wealthy home the husband's secretary, a silent, shadow-like, humble man like the wife. He and she, without even the thought of evil, understand each other because they are kindred souls. The husband, under the urge of his moral sense, makes himself believe that his wife cannot be happy with him. They are too different, he with his searching, subjective intellect, she with her humility and silence, her spontaneity and simplicity. He feels that the real mate for his wife is his secretary. He provides a home for the two of them and has them live together. He does this, urged on by the "demon of experience," one of the demons, popularized copies of the Greek *daimon,* so dear to the intellectual class of D'Annunzio's days. The "demon of experience" is just a phrase according to the Son and to the other members of the family. The Father rebels: "Phrases! Phrases! As if it were not everyone's consolation, before a fact that cannot be explained, before a disease that destroys us, to find a word which says nothing and in which we find quietude."

Both Pirandello and the family question the validity of the Father's acts because they are determined by his tortuous reasoning and not by real sentiment. How can one believe him when he says that he feels sorry for his wife's loneliness and therefore sends her away to live with the secretary? Does he not do it because he has tired of a woman with whom he has nothing in common? Does he not mention the "stifling atmosphere of his home life," mixing truths and lies and believing them all true? It is useless for him to put lofty motives into his acts after his poor and humble wife goes to live with the other man. He continues to watch over her out of a sense of responsibility, and, for the same reason, he is interested in the new family of three children. When the little girl grows up, he goes to meet her after school, taking her gifts as if she were his own. One day the family disappears from the town and does not return until after the secretary's death, many years later. The Father's torment and loneliness become greater. His Son is as if not his own; his house is empty and barren. The Stepdaughter voices Pirandello's revolt against the Father's attempt at philosophizing about human acts. "How sickening, how sickening, are all those intellectual complications, all that philosophy that uncovers the beast and then attempts to save it and excuse it. When we are compelled to 'simplify' life in such a beastly manner, casting away all the 'human' encumbrance of every chaste aspiration, of every pure sentiment, ideal, duty, shame, modesty, nothing moves us to rage and nausea more than certain remorses: crocodile tears!"

Some years later the Father visits a bawdy house where he finds himself face to face with the Stepdaughter, whom he does not recognize. The arrival of the Mother saves them from a greater disgrace. After the identification stamps their faces and hearts with burning shame, the Father takes the new family to his home and there they live under an evil spell, in a light of tragic exasperation.

Each has his own tragedy, and the tragedy of one merges with the tragedy of all. The Father refuses to have his whole life caught in that shameful moment as if his entire existence were summed up in that act. But he protests in vain to the Stepdaughter, who sees in him the cause of all her shame and misfortunes. The Adolescent is lost in that tormented life. The Son sees half-bred intruders in them all, and looks with cold, indifferent eyes at his Mother. She has belonged to another man. His Father is a libertine. The Son feels that his life depends on them "as a putrid shame which must be hidden." The Mother's tragedy is that of any mother who feels estranged from her son. All this shame and misfortune is summarized in that moment in which Father and Stepdaughter find themselves face to face as man and woman: he a man nearing sixty, she a young girl of eighteen. Now, the Six Characters are gathered in a tragic huddle around that scene. This scene is a flame kept alive by hatred, rebellion, and remorse.

As the subtitle suggests, the comedy is yet to be made. The rough copy is in them—in the Six Characters. "It is in us, sir," announces the Father while the actors laugh. "The drama is in us. It is we and we are eager to enact it, urged on by the passion within us."

They present their drama to the Director. Why does he not attempt to make of it a dramatic work? His task will be very simple, since the characters are there before him. Instead of being written, the work will only be transcribed, scene by scene. As the Characters enact their tragedy, the professional actors will observe how real characters act, and will attempt to reproduce their acting. The Director, with the assistance of the Six Characters, gives a certain plan to the action to which they are to give life.

The first act presents the fashionable establishment of Madame Pace, where elegant garments are sold, together with the honesty and youth of poor girls. The Stepdaughter insists that the stage furniture be the same as that in Madame Pace's room. The furniture is engraved in her memory, and it disturbs her to see anything different. The Father rebels because another person will play his part and the various characters will receive names other than those which they bear in real life. The Stepdaughter laughs at the thought of the First Actress attempting to portray her passion. The first scene is to bring together Madame Pace and the Stepdaughter. The distance between the plane of life and that of artistic reality is so slight that Madame Pace arrives attracted by the divine afflatus of the tragic reality that the Six Characters are living. The Stepdaughter dashes towards her and they talk in a low voice. The Director wants them to talk loud enough for the public to hear. But can one utter aloud the words that are used to persuade a girl to prostitute herself? Are these words said aloud in real life? Pirandello makes Madame Pace speak in a queer mixture of Spanish and Italian to give a complete rendering of the actual reality. As the Mother sees her, forgetting that they are only acting, she shouts, "Monster, monster! Assassin! My daughter!" Reality refuses to be contained within the artificial mold of fiction. Madame Pace leaves, and the scene between the Father and Stepdaughter takes place. The play pivots around this scene as the life of the Six Characters centers around it. Pirandello lets their shame fall drop by drop over his sorrowing but steeled heart. The two characters are full of the impetus of reality. To them that scene is torment and life. They go through it word by word, stage by stage, partaking with cruel pleasure of the shame and nausea that it exudes.

After the Father and Stepdaughter enact their parts, it is the turn of the First Actor and First Actress to reënact them, but they fail miserably. How can it be otherwise when that scene is but mimicry to them? Small wonder that they indulge in exaggerated tones and conventional postures that create a banal uniformity. It is but natural that the Father and Stepdaughter are unable to recognize themselves in those puppets. With impatient, ill-restrained gestures, with half amused smiles, openly with words, they express first their astonishment, then their wonder, and finally their disgust. Both the Director and the actors are, by eliminating the truth, making of that tragic scene a romantic concoction: "Of my nausea, of all the reasons, one crueler and viler than another, which have made this of me, have made me just what I am, you would like to make a sentimental, romantic concoction." The Stepdaughter wants the truth. When she had told the man, her stepfather, that because of mourning she could not accept a charming little hat that he, with a lewd smile, wished to present to her, he replied, "Good! Then let us quickly remove that little dress." The Director does not want to have that phrase included. He wishes to replace it by making the man sympathetically inquire for whom she is wearing mourning. Pirandello is disgusted with this hypocritical sentimentality. The Director is afraid of the truth. Why hide the dregs of human lust when man is made insensitive to everything gentle and human, to the youthfulness of the victim, to the nausea of her paid flesh, even to her heart bleeding for a recent death? "I," shouts the Stepdaughter, "with the wound of a recent death in my heart, went, you see, there behind that screen, and with fingers that faltered with shame and repugnance, I undid my dress, my corset."

There is a greater moral lesson in this scene than in a hundred volumes of tiresome moralists. Pirandello does not shrink from the truth, no matter how bitter. He wishes to have faithfully reënacted to the very end the scene in which the Stepdaughter is shown standing before the man, her head resting on his chest. In presenting the scene the Stepdaughter wants her arms bare because "while standing so with my head resting on him and my arms around his neck, I saw a vein throbbing here in my arm and then, as if only that pulsating vein awoke repugnance in me, I looked at him wantonly and buried my head in his chest! [*and turning towards her mother*] Shout, Mother, shout! [*she buries her head in the Stepfather's chest with her shoulders hunched as if not to hear her mother's shout; then she adds in a voice vibrating with stifled anguish*] Shout as you shouted then!" The Mother, carried away by the power of truth and reality, cries, "No, my daughter, my child! [*and after having separated her from him*] You brute, you brute, she is my daughter! Don't you see that she is my daughter?" "Good," exclaims the Director. "The curtain can fall right here." The stage hand is so gripped by the reality of the drama that he actually lowers the curtain.

The next act presents the two families living in the home of their father a life of unspeakable tragedy that weighs on them like a leaden cloak. The Father stares with lucid eyes into the darkness of his studio at the heavy, useless burden of his life. The Stepdaughter is still haughty and arrogant; the Mother is crucified by the indifference of her Son who continues to be silent and disdainful. The Adolescent, meditating suicide, moves like a ghost in the spacious and beautifully furnished rooms of his stepfather. That thought absorbs him and destroys him. The only delicate note is afforded by the Little Girl, who can wander in the lovely gardens, a flower among flowers. As the act progresses, the Little Girl is drowned in the pool which has been placed in the garden scene. The Adolescent stares at her, and shoots himself.

The tragic end of the play reintroduces the original theme of the relation between art and life. Life enclosed in the artificial mold of art breaks its narrow walls, sweeps away fiction, and rules with tragedy and grief. In the wake of a tragic life there lurks death.

Outwardly we find ourselves before a play within a play, a situation that has often been resorted to by playwrights. Actually it is a cleverly constructed play in three acts in which the first act gives the background, the second reënacts the ghastly scene between the Father and the Stepdaughter, and the third presents the life of the Six Characters in the home of the Father where tragedy overtakes them.

What makes the play difficult to understand and most difficult to act is the fact that Pirandello has unveiled before us his secret concern as an author, together with his sympathy for the pitiful plight of the Six Characters. "Authors usually hide the travails of their creation," departing from their custom he tells us through the lips of the Father. He has dramatized the life of a character by portraying him as he is when he leaps into existence in the imagination of his creator, and what he becomes when he is presented by professional actors. The reality of the actor's rôle is fleeting. At best it lasts as long as he plays, and it changes from one actor to another and even from day to day in the same actor. But, in a true character, his reality is the same forever. The rebellion of the Six Characters is that of Pirandello, the playwright, who sees the reality of his characters offended by the interpretation of the professional actors. Characters, as characters, live in the mind or in the book of the author, not in the interpretation given by actors.

Pirandello has also expressed here the feeling of resentment that an artist experiences against the limitations of dramatic art. Why should characters utter aloud what is meant to be a terrible secret between them? Here art offends life, which is truth, in that, for the sake of the spectators, it makes actors proclaim aloud what should be only whispered. All through the play the acting of the Six Characters is closer to real life than that of the professional actors. There is also the resentment of the artist against his inability to take the tangibility of life and transport it into his art. Life as life is, and as such it needs no artistic representation. As soon as we translate it into art we can render but a pale reflection of it. The Father is the spokesman for Pirandello's anti-intellectualistic trend when he says, "You know that life is full of infinite absurdities which have no need whatsoever of appearing verisimilar because they are true. It is really madness to toil in doing the contrary, that is, to invent verisimilar situations and attempt to make them appear true." He contrasts life and art, identifying life with the vehement, maddening passion of the Six Characters, and voicing disdain for the art of the actors which is but form with no real human content. Pirandello feels that the concern of the verisimilar is a hypocritical contrivance, centuries old, to justify the lack of true creation. Men have created always verisimilar situations in the hope that they may seem true.

There is in the play the clash between reality and the perfect illusion of reality. If art is a perfect illusion of reality, then it is not reality; indeed, the more perfect the illusion, the more removed from reality it is. At the same time, if art is perfect reality, it identifies itself with the living actual reality, and it is no longer art. Pirandello has broken the *impasse* by widening the boundaries of what we call reality and giving a paramount place to imagination. "Nature uses the instrument of human fantasy to continue, even in a higher form, her creative work." Confronted by the angular, solid, unwieldy, prosaic reality of material facts and by the vain, empty life as portrayed by the artificial art of the professional actors, he takes refuge among the Six Characters and entrusts to them his own meaning of reality, which is life lived with passion illuminated by fancy, made immortal by true art.

These æsthetic considerations constitute the background

against which Pirandello has projected a highly dramatic life. It is truly a *tour de force* to have been able to keep the intellectual genesis of the play from crowding out or weighing down the emotional element centering about the pitiful and great figures of the Six Characters.

XXXIV

A Play in the Making

TONIGHT WE IMPROVISE

(*Questa sera si recita a soggetto*)

The *motif* of the closeness of art and life is ever recurring in Pirandello. It takes a strange form in that the man in him longs for life lived as actual experience, while the artist is fully conscious of the great power of art considered as a reflected activity.

The framework of *Tonight We Improvise* is constituted by showing a play in its making. The author contrasts the passion of the characters with the artificiality of the stage director in presenting a slight dramatic event that the latter has to stage. In its procedure and structure it bears a marked resemblance to *Six Characters in Search of an Author,* with the fundamental difference that it does not possess the striking characters that create the strength of that celebrated play.

The *deus ex machina* of the play is Dr. Hinkfuss, a stage director who in his physical traits and mannerisms has all the marks of a grotesque character. He is presented as a tiny man "who vents his rage for being short by wearing incredibly long hair. His hands are delicate with small, pale fingers as hairy as caterpillars."

Pirandello places before Dr. Hinkfuss a simple short story and bids him make it into a play. He wants to amuse himself in seeing how the stage director will acquit himself of this task. He patiently listens to the tiny, but fiery doctor who shouts that in the theatre he, as stage director, has a greater rôle than the playwright, in that he makes alive the stilled life that the playwright has enclosed in his written work.

The theme of the play is that of jealousy, the most fearful kind of jealousy, that of the past, felt by a husband who feared that his wife, no longer young or attractive, may still dream of the days when she was both young and gay. Before such a jealousy and before the events that accompany it, what will an artificiality-loving stage director do and what will real characters do? Pirandello does not trust Dr. Hinkfuss. Instead of allowing the dramatic action to weave itself naturally into the atmosphere created by the presence of the public and by the expectation aroused by the long prologue, Dr. Hinkfuss, obeying his instinct for systematized division, breaks it into various tableaux which are to take the place of the traditional acts. In his desire for novelty he has a new scheme—that of introducing the actors by their real names, although they are disguised as the characters that they are to impersonate.

The first actor, who is to play the rôle of the jealous husband, comes on the stage at the bidding of the director but rebels at hearing his name: "You must only believe that here, under these trappings, there is no longer Mr. [*he will say his name*]. He must live the character of Rico Verri, be Rico Verri: and he is, he already is." As Dr. Hinkfuss continues the presentation of the other actors, these, urged by the passion with which they live their rôles, begin to act independently of the director's plans. These actors are characters and not merely paid mannekins. They refuse to give a well-arranged and preordained action. Life in its impetuosity will present men and events better than the cold wisdom of a playwright or a stage director.

The setting is in a small provincial town in the interior of Sicily, where "passions are strong and they smolder in darkness till they flare up violently: most ferocious among them all, jealousy." People live a sluggish life there and they are ready to gossip, especially about a middle-class family whose actions are not very exemplary.

The family is composed of the father, the mother, and four daughters: Mommina, Totina, Dorina, and Nenè. The father, Signor Palmiro, a mining engineer, is a small man. They call him Sampognetta (little bagpipe) because he falls into lapses of absent-mindedness and whistles. The mother, Signora Ignazia, is an enormous woman who beats her husband and instructs her daughters in modern ways of making life pleasant and easy. She comes from Naples and is generally known as "the General." Her four daughters are "very beautiful, plump, sentimental, vivacious, and passionate." Their mode of living is in sharp contrast with the rigid watch that Sicilian families used to keep on their daughters. Pirandello, a Sicilian, has made Signora Ignazia come from Naples.

There are five young aviation officers who play with Signora Ignazia's beautiful, free-and-easy daughters. Only one, Rico Verri, is ill at ease among them. Where women are concerned he is not used to the freedom of the continent. He is shocked upon hearing the mother's ideas: "Do you expect me to keep them in a convent to learn the catechism and embroidery? That time is gone forever." In spite of their worldly ways, the daughters possess the virtues that they will need when they have homes. Mommina knows how to cook; Totina how to mend, how to make dresses, how to keep a budget. The daughters do not want people to know that side of their life; they keep it carefully hidden under another side: the theatre, opera, music. How they love music! Music opens new vistas for them, especially for Mommina. She sings *Trovatore* very beautifully, and as she sings she weeps.

Are there not enough dramatic elements in this simple setting? For Pirandello there are, but not for the stage director who wants his play to be highly melodramatic and picturesque. What would Christmas be without the customary tree, the lights, the gifts, and wishes? Since the story deals with Sicily, Dr. Hinkfuss thinks that "it will be appropriate to have in the beginning a small religious procession—a synthetic representation of Sicily. It will add color." There will be four choir boys in black cassocks and white cottas; four girls dressed in white and enveloped in spotless veils; then a canopy carried over the Holy Family represented by three people who impersonate Saint Joseph, the Virgin, and the infant Jesus.

A small portion of the stage is to be occupied by the entrance to a cabaret. Against the intention of Dr. Hinkfuss the events pertaining to the drama crowd out the sentimental and

305

picturesque setting which really has nothing to do with it. What part can a formalized procession take in an atmosphere where the most violent and barbaric passions are smoldering and are ready to burst into flame? In the cabaret a great confusion arises, brought about by a jest of very questionable taste played by some youths on poor Signor Palmiro who had gone to hear a chorus girl who touched him deeply because she sang like his eldest daughter and cried while she sang, just as Mommina did.

Verri becomes more gloomy and more intractable as he comes to know the ways of those girls better. He resents the liberties that they allow the boys. It makes "his nasty Sicilian blood" boil in his veins. He is not like the other officers. To these, fooling with one is the same as fooling with another. He is attached only to Mommina, who is the wisest of the four girls. She is the one who has been sacrificed, "she has always prepared amusements and parties for the others, and has always been excluded from them." Mommina must be his, only his, and although not even engaged, she must not so much as look at the other officers. One day he finds Mommina singing the second act of *Trovatore,* surrounded by the aviation officers and her sisters. Verri goes into a rage, quarrels with his comrades, beats one of them, and justifies his conduct by asking Mommina to marry him.

As Dr. Hinkfuss continues to arrange his tableaux, almost in despair in his inability to match the impetuosity of events as lived by the characters in their assumed, yet real, life, Signor Palmiro is brought home mortally wounded. Dr. Hinkfuss had planned a dramatic entrance for him. The maid was supposed to shout: "Oh, the master is wounded! The master is wounded! They are carrying him upstairs wounded!" Signor Palmiro enters, carried by the chorus girl and a gentleman. He had gone again to the cabaret to hear her sing, because he found sympathy in her while at home there was only that big woman, his wife, with her violence, and his four daughters with their questionable conduct. A man in the cabaret had offended the chorus girl. Signor Palmiro had taken her part, and the thug had wounded him mortally. All the dramatic effect that Dr. Hinkfuss had planned is absent. There is nothing but death, with Mommina crying real tears. Death is not dramatic. It is ghastly.

Now there is want at home, and want does not encourage virtue in four girls with a mother like Signora Ignazia. What else can Mommina do except marry Verri, even knowing what sad fate awaits her? He will be more jealous than before. Everybody in his home town knows the reputation of his wife's family, and he will show all whether she is modest and virtuous or not.

If what is being enacted does not have all the impetus of life, it is because Dr. Hinkfuss interferes with his "cursed theatre that may God destroy." He only cares about effects when life is roaring in the characters, in their blood, while passions ride gigantic black horses with them; and their bodies are all aquiver and their souls are in fever and agony. Mommina and Verri must remain alone. Their grief must be stripped of any veneer to be seen in all its pathos and tragedy.

The characters insist that Dr. Hinkfuss go away. Since it was the final scene, and since it was their passion, while he was doing his part merely for art's sake, they cannot stand his presence there. Mommina is now about thirty; has been married to Verri for several years and has two little girls. Dr. Hinkfuss would have used powder in her make-up in order to give the impression of age. There is no need of make-up for Mommina. She is already old; she is pale, di sheveled; some of her teeth are out; her body has been made ungainly by motherhood. Her husband is violent, forbidding, gloomy. His jealousy continues; he forbids Mommina to go out, and since he cannot be jealous of the present, and no man ever sees her, he torments her and himself with the jealousy of the past. He tries to pry into her secret thoughts; he wants to know what she dreams. It is useless for Mommina to tell him that she does not have dreams; that if she did, when she opened her eyes again, her present life would be more unbearable to her; that he wants her death; that he does not want her even to think or to dream. That infuriates Verri more. He moves like a beast in a cage: "It is that, it is exactly that! I

bar doors and windows and to what avail if I am betrayed
here in this very prison? Here in her, within her—in this
dead flesh of hers which makes her betrayal alive, alive, if
she thinks, if she dreams." Verri is powerless: "Even if I
blinded you," he says, "what you have seen, the remem-
brances which you have in your eyes would remain in your
memory; and if I should tear your lips, these lips which
have been kissed by others, you would continue to feel the
pleasure, the taste, that they experienced in kissing, to the
point of dying of this pleasure."

Now poor Mommina is dying, but not of the pleasure derived from the remembrance of the kisses she has received.
She has heart trouble, and Verri is killing her with the
savage fury of his jealousy. The images of her mother and
sisters float before her, and they assume a tangible existence
on the stage.

After Mommina had married, they had continued to live
the same life. Totina had become a great opera singer; Nenè,
a fashionable harlot. Now Totina is singing in the town where
Mommina and Verri live, so a program has announced.
Totina will sing in *Trovatore*, the opera that Mommina sang
so beautifully.

Verri knows that his wife's family is in town. The past has
surged like a polluted tide over him, and is stifling him.
He goes to Mommina's room and reproaches her again for
the liberties that the girls took in her house before they married. In his over-excited mind, he sees again how those aviation officers embraced her, how they kissed her. He is like a
madman; he kisses her, bites her, sneers at her, pulls her
hair. Mommina calls for help, and her two little girls hasten
to her side in their long nightgowns, pale, frightened, while
Verri flees, shouting: "I am going mad! I am going mad! I
am going mad!"

The past, her love for music, the thought of Totina and of
her mother are so vivid in Mommina's mind that her mother
and sister appear before her. Reality is obliterated by her
dream. Drawing her daughters close to her, she tells them
how Totina has come to sing in *Trovatore*. She tells them of

the beauty of a theatre on an opera night, as she had always dreamt of it in wishing to dedicate herself to singing. Had she not married Verri, she would have sung in *Trovatore*, because her voice was more beautiful than Totina's. Now Totina sings while Mommina's heart is giving way. But she clings to life, happy in her music and in having her little daughters near her, loving her, all three happy, at least for a moment while the little girls' eyes shine like stars in their pale faces. She feels that life is ebbing away. She sings her favorite aria desperately, with all her voice, and dies.

This is the play as we have laboriously reconstructed and interpreted it. The dramatic events are stifled by the technique that occupies a paramount part in the play. The constant clashes between Dr. Hinkfuss and the characters interrupt the action and prevent that unity which is so often admired in Pirandello and which is a direct derivation of the intense passion that stirs his characters. In reality there are two centers in the play: one that of the author who rebels against the artificiality of the stage director, and the other that of the pitiful story of Mommina, her family, and Verri. These two centers, often clashing and interfering with each other, rob the play of unity.

The play would not please a modern audience. The differentiation between actual life and life in the passionate characters is so slight that events can happen on each of the two planes without jarring the author who wishes to stress this closeness, but naturally they would jar the onlookers. What remains with us after reading the work is the drama of Pirandello, the playwright, in the torment of creating his play, rather than the drama of Mommina and Verri. One feels, to be sure, the pitiful condition of that poor human being tortured by jealousy, and the self-tormenting hatred of Verri, but one sees them in the distance, as if looked at through the wrong end of the opera glasses.

The author's mind is returning with excessive insistence to the theme of the making of a play, a theme which attracted his attention both in *Six Characters in Search of an Author* and in *Each in His Own Way*. In the endless series of æsthetic

309

recriminations, the stage director calls the playwright artificial; in turn, the characters call the stage director artificial, and Pirandello seems to suggest sadly that life calls all of them artificial. In doing it he attacks himself, and his autocriticism explains the weakness of the play. He has shown all the tricks of the trade, just as in *Six Characters in Search of an Author* he has shown the tormented travails of dramatic creation.

As in everything that Pirandello has written, there are beautiful pages and situations, and there stand out his beautiful and exquisite thoughts on art.

In spite of the negative reactions that the play has inspired in us, we see in looking at it in retrospect that the play has a prologue that is followed by a first tableau introducing the characters and giving the situation as it stands when the drama begins. Then new tableaux give the death of the father, the marriage of Mommina, and the rage of the jealous Verri that leads to Mommina's death.

Over the æsthetic consideration, over the tragic life of modest and romantic Mommina, there floats the infinite sadness of the author before the mystery of life: "Life must obey two necessities that, because they are opposed to each other, do not allow it either to assume a definite form or to be forever fluid. If life moved eternally it would never acquire consistency; if it acquired consistency, it would never move. And yet life must have both consistency and motion." Still he realizes that life has ebbed away from the art that encloses Mommina's tragedy. Nothing will ever equal nor make live again the anguish of the poor girl who sang so beautifully the aria of *Trovatore* and shed real tears as she sang.

XXXV

Life Rebels Against the Fixity of Art

DIANA AND TUDA

(*Diana e la Tuda*)

Diana and Tuda is another play dedicated to Marta Abba. The heroine, Tuda, has auburn hair like Marta's in *The Wives' Friend*, and is as beautiful as Donata Genzi in *She Wanted to Find Herself*.

Reduced to the main threads that the author has woven into the play, *Diana and Tuda* is the delicate and pitiful story of a young model who could not bear to be only a model, a statue, for the artist she loved. Her life wavers between two men: Nono Giuncano, an old and celebrated sculptor, and Sirio Dossi, his pupil. Giuncano is one of the many characters created by Pirandello to represent his absolute and irrational idealism. In his long and glorious career the old sculptor has made numberless statues, but he has always been tormented by the thought that his statues, since life is really fluid, voluble, and chaotic, were lives fixed unto death.

As an artist who lives his art in his very flesh, as an intimate part of himself, he has suffered before the stony silence and immobility of his statues as before something that was once throbbing with youth and is now cold and stiff. It has been tragic for him to take the life of a model and imprison it in clay or marble. A feeling of revolt has spread its cold tentacles over him as he has realized that death too makes a statue of a man. His own body is the model that death is using to transform him into a statue. The process is slow but fatal. As the years have passed, his hands, his face, and his limbs have been assuming the stiffness of what is dead. As this realization grew in him, a gust of folly passed roaring by him; it enveloped him; it compelled him to break and shatter his own statues to which he had dedicated his youth.

311

He saw his own death in them. He shouts to Sirio Dossi, the great believer in art: "It will make of you as well as of me a statue, when you lie on a bed or on the naked earth, stiff." The two artists are perfectly described in these words of Giuncano: "When I hear someone talk, when I look or go somewhere, in the words I hear, in what I see, in the silence of things, I have always the suspicion that there may be something unknown to me from which my spirit, though present, runs the risk of remaining excluded. Then I stand there with the longing that, if I could penetrate into it, my life would open to new sensations that would give me the feeling of living in another world.—This man [Dossi], on the contrary —I don't know—he is just like that; with blinkers on. He does not feel, he does not see anything. He wishes only one thing."

The all-absorbing interest of Sirio Dossi is a statue of Diana that he is molding. He wants it to have the same winged beauty and the same posture as the one attributed to Cellini that is admired in the Brescia Museum. He is using beautiful Tuda as a model. Behind a curtain which extends across the stage Dossi is working and Tuda is posing. Before the curtain is seated Giuncano. He is "gloomy, restless. He is in his sixties; powerfully built, with his white beard and hair in disorder. His face is haggard, but his eyes are very young and full of life. He dresses in black." He loves Tuda, but he would never reveal his feelings to her because he would not want to contaminate her life and youth. Dossi is feverishly working while Tuda is begging him to stop because her posture is very tiring and her arm is absolutely numb. He refuses to stop; the hour is not up yet. Giuncano violently demands that Dossi allow Tuda to rest. To Giuncano the art of statuary appears futile and sinful before the supple beauty of Tuda's body; and he resents Dossi's so torturing her exquisite limbs. But Dossi is deaf to his voice. At Tuda's slightest movement he shouts and threatens her. He has made four sketches of his Diana and has thrown them away. Now he hopes to have the statue as he sees it in all the purity of its contour and in its perfection. A fever for work burns in him.

Dossi is tormented too, as are all true artists, but his torment is brought about by reasons that are antithetical to those of his master. While Giuncano is haunted by the immobility of death, Sirio Dossi is harassed by the mutability of life. The body of Tuda appears to him in all its changing forms as he works at his statue. That is life which is never the same. In his rebellion he wants to give to that body the immortality of the unchanging and divine character of art.

Tuda suffers in being only a perfect, cold, and distant body towards which Dossi often has a sort of hatred. She is presented to us in the glory of her loveliness as follows: "She is very young and marvelously beautiful; auburn hair, curly, arranged in the Greek fashion; green eyes, long, large, and luminous, that at times, in a passionate mood, gaze limpidly and sweetly like a dawn; at times, in sadness, they have the grieving, opaque character of a turquoise. Her lips often have a sorrowing expression, as if she views life with a disdainful bitterness; but if she laughs, she is suddenly enveloped in a luminous grace that seems to spread light and life on everything."

The play moves on two planes, one serving as a background formed by Giuncano's and Dossi's ideas about art and life, another where the dramatic action develops. The main characters, with the exception of Tuda, who is a model with a soul that Pirandello has lent to her, are people who live in the storm of a sensuous social life out of which they must come because in their soul there is an aspiration to something higher than social intrigues and love affairs. The higher life is represented in the play by art, much as in the old days religion was the beacon that led men out of the stormy waters of sensuality.

Dossi has a mistress, a society woman, Sara Mendel. It is one of those relations that are obscure, especially to those who writhe in them; filth that sticks, loathing that gurgles in one's throat.

Tuda tries to remove Dossi from the abstract and rarefied atmosphere where he lives with his statue of Diana. She wants him to see that she is alive: "Alive! eyes, mouth, arms, fingers, legs, look at them. I move them, and this is flesh, feel it: warm." Dossi cannot see the living being in her. She must serve only his art: "But what have you to do with me, as a living being?" he says. "What counts is the statue—not you. Marble; it's matter; not your flesh."

A mere chance gives Tuda the opportunity to force Dossi to give her more attention. Another artist, Caravani, has decided to make a painting of Diana with Tuda as a model. It has been a scheme of Tuda's to compel Dossi to marry her. She has already had a few sittings with Caravani. The picture is half finished. Dossi, upon learning of this, is furious. In her free way Tuda says to him, taunting him: "When an artist wants a model all to himself, do you know what he does? He marries her, my dear." In her words, however, there is more than a caprice and a challenge. She loves Sirio Dossi, even if her wounded vanity and pride mingle with her feelings.

Dossi agrees to marry her. He will marry her to compel her to be a model for him only. There are so many erratic arrangements and situations under the cloak of matrimony, especially among people of Dossi's social circle, that at the most his friends will but laugh. He and Tuda will be free to live as they wish, since he marries her only as a model. To prove to his friends and acquaintances that Tuda is only a model to him, the model for his statue Diana, he continues his relations with Sara Mendel. Dossi is blind to the humble offer that Tuda has made of herself. He does not see the woman in her. She longs for a bit of real affection. She wants to be alive for him and to give him joy, but she is rejected and spurned.

As soon as Tuda is married she becomes more and more hurt and despondent. Her dressmaker, who has gone to her house to try on new dresses, finds her very much thinner. She is pale and haggard. The wife is taking her revenge on the model. Having assumed the form of a wife and not living as one, it is natural, human, and logical that she should suffer.

She even abandons herself to grotesque acts. She goes to the studio and puts her numerous dresses on the various statues that Dossi has created of her. She is a statue like them. "Very well," she says, "I shall see to it that he will find them so. You can imagine how he will shout that I have desecrated them! As if what he is doing to me were not worse than this! Must I be only a statue here? Like a sister to these? Well: I am dressed, but I want them to be dressed too." People around her laugh at this outburst, but there is in these words an anger that lacerates something in the human breast, the resentment of a woman scorned, whose love gradually turns to hatred.

The chief sufferer in this situation is Dossi. It is his penalty for trifling with a human heart and with a life. His Diana is not finished, and whatever there is of it is not the copy of the beautiful, young, and happy Tuda of former days. Dossi has uncovered the human being in her, has wounded her, and in so doing he has destroyed the model in her. In the features of the statue Tuda sees herself as she has been made to suffer by Dossi and her rival, Sara Mendel. She sees in the eyes "hatred for the torture that they have given me. Before, it did not have eyes like these—its eyes were different, quite different . . . and that hand that touches its side—do you see it?—that hand was open before! Do you see now? It is closed tight like a fist. . . . It is no longer the one that he wanted to make. It is I now there, do you understand?"

One day poor Tuda finds Sara Mendel in Dossi's studio and learns that he has given her the key. She rebels with a violence that the other woman cannot understand, but which is clear to the logical mind of Pirandello, who sees in Tuda the model only. Since she had failed to be a woman, a wife, to Dossi, and had to be reconciled to be a model, the studio is her kingdom and Sara should not violate it with her presence. She can go to Dossi's rooms, if she wishes, since Tuda is not really his wife, and he is completely free. But there in the studio, no; Tuda has a right there. She sees the subtle scheme of Sara Mendel. She has succeeded in keeping Dossi chained to her, thus defeating Tuda as a wife. Now she wants to defeat her also as a model, wound her in the only prerogative she has before the man whom she loves.

How can Tuda remain in Dossi's home now that he, by giving a key to her rival, has offended her and destroyed her even as a model? She offers herself to Giuncano in a fit of desperation, and also because she feels sorry for the man who has borne in silence and with reserve his love for her. The old master nobly refuses because he knows that behind Tuda's offer there is only "a little compassion" for him. His soul is still young, for he remarks: "I stir too—yes, within— I still feel, I still feel. I feel with all the forces of my soul; but here, now—do you see? I have this body that I hate, in which I was never able to recognize myself." He reveals to Tuda the tragic story of his life. His father had been a profligate man, and no tie of affection had ever existed between father and son. He had been the cause of the death of Giuncano's mother. Giuncano hated himself, his body, because it resembled his father's: "It is horrible, yes," he says. "It grows old, and it becomes his more and more as my features become more pronounced and the lines of my face deepen." Giuncano has placed himself outside of life, like so many of Pirandello's characters to whom life has been too unkind and cruel, but he has the strength to shout to himself and to the woman who has offered herself to him: "Life must not take hold of me again! It must not take hold of me again!"

Tuda has decided to leave Dossi at any cost. She has written to Caravani that she is ready to be his model that he may complete the painting of Diana that was left unfinished because of her sudden marriage. Caravani accepts, all the more that a gentleman from Chile wants to buy the work. He goes to Dossi's studio and finds Tuda steeped in deep thoughts imbued by Giuncano's tragic confession. He tiptoes over to her and tries to kiss her. A slap reveals to this modern Don Juan that love redeems Pirandello's women from the baseness of the flesh. She tells Caravani: "Woe unto you if you touch me. I come only to be your model." And she leaves Dossi's house.

Dossi is frantic. He cannot finish his Diana without Tuda. He has attempted to work with other models, but in vain. He has fought a duel with Caravani and has wounded him. Now he is seeking Tuda everywhere because he must have her, only her, to finish his statue. After many days he finds her, worn out and haggard, the shadow of her former self. Dossi, Giuncano, and Tuda enter the studio. She tells Dossi that she cannot be the model for his Diana any longer. She tries to go over to the statue. Dossi, thinking that she wants to destroy it, threatens to kill her. Giuncano, like a wild beast, leaps on him and strangles him. Now Tuda is nothing at all; neither wife nor model; just nothing.

There are several situations that make one wonder whether Pirandello had not in mind D'Annunzio's *Gioconda* when he was touched by Tuda's sad plight. The similarity, however, is only in elements concerning the plot, since Pirandello's characters do not possess the Olympian calm nor the æsthetic nature that D'Annunzio has given to those who create the drama of Gioconda. It is very interesting to note the contrast in the development of the plays by two authors so strikingly dissimilar as D'Annunzio and Pirandello. The different treatment of the love theme constitutes the basic difference between them. In D'Annunzio, eroticism makes the long disquisitions about art empty and cumbersome; in Pirandello, the tormented concern about life tinges with sincerity and pathos the art and love *motifs*. Passions play a large rôle in Pirandello's play, too, but only as a vital part of life and not for their own sake.

Critics may accuse Pirandello of being abstract in this play. Often the concept has obscured and overpowered the poetic element in the situations. Often the distance between the background and the action jars the audience, as when one passes from Giuncano's or Dossi's beautiful discussions of art to the petty jealousies between Tuda and Sara. However, it should not be forgotten that Pirandello has never failed to endow his characters with a sincere thirst for life. The lucid lucubrations of these people, excluded from a normal existence, constitute all their life, and it is pitiful to see them suspended in a harrowing emptiness. Giuncano and Dossi are both perfectly aware that before them lies the possibility of letting themselves be engulfed by the muddy marshes of a commonplace existence or of living in the torment of their intellect. Referring to what people call "living," Dossi asks: "What is it? To travel, . . . to gamble, to love women, a beautiful home, friends, fine clothes, to listen to the usual gossip, to do the usual things? To live for life's sake?" They refuse to live such a life, and they naturally find themselves in a world of lucid concepts where the intellect is forced to take a paramount rôle.

The gloom of Giuncano is not cerebral. One feels a real and genuine flame in his utterances because they reflect the thoughts of Pirandello. Man is caught in a trap—the trap of life. "Call it life," says Giuncano to Tuda. "As a child you moved more easily; you darted here and there—now a little less—always less, always less, till—do you think that you have lived?—You have finished dying." It is the thought that life is a slow, continuous, but inevitable death—a thought so dear to those who have been excluded from the feast of life, be they ancient philosophers or solitary saints. Giuncano, too, re-echoes the feeling that the author has expressed through other characters: "I am thus: with my wide-open eyes that would not like to know what they see: things as they are that bear the punishment of being as they are and of not being able to be otherwise."

Pirandello's ideas of art and life pass over the play like luminous beams moving in the night, but the sad plight of poor Tuda is never obscured before us.

XXXVI

Renunciation

SHE WANTED TO FIND HERSELF

(*Trovarsi*)

The thought of the effect of dramatic acting on personality has often appeared in a veiled or open way in Pirandello's theatre. The problem can be briefly stated thus: When we act we assume, be it but temporarily, a personality different from our own. To what extent does it become ours? Does it have any lasting effect on us?

She Wanted to Find Herself is dedicated to Marta Abba, whose dramatic art Pirandello admired very much. What would be the effect of an assumed dramatic personality on the life of an actress like Marta Abba or of Donata Genzi, if you prefer to disguise her under that name? Pirandello presents the thesis that a true artist such as Abba must deny herself her own personality, must give up the fullness of her natural existence for her art. When she lives entirely absorbed by the present reality, as a perfectly normal human being, constantly and deeply herself, she cannot be a true artist. To be truly great she must live in the characters that she impersonates, and if she does, she necessarily renounces her own personality and life. It is natural that a person who has had such a great interest in the theatre, who has known and lived among actors for years, should consider such a problem.

Donata Genzi bears the characteristic traits, both physical and mental, that Pirandello lends to his typical characters: "She is pale, perturbed, with a grieving expression on her strange, tragic lips. In her large eyes with very long lashes there is something gloomy and lost." She is one of the great individuals before whose depth and beauty Pirandello ceases to be a humorist and becomes a tragic writer in the loftiest and best sense of the word. It is due to this afflatus of his art that he sought his setting and characters in an aristocratic place

319

and among distinguished people whom he uses to express his
new mood. The tone of the conversation is higher than in earlier plays; as brilliant as ever, but more contained and reserved. We are led to the Villa Arcuri on the Riviera. Modern
life has entered the play without Pirandello's recriminations,
and its exponents are sympathetically treated. Nina, who represents a modern girl, athletic and outspoken, Giviero, a distinguished psychologist, and Count Mola, a friend of the
hostess, Elisa Arcuri, are all presented in a favorable light in
accordance with the distinction and good taste that are often
found among people of their class. There are also among the
guests two writers, Salò and Volpe. Volpe stands for the narrow, meticulous "realist." He is a great believer in experience, a convinced follower of instinct: "dark, untidy, he often
pulls his lower lip with two fingers." Salò expresses the
author's belief in imagination that dwarfs experience: "under
his flying hair, long and gray, he has a penetrating, luminous,
youthful countenance."

These members of the best society that crowd the Riviera
are gathered at the Villa Arcuri to meet the great actress,
Donata Genzi, who is visiting the hostess. Donna Elisa Arcuri
and Donata had gone to school together. When Donata became famous, Donna Elisa had written to her. They had remembered each other, and a warm friendship had begun.
Now, Donata is tired, almost sick. She has come to spend a
few weeks with her friend to restore her health.

Elj Nielsen is the only guest who has not arrived. He is a
blue-eyed youth, son of a Swedish sailor and of Count Mola's
sister; now an orphan entrusted to the Count's care. "He is
twenty-six years of age, very blond, but bronzed by the sun,
with clear eyes and an exotic countenance. He is dressed as
people dress at a summer resort; he is simple mannered,
abrupt, and yet dreamy." He passes his days in his sailboat,
roaming over the sea, happy in its blue immensity. Nina
hopes that he does not come. She is desperately in love with
him, as love flares up among the free, unconventional young
people of today. She is afraid that Donata and Elj, upon see-

ing each other, will fall in love. It will be fatal, because they are two creatures of perfection.

We are introduced into the drama by the curiosity of the Marchioness Boveno, another guest, who asks what sort of woman Donata Genzi is. She is informed by Salò that she is not one of those persons who act in life, too, not one of the common, hateful variety that can be easily defined as "a woman who acts even off stage." To Salò an actress, a true actress like Donata Genzi, lives on the stage "and as such she does not act in life. She is not one woman, one person—but many, as many as are the women whose rôles she takes." He ends: "And perhaps—for herself, no one." When she becomes a woman like all others, and makes a life for herself and enjoys it, she will cease to be an artist in the same measure as she allows life to absorb her. An artist, according to Salò, must "deny herself, her life, her person, give herself and her life completely to the character that she impersonates." Volpe, the one who believes in experience, wants to know how an actress could enact a love scene if she had never loved in her life. Salò, furious, retorts: "Oh, I had forgotten that you believe in experience—that in order to know, you must experience. I know, on the contrary, that I have always experienced only what I imagined beforehand." Experience is to him a synonym of disillusionment. Facts are disillusioning because they do not correspond to the idea that we have formed. It is the same with love. Those who love are not conscious of their emotion. Sentiment is blind. In the depth of love we close our eyes.

The guests are interested in this discussion when Donata arrives. They ask her opinion. She agrees with Salò. It is enough for her to project herself intuitively into the characters that she impersonates. She confesses: "I am each time as my rôle wants me to be, with the greatest sincerity." Since they are talking of love, that devilish chap Salò points out to her that if some day she falls in love, she will copy herself as she was when enacting her love scenes. Donata Genzi admits that. She is conscious of the fact that to deny herself a personal life is the penalty for the privilege of living her many lives on the stage. She has always lived a lonely and secluded existence; the warmth of love has never cheered her heart. Art is not fiction for her: "It is life that is revealed to us. Life that has found expression. It is no longer feigning when we have made this expression our own to the point that it becomes fever in our veins, tears in our eyes, smiles on our lips." Art is to her exaltation, but also renunciation.

As she becomes more and more conscious of the limitations that her art has imposed on her personal life, a deeper light gathers in her eyes. Her inner torment becomes clearer as she clothes it in sharp, lucid words before the guests, and she sees it in the transparent consistency that words give to ideas. She knows that an artist cannot have secrets, that she belongs to the public, that all claim the right to fall in love with her, while her heart is lonely and cries for a bit of warmth that she knows she must deny herself. She knows that to really live, fully, instinctively, one has to throw oneself headlong into the abyss of life. She is aware that it is not really living to be suspended as she is, caught between the powerful mirror of art and the swift river of life, "ready to answer in her mind the call of every sensation, of every impression, of so many images that a sudden longing may kindle." Her life is as evanescent as that of one who wanders among memories. She is like a flower that has not been able to blossom. She knows it, yet she has denied herself to love in order to offer all the thirst of her whole self to her art.

After this sincere and dramatic outburst, she is too excited to have dinner with the other guests. She begs to be excused, and retires to her room, only to come downstairs after a while to go down by the sea, seeking solace in its immensity for the torment of her soul. In the hall she meets Elj Nielsen, who has arrived in the meantime. He has preferred to stay there, alone, glancing at a magazine, while the guests are having dinner. His plans are to wait until his uncle goes to bed, then sail his boat, defying the roaring, stormy sea. Donata asks him to take her with him now on his sailboat, to face danger in the storm that is growing worse. Elj is at first surprised;

the request, the look of the unknown lady, and her daring spirit move him from his customary indifference. He tells her that he has "courage for himself, but fear for her." Donata insists. They go. Elj's sailboat is too fragile to withstand the mighty waves which batter its slight hull to pieces. Elj saves Donata by a miracle. They fall in love.

Elj is the very antithesis of Donata. She has the restrained consciousness of acts, postures, even ideas that her art has given her. He is fluid, spontaneous. He has in his blood the adventurous spirit of his father. He confides to her that he does not like commercialized sport: "I detest it as it is practised: imposture, mania, or speculation. I want my eyes to remain eternally new. I live with nature. I keep away from every intimacy as from a plague. I don't want disappointments. I want other people to remain new for me. Everything new. Only what is sudden is beautiful for me—what does not seem true—the continuous surprise that overtakes us. If I look closely at something and think of it, I am lost." His spontaneous temperament is revealed more clearly now that he is in love with Donata. She is convalescing in his studio where he had taken her on that harrowing night. He wants Donata and himself to be always new to each other: "You must never know what may come to you from me: acts, thoughts, surprises; things do not seem true to you in one like me." He paints. To be out at sea before the always different aspect of nature is to him a moment of supreme joy in which he finds the best in him: exaltation, rapture, courage to conquer all difficulties. His painting falls short of his expectations and desires because life appears to him a bursting shell, a continuous blossoming, a stupefying miracle. Donata, too, is new to him, and he is lost in her love. Elj knows that his instinctive, complete abandonment to her is the secret of his joy.

Donata is not less happy than Elj. She confesses to him that she has never belonged to herself. "But now that is over, all over. This is life and I want to see and feel my life only in you. To touch it in you, so: the light of your eyes [*she passes loving hands over them*], the taste of your lips [*she passes her fingers gently over his lips*]. Now I live, now I

323

live." She wants to find herself—her real self—not the one that she has transfused into her acting. She hopes to find her deep self and offer it to Elj. This is the meaning that "to find herself" has for Donata Genzi. Will she find herself in Elj's love? Will that love be greater than her art, absorb her so as to make a new being out of her, a perfect being not only in the eyes of others but before herself in the light of her own limpid eyes?

One day while caressing Elj's hair she becomes conscious that her caress is exactly the same as that which Giviero, one of the guests, had told her he had noticed in her acting. She is horrified. She begs of Elj: "Don't let me think of how I am, how I move, how I look at you, the gestures I make. I don't want to see myself. I know my face too well. I have always made it up. Now I want mine as it is, without my seeing it."

She, too, would like to be entirely new, but she cannot. She must use the same voice, the same words, the same gestures that she has so many times used in her love scenes. She becomes more and more conscious of the futility of her attempt at being as spontaneous as Elj. She has thrown herself blindly into life just as that night she threw herself into the slashing fury of the storm. She has realized that that is the way of life and of love: to close her eyes; and she has obeyed. She now awaits with fear the moment when her eyes will be open, when a man as spontaneous and rebellious as Elj will see her on the stage. She tells him: "You are like a child who perhaps will be frightened as many children are when they see masks."

She considers giving up her career, but she realizes that it would be too great a sacrifice. Elj's love cannot fill her life. He represents only instinct, fluidity, even gentleness and purity of instinct, but that is all. Grievingly she admits that she has not found herself in that love. Life is still to her the beating of quivering wings, the aspiration towards a goal which is never attained. It was that feeling that made her acting so beautiful and appealing. Perhaps all in the darkened theatre recognized themselves in the passionate expression of her vain aspiration. She sees her failure in the light of the struggle that goes on in the whole universe when what is unformed is constantly striving to take shape, to be something definite, unaware of the fact that at the end of that transformation lurk death and destruction.

Through this realization her faith in art is strengthened. She reaches the conclusion that only art affords a perfect creation, finished unto itself, yet not dead but gloriously living. She is terribly unhappy now. Before she met Elj the thought had often come to her mind that her unhappiness was due to the fact that she had denied herself the experience of actual life, love, and passion. She has to confess that it is worse now: "It is worse, worse to have a life of your own. If you abandon yourself completely to it, you can no longer understand anything at all. You reopen your eyes, and if you don't wish to be engulfed by all that is commonplace, by all that becomes habit, a rut, monotony without color or taste, everything is again uncertain, unstable. With this difference that you are no longer as before, but you have tied yourself, compromised yourself, through what you have done without having succeeded in finding yourself." Love has been a disappointment to her because it has fallen short of her imagining —the imagining that art had enriched for her.

Uncertain, trembling, almost groping, she returns to the stage. The first time that Elj sees her act will be the crucial test. What she feared happens. Elj goes to the theatre and sees her as she had been with him in their intimacy. He feels that his love cannot stand this. He leaves the theatre before the play is over, and returns to his sea, to his nature, away from the painted masks that make him shudder. Donata too had suffered. In the first two acts she had felt lost. She confesses: "I felt dragged down by the public with which I had lost contact. What silence! What emptiness! I sweated blood—a torture, a torture!" But all of a sudden in the third act she really found herself: "A sudden jerk, here, within me, and freedom was mine. I forgot everything. I felt myself taken, carried away. Life flowed back into all my senses, my ears could distinguish sounds again, and everything was again clear and sure, sure. I possessed life again and so full, so full, and so easy—in such complete intoxication of happiness that everything glowed, burned, lived, and grew with me."

Donata had found herself in her art, but through Elj's love. She had fled to his room without even changing her costume to offer to him her triumph. He had already left. She had hoped that he would understand that it was possible for her to have her experience as a woman merge with her experience as an artist. Only so could she have the complete experience of his love. That night she had felt that she had "found not only the fullness of her art as an actress but the fullness of her life as a woman." Elj had not understood. His blindness condemned her again to the painful loneliness, the haughty disdain, and the isolation on the lofty peak where she nurtured her art with the sacrifice of her womanhood. She realizes that she cannot find herself in instinctive and complete life as she had longed to do. She accepts her hard but luminous destiny: to create, to re-create in her acting the lives of the great heroines of drama.

In this play we find the same *motif* as in *Right You Are if You Think You Are,* but accorded an entirely different treatment. Here, too, echo the words of Signora Ponza, "I am no one for myself." Donata Genzi had condemned herself to an impersonal life, to the negation of her identity, for the sake of her art. After the brief interlude of her love for Elj, she returns to the stage, grieving as Signora Ponza did but, being an actress, with more theatricality.

In humble terms, the problem of Donata and Elj is that of people who want to reconcile marriage and career. Pirandello has naturally made it more complex according to the nature of the two characters around whom the drama pivots.

The play is also a defense of the life of an actress against the stupid, current opinion that imagines that every actress must be corrupt: "The normality of a chicken cannot understand the flight of a crane. The chicken stands for current morality, *bourgeois* morality with all its preconceived ideas and prejudices," explains the humorous Salò.

Donata Genzi shares Pirandello's lofty idealism which at

times becomes exasperated and tormented, bordering on irrationality. She revolts against the limitations of the everyday life and looks on her body as on a clumsy impediment: "Seeing myself called back to reality by certain glances directed at my body, finding myself a woman—well, I don't say that it displeases me—but it seems an almost hateful necessity, in certain moments, and I feel the impulse to rebel against it. Candidly, I do not see the reason why my body should be for me my most personal possession." The author has placed in her not only his admiration before an exquisite and perfect embodiment of womanhood, but also his tragic wavering between art that has consistency and life that is fluid. Life is Elj Nielsen; art is Donata Genzi.

The idealism of Pirandello before alighting on the blue waters of the Riviera and tarrying for a brief moment on the love of two perfect creatures, has soared to a dizzy height. Pirandello has voiced here his rebellion at the very fact that we are who we are because this fact precludes the possibility of our being innumerable other beings: "Once life has become caught in this mold, in us, that's the end. It is fixed." Pirandello is tormented here by the fixity of universal life. He has revealed his grief through Donata Genzi's words: "When we perform an act, it is not our whole being which performs it, all life which is in us—but only what we are in that moment—and yet that act, once accomplished, immediately imprisons us—stops us with obligations and responsibilities, in that given way and in no other, irreparably." Every possibility of action is precluded from us then: "and of so many germs that could create a forest, only one germ falls there, the tree grows there, and will not be able to move from there, there in its entirety forever."

We hear in this play many of Pirandello's ideas on art in general and on dramatic art in particular. There are clever and witty statements such as the one that Salò voices: "Art, being eternal, should have no age. But the trouble is that, being a woman, it loves fashion." There are also exquisite pages in which Donata Genzi reveals the exaltation and solace that she found in art.

The ever recurring *motif* in the play is the author's wavering between yielding to the fetters of a dwarfing experience and entrusting himself to the freedom of a daring imagination. He has revealed his idealistic mood by leading his heroine to a lofty region where only a few superior beings such as Donata Genzi and Marta Abba can abide.

XXXVII

The Misery of Fame

WHEN ONE IS SOMEBODY

(*Quando si è qualcuno*)

The keynote of *When One Is Somebody* is the misery of literary fame. The author studies the life of a poet who has found that respect, admiration, and glory are "all things that kill." His family, his admirers, the whole country have immobilized him in a given image that has blurred his real features by sealing them in a painful fixity. Although in his fifties, he seems to have lost the possibility of looking any age. They have molded him much in the fashion in which a puppet is made. He is almost embalmed alive. His life is no longer his own, nor are his acts or his feelings. He is tired of being followed by the eyes of the public: "They are as many mirrors before you, those eyes that stare at you. They make a statue of you, always composed in a fixity of perfection that is very tormenting."

His literary fame has established a certain form and style in his art from which he cannot depart. His head with his long hair brushed sweepingly back from his forehead in the fashion of all poets has become "of public ownership like the head on a coin." But he suffers, since behind that stereotyped image there is a soul that rebels: "No other image of me is admitted. I have expressed what I have felt, and there—crystallized—I cannot be different. Woe unto me if I am! They do not recognize me any longer. I must not move from the precise, definite concept which they have formed of me: there, that one, motionless, forever!" He confides his sorrow in these terms: "How many times, at night in my studio, do I feel oppressed beyond endurance: a puppet, to be left there, before my desk, in the light of the lamp, with its wig, its wax face, its wax hands, its lifeless eyes—there, motionless."

Pirandello has derived his theme and feelings partly from

329

his own experience, and he embodies the misery of greatness in a character that has even been deprived of a name. His speeches are marked by three asterisks. (We shall follow the author's procedure in using them.) Fame has destroyed his identity. It is natural that he should have no name.

When we meet his family we do not wonder why he has assumed his stilted and statuary coldness, his unchanging impassivity that makes one think of a mask. "Giovanna, his wife, is a large-boned woman, a rigid personification of the official glory of the husband; she has a very low forehead, austere oval eyes, a solemn look, a strong, imperious nose, a firm chin; she dresses pompously in black and silver." The children, Valentina and Tito, are as formal and hollow as their mother. Tito basks in the glory of his father, and he always has the words "Papà, papà," on his lips. We learn that "when he has said 'Papà' he has said everything." Valentina, the daughter, already in her thirties, seems unapproachable, like a figure descended from a picture. She is painted with painstaking artifice. She has an air of supreme absentmindedness. These people have solidified the father's fame into a block of marble.

The poet lives in an ancient house, and his library "smells of the musty air of old prints and of the closeness of churches. It gives a stagnating sense of solemn oppression." When one sees him seated before his desk, he looks as if crushed by the artificiality of his life. He is not as alive as the pictures of four great men of letters that he keeps in his library: Dante, Ariosto, Foscolo, and Leopardi. They are the only people with whom he can communicate, but they do not give much encouragement. Pirandello has treated their four figures symbolically and when * * *, the man without name, is in the library, they move from the panels where they are portrayed and they enact a sort of mute scene in which they appear in the typical postures that tradition has attributed to them. They, too, have been immobilized by their fame: "In an absolute silence, they will, all four at the same time, gesticulate most excitedly: Foscolo, all aquiver, with his arm raised and his palm up, invites Dante to speak of the new destinies of

Italy, as he would like to; but Dante, forbidding and disdainful, shakes his shoulders peevishly and with an outstretched finger says, 'No, no,' most energetically. On the other hand, Leopardi disconsolately shakes his head and opens his arms in desperation, as if to say that everything is useless and vain; while Ariosto, with a smile of knowing indulgence, makes to the unhappy poet gestures of exaltation with his head and arms, as if to say: 'Well, find solace in yourself.' " The admonition is lost on the downcast poet, as it is lost on Leopardi.

The sudden return from the United States of a nephew of * * *, Pietro, with his wife Natascia, a beautiful Russian girl, and her sister Veroccia, leads * * * to the realization of his living death. Pietro, Veroccia, and Natascia represent youth, the youth of the new continent where races by intermingling are creating a new human type: "Russia, America, humanity that is blossoming anew."

Pietro, in his thirties, is blond, "speaks with great vim, then suddenly closes himself in a watchful silence of expectation while his eyes dart here and there." Only Natascia knows how to calm him with her beautiful, strange eyes. "Natascia is terribly calm. The strange ideas that pass through her mind are visible only in the designs of her embroidery, which no one can understand at all. That's the way in which she finds relief in order to play the part of a wise little wife and affectionate sister" to Pietro and Veroccia. The latter is hardly in her twenties, with auburn hair. She is the very embodiment of vivacity, youth, and life.

Invited by Pietro, * * * has gone to the latter's villa as a guest in order to rest, and he has found a great and beautiful love in Veroccia. She has discovered that under the dead crust there is a living soul. The poet tells her: "A moment was enough for you to search into my eyes and see that I was alive." That love has brought a new youth to him, a love that he has kept on a spiritual plane only because it would have seemed to him, a man in his fifties, to contaminate her pure and supple youth, had he yielded to his passionate desire. His whole self seems changed. He dresses in sport clothes; he moves with agility; he knows again the beauty of being natu-

ral, the joy of laughing and hearing other people laugh, especially if in their laughter tinkles the joyousness and freshness
of youth. Veroccia is joy for his eyes and delight for his soul.

Since knowing Veroccia, he has written poetry permeated
by the fire that she has awakened in him, waking the dreams
of the poet. Near her, it was natural for that fire of youth and
for those dreams to flame into poetry. It was a new poetry, a
reflection of the thoughts and sentiments that Veroccia had
awakened in him.

The poems in which * * * has expressed that interlude of
love and youth have been collected in a volume under the pen
name of Délago. The book has been an editorial venture of
Pietro. He has followed the clamorous and striking methods
of American advertising in presenting the volume to the public. He has designed a gorgeous and varicolored poster with
two portraits of the author. On the right there is the familiar
one of * * * "in his posture, famous because thousands of
times reproduced in books and prints of every kind; at the
left that of the imaginary Délago, a fine-looking youth in his
twenties who might even be a distant image of * * * when
young, unknown to all and unrecognizable." Pietro has disguised the identity of * * * under that of a young American
poet of Italian extraction.

The book is a real event in the world of Italian letters. The
young generation feels that it has found in Délago "its own
voice; . . . a voice that Délago has found for all of us there
in America, in the clash of new forces." Three representa-
tives of this new generation go to Pietro's villa to make in-
quiries because they have heard that Délago has arrived at
Genoa on the steamship *Roma*. Quite frankly they contrast
the glory of Délago with that of * * * in his very presence. He
suffers unspeakably.

He cannot reveal the truth; he cannot tell that he is Délago.
Délago, fantastic and unreal, is crushing him, the real author.
There is a mocking irony in that fact. "You," remarks * * *
to Pietro, "deprive me of my life to clothe another man
with it."

Veroccia wants the truth to be known: "I want you to be

332

Délago for all," she says. "You feel this impossibility because you have chosen to be hidden in him, and now you feel
that he stifles you, and you rebel."

Can the old poet reveal his young soul to his admirers? If
he should tell them that he is Délago, he would kill Délago;
"I am not nobody. I am somebody. I am I, as I am for everybody, and I cannot be another. If I say that I am Délago, if I
shout that I am Délago, Délago is done for. He becomes just
my mask, don't you understand? A mask of youth which I put
on for mockery." To his dismay there rises clearly before him
the vision of his self unnaturally divided into two beings, contradictory and hostile. Either he agrees to be Délago or the
old Somebody. Veroccia is not his. She is Délago's, and to
Délago belongs that brief moment in which youth and love
have flared again. Veroccia granted him a short interlude in
which he was allowed to bask in the warmth of her youth, but
there was to come a sad end to that short-lived dream.

In fact, his family goes to Pietro's villa to interrupt this
midsummer night's dream of poetry and youth. His wife and
children have come to protest against the fact that * * *
wishes to publish a new volume of verses that show a decided
similarity to Délago's poetry. Even Giaffredi, a minister of
state and friend of the family, has gone there because the
Italian Government, on the occasion of the fiftieth birthday
of the poet, wants to bestow on him the title of count for his
literary merits, and could not do so if his poetry changed.
Glory, especially if officially consecrated, is of one kind and
one only.

A difficult choice lies before * * *: either he must be young
with Veroccia or he must reënter the groove of his stilted
existence with his family and with his glory. He yields to the
pressure of his family and friends, and returns to the musty
atmosphere of his home. He appears "as if he has reëntered
his immutable image, universally known to all. He is pale
and as if dulled into the rigidity of a stone."

He also agrees not to publish the manuscript of the new
lyrics that he had put in Pietro's hands. Pietro, however,
against his wishes, publishes them as new lyrics by Délago

and reveals that Délago is one person with the old poet. The new generation turns against him: "For us, the poet—it is well that you know it—is no longer the wise man of letters, one who can amuse himself by appearing young when he is not. Knowing that you are Délago is enough for us to disown you. The poet for us must be above all a man." Délago has been killed by Somebody. * * * has to confirm even to the press that Délago is only a mockery; a mockery, and it was his whole life, the purest part of his soul. He had wanted Délago to obscure his previous fame. He had wanted to live in Délago because Délago was still alive and represented the eternal youth of his soul.

His friends and his family see only the mockery in his literary hoax. They insist on finding mirth in it, and they are blind to the fact that it is only tragedy to the poet. He sadly comments in despair: "The hoax! The hoax! You only see the hoax, you! It is incredible to you that I may still feel alive; evade this prison of myself! I am closed in, walled in! And I stifle! I stifle! I die!"

The celebration of * * *'s fiftieth birthday is a national event. They have reproduced his voice on phonograph records that all in the land may hear him. It is a tragic sensation for him to hear that voice which awakes a feeling of hatred in him. Photographers arrive to take his picture and flash it all over the country. They celebrate the rebirth of the old poet, and they do not realize what that rebirth has meant to him. He submits to everything, even to the torture of having to pose several times with his editor, with his friends, with his dignified family.

Pietro, Natascia, and Veroccia go to see him. They have read in the papers his statement about Délago. Veroccia is deeply hurt that he has declared that Délago's poetry and person are nothing but a joke. Had she been to him nothing but a jest? She leaves him indignantly, while he is unable to say a word, petrified in his grief. After Veroccia leaves, he talks to her tenderly and sadly as if she were present. He cannot be alive as she wanted him to be alive. She was only the youth of his spirit and he would have contaminated her young body had he accepted the offer of herself that she made to him: "You have not understood this restraint in me, of my shame in being old before your youth."

* * * is ready to accept the final humiliation: the official conferring of the title of count. A solemn festival is given in which high dignitaries of the political and literary worlds take part. Giaffredi is the official orator. * * * listens to his own funeral oration. "He is dead." So cries Veroccia as she gets a glimpse of him, moving as an automaton. After the official ceremony is over, he wanders in the garden alone and sits on a bench, a living statue of his useless and empty glory.

Is it indiscreet to ask whether this is one of the plays conceived and written when the beauty and charm of Marta Abba illuminated the pages of the playwright? Veroccia, in whom * * * found the last flare of his soul, has auburn hair like other noble heroines that have appeared in Pirandello's theatre. Has the author meant to silence the stupid innuendoes of people who surmise wrongly in their inability to feel the presence of something finer and loftier than the crude sensuality to which they reduce life?

Perhaps Pirandello has also tried to express humorously here the contrast between the new and the old generation. Newspapers in Italy a few years ago often used to carry attacks, and even do today, against the writers of the last century while exalting those of the present. To a superior mind like Pirandello's this literary clamor is foolish and amusing because he is not ready to countenance artificial divisions that are meaningless in the serene world of poetry. Only in this way can we interpret the benevolent irony towards the young generation, irony that is found behind the literary hoax of Délago. Pirandello seems to say to the younger generation: "Do you see? You believed that Délago was one of you, and the truth is that he was a man of the older generation." To Pirandello great art is life, and life in its cosmic reach does not know this or that generation.

Resuming the theme of *Diana and Tuda,* he has forcefully, but with greater pathos and serenity, expressed the tragedy of a man whose body begins to wither while his heart is still young and warm. The attitude assumed by * * * towards Veroccia, and his behavior, are proofs of Pirandello's deep sense of humanity and of the nobility of his art and life.

In this play, which is one of the latest and finest, every trace of self-deception, of intellectual dishonesty, has disappeared. At an earlier stage of his development Pirandello would have accused the poet of having contributed with his tortuous intellectualism of his own fixity. Here the family, his friends, and life, are responsible for that fixity. Pirandello, sobered by experience, deepened by it, is no longer capable of laughing, albeit sadly, at his characters. He is completely penetrated by the tragedy of * * *, a man who has lost his identity to the point of having even his name obliterated.

CONCLUSION

Conclusion

In the course of this study of the dramatic works of Luigi Pirandello we have emphasized the tragic character of his life and have identified it with his art rather than stressing either his humor or his idealism. Both humor and idealism are the forms assumed by the grief that oppressed him. Critics are likely to take one outstanding characteristic and to insist on it to the exclusion of all others, thus neglecting what is basic and stressing unduly what is external and formal.

I have passed several months steeped in the dramatic works of Pirandello. It was as if I lived in the intimate communion of his soul. I met the characters that he has created, I learned how to look into their hearts, to suffer with them, and I feel that they have allowed me to penetrate into the heart of their creator. Those characters are now around me. They look at me with a resigned and sad air, and they tell me the secret anguish of the man who has mirrored himself in them. In our intimacy, I see no longer the grimace and the painful tic with which nature has marked them. They are human, deeply human beings, especially in their tragic grief.

Many people find Pirandello's pessimism excessive, and they resent it. They must belong to the class of those who think of man as a being endowed with eyes, nose, mouth, and a clear-cut profile, who quietly passes through life like an engine of which they definitely know the horsepower and the output. It is possible that they have the luck—if it is luck—of seeing themselves in the concept of a perfectly normal man. But let us suppose that another individual does not feel himself normal; that in place of his intellect there is a hostile force, a kind of motor whirling at terrific speed, and that his heart is full of rebellion and of tumult, that his brain is cold and sharp like a blade. Would we then have the courage to reproach this individual for seeing himself in characters to whom life is unbearable and who aspire in vain to free their

339

wings from the mire that weighs them down? Would it not be cruel to deny such an individual the possibility of finding in art the solace that life has so cruelly denied him? Who could reproach Leopardi his pessimism? Pessimism is as natural in him as optimism is in a healthy and happy individual. It is equally natural for Pirandello who, in the name of the agonizing torture of his life, can claim the right to present characters that have not been blessed with the gift of joyousness.

Pirandello is a modest man, given to thought. A few years ago he came to New York, and the Chamber of Commerce invited him to be one of the guests at a banquet where former Mayor Walker was present. Both Pirandello and the debonair mayor were called upon to talk. Pirandello said a few words and modestly sat down. Mayor Walker engaged in a humorous speech that brought on applause that rocked the house. Pirandello, so an eye-witness has related, sat quietly by, his chin resting in his hand and his arm propped on his crossed knee, gazing in amazement as if he could not understand. In that perplexed and thoughtful attitude there is a great deal of his personality and of his art.

It may be that someone will scoff at certain facts that form the plots of Pirandello's plays. Yet life offers stranger vicissitudes than those presented by him. In August 1934, the Philadelphia papers spoke of a boy in whom nervousness had taken the form of constant singing that could not be stopped for nine days and nights. The same papers in the same month spoke of a former beauty queen who felt such revolt for the physical side of love that she had lived for three years in a kissless marriage. Imagine the sensual clamor of Atlantic City on the night that she was crowned queen, and then see her and her husband struggling in a situation that no one could easily project against such a background. Of such cases as life offers unrequested is made up the grotesque element in Pirandello's plays.

As I look at the crowd of characters who gesticulate and move in a frenzy in the perspective afforded by Pirandello's dramatic works, I think of the forest where Dante enclosed those who committed suicide. Dante created in it one of the most ghastly and powerful scenes of the *Commedia*. The poor human soul has been caught in the texture of the tree, becoming one with it, and writhing in it. On the judgment day those souls will reclaim their bodies, and they will hang them on the branches from which they will dangle all through eternity. Dante has been more compassionate than Pirandello. He has punished his characters after they have committed suicide, thereby dividing life and his inferno; Pirandello has denied his characters the interlude of a peaceful existence, and has obliterated the boundaries between life and suffering.

I have tried to present the forms that the thoughtful and deep humanity of Luigi Pirandello has assumed in his theatre. By his intellectual aloofness, by the creations to which his sense of grieving isolation has given life, by his art that is as serene as it is unadulterated, Pirandello deserves a prominent place among the great spirits who have honored Italian letters and, indeed, since art is universal, the literature of the world. He has written in one of his short stories: "The characters of my fiction are spreading all over the world the rumor that I am a most cruel and heartless writer. I need a sympathetic critic who will show how much understanding there is beneath my laughter." [1] Nothing would give me greater joy than to have succeeded, no matter in how small a degree, in rendering justice to the great mind and to the great heart of Luigi Pirandello.

[1] *Novelle per un anno.* Vol. IV, p. 238.

BIBLIOGRAPHY

Bibliography

PIRANDELLO'S WORKS USED IN THIS BOOK

In a Sanctuary. Bemporad. Firenze. 1925.
The Other Son. Bemporad. Firenze. 1925.
The Patent. Bemporad. Firenze. 1926.
The Jar. Bemporad. Firenze. 1925.
Limes of Sicily. Bemporad. Firenze. 1926.
At the Exit. Bemporad. Firenze. 1926.
The Vise. Bemporad. Firenze. 1926.
The Duty of a Physician. Bemporad. Firenze. 1926.
Liolà. Bemporad. Firenze. 1928.
Cecè. Bemporad. Firenze. 1926.
The Imbecile. Bemporad. Firenze. 1926.
The Man with a Flower in His Mouth. Bemporad. Firenze. 1926.
Man, Beast, and Virtue. Bemporad. Firenze. 1925.
Cap and Bells. Bemporad. Firenze. 1925.
All for the Best. Bemporad. Firenze. 1923.
Each in His Own Rôle. Bemporad. Firenze. 1925.
Right You Are If You Think You Are. Treves. Milano. 1918.
Each in His Own Way. Bemporad. Firenze. 1926.
Naked. Mondadori. Milano. 1927.
Henry IV. Bemporad. Firenze. 1923.
As You Desire Me. Mondadori. Milano. 1930.
One Does Not Know How. Verlag. Wien. 1935.
The Pleasure of Honesty. Treves. Milano. 1918.
Think It Over, Giacomino. Treves. Milano. 1918.
The New Colony. Bemporad. Firenze. 1928.
Lazarus. Mondadori. Milano. 1930.
As Well as Before, Better than Before. Bemporad. Firenze. 1923.
It Is Only in Jest. Bemporad. Firenze. 1926.
Either of One or of No One. Bemporad. Firenze. 1929.
Other People's Point of View. Mondadori. Milano. 1925.
The Wives' Friend. Bemporad. Firenze. 1927.
Mrs. Morli, One and Two. Bemporad. Firenze. 1925.
Grafting. Bemporad. Firenze. 1926.
The Life That I Gave You. Bemporad. Firenze. 1925.
Six Characters in Search of an Author. Bemporad. Firenze. 1928.
Tonight We Improvise. Mondadori. Milano. 1930.
Diana and Tuda. Bemporad. Firenze. 1927.

She Wanted to Find Herself. Mondadori. Milano. 1932.
When One Is Somebody. Mondadori. Milano. 1933.

TRANSLATIONS OF PLAYS

Sicilian Limes. *Theatre Arts Magazine* 6: 329–44. Oct. 1922.
Three Plays of Pirandello. E. P. Dutton and Co. New York. 1923.
Six Characters in Search of an Author. Tr. by E. Storer.
Henry IV. Tr. by E. Storer.
Right You Are if You Think You Are. Tr. by A. Livingston.
Man with a Flower in His Mouth; dialogue. *Dial* 75: 313–22. Oct. 1923.
Each in His Own Way and Two Other Plays. (The Pleasure of Honesty and Naked.) Tr. by A. Livingston. E. P. Dutton and Co. New York. 1925.
Three One-Act Plays. Tr. by Elizabeth Abbott, Arthur Livingston and Blanche V. Mitchell. E. P. Dutton and Co. New York. 1928.
As You Desire Me. Tr. by S. Putnam. E. P. Dutton and Co. New York. 1931.
The New Colony. Tr. by S. Putnam for the Shuberts. Not yet presented. 1931.
Tonight We Improvise. Tr. by S. Putnam. E. P. Dutton and Co. New York. 1932.

TRANSLATIONS OF OTHER WORKS

The Late Mattia Pascal. Tr. by A. Livingston. E. P. Dutton and Co. New York. 1923.
Fly. Story. Tr. by R. Wellman. *Forum* 71: 220–8. Feb. 24, 1924.
Shoes at the Door. Story. *Living Age* 323: 371–5. Nov. 15, 1924.
Goy. Story. Tr. by A. Livingston. *Menorah Journal* 10: 15. Feb. 1924.
The Outcast. Tr. by Leo Ongley. E. P. Dutton and Co. New York. 1925.
Mere Formality. Story. *Golden Book* 2: 399–410. Sept. 1925.
Shoot. (Si Gira). Tr. by C. K. Scott Moncrieff. E. P. Dutton and Co. New York. 1926.
Reserved Coffin. Story. Tr. by J. G. Harry. *Golden Book* 3: 122–7. Jan. 1926.
The Old and the Young. Tr. by C. K. Scott Moncrieff. E. P. Dutton and Co. New York. 1928.
Portrait. Story. *Living Age* 337: 300–6. Nov. 1, 1929.
Horse in the Moon. Tr. by S. Putnam. E. P. Dutton and Co. New York. 1931.
Two Double Beds. Story. *Spectator* 151: 764–6. Nov. 24, 1933.

346

BIBLIOGRAPHY

Through the Other Wife's Eyes. Story. Tr. by J. Redfern. *Fortnightly Review* 139: 503–10. April 1933.

Here's Another! Story. Tr. by J. Redfern. *Fortnightly Review* 140: 599–606. Nov. 1933.

One, No One and a Hundred Thousand. Tr. by S. Putnam. E. P. Dutton and Co. New York. 1933.

Sicilian Limes. Story. *Golden Book* 21: 1–9. Jan. 1934.

Truth. Story. Tr. by J. Redfern. *Fortnightly Review* 141: 658–65. June 1934.

Dinner Guest. Story. *Golden Book* 20: 50–7. July 1934.

Miss Holloway's Goat. Tr. by J. Redfern. *Golden Book* 19: 586–9. May 1934.

Better Think Twice About It. Stories. Tr. by Arthur and Henrie Mayne. E. P. Dutton and Co. New York. 1934.

Naked Truth. Stories. Tr. by Arthur and Henrie Mayne. E. P. Dutton and Co. New York. 1934.

CRITICISM

United States

Two Noisy Roman School Masters. J. Collins. *Bookman* 51: 410–16. June 1920.

Grotesques of Pirandello. E. Storer. *Forum* 66: 271–81. Oct. 1921.

Luigi Pirandello. J. C. Grey. *Theatre Arts Magazine* 6: 317–28. Oct. 1922.

Six Characters in Search of an Author. S. Young. *New Republic* 32: 335–6; 33: 97. Nov. 22, Dec. 20, 1922.

Floriani's Wife. S. Young. *New Republic* 36: 207. Oct. 17, 1923.

Luigi Pirandello and His Writings. B. Crémieux. *Living Age* 318: 123–6. July 21, 1923.

Luigi Pirandello, Dramatist. *Review of Reviews* 68: 440–1. Oct. 1923.

Six Characters in Search of an Author. J. Crawford. *Drama* 13: 130–1. Jan. 1923.

Six Characters in Search of an Author. E. Wyatt. *Catholic World* 116: 505–7. Jan. 1923.

Eleanora Duse, Actress Supreme. Luigi Pirandello. *Century* 108: 244–51. June 1924.

Living Mask. B. De Casseres. *Arts and Decoration* 20: 32. March 1924.

Living Mask. S. Young. *New Republic* 37: 287. Feb. 6, 1924.

Living Mask. H. Kellock. *Freeman* 8: 544–5. Feb. 1924.

Luigi Pirandello, Dramatist. E. Storer. *Fortnightly Review* 122: 227–41. Aug. 1924.

Pirandello Hacks at Life. *Current Opinion* 76: 457–8. April 1924.

Pirandello's Warning. A. Rotre. *Forum* 71: 791–4. June 1924.

LUIGI PIRANDELLO

Portrait. *Theatre Arts Magazine* 8: 149. March 1924.

And That's the Truth, if You Think It Is. J. Crawford. *Drama* 16: 51. Nov. 1925.

Italian Letter. R. Piccoli. *Dial* 78: 43–50. Jan. 1925.

Pirandello on Writing Plays. *Living Age* 326: 473. Aug. 1925.

Plays of Luigi Pirandello. J. Palmer. *19th Century and After* 97: 897–909. June 1925.

Some Plays of Pirandello. B. Causton. *Contemporary Review* 128: 229–36. Aug. 1925.

Pirandello Confesses . . . Why and How He Wrote Six Characters in Search of an Author. Tr. by L. Ongley. *Virginia Quarterly Review* 1: 36–52. April 1925.

Luigi Pirandello. Walter Starkie. Dutton and Co. New York. 1926.

Naked. J. W. Krutch. *Nation* 123: 539–40. Nov. 1926.

Pirandello Interviewed. *Living Age* 331: 80–1. Oct. 1, 1926.

Pirandello, Man and Artist. E. Storer. *Living Age* 329: 415–19. May 22, 1926.

Jesting Pilate. J. W. Krutch. *Nation* 124: 295. March 16, 1927.

Luigi Pirandello. D. Rops. *Living Age* 332: 1001–7. June 1, 1927.

Masks: Their Use by O'Neill and Pirandello. G. Anschutz. *Drama* 17: 201–2. April 1927.

Pirandello and the Italian Stage Crisis. *Literary Digest* 93: 36–8. April 23, 1927.

Pirandello, Prophet of Unreality. *Review of Reviews* 76: 212. August 1927.

Pirandello's Plans. *Living Age* 333: 365–6. Aug. 15, 1927.

Right You Are, if You Think You Are. S. Young. *New Republic* 50: 141–2. March 23, 1927.

Pirandello's Humor. M. Y. Hughes. *Sewanee Review* 35: 175–86. April 1927.

La Nuova Colonia. *Living Age* 334: 955–6. June 1928.

Pirandello, Paradox. T. V. Blankner. *Theatre Arts Monthly* 12: 891–902. Dec. 1928.

New Pirandello in Diana e la Tuda. F. Blankner. *Poet Lore* 40: 215–22. June 1929.

Modern Italian Novel. Domenico Vittorini. University of Pennsylvania Press. Philadelphia. 1930.

Pirandello Quits Europe. *Living Age* 339: 317. Nov. 1930.

Pirandello Without Honor. *Living Age* 337: 544. Jan. 1930.

As You Desire Me. *Living Age* 338: 290–1. May 1, 1930.

Pirandello on America. *Living Age* 339: 541–2. Jan. 1931.

Actor Looks at Pirandello. H. Miller. *Canadian Forum* 12: 78–9. Nov. 1931.

As You Desire Me. *Commonwealth* 13: 415. Feb. 11, 1931.

As You Desire Me. *Nation* 132: 198. Feb. 18, 1931.

BIBLIOGRAPHY

As You Desire Me. *Catholic World* 132: 721. March 1931.

As You Desire Me. *Arts and Decoration* 34: 84. April 1931.

As You Desire Me. *Drama* 21: 9. April 1931.

As You Desire Me. *Theatre Arts Monthly* 15: 277. April 1931.

As You Desire Me. *Theatre Magazine* 53: 26. April 1931.

As You Desire Me. *New Republic* 66: 209. April 1931.

As You Desire Me. *Outlook* 158: 36. May 13, 1931.

As You Desire Me. *Bookman* 73: 409–10. June 1931.

Broadway to Date; Whither Masks? B. De Casseres. *Arts and Decoration* 35: 82. Oct. 1931.

Six Characters in Search of an Author. *Arts and Decoration* 35: 46. June 1931.

Six Characters in Search of an Author. *Theatre Arts Monthly* 15: 450–1. June 1931.

Tonight We Improvise. S. Young. *New Republic* 71: 44–6. May 25, 1932.

Pirandello in Search of Himself. *Literary Digest* 114: 18. Oct. 1, 1932.

Only Women Will Challenge the Mailed Fist; interview. R. Bercovici. *Pictorial Review* 35: 4. Oct. 1933.

Award of the Nobel Prize to Pirandello. *New Republic* 81: 30–1. Nov. 2, 1934.

Awarded Nobel Prize for Literature for 1934. *Publishers' Weekly* 126: 1749. Nov. 10, 1934.

Nobel Prize. *News-Weekly* 4: 42. Nov. 17, 1934.

Nobel Prize Author. *Commonwealth* 21: 120. Nov. 23, 1934.

Nobel Prize for Literature Awarded to Pirandello. *Nation* 139: 577. Nov. 21, 1934.

Nobel Prize Winner. G. A. Borgese. *Saturday Review of Literature* 11: 305. Nov. 24, 1934.

Portrait. *Rotarian* 46: 21. Jan. 1934.

Wins Nobel Prize. *Literary Digest* 118· 8. Nov. 17, 1934.

Tendencies of the Modern Novel. *Fortnightly* 141: 433–40. April 1934.

Pirandello, Italy's Man of Letters. G. J. Lux. *Richmond Times Dispatch*, Sunday Magazine Section 3, Dec. 16; 8, Dec. 23; 9, Dec. 30, 1934.

Conversation with Pirandello. A. Rousseaux. *Living Age* 347: 512–14. Feb. 1935.

Nobel Prize Winner. S. D'Amico. *Theatre Arts Monthly* 19: 114–21. Feb. 1935.

Pirandello in Search of an American Theatre; interview by S. Putnam. New Hope. Aug. 1935.

Metaphysics and Pirandello. E. C. Knowlton. *South Atlantic Quarterly* 34: 42–59. Jan. 1935.

LUIGI PIRANDELLO

England

Letter from Italy. M. Praz. *London Mercury* 6: 35–7. Sept. 1922.

Something New. D. MacCarthy. *New Statesman* 18: 618–19. March 4, 1922.

Luigi Pirandello. D. Williams. *Cornhill Magazine* 55: 268–83. Sept. 1923.

Henry IV. F. Birrell. *Nation* (London) 35: 379–80. June 24, 1924; Reply. F. Birch. 35: 407–8. June 28, 1924; *Rejoinder* 35: 437. July 5, 1934.

Henry IV. H. Wolfe. *Spectator* 132: 954–5. June 14, 1924.

Pirandello. F. Birrell. *Nation* (London) 34: 634. Feb. 2, 1924.

Henry IV. F. Birrell. *Nation* (London) 37: 399–400. June 27, 1925.

Henry IV. D. MacCarthy. *New Statesman* 25: 309–10. June 27, 1925.

And That's the Truth (If You Think It Is). *Outlook* (London) 56: 202. Sept. 26, 1925.

And That's the Truth (If You Think It Is). I. Brown. *Saturday Review* 40: 334–5. Sept. 26, 1925.

And That's the Truth (If You Think It Is). W. J. Turner. *New Statesman* 25: 694–5. Oct. 3, 1925.

Henry IV. N. G. Royde-Smith. *Outlook* (London) 56: 57. July 25, 1925.

Henry IV. H. Shipp. *English Review* 41: 437–40. Sept. 1925.

Six Characters in Search of an Author. D. MacCarthy. *New Statesman* 25: 282–3. June 20, 1925.

Pirandello. N. G. Royde-Smith. *Outlook* (London) 55: 429. June 27, 1925.

Pirandello. M. Waldman. *London Mercury* 12: 396–405. Aug. 1925.

Pirandello Season. I. Brown. *Saturday Review* 139: 670–1. June 20, 1925.

Plays of Signor Pirandello. *Spectator* 135: 11–12. July 4, 1925.

Man With a Flower in His Mouth. N. G. Royde-Smith. *Outlook* (London) 57: 393. June 1, 1926.

Pirandello, Man and Artist. E. Storer. *Bookman* (London) 70: 8–11. April 1926.

Naked. F. Birrell. *Nation* (London) 40: 924–5. April 2, 1927.

Naked. H. Horsnell. *Outlook* (London) 59: 330. March 26, 1927.

Naked. D. MacCarthy. *New Statesman* 28: 732–3. March 26, 1927.

Six Characters in Search of an Author. H. Shipp. *English Review* 47: 113–14. July 1928.

The Life That I Gave You. R. E. Roberts. *New Statesman and Nation* 1: 425. May 16, 1931.

Secret of Power. *Saturday Review* 152: 554. Oct. 31, 1931.

What is genius? *Bookman* (London) 81: 6–7. Oct. 1931.

Luigi Pirandello. A. Wareing. *Bookman* (London) 81: 190. Dec. 1931.

Portrait. *Bookman* (London) 84: 62. April 1933.

The Life That I Gave Him; adapted by C. Bax. D. Verschoyle. *Spectator* 153: 521. Oct. 12, 1934.

Italy

Bibliografia di Pirandello; edited by Manlio Lo Vecchio Musti. A. Mondadori (Milan). Idem. Bibliografia di Pirandello. A. Mondadori (Milan), 1952.

APPENDIX

Appendix

PIRANDELLO AND THE ITALIAN THEATRE*

By Domenico Vittorini

THIS brief essay on Luigi Pirandello as a dramatist has been written with the conviction that the task of criticism follows two parallel lines of investigation. One is objective and aims at singling out the aesthetic and ethical principles shared by the author; the other is subjective and enjoins the critic to state whether or not, in his opinion, without the slightest shadow of dogmatism, the author has reached the goals that he assigned to his art, and whether or not his works have attained artistic significance.

This is the modest task that I have set before me in sketching the outwardly quiet and inwardly tormented figure of the man who in our lifetime called the attention of the entire world to the literature of Italy. The Nobel Prize that he received in 1934 was a clear recognition of the universal appeal and significance of his art.

Born in Sicily in 1867, Luigi Pirandello lived through two very different epochs of Italian history; one represented by the civilization that appeared after Rome became the capital of his unified country, the other encompassing the years in which Italy, following the urge of the "sacred egotism" of nations, grew of age, expanded economically and politically with that mixture of good and evil that is inherent in all change and growth. Pirandello died in 1936, before his country was engulfed in the tragedy of the second World War. Had he lived, I feel confident that he would have raised his stooped shoulders and, faintly smiling, with arms outstretched in the manner so peculiar to many of his characters, would have said: What can you expect, life, history and man being what they are?

*Read at the Casa Italiana of Columbia University on Saturday, April 19, 1952.

Culturally speaking, Pirandello bridged the Verismo period and our own age. The critic has two main sources at his disposal among Pirandello's writings: his *Umorismo*, published in 1908, and the preface to *Sei personaggi in cerca d'autore*, penned in 1925, as well as the numerous passages in the dramatic works of this period.

The basic aesthetic ideas expressed in *Umorismo* link Pirandello with the Verismo movement. His later utterances show that he departed altogether from the tenets of that school in order to veer towards an art more universal, complex, and psychological.

It is unquestionably true that Pirandello had definite links with Verismo, the main, but by no means the only, stream of literary life in Italy in the nineties. Nor was there any reason for Pirandello to resent this. He learned from that movement how to use in his fiction a landscape that he knew intimately, his native Sicily, and how to adhere to the human traits of his characters, two basic characteristics that served him in good stead, as he reflected in his art his own quixotic temperament and the strange vicissitudes of his existence. Let us not forget that he lived for years with a demented wife and that he greatly resented the indifference of the Italian public.

Yet, Pirandello's protest had a basic justification in the fact that he had not slavishly followed the footprints of Giovanni Verga, his master and friend. He had, instead, created a type all his own of realistic fiction by injecting humor into the material that the Verismo of his Sicily offered to him. He had transformed the objective and wistful naturalism of Giovanni Verga into a more searching and subjective study of man and life.

His *Umorismo* clearly documents the new treatment that he accorded to the realism of his age. Art, so he tells us, appeared to him in the light of contrast between being and seeming, between life as a cosmic force and human existence as a personal experience. But that critical essay on humor shows also, or rather, leads one to conclude that the world of naturalism was not suited to Pirandello's philosophical temperament. Who would ever have surmised that behind the grotesque figures that moved in the early works there was a deep philosophical intuition? The average reader only laughed at the vicissitudes of those little men and women whom the author paraded before him with the only purpose, so it seemed, of ridiculing them. How could the average reader, or even the critic, correlate the events of Pirandello's early fiction with such statements as these: "Life is a continuous and fluid entity that we try to stop, to fix in unchanging and definite forms, inside and outside of us, because we all are fixed forms, forms which move along others equally fixed." We are, he continues, the result of concepts reached through an infernal machine called logic, which pumps our sentiments from our hearts up to our brains and reduces them to lifeless abstractions. Only now and then, in rare moments of inner illumination, do we resume contact with real life, life as a cosmic flux that suffers in being enclosed in its human molds: rocks, plants, animals, men. Then we experience a terrifying shock, as we see ourselves live suspended in the inner void created by the contrast between cosmic life and its earthly and human forms. Pirandello's fiction reflected in his puny and strange-looking characters the ludicrous embodiments of this ideal life-concept. We must not wonder that this fiction was never popular.

We can appeal directly to him to prove that he considered himself a philosophical author. In the preface to his *Sei personaggi in serca d'autore*, he wrote: "I have never been satisfied with representing the figure of a man or of a woman for the sheer pleasure of representing it; nor with narrating a specific event, gay or sad, for the sheer pleasure of narrating it; nor with describing a landscape for the sheer pleasure of describing it." He attributes to such authors the quality of being "historical" or "descriptive." But he points out that there are other writers for whom "a human figure, an event, a landscape become enriched with a peculiar life-sense that lends to them a universal value. These are writers of a nature strongly philosophical." He adds: "I have the misfortune of belonging to the latter type." It was but natural that an author, who took his art so seriously and who had studied himself so clearly, should seek a more congenial medium of expression.

In his first attempts Pirandello did not abandon the themes dear to Verismo. His *Lumie di Sicilia* testifies to this. Indeed, he often returned to that small, yet unforgotten world, even in later years, when he dramatized short stories previously written. These plays constitute a very readily distinguishable section of his dramatic work. Many of the one-act plays belong to it. Most of them are characterized by a Sicilian setting, a language that achieves effectiveness through a restrained and consciously simple vocabulary, by elementary passions as material for the plot. *La patente*, *La giara*, *L'altro figlio*, *Liolà* are typical of this activity. Many of them can be very successfully staged, but they all show a deep contrast between the simple figures that move in them and the philosophical utterances that they are made to voice. Imagine Ciampa, a small-town bookkeeper, the hero of *Il berretto a sonagli*, who suddenly sallies forth with these words: "We are puppets, dear Mr. Fifi. The Divine Spirit enters into us and it becomes dwarfed." And, as if this were not enough, Ciampa proceeds to refer to that processs of "building one's self up" which plays such a large part in the major works of our author. The thoughtful reader cannot help noticing the dualism that besets this and similar plays, gems of dramatic art as some of them are. Of this contrast, the author himself must have been conscious, for he changed to a new dramatic form in which this jarring discrepancy was eliminated. Of *L'uomo, la bestia e la virtù* he said: "It is tragedy stifled by the traditional Italian comedy." Pirandello uncovered the limpid stream of his creativeness when in his major plays he forsook the realm of comedy and entered the precincts of stately tragedy. Then he penned such works as *Sei personaggi in cerca d'autore*, *Enrico IV*, *Come tu mi vuoi*, *Quando si è qualcuno*. His fame is especially evidenced in these works, the most significant of modern Italian dramatic literature. As a result of these plays, he was recognized as the dominant figure of the European stage from 1920 until his death.

He expressed the torments of the intellectual men of our time more fully than any other contemporary playwright. His characters became the lucid and perfect projection of the same tragic sense of life that he had expressed less perfectly in the works of his youth. In this sense, he was right when he insisted that his art had never changed. It had changed only in that now his new characters were possessed of a rich personality and of a stature that was consonant with the message that Pirandello entrusted to them. The author himself states that he gave to the unforgettable Father of *Sei personaggi in cerca d'autore* the task of conveying the impossibility of human comprehension, of the multiple character of human personality and the "tragic conflict between life as a fluid entity and life as a fixed and immutable form." The main characters of his plays have absolved this function with a perfection that assigns to Pirandello a place among the great dramatists of all times.

The theme of "costruirsi," of building oneself up, rises with a clearcut contour in these major plays and it conveys with compelling force the conviction of the author concerning the tragedy of being human. The plight of the characters has become one and the same with that of the author, and the reader is carried away by the passionate pleading of the latter. The conscious madness of Henry IV is not conceivable in a less complicated character, for complication presupposes a great wealth of psychic power, even if misdirected. Henry IV, like Mrs. Morli in *La Signora Morli, una e due* or like Baldovino in *Il piacere dell'onestà,* is an exemplification of "costruirsi," but what a difference from Ciampa, Cecè, or even Mattia Pascal! What tragedy and what agonizing torment Pirandello has been able to create in him, a man who, masquerading as Henry IV, becomes unconscious as the result of a fall from his horse, and wakens into the belief that he is actually the German Emperor. For fourteen years he vegetates in the neutral state

of his madness, when suddenly he reopens his eyes on the
horrible spectacle of his true identity. His cry of terror
conveys with an overpowering impact the tragedy of being
himself. Seldom have imaginary tortures been made so real
in the limpid mirror of art! Henry IV, too, like Mattia
Pascal, has remained excluded from life but his loneliness
is of a different nature and is conveyed in a different style
with a different poignancy. The Unknown woman in *Come
tu mi vuoi* is also a "costruzione" when she tries to live
again in herself the soul of Cia, but what a difference from
the wanton women of earlier works who "built themselves
up" in deceit and perversity! The soul of Cia cannot live
again on this earth because, upon her return, her husband
and relatives are more interested in her body than in her
soul and so the Unknown goes back to her destiny of world-
liness and tragedy. Did the literal identity of the Unknown
really matter since she was bringing back to them the soul
of Cia? Had the literal identity really mattered for mothers
who during the first World War, fought over a torso that
each believed to be her son maimed on the battlefield?

One of the best exemplifications of Pirandello's intuition
of "costruirsi" is found in *Quando si è qualcuno* in which
the author reflects his own reaction to the literary fame
that the world accorded to him after his plays were given
both in Europe and America. Pirandello's hero had reached
the conclusion that respect, admiration, and glory are "all
things that kill." His family, his admirers, the whole country, had immobilized him in a given image that had blurred
his real features by sealing them in a painful fixity. The
main character concludes that he has been embalmed alive
and confesses: "They make a statue out of you, always composed in a fixity of perfection that is very tormenting." He
had to dress, to wear his hair long, to speak, even to write
in the form that his contemporaries associated with the
idea that the public had conceived of him. Was that living?
He adds: "How many times, at night in my studio, do I
feel oppressed beyond endurance: a puppet, to be left
there, before my desk, under the light of the lamp, with its

wig, its wax face, its wax hands, its lifeless eyes — there, motionless." Pirandello presents the speeches of the hero by marking them with three asterisks, since he has not given him a name in the play. He is a Somebody, a shadow entity which gradually has become synonymous with Nobody. When the Italian government, on the occasion of the hero's fiftieth birthday, decides to honor the poet by making him the spokesman of the regime, the latter passively acquiesces. His passiveness is so complete that it becomes very plausible when he is seen rising with the stand on which his statue was supposed to rest. This play constitutes one of the last expressions of Pirandello's meaning of "costruirsi." He embodied in it the most personal and fullest idea of the tragedy of not being oneself. His last words have a poetic and human resonance which is not easily forgotten: "Puerizia — arcana favola — ombra chi a te si avvicina — ombra chi da te s'allontana — " ("Childhood — mysterious fable — a shadow is he who draws near you — a shadow is he who draws away from you.") These are the words which, as the hero speaks, become engraved on the stone that contains his epitaph. What greater tragedy for fluid life than that of becoming petrified, for a living man to become "the statue of himself!"

Playwrights are generally remembered because of the dramatic forms which they have introduced, for the novelty of the material used, for the characters that they have created. Pirandello deserves to be remembered for these reasons, too. But, as time passes, I believe that he will be remembered, at least by thoughtful readers, for the many pages that he has dedicated to man who feels lost before the mystery and wonders of the universe, to the study of the real meaning of living on this planet, to the singling out of quiet moments in his existence in which, against and beyond the social hypocrisies that surrounded him, he reached the simple truths, spontaneous feelings, and unadulterated sentiments that represented for him a true pattern of living. Here is one of the passages that reveal the basic character of Luigi Pirandello: "We advance sadly along a road already invaded by the shadows of the evening. It is enough to raise our eyes to a little loggia still illuminated by the setting sun, with a red geranium that glows in that light — and suddenly a distant dream touches our hearts." This passage is taken from *Ciascuno a suo modo*, one of the most tormented plays that he wrote; a play in which characters are shown as deceiving not only others, but themselves; a play in which everything is tortuous, spasmodic, torturing and tortured, because there is no basis for the thinking and acting of those who, though they proclaim very vociferously and excitedly their sincerity, are deprived of opinions and beliefs, even of conscience. The title is at first very baffling, until one reads passages like the following: "Detach from yourself the little puppet that you create with the fictitious interpretation of your acts and your sentiments — and you will immediately see that it has nothing to do with what you are, or what you may truly be — with what abides in you without your being aware of it, and which is a terrible god, understand, if you oppose him, but which becomes immediately compassionate of every guilt if you abandon yourself to him, and do not wish to find excuses." With these words comes the admonition that everyone of us has to create his own reality through spontaneity of feelings and through humility.

Other memorable words in their human resonance are those of Ersilia Drei in *Vestire gli ignudi*, the forlorn and forsaken heart that longed so for a bit of love that she, through a lie, prepared to take her life by poison in order to replace with the tinsel of her story the white garland of orange blossoms that she had so desperately hoped would one day rest on her brow. But everyone refused to see the reason for her lie. So, desolate and alone, she took poison again and announced that she had lied not in order to live but in order to die. "Well, yes, . . . I tried to make a decent little garment for myself, at least, for my death. That's why I lied. I swear it to you. In my life I had never been able to put on a little dress without having it torn by the many dogs that have always attacked me in every street; without having it soiled by the basest and vilest miseries. So I attempted to make myself one — to die in — that of a bride, in order to die in it with a little sympathy and pity from everyone. Well, I have not been able to have even this! It has been torn from me, cast into the gutter and spurned . . . Now go. Let me die in silence: stark naked. Go and tell . . . that this poor girl died naked."

Allow me to quote from *Come tu mi vuoi* and let us take notice of the deep chords that Pirandello reached in justifying the Unknown for assuming the personality of Cia: "Many an unfortunate one, after years, has returned just like that (she points to the Demented One, the pitiful body of Cia, once beautiful and all perfection of soul and mind); many an unfortunate one has returned with features obliterated, unrecognizable, without any memory, and sisters, wives, mothers, have fought to have the unfortunate one with them. Not because they have recognized him, no (cannot the son of one resemble that of another?), but because they have believed him to be their own. And there is no contrary proof that may be valid when one wishes to believe! Is it really he? But for that mother, it is he; yes, it is he! What does it matter if it isn't he, if a mother keeps him and makes him hers with all her love? Against every proof she believes him to be hers." And yet, the author of such passages has been called cerebral and abstract!

In his concept of the impersonality of love, Pirandello joins Plato who, in his ideal republic, wanted a communal possession of wives and children, that one would love all the children in the state and not only one's own. If we preface the reading of *L'innesto* with this thought, we shall understand better the theme of mystic parenthood that is the kernel of the play. We shall, at least, heed the pathos of the words of the woman who, loving her husband in an absolute way, couldn't conceive that the child that she was bearing as the result of a brutal attack by an unknown individual, should be considered the child of any man other than her husband. These are her words: "I want you to see in your son all of me; he is yours, because he is proof of all my love for you." Naturally enough, Giorgio, the husband, does not understand. Pirandello condemns him to losing Laura, who proves too imaginative and too lofty for his practical mind.

Time does not permit a discussion of Pirandello as a social critic, of his theme of conscious illusion that makes the wearing of a mask so painful for his characters, of his abstract idealism that leads him to justify even adultery as he does in his last play, *Non si sa come*, to mention only a few of the many aspects of his art.

However, consideration, be it brief, must be given to Pirandello's place and role in the Italian drama of our time. It was certainly the impact of his work that caused a large section of Italian drama to forsake the modes as exemplified by Giacosa, Bracco and Sem Benelli and to replace them by a fantastic setting whose dimensions and rhythm are not regulated by ordinary logic. The "Teatro del Grottesco" that flourished during the first World War and in the interlude between the two wars was closely connected, historically and culturally, with Pirandello's intuition of life and art. In fact, Pirandello was an intimate friend of Luigi Antonelli, one of the leading figures of the group of the Grotteschi, which looked upon *Umorismo* as its guiding light. Pirandello did not belong officially to this group. His position was somewhat like that of Alessandro Manzoni who influenced Italian Romanticism, although he refused to be officially linked with the movement. Pirandello's influence on the revival of Italian art in the 1920's was very effective, and was carried out through the formation of his own troupe with which he toured both Europe and the Americas.

It is more difficult to single out what specific influence Pirandello had on playwrights of other nations. He exemplified the interest of our time in probing into the psychological and the subliminal, and contributed to the popularity of such themes. More than of influence, I believe it is proper to speak of similarity of intuitions between Pirandello and Eugene O'Neil, Fernand Crommelynck and Jean Sarment. They all used themes to which they were attuned by the history of their time, their personal experiences, and, above all, by their oversensitive temperaments.

Pirandello's work was far from done, so he felt and confided to his friends, when death overtook him in his sleep. He was buried without pomp, as he had requested. With him disappeared the most significant Italian literary figure of our time.

Criticism has not stressed enough the intimate note of admonition that lies very unobtrusively but deeply in the art of the Maestro. We know so little of ourselves, of the Universe, and of our fellow-men; life is so fleeting, indeed, so ruinous that only humility and sentiment can save and console us. The world of his art is populated by strange-looking characters whose eyes are wide open, whose nerves are tense, whose hands are contracted as if in fear of losing control over themselves, and who, nevertheless, manage to look normal, and walk with seeming indifference and even dignity among other men sharing their lot and feigning with equal success. Pirandello still lives in the creations of his fancy, possessed now of a peace that he never knew on this earth.

LUIGI PIRANDELLO AS I SAW HIM*

Domenico Vittorini

University of Pennsylvania

T HE following are recollections of my meetings with
Luigi Pirandello in New York during the months of
July and August, 1935, offered here as an historical
document of what he said in many hours of intimate conversation. The term "historical" is used advisedly, in humble awareness of the tenuous data upon which the historian
is often compelled to rely for his reconstructions of the
past. That Pirandello belongs to the literary history of the
last fifty years, there is no doubt. He created such a stir in
the dramatic circles of our time as to cause his name to be
widely known outside of Italy; and enough playwrights
were influenced by his intuitive grasp of human personality
that "Pirandellian personality" has become a byword in
our generation.

I first met Luigi Pirandello at the reception that was accorded him aboard the steamship *Conte di Savoia* at the
18th Street dock on July 20, 1935, when he arrived in New
York for a three months' stay in the hope of having his
well-known play *Sei personaggi in cerca d'autore* (Six
characters in search of an author) made into a film. As I
stepped on the ship, the thought that I was shortly to see
the man whose work I had always admired keyed me to a
nervous tension. When I confided my nervousness to a
young colleague of mine, he, with characteristic modern indifference toward greatness, exclaimed, "For heaven's sake,
man, do you think that Pirandello is a god?" Being aware
that reality is something very subjective, I did not answer
and hastened toward the other end of the hall where the

* From SYMPOSIUM, Vol. VIII, No. 1. Syracuse University, Syracuse, N. Y.

smiling and wistful countenance of the playwright had appeared. He was accompanied by the ship's officers and the New York City dignitaries who had gone to meet him at quarantine.

Pirandello was of medium height, rather heavy-set, with an oval face and a short, pointed, gray beard. Although sixty-seven years of age, he was quick in his movements, and his person bore the marks of a robust manhood. What attracted me more than anything else were his mobile eyes. They had a way of their own of converging on you as if to penetrate your innermost thoughts, and then they suddenly became hidden by an impenetrable veil as he relaxed his attention and withdrew within himself. Introspection was not a pose with him. It was an instinct and a habit reflected in many of his characters. Shy and timid, he stood in the midst of the reception committee. While grateful for the recognition accorded him, he seemed to have to force himself to listen to the oratory lavished in his praise.

As I stood a little to one side, interested in seeing his reactions in meeting people, I saw him turn and beckon to me with his finger. He must have been told that I was eager to have an interview with him. He was very cordial in thanking me for my interest in his writings and expressed gratification at the manner in which I had presented him in a long article that had recently been published in the *Ateneo veneto* of Venice.[1] He gave me an appointment for the following day at the Waldorf-Astoria.

The next morning, as I waited in the lobby of the Waldorf-Astoria, it was hard for me to picture Pirandello, who had always indicted the splendor and the hustle of modern civilization, on the forty-first floor of a hotel that has no rival anywhere for size and luxury. He received me in the large living-room of his apartment. He seated himself in a rather high armchair against the open window, and I was happy to look up to him. As we discussed his art and plays, he seemed gradually to recede miles and miles from the luxury that surrounded him. I had with me the page proofs of a volume that was to appear a few months later.[2] I submitted to him my plan of work, my interpretations of his plays, and my main conclusions. He was very interested and eager to hear what I had written. I translated into Italian the passages in question, because he confessed that, although he could read English, he found it difficult to understand when spoken.

My first interview almost went awry at the very outset when I showed him the index of the various chapters of my book and told him that in the first chapter I dealt with his contacts with naturalism. Pirandello was very indignant. "My art has no connection whatsoever with naturalism," he almost shouted. "Giovanni Verga, the great representative of that movement, wrote me that there was a new force and a new light in my art. I have a letter written to me by him after the publication of my novel *L'esclusa* (The Outcast). Indeed, I feel that I am at the opposite pole from naturalism. I have battered down blind faith in clumsy, tangible reality. My characters, through imagination, conquer and break the fetters of everyday reality. I have shown the stupidity of placing our sense of reality in this material world of ours, which was the pivotal point of the art-mode created by the naturalists." I pleaded that I considered naturalism only as a point of departure for his art, and that my book aimed at showing how he had developed later into the artist so uniquely psychological that we all admired. I cannot say that the Maestro looked convinced, but he became more approachable.

"Certainly, it was due to naturalism," I continued very cautiously, "if your early characters are small figures caught in the ebb and flow of everyday life. Indeed, I feel that they are not capable of carrying the intellectual motivation of your art as are the more complex personalities that one finds in your later works." I referred to the dramatization of early short stories that are typically naturalistic, and I singled out *Liolà* (Liolà) and *L'uomo, la bestia e la virtù* (Man, beast, and virtue).

"Yes," agreed Pirandello. "These are developed along the lines of the traditional comedy of the XVIth century." Of *L'uomo, la bestia e la virtu* he said, "It is tragedy stifled by comedy."

The reason that Pirandello was so resentful about my mention of his contacts with naturalism was that Benedetto Croce, in an article published in *La critica*, had reduced Pirandello's art to the form and substance of the naturalism of the eighties.[3]

"Croce, in his obtuseness," said Pirandello with ill-repressed anger, "has failed to see the human strain that runs through my art. He has always been unable to see that I have been and am an enemy of formalism and hypocrisy. Basically, I have constantly attempted to show that nothing offends life as much as reducing it to a hollow concept. My idea of *costruirsi*, of building oneself up, is the fundamental tenet of my art. Marriage, fatherhood, motherhood, and personality have no meaning except that which we give to them. In my plays I have shown how unreal marriage is, if held together only by civil and religious ceremonies. I have shown couples who quarrel at home but stroll through the city streets arm-in-arm as the embodiment of marital perfection. Such people are not alive nor real. They are self-constructed, empty concepts. I have compared one such man with a cigar that has smoked itself out, keeping its shape but being only ashes." He was referring to Lello Carpani, an important character in *La Signora Morli, una e due* (Mrs. Morli, one and two).

I told the Maestro that I had taken the liberty of pointing out in my book the anti-social undercurrent of his thought. A slight expression of resentment passed over his face as he replied, "Society is necessarily formal, and in this sense I am anti-social, but only in the sense that I am opposed to social hypocrisies and conventions. My art teaches each individual to accept his human lot with candor and humility, and with full consciousness of the imperfections that are inherent in it."

Pirandello was very happy when I showed him I had strongly stressed the positive side of his thought, quoting especially from the interludes of *Ciascuno a suo modo* (Each in his own way). "All true art contains a philosophy of life that tends toward sound and noble living," he concluded.

"What about the 'drama of mirrors' as your drama has often been characterized?" I asked on another occasion.

"It is an exaggerated view of a situation that exists in many of my plays," he answered. "If we present ourselves to others as artificial constructions in relation to what we really are, it is logical that upon looking at ourselves in a mirror we see our falseness reflected there, made galling and unbearable by its fixity. That is all that I mean by placing my characters before a mirror and making them say that they would like to spit at themselves." Pirandello had a very intense manner of speaking in discussing his plays. One could see that he lived for his art.

He complained of having been misunderstood, or not understood at all, especially in Italy. "How many do really understand what I have tried to do and say?" he asked, raising his shoulders and closing his eyes in the typical Italian fashion that expresses resentment and mortification, as well as a bit of contempt. I called to his attention how much the criticism of Adriano Tilgher in *Voci del tempo*[4] and in *Studi sul teatro contemporaneo*[5] had contributed toward blurring the clear profile of his drama. Pirandello seemed unwilling to dwell on Tilgher, undoubtedly because he had accepted Tilgher's presentation of his art as final in the early twenties. However, he agreed with me that Tilgher had unintentionally misrepresented the philosophical content of his drama by stating that his art pivoted on the obliteration of reality and of human personality. He also agreed that dramatic art is not conceivable without a clear-cut personality, and that the conscious madman that appears so often in his plays is a well-defined dramatic character. He added with a gesture of resignation, "Tilgher is not the only one." Yet, I had a slight suspicion that at least his managers, if not he himself did not regret the quibbling and shouting that accompanied the performance of his early plays after the first World War. It certainly helped theatre receipts. One finds an echo of those disputes in two of Pirandello's plays: *Sei personaggi in cerca d'autore* and *Ciascuno a suo modo.*

Pirandello departed from the discussion of Tilgher to inform me that what he thought of life and art had been expressed by him in a book that bears the title of *L'umorismo* (Humor)[6] published back in 1908. He insisted that neither his life concept nor his art had substantially changed, and he plunged into a wonderful discussion of what life was to him. He said with a force that bespoke his inner conviction: "Man moves in an impalpable atmosphere of dreams, whether he is conscious of it or not. Because of this he walks over the bleak planet of the eacth as a bewildered stranger and a grieving vagabond. Beyond the boundaries of time and space, above the arched, blue curve of the sky, there is life, unformed and unfettered, life out of which a strange god has carved the earth and the universe. No laws, no limitations, no boundaries exist there. Life is a ruinous stream that roars into dazzlingly white stretches of infinite space. Woe to us if we have a glimpse of that primeval life! We become both terrified and deified by it. We cease to be human, and our contact with the average man becomes impossible. My art is the expression of what happens to universal life when it becomes individual existence."

I showed him various passages in my page proofs that brought out the tragedy of being human as he had expressed it. He added, "There are four great forces in life whose urge man constantly feels: love, hate, mystery, and the acquisitive instinct." He turned toward the little table near which we were seated and grasped a small and exquisite ash tray that was there: "We say as fiercely as in the days of the cave man, 'This woman is mine!' As to mystery, this is to me the greatest force of all. Man speaks, and he does not know whence his words came. We are the prey of forces that emanate from a world that we feel moving beyond time and space, a world whence all the forces of instinct issue."

This was a golden opportunity to have Pirandello explain his concept of personality. Here are his very words as they survive in my notes: "That last generation looked upon nature and man as something existing in unchanging, clear-cut, and solid form outside of us. To me, reality is something that we mold through the power of our imagination. I have given a quixotic treatment to this concept, especially in *Cosi è, se vi pare* (Right you are if you think so); but this idea is fundamental in my art and it enlivens most of my work." He insisted on the reality of the split shown in *La Signora Morli, una e due.* "Hasn't it ever happened to you," he queried, "that you feel one way with one person and another way with another?" Fully in agreement with him, I showed him what I had quoted from his *Umorismo*s "Man does not have an idea, an absolute concept of life, but rather a changing and varied sentiment according to time, cases, and circumstances."[7]

With a slightly ironical smile, Pirandello countered: "You see that I said that long ago, and that applies also to my idea of personality. We say 'I am one,' and we look upon ourselves as well as upon our fellowmen as solid and clear-cut personalities, while in reality we are the juxtaposition of infinite, blurred selves. Take the case of Mrs. Morli in the play we have mentioned. Yes, she was one while in the company of her husband Ferrante and another when she was with her lover Lello Carpani. That is an experience we all have." He was so serious as to seem almost aggressive. "Those who deny the reality of Mrs. Morli are deprived of understanding and feeling," he stated with explosive emphasis.

"The strange thing in that play," I added, "is that she is carefree with her husband, and serious, almost sullen, with her lover."

With a gleam of mischief in his eye, Pirandello said, "That's a trick of the trade!" He went on, "My idea of personality is clearly presented in my latest play *Non si sa come* (One does not know how)."

I had not read the play and felt lost. I thought that I had perused all of his plays. He informed me that the play had been given in Germany before being performed in Italy. Stefan Zweig had beautifully translated it. Pirandello gave me the German translation that I might add the analysis of that play to my book.

"Yes," continued Pirandello, "we pass most of our time outside of ourselves rather than in a state of full consciousness. We constantly lapse into subconscious reveries that detach us from our surroundings. It is the call of primeval life. How can our personality be one when so suddenly we are capable of reentering primeval life and of being absorbed by it?"

When I told him that this seemed a sort of flimsy mysticism that clashed with the central theme of the play in question, which represents a strange case of adultery, he exclaimed, "Sexual instinct in its origin is a cosmic force, yet when it enters individual life it leads to the most terrifying complications. It makes us betray our friends, break moral laws, and disregard conventions."

"But you thus destroy the moral code," I interjected.

Pirandello was on the defensive. "I cannot help it," he said. "There are emotions and acts that are uncontrollable because of the blurred character of our personality. It is so, and I should not be honest with myself and with my art if I did not say so."

"You actually reach the same conclusions as D'Annunzio," I added.

Pirandello was furious. "No, no," he shouted. "D'Annunzio is immoral in order to proclaim the glory of instinct. I present this individual case to add another proof of the tragedy of being human. D'Annunzio is exultant over evil; I grieve over it."

I remained silent and convinced in the face of this rebuke.

This discussion brought us to Pirandello's religious point of view. He stated that Pietro Mignosi of the University of Palermo was trying to make a Catholic mystic out of him, but he added that he could not recognize himself in that role. "In my system of thought," he said, "there is no place for any organized religion." Then turning sharply toward me, he added very seriously, "Don't you see that even God has built Himself up?" I must have looked puzzled, for he continued, "I am not sacrilegious. I mean that God is a universal concept existing outside the partial constructions of Him that each religious sect makes. When this universal concept is enclosed in the Christian God, the Hindu God, and in as many gods as there are tribes in Africa and peoples on this earth, the universality of that concept is necessarily offended and dwarfed." I understood and, by way of comment, added that there was the same relation between the concept and the many gods that man has fashioned as between universal life and individual existence.

"This relationship exists also between the ideal state and the actual realization of a form of government, whether you call it democracy, fascism, or communism," said Pirandello another day in telling me of a request that he had received to grant an interview to a group of American newspapermen who wanted to know what he thought of the Ethiopian campaign. In spite of his political relativism, he took the defense of Italy with the result that the American press assumed a very hostile tone toward him. He explained to me that, since he was a member of the Fascist party and traveled with the permission of the Fascist government, he had no alternative. I could see, however, that his political faith was not very deep.

He was actuated by the same practical considerations in refusing to see Samuel Putnam, the translator of *Come tu mi vuoi* (As you desire me), who had recently joined the Communist party. Pirandello had the deepest affection for

Samuel Putnam, whom he had known many years before in Paris, but he confided to me that he could not see him because of his political affiliations.

Concerning *Come tu mi vuoi*, he was indeed provoked upon hearing that in the version offered on the American stage the identity of Cia and Elma had been purposely blurred. In the Italian original, there is not the slightest doubt about the identity of the actual Cia and of Elma, who consciously sets before herself the task of reincarnating the soul of Cia. I told Pirandello that I had set the question right in my book, and he was very grateful.

Another play on which his comments should be recorded was *Come prima, meglio di prima* (As before, better than before). In my analysis of it, I had failed to see the point in the dénouement of the play. Fulvia, the heroine, leaves the home of her husband, a famous surgeon, but a man of very low moral principles, and lives as a common-law wife of Marco Mauri, a quixotic dreamer who can offer her only an existence of passion and torment. When she returns home after many years, she discovers that her husband has poisoned the mind of their daughter Livia by distorting the truth about his wife. He has molded her into the conventional figure of a saintly woman who died when Livia was born. It was quite natural for Fulvia to be treated as an intruder by her daughter who hated her as much as she loved the false image of her saintly mother. When a new baby was born to Fulvia, she decided to leave her hated husband, but this second time she took with her the child, something she had not done the first time. What I had not perceived was the significance of her taking her child with her. Pirandello explained, "Don't you see? The first time she had left her daughter Livia with her husband who, not desiring to tell the truth of the situation, allowed Livia to grow up in the belief that her mother was a saintly woman now dead. Fulvia rebelled at the idea of having lived in this conventional and false concept in the memory of her daughter. That was an imposture, and had made a puppet out of the living Fulvia. This time her husband will not have the chance to contaminate her child's mind and falsify her personality." As to Mauri, Pirandello said, "I actually met that man in a small town in Umbria. I transported him into my play as I studied him in real life."

He spoke at length of *Sei personaggi in cerca d'autore*. He did so especially one afternoon after having had a long conversation the previous evening with Mr. Selznick concerning the possibility of filming the play. Pirandello was highly excited. "I could not convey to him, no matter how hard I tried, my idea of the three planes," he kept saying. I read to him what I had written in my book, after having asked him whether I was correct in believing that the nucleus of the play was the clash between actual reality and reality in art. I translated for him: "The six characters oscillate with perfect balance between the artificial life of glorified marionettes and the moving, stirring existence of tragic human beings."[8]

"Yes," interrupted Pirandello, "but it is more than that. I have portrayed their life on three planes that could be expressed in the cinema even better than on the legitimate stage."

I agreed, and I added that to me the three planes were that conveyed by the six characters portraying the solid and angular reality of actual life, that of the actors who take the roles of the six characters in re-enacting their tragedy, and finally that of imagination that bridges the former two, thus creating a new reality which is "life lived with passion, illumined by fancy, made immortal by true art."[9]

Pirandello commented that this sort of three-dimensional art was the salient feature of that play, and expressed disappointment that I had not read this to him before his meeting with Mr. Selznick. From his rather bitter reference to his conversation with Mr. Selznick, it was evident that he had no desire to re-open his negotiations with the motion picture magnate. In fact, *Six characters* was not filmed.

Pirandello also commented on *La vita che ti diedi* (Life that I gave you), that had failed even in England where his plays had usually been very well received. "They do not understand the fact that for that poor mother who had lost her son the only reality was the image of her son as a child that she held in her memory. After all, that was all that was left of him."

In reply to my question as to which of his plays he considered the best, he showed his preference for *Enrico IV* (Henry IV).

It may be of interest to record what he had to say about Italian literature in general and about criticism. When I asked him to give me accurately the date of his plays, he was quite impatient. "What does it matter?" he asked. I told him that one could thus trace better the development of his art. He retorted, "Dates do not count. An author should stand before the critic as a complete whole." He added that he would soon write an autobiography, the title of which would be *Of my unasked-for visit on this planet*. He continued to speak animatedly and even volubly of his future plans, but I never got the dates of his plays.

He was very happy when I told him that I had presented him, in the introduction of my book, as the antithesis of D'Annunzio, and he added, "In the whole course of Italian literature, one constantly finds such contrasts: Dante and Petrarch, Ariosto and Tasso, Goldoni and Metastasio, Leopardi and Monti, and today myself and D'Annunzio." He had words of deep contempt for D'Annunzio.

Of contemporary writers in Italy who had significance for him, he mentioned Alberto Moravia, author of *Gli indifferenti* (The indifferent ones), and his own son, Stefano, who writes under the pen name of Stefano Landi in order not to exploit the renown of his father. He spoke with great admiration of the American authors Edgar Allan Poe and Mark Twain. He referred with a lack of admiration to Sherwood Anderson's play *If this be treason*, whose first performance he had seen the previous evening.

Of his personal life he said little. He appreciated greatly my defense of his relationship with the actress Marta Abba in a conversation with ex-ambassador to Italy Washburn Child. It happened in 1927 at a luncheon at Buck Hill Falls, where I had lectured on modern Italy and had presented Pirandello as the embodiment of the new consciousness that had emerged from the tragedy of the first World War. Mr. Child, with cynical humor, warned me not to be so sure about the new consciousness as embodied in Pirandello, and added, "He is having a good time just now with a young and beautiful actress."

Pirandello interrupted me, "Why didn't you tell him that Pirandello has never had a good time in his life?" In those words I felt the moral texture of the art of Luigi Pirandello as never before. He then confided to me, "She is like a daughter to me. She is younger than my own children. She is twenty-seven years of age and I am an old man, nearly seventy."

I told him that I had singled out the plays in which I had felt the presence of Marta Abba: *L'amica delle mogli* (Their wives' friends), *Trovarsi* (To find oneself), *Quando si è qualcuno* (When one is somebody). He confessed that he had written them thinking of her, and a smile shone in his brown eyes that were now soft and affectionate.

I never realized more clearly than in those conversations the close relation that exists between Pirandello the man and Pirandello the artist. I felt it again when with grief I read in our newspapers that in December, 1936, Pirandello was taken to his last resting place in a coffin of plain wood, in accordance with his request that he be buried without any pomp and ceremony whatsoever.

1. Vol. 117 (1934), 81-94.
2. *The drama of Luigi Pirandello*, University of Pennsylvania Press, Philadelphia, 1935.
3. Republished in *La letteratura della Nuova Italia*, Bari, Laterza, 1949, VI, 359-377.
4. 2nd ed., Rome, Libreria di Scienze e Lettere, 1923, pp. 92-102.
5. Rome, Libreria di Scienze e Lettere, 1923, pp. 135-193.
6. Venice, La Nuova Italia, 1908. It is now included in the volume edited by Manlio Lo Vecchio Musti and published by Mondadori of Milan in 1939.
7. *L'umorismo*, p. 138.
8. *The drama of Luigi Pirandello*, p. 202.
9. *Ibid.*, p. 301.

PIRANDELLO AND THE CONCEPT OF REALITY*

Domenico Vittorini

THIS short article is primarily concerned with the meaning that such terms as *real, reality,* and *realism* assumed in the mind and art of Luigi Pirandello.

The meaning of these terms has varied throughout the ages. One of the first to focus his attention on the relationship between life and art was Aristotle, one of the great men of Antiquity. In his famous booklet, *Poetics,* he defined poetry as "mimesis or imitation of nature." By nature, however, he meant the immutable and eternal pattern that underlies the phenomenical world. He followed the Platonically conceptual point of view that had blossomed in the perfect creations of the Classical era, represented by Homer, Phidias, and Sophocles. Not much was added to this investigation during the centuries of the Renaissance, when the term *verisimilitude,* as applied to art, reflected the same attitude as that of the author of the *Poetics.*

Pirandello, as a teacher of Italian literature in the *Istituto Femminile di Magistero,* a sort of Teachers' College in Rome, was very much interested in aesthetics and reacted against the Renaissance sense of realism as well as that of the naturalism of the late nineteenth century. He pronounced himself, with unmistakable clarity, against both the humanistic trend in the Italian literature of the Renaissance and against the narrow sense that the naturalists of the late nineteenth century gave to the term *realism.*

Luigi Pirandello was born in Sicily in 1867 and died in Rome in 1936. He was awarded the Nobel prize in literature in 1934, a clear recognition of the universal appeal and significance of his art. Pirandello lived his not too happy life astride the last century and our own, bridging two very

* From *Pennsylvania Literary Review,* Vol. 5, No. 4, 1955.

distinct ages, that of the objective naturalism of the late nineteenth century and that of the imaginative or subjective naturalism of our own. His early literary work, short stories and novels, bore marked traits of the objective naturalism of the last century. His later works, most in the field of drama, were and still are an outstanding exemplification of the literature of our epoch.

Pirandello's major and significant plays can be best understood if viewed as the projection of a theory of art that has distinguished modern aesthetics from those of the Ancients and from those of the late nineteenth century. He has contributed to both the modern concept of art and its reflection in works in which we men of today can recognize ourselves in ideas, feelings, and passions.

Pirandello was so deeply concerned with the creative character of art as to believe that the influence of Classical Antiquity on the Romance literatures had been very obnoxious. In 1906, he wrote a critical study that serves as a preface or introduction to a novel by an Italian humorist, Alfredo Cantoni (1841-1904), whom Pirandello admired very much. Regretting the vast role that rhetoric had played in Italian literature, he stated: "The harm that it (rhetoric) has caused in every age, not only to our literature but also to Latin literature and, hence, in varying degrees, to all Romance literatures, is incalculable." The pages that follow this statement insist on the necessity of originality in art. Condemning imitation, he stated: "In imitating a preceding model, one denies his own identity and remains of necessity behind his pattern. The best is to affirm one's own sentiment, one's own life." He believed that each work of art has in itself its own laws and rules. There are no "eternal principles" in literature. The task of criticism consists in "discovering the principle that determined and gave a personal character to the specific work of art." And again: "The work of fancy is a work of nature, an organic and living whole. . . . A work of art is nature itself that makes use of the instrument of human fancy in order to create a work of a higher order, more perfect because elements that are too common, obvious, and fleeting have been pruned away. A work of art lives by its own essential ideality."

As to the attitude of Pirandello towards the aesthetics of the Naturalists, to hear himself classified as a Naturalist was enough to cause him to explode with typical Italian vehemence. His art, he believed, was a complete departure from the aesthetics of the Naturalistic School as exemplified by his personal friends and predecessors, Giovanni Verga and Luigi Capuana. He was wont to quote from Verga who, upon reading his novel *L'Esclusa* (The Outcast), had written to him that with his novels a new light was shining in contemporary fiction.

Pirandello, in his aesthetic views, resumed contact with Gian Battista Vico (1688-1744), who ushered in the Romantic Age with a fundamental distinction between the role of logic and fancy in art, a distinction that is still the corner-stone of modern aesthetics. Vico proclaimed in his *New Science* (1725) that art is the product of fancy and, if so, by inference, art is not conditioned by actual life. A character is not *real* simply because it is modeled on a man actually existing, actually known and studied in the world close at hand. If art is the product of fancy, Pirandello felt, a complete definition of aesthetics should embrace not only the use of Greek myths (Classicism), not only historical material (Romanticism), not only material observed in the society and environment in which the artist lives (Naturalism), but also whatever dreams and enchanted or awesome places the artist evokes from his imagination (Contemporary Art). *Reality* resides not in the material used, but in the life that the magic power of imagination can awaken in it.

In many of Pirandello's plays, *Six Characters in Search of an Author, Henry IV, Tonight We Improvise, When One Is a Somebody, To Find Oneself*, and others, one reads beautiful pages dedicated to his art concept. I quote at random a passage from *Six Characters*, that echoes the very words of the essay on Cantoni: "Nature uses the instrument of human fancy to continue, even in a higher form, its creative work." Art rests on a higher plane than actual life. It is capable of giving to the creative artist a completeness of existence that actual life does not give him. The vision and realization of this more complete and different form of life constitutes *realism.*

Realism is an aesthetic category and not the material that some artists have used. An artist can reach realism either by using ideal patterns or actual ones. He is completely free in his choice that is dictated only by his own temperament, mood, and experience.

The clash between Benedetto Croce and Luigi Pirandello that started with the publication in 1902 of the *Aesthetics* of the Neapolitan philosopher, ultimately rested on the fact that Croce, through his definition of art as expression of a subjective intuition of reality, still clung to *objective reality* as the model or pattern of art. Pirandello felt that *imaginative reality* is as real as the tangible, solid, and angular reality of the world close at hand. Hence, the insults and recriminations that each heaped upon the other until the very end of their lives.

The new meaning of reality in art is more than a theory in the late Pirandello. It served as the fertile seed from which developed the new drama that our age has admired with almost universal consent.

Pirandello was a very patient and stubborn worker. He worked very slowly, and his plays clearly show the moment when he departed from the Naturalism of his youth, as exemplified in his short stories, *The Old and the Young,* and even in *Mattia Pascal,* in order to rise towards a type of realistic drama, the glory of which is a more searching and subjective study of man and life. His essay on humor, written in 1908, can only serve as a basis for his fiction and for the section of his drama formed by plays that were the dramatization of previously written short stories. An attentive study of the two sections would show how close Pirandello was, in inspiration and technique, to the tenets of

Naturalism, and how different and new are such plays as *Henry IV* and *Six Characters*. Naturalism, with its precepts of closeness to actual life, hindered and fettered Pirandello in realizing an ideal of art that had loomed even in the days when he wrote his *Umorismo*. How is it possible to correlate the events in Pirandello's early fiction and old plays with statements such as the following that are found in these critical works? Here we read: "Life is a conscious and fluid entity that we try to stop, to fix in unchanging and definite forms, inside and outside of us, because we all are fixed forms, forms which move along others equally fixed." We are, he continues, the result of concepts reached through an infernal machine called logic, which pumps our sentiments from our hearts up to our brains and reduces them to lifeless abstractions. Only now and then, in rare moments of inner illumination, do we resume contact with real life, life as a cosmic flux that suffers in being enclosed in its human molds: rocks, plants, animals, men. Then we experience a terrifying shock, as we see ourselves live suspended in the inner void created by the contrast between cosmic life and its earthy and human forms. Pirandello's fiction reflected in his puny and strange-looking characters the ludicrous embodiments of this ideal life-concept. We must not wonder that this fiction was never popular. It was this intuition of life that was developed in the works written after the First World War. He uncovered a new and deeper stream of creativeness only when he forsook the tenets of Naturalism and entered the precincts of stately tragedy. Then he penned such works as *Henry IV*, *Six Characters*, *As You Desire Me*, *When One Is Somebody*.

A perusal of the Preface to *Six Characters*, written in 1927, seven years after the play which had sent the name of the author all over Europe and South America, can serve as a document to illustrate the art concept that led to the new art. Here Pirandello differentiated between "historical" or descriptive authors and "philosophical" ones. He ranked himself as one of the latter type. Art had become

for him the medium of expression of the unspeakable loneliness of his soul, as befitting a man who had lived for years
in the company of a wife who was demented and in a period
of history made up of wars, hatred, and destruction.

Such an intuition of art as Pirandello revealed in his new
plays helps us to understand our contemporary art or, at
least, that section of it that refuses to accept the principle
that art must be molded on models found in actual life.

Pirandello's theoretical attitude, as exemplified in works
that men will never forget, shows how limited is the current
use of the term *realism*. If realism is associated with the
idea of art as the closest approximation to actual models,
then the significance of art rests on accuracy and not on
creativeness. In a way, such a restricted view of realism
proclaims the uselessness of art in that it is unquestionably
true that no reflected object is more similar to itself than
the very object that the artist wishes to represent. Why
waste time in reproducing imperfectly in art what exists
perfectly in life?

In our discussion, it became clear that the term *reality*,
as used in his works, was often confusing. Drawing on what
I had learned from him more than from any other author,
I suggested to him that in order to distinguish between
reality in life and *reality* in art, one could use the term
actuality for the former and *reality* for the latter. Art transforms the actual into the real. The actuality of life is outside
the realm of art until the fancy of a poet gives to it the new
life to which Pirandello constantly referred. The logic of
life is different from that of art in the same way as that of
primitive peoples and children is different from that of
highly civilized beings. "Vico discovered this long ago,"
interjected Pirandello, looking very wistful.

Our conversation resumed its usual pleasant character
when we returned to the discussion of *Six Characters*, and
I told him, much to his satisfaction and even joy, that, to
me, the three planes were conveyed by his consideration of
the characters as actual human beings in the snares of

nature, by their resentment upon seeing themselves represented by professional actors when the stage director decides to use their tragic case as art material of an improvised play, and, finally, as they live now in Pirandello's play.

To understand fully Pirandello's art one must be aware of the efforts through which his characters are made to replace their actual existence by one created through illusion and fancy. The two planes are constantly and clearly visible in his best plays. To restrict ourselves to *Naked Masks*, a collection of his plays translated into English and now available in the Everyman's Library edition, one finds a great variety of situations, all characterized by this pitiful attempt to put on a mask that covers a scarred human countenance, seared by shame and contorted by suffering.

The central nucleus of *Henry IV* is precisely this: an imaginative and hypersensitive gentleman who, while impersonating the famous emperor, Henry IV of Germany, falls from his horse, strikes his head, and, when he opens his eyes, he has lost the consciousness of his actual personality, as a man of today, and feels that he is the historical character of the eleventh century, who lives again in his mind the struggles against Pope Gregory VII, the other rulers of the time, and the intrigues of Peter Damian. A wealthy sister places him in a palace and surrounds him with counselors, guards, and pages who keep that illusion alive. One day he recovers consciousness of his actual identity. Never has human fancy so exploited the artistic possibilities of the clash of the two planes, the actual and the fantastic, and seldom have the two planes merged into a more tragic and heart-rending unity of artistic reality than in this play.

In *Naked*, the contrast between the actual and the self-imposed illusion is projected into the attempt of Ersilia Drei to fabricate the tale of a little romance in a life that has never known the joy of love. When the iridescent bubble of the fiction that has become her whole life is destroyed, she commits suicide.

In *The Pleasure of Honesty*, Baldovino, at the end of his resources financially and intellectually, decides to become the husband of a young woman with social position and wealth who has had to hide the fact that she, unwed, is going to give birth to a child. Baldovino is fully conscious that he wears only the mask of a husband, and that he lives in the home of Agata as a phantom. Pirandello makes him take his role as a husband so seriously and with such telling effect that eventually the form of the husband in Baldovino becomes the reality of the husband of Agata Renni.

The nucleus of Pirandello's dramatic art lies precisely in the transformation of the *actual* into the *real*. It represents one of the most beautiful and perfect embodiments of realistic art, as the playwright understood realism. He was so successful in presenting this to his readers because existence and art in him became fused into one. Confronted by the angular and hard existence that was his because of his temperament, sensitivity, and the circumstances that surrounded his life, he took refuge in the reality of art, just as his characters took refuge in the reality of illusion. He lived the last years of his life believing that true art portrays life lived with passion, illumined by fancy and solidified in the joy of creative art.

It was an unforgettable experience to have been privileged to know one of the greatest men of our time. In my personal life it has been an even greater gift to have been able to study the work in which he still lives, the only kind of survival in which he believed.

PIRANDELLO IN EVERYMAN'S LIBRARY*

T HE recent publication of five of Pirandello's plays
edited by Eric Bentley (*Naked Masks*, Everyman's
Library, 1952) is truly a happy event for those who
are interested in dramatic art in general and in Pirandello's
drama in particular.

In this book, the best of Pirandello's works are made
available to the average reader in England and America,
while the introduction and three apendices, with their carefully checked biographical and bibliographical data, are of
particular interest to scholars. The first appendix contains
an accurate and lucid translation by Eric Bentley of Pirandello's preface to *Six Characters in Search of an Author*,
which is a major declaration or the dramatic principles that
apply to Pirandello's late plays, just as *Umorismo*, written
in 1908, casts a revealing light on the earlier works that
show the author's contact with, and departure from, the
Naturalism of Verga and Capuana.

There are two statements in Appendix II (p. 379) that
are open to question. One refers to the *New Colony*, a play
that, according to Mr. Bentley, shows a "definite fascist
mentality," just as *Lazarus* is "miracle mongering." Since
both Fascism and Christianity are positive and dogmatic
systems, they could not be accepted by Pirandello who
believed that the essence of Life is unfettered and fluid, and,
therefore, every "form" that encloses it gives to it a fixity
that dooms it to disintegration and death. This is the basic
and unchanging principle of Pirandello's system of ideas.
Accordingly, he presents in the *New Colony* the thesis of the
impossibility of realizing a perfect government and society
on this earth. Likewise, in *Lazarus*, since all religions are
"constructions" of the universal concept of God, Pirandello

* From Yearbook of Comparative and General Literature No. 2, Chapel Hill,
North Carolina.

rejected the Christian belief in the personal survival of the soul. For Pirandello, the soul longs to re-enter cosmic Life, whence a strange God detached it to make it live on the bleak desert of this life. Personal form is for him the chief factor in the tragedy of being human.

The second statement of Mr. Bentley to which I take exception refers to Pirandello's *grande passion* for Marta Abba. My exception is based on Pirandello's own words when he expressed to me, in 1935, during an interview with him in New York, his great resentment against the misconception of his relationship with Marta Abba. I had mentioned to him that the ex-ambassador to Italy, Washburn Child, had cynically referred to that relationship. Whereupon, Pirandello exclaimed, "She is younger than my own children. She has always been like a daughter to me."

The major contribution of Mr. Bentley in this book is his translation of *Liolà*. It is an entirely new translation and it has been beautifully and accurately done by one who knows both Italian and English perfectly. Moreover, Mr. Bentley has a truly lyrical temperament, and he is in love with Sicily. Only a poet can describe the Sicilian landscape as beautifully as this: "Sicily is like that: the African sun shines, the hard rock takes on the soft color of honey, the trees are laden with almonds and oranges, and vagabonds sing." (ix). However, again, I must be allowed to courteously disagree with Mr. Bentley as to the central interpretation of this play. He states that *Liolà* is "Pirandello on holiday. . . . truancy on Pirandello's part, an exception to the rules of the maestro's art" (ix-x). To us, *Liolà* presents the positive aspect of Pirandello's central intuition of life. Liolà, the main character, is primitive, spontaneous, fluid, and, is close to primeval life, and capable of living with joy. He is not so tortuous and "cerebral" as many, although not all, of Pirandello's characters. According to Pirandello, by applying the "infernal machine of logic," man forsakes sentiment and offends life in its very essence. Thinking is not a "gift" for man. Since it implies objectivity and consciousness, it leads to our "constructing ourselves," and, hence, is a negative force. Pirandello, while of necessity indulging himself in thought, punishes his characters by showing their tortuous thinking through which they "immobilize the continuous flux of life through concepts" (*Umorismo*, p. 214). By denying to his characters the gift of logical thinking, Pirandello reaches the absolute in his system of tragedy, the essence of which lies in incomprehension of others as well as of ourselves. In his plays, it is primarily the incomprehension of the characters of the plight in which they find themselves that creates tragedy.

In *Liolà*, the main character is the opposite of being "constructed." The characters that are "constructed," although they are too elementary to be aware of it, are Zia Croce and Zio Simone. Zia Croce conceives the scheme of attributing to Zio Simone, her wealthy cousin, the fatherhood of the baby that her unwed daughter Tuzza is going to have by Liolà. She not only wants to save appearances but also hopes to get her cousin's money. The latter, since he has not been able to have a son from his young wife Mita, agrees to the base pact in order to save his masculine pride. Liolà realizing that this offends and ruins Mita, a former sweetheart of his, intervenes and spoils the scheme. Unsuspectingly, Zia Croce and Zio Simone have thrown Liolà and Mita into each other's arms. Mita, too, is soon expecting a baby by Liolà. Zio Simone will now appear to be the father of two children who are in reality of Liolà. The only person who is left defenseless and exposed is Tuzza who in the very end tries to stab Liolà, but in vain. All this is very far from being an idyll, "the last Sicilian pastoral" (x). Indeed, *Liolà* bears a marked resemblance to the traditional Italian comedy and particularly to Machiavelli's *Mandragola*. In both works, the plot is basically the same and the two dishonest husbands, Ser Nicia and Zio Simone, are punished through the triumph of the romantic lovers Callimaco and Liolà.

An objective and critical reading of the text makes it questionable whether this play can be included among those that deal with the contrast of truth and appearance. It is difficult to agree with Mr. Bentley that in *Liolà* Pirandello wanted to prove that "reality is not more real than appearance" (xii)' (Tuzza would not grant this) and that Zio Simone "only appears to appear to be the father" (xii). Basically, Zio Simone wants to appear to be a father, but Pirandello unmasks him and holds him up to ridicule. This is all. More simply, *Liolà* belongs to that section of Pirandello's drama that is closely related to his early contacts with Naturalism. Even in technique, like many plays of this group, *Liolà* has been given a solid background, and its characters possess traits quite different from those so effectively described in the above-mentioned preface to *Six Characters*. The theoretical roots of *Liolà* are in *Umorismo*, just as those of the later play are in the preface of *Six Characters*.

In discussing *It is So (If You Think So)*, the term "reality" is rather misleading. In Pirandello, what exists in the observable and tangible world is an *actuality* that the artist uses in order to transform it, first into a psychological, and then into an artistic reality. The epilogues of many of Pirandello's plays contain in a very living and human manner the result of this transformation. The playwright is not at all interested in the actuality of the situation presented. It does not matter to him whether Ponza's wife is Lina or another person. Indeed, if this be ascertained, the play would lose its *raisin d'être*. What counts is the nobility of the veiled wife who proclaims that she is, to Ponza and to Signora Frola, what each wants her to be, and she is nobody to herself. With infinite compassion she has obliterated her own identity and consciously has lent herself to be whatever the two want her to be. This is a new type of "construction" in Pirandello. It possesses positive connotations and it is distinguishable from that of the comedies conceived under the guidance of the artistic principles contained in *Umorismo*. Tragedy shuns laughter and this is the ancient principle that Pirandello followed only in the later period of his *(If You Think So)* is "outside the boundary of realism" artistic career. In this context, the statement that *It Is So*

(xviii) clashes with the deep significance of the play. Pirandello's system of ideas, far from being abstract, is full of human understanding. Life being what it is, only simplicity, humility, kindness, and, especially, illusion, help us to bear its burden.

One of the merits of Mr. Bentley is to have championed the reality of Pirandello's ideas. This is precisely what Adriano Tilgher had failed to do in his essays written in the twenties. Pirandello was fully aware of this when he came to the United States in 1935, at which time he, in accepting my own analysis of his dramaturgy, repudiated Tilgher's theory to which he had previously given official sanction.

The greatest praise that can be rightly and gladly given to both Mr. Bentley and Everyman's Library rests on the fact that this new volume serves the average man as well as the scholar. This combination is befitting democratic society that constantly aims at raising the intellectual level of its citizens.

DOMENICO VITTORINI

University of Pennsylvania